Humanitarian Photography

For well over a century, humanitarians and their organizations have used photographic imagery and the latest media technologies to raise public awareness and funds to alleviate human suffering. This volume examines the historical evolution of what we today call "humanitarian photography" – the mobilization of photography in the service of humanitarian initiatives across state boundaries – and asks how we can account for the shift from the fitful and debated use of photography for humanitarian purposes in the late nineteenth century to our current situation in which photographers market themselves as "humanitarian photographers." This book is the first to investigate how humanitarian photography emerged and how it operated in diverse political, institutional, and social contexts, bringing together more than a dozen scholars working on the history of humanitarianism, international organizations and nongovernmental organizations, and visual culture in Africa, Asia, the Middle East, Europe, and the United States. Based on original archival research and informed by current historical and theoretical approaches, the chapters explore the history of the mobilization of images and emotions in the globalization of humanitarian agendas up to the present.

Heide Fehrenbach is Board of Trustees Professor and Distinguished Research Professor in the history department at Northern Illinois University. She is the author of three books: *Cinema in Democratizing Germany; Race after Hitler: Black Occupation Children in Postwar Germany and America*; and *After the Nazi Racial State: Difference and Democracy in Germany and Europe* (with Rita Chin, Geoff Eley, and Atina Grossmann). She is also coeditor, with Uta Poiger, of *Transactions, Transgressions, Transformations: American Culture in Western Europe and Japan* (2000).

Davide Rodogno is professor of international history at the Graduate Institute of International and Developmental Studies in Geneva, Switzerland. His books include *Fascism's European Empire; Against Massacre: Humanitarian Interventions in the Ottoman Empire (1815–1914)*; and, as coeditor, *Shaping the Transnational Sphere: Transnational Networks of Experts in the Long Nineteenth Century*.

Human Rights in History

Edited by

Stefan-Ludwig Hoffmann, *University of California, Berkeley*
Samuel Moyn, *Harvard Law School*

This series showcases new scholarship exploring the backgrounds of human rights today. With an open-ended chronology and international perspective, the series seeks works attentive to the surprises and contingencies in the historical origins and legacies of human rights ideals and interventions. Books in the series will focus not only on the intellectual antecedents and foundations of human rights but also on the incorporation of the concept by movements, nation-states, international governance, and transnational law.

Also in the series:

Humanitarian Photography

A History

Edited by

HEIDE FEHRENBACH
Northern Illinois University

DAVIDE RODOGNO
Graduate Institute of Geneva

CAMBRIDGE
UNIVERSITY PRESS

CAMBRIDGE
UNIVERSITY PRESS

32 Avenue of the Americas, New York NY 10013-2473, USA

Cambridge University Press is part of the University of Cambridge.

It furthers the University's mission by disseminating knowledge in the pursuit of education, learning and research at the highest international levels of excellence.

www.cambridge.org
Information on this title: www.cambridge.org/9781107639713

© Cambridge University Press 2015

First published 2015
First paperback edition 2016

A catalogue record for this publication is available from the British Library

Library of Congress Cataloguing in Publication data
Humanitarian photography : a history / Heide Fehrenbach, Northern Illinois University, Davide Rodogno, Graduate Institute of Geneva.
pages   cm. – (Human rights in history)
Includes bibliographical references and index.
ISBN 978-1-107-06470-6 (hardback)
1. Photography – Social aspects – History.   2. Documentary photography – History.   3. Humanitarian assistance – History.   I. Fehrenbach, Heide, editor of compilation.   II. Rodogno, Davide, 1972– editor of compilation.
III. Series: Human rights in history.
TR183.H86   2014
779′.936126–dc23   2014032388

ISBN 978-1-107-06470-6 Hardback
ISBN 978-1-107-63971-3 Paperback

Contents

Illustrations

Contributors

Peter Balakian is the author of *Black Dog of Fate: An American Son Uncovers His Armenian Past* (Basic Books), winner of the PEN/Martha Albrand Prize for the Art of the Memoir, and *The Burning Tigris: The Armenian Genocide and America's Response* (Harper Perennial), winner of the Raphael Lemkin Prize. Among his seven books of poems are *Ziggurat* (Phoenix Poets) and *Ozone Journal* (Phoenix Poets). He is also the author of *Vise and Shadow, Selected Essays* (University of Chicago Press). He is the recipient of many awards including a Guggenheim Fellowship and a fellowship from the National Endowment for the Arts. Balakian is Donald M. and Constance H. Rebar Professor of the Humanities in the department of English at Colgate University.

Heather D. Curtis is associate professor in the department of religion at Tufts University, where she also serves as a member of the core faculties for American Studies, International Relations, and the Tisch College of Citizenship and Public Service. Curtis received her doctorate in the history of Christianity and American religion from Harvard University in 2005. She is the author of *Faith in the Great Physician: Suffering and Divine Healing in American Culture, 1860–1900* (Johns Hopkins University Press), which was awarded the Frank S. and Elizabeth D. Brewer prize from the American Society of Church History for the best first book on the history of Christianity. Her current research project, *Holy Humanitarians: American Evangelicals and Global Aid* (under contract with Harvard University Press) examines the crucial role popular religious media and evangelical missionaries played in the extension of U.S. philanthropy at home and abroad from the late nineteenth century to the early twentieth. Articles on aspects of this research have been published in *Material Religion, Church History*, and *The International Bulletin of Missionary Research*.

Thomas David is professor at the Institute of Economic and Social History at the University of Lausanne and director of the College of Humanities at the Ecole Polytechnique Fédérale de Lausanne (EPFL). He is coauthor of *The Invention of Race. Scientific and Popular Representations*, with N. Bancel and D. Thomas (Routledge), and *The Power of Corporate Networks: A Comparative and Historical Perspective*, with G. Westerhuis (Routledge).

Heide Fehrenbach is Board of Trustees Professor and Distinguished Research Professor in the history department at Northern Illinois University. She previously taught at Emory University and Colgate University. She is the author of three books: *Cinema in Democratizing Germany* (UNC Press); *Race after Hitler: Black Occupation Children in Postwar Germany and America* (Princeton University Press); and, with Rita Chin, Geoff Eley, and Atina Grossmann, *After the Nazi Racial State: Difference and Democracy in Germany and Europe* (University of Mich. Press); with Uta Poiger she edited *Transactions, Transgressions, Transformations: American Culture in Western Europe and Japan* (Berghahn). Her research has been supported by fellowships from the American Council of Learned Societies, the John Simon Guggenheim Memorial Foundation, the National Endowment for the Humanities, the American Academy in Berlin, and the Deutscher Akademischer Austauschdienst. She is currently at work on a book-length study of child-centered humanitarian imagery in the twentieth century.

Kevin Grant teaches history at Hamilton College. He is the author of *A Civilised Savagery: Britain and the New Slaveries in Africa, 1884–1926* (Routledge), and co-editor, with Philippa Levine and Frank Trentmann, of *Beyond Sovereignty: Britain, Empire and Transnationalism, 1880–1950* (Palgrave Macmillan). He is currently writing a comparative history of hunger strikes in the British Empire.

Lasse Heerten is a postdoctoral Fellow in human rights at the University of California at Berkeley, where he is completing a book manuscript on the international history of the Nigerian Civil War. He holds graduate degrees from the Humboldt-Universität zu Berlin (MA, 2008), the University of Oxford (MSt, 2009), and the Freie Universität Berlin (Dr. Phil, 2014, summa cum laude). Heerten's research has appeared in peer-reviewed journals, edited volumes, and anthologies. Most recently, he coedited an issue on the theme "The Nigeria-Biafra War: Postcolonial Conflict and the Question of Genocide, 1967–1970" with A. Dirk Moses for the *Journal of Genocide Research* 16, nos. 2–3 (2014), for which he also coauthored the introductory article.

Henrietta Lidchi works at the National Museums Scotland, Edinburgh, as Keeper of the Department of World Cultures. Her postgraduate research considered the types of visual images produced by British non-governmental organizations in the context of debates regarding the ethics and politics of representation. Since 1994 she has worked in museums, specifically on Native American art and material culture, visual anthropology, and museology, on which she has published in journals and edited collections. She is coeditor of two volumes examining photography: *Imaging the Arctic* (University of Washington Press) and *Visual Currencies* (National Museums of Scotland). In 2015, her research on the production and consumer appeal of Native American jewelry of the southwestern United States will be published by the British Museum Press as *Surviving Desires*.

Sanna Nissinen is a sociologist with extensive experience working in program evaluation and communications with United Nations agencies on issues of commercial sexual exploitation of children and child trafficking. As a researcher, she focuses on the role of photography in the production of "humanitarian" culture; as a practicing photographer, she explores in her work the social lives of images. Nissinen holds a PhD from the Open University (UK) and has published on the ethical tensions in the production of contemporary humanitarian photography.

Francesca Piana received her doctoral degree in international history from the Graduate Institute of International and Development Studies in Geneva, Switzerland, in 2013. She was Swiss National Science Foundation postdoctoral Fellow at Columbia University during 2013–2014 and at the University of Michigan during 2014–2015. Her doctoral research, "Towards the International Refugee Regime: Humanitarianism in the Wake of the First World War," is forthcoming as a monograph. She is currently working on comparative biographies of female missionaries and humanitarians from the end of the nineteenth century through the Second World War. Her recent publications include "L'humanitaire d'après-guerre: prisonniers de guerre et réfugiés russes dans la politique du Comité International de la Croix-Rouge et de la Société des Nations," *Relations Internationales* no. 151 (2012–2013): 63–75 and "Two Eras of Refugee Policy: The Legacies of the League of Nations in the 1940s," in Jaci Eisenberg and Davide Rodogno, eds., *Ideas and Identities: A Festschrift for Andre Liebich* (Peter Lang).

Caroline Reeves is Associate in Research at Harvard University's Fairbank Center. Her expertise lies in the history of Chinese philanthropy and China's early involvement in transnational processes, including the global spread of international humanitarian norms. Recently awarded an ACLS grant to develop a project on "The Social Lives of Dead Bodies in Modern China," she has published and been interviewed in numerous books, journals, and other media on Chinese philanthropy and the history of the Chinese Red Cross Society. She is currently working on a book on Chinese philanthropy.

Davide Rodogno is professor in the international history department at the Graduate Institute of International and Development Studies, Geneva. Rodogno was a research Fellow at the London School of Economics (2002–2004); foreign associate researcher at the Institut d'Histoire du Temps Présent in Paris (2004–2005); academic Fellow, Research Council United Kingdom, at the School of History, University of St. Andrews (2005–2010); and Fonds National Suisse Research Professor (2008–2011) affiliated with the Graduate Institute. Professor since 2014, he is currently preparing a monograph tentatively entitled *From Relief to Rehabilitation: The History of International Organizations' Humanitarian Programmes in the Interwar Period*. His recent publications include *Against Massacre: Humanitarian Interventions in the Ottoman Empire (1815–1914)* (Princeton University Press) and *Fascism's European Empire* (Cambridge University Press). Rodogno is also author and editor with Bernhard Struck and Jakob Vogel of *Shaping the Transnational Sphere: Experts, Networks and Issues from the 1840s to the 1930s* (Berghahn).

Silvia Salvatici is associate professor in modern history at the University of Teramo (Italy). She was associate research Fellow at the Italian Academy of Columbia University (2009), Fernand Braudel Senior Fellow at the European University Institute (2010), and visiting professor at the California Polytechnic State University SLO (2011). Her research interests focus on individual and collective memories in postwar societies, women refugees in the twentieth century, gender and human rights, European displaced persons in the aftermath of World War II, and the history of humanitarianism. Among her most recent publications are *Senza casa e senza paese: Profughi europei nel secondo dopoguerra* [Without Home and Without Country: European Displaced Persons in the Aftermath of World War II] (Il Mulino); "'Help the People to Help Themselves.' UNRRA Relief Workers and European Displaced Persons," *Journal of Refugee Studies* 25 (2012); "Between National and International Mandates: DPs and Refugees in Post-War Italy," *Journal of Contemporary History*, special issue "Refugees and the Nation State," 49 (July 2014).

Christina Twomey is professor of history at Monash University. She is the author of three books: *A History of Australia* (Palgrave Macmillan), coauthored with Mark Peel; *Australia's Forgotten Prisoners: Civilians Interned by the Japanese in World War II* (Cambridge University Press); and *Deserted and Destitute: Motherhood, Wife Desertion and Colonial Welfare* (Australian Scholarly Publishing). Twomey has also published widely on the cultural history of war, with a focus on issues of imprisonment, captivity, witnessing, the photography of atrocity, gender, and memory. Currently an Australian Research Council Future Fellow (2012–2015), she has been researching civilian internment and concentration policies at three different colonial sites in the late nineteenth century: South Africa, Cuba, and the Philippines. She is also completing a book-length study, provisionally entitled *Scars: POWs in Post-War Australia*.

Acknowledgments

Historians are suckers for origin tales, or at least inveterate spinners of them. Here is ours.

The seeds for our volume were first sowed around a dinner table at a London restaurant in May 2011. A group of us – Davide Rodogno, Heide Fehrenbach, Silvia Salvatici, Caroline Reeves, and Francesca Piana – were participating in a conference on humanitarianism at the German Historical Institute organized by Johannes Paulmann. In becoming acquainted and discussing our research interests that evening, we reached a vague consensus that the visual culture of humanitarianism was not only something worth pursuing, but something we should pursue together. Returning home, Davide and Heide fell into a correspondence about the idea and resolved to seek funding for a workshop on the topic. Grant applications were written, a guest list was brainstormed, participants were recruited, and by December 2012, the project germinated at a stimulating workshop at the Graduate Institute of International and Development Studies in Geneva, Switzerland – the historical seat of internationalism. Impressed by the topical range and originality of research presented at the workshop, we resolved to publish a book. You hold the harvest in your hands.

For crucial financial and institutional support for the workshop, we thank the Fonds National Suisse de la Recherche Scientifique and the Graduate Institute, Geneva; its director Philippe Burrin; and its International History Department. In addition, we gratefully acknowledge the generous Opportunity Grant provided by Northern Illinois University, along with the ongoing support of Provost Lisa Freeman and Vice President for Research Lesley Rigg, which allowed us to see this project through from workshop to publication.

For early input that enriched both the workshop and the conceptualization of the volume we thank Stefan Ludwig Hoffmann and Julia Adeney Thomas. We also recognize the intellectual contributions of Felix Ohnmacht and Laura Iandola, who attended the workshop, and extend our hearty thanks to Felix for his excellent work coordinating the workshop and expertly handling organizational details with good humor, while participating actively in it.

For critical intellectual feedback and support, we thank series editors Samuel Moyn and Stefan-Ludwig Hoffmann, as well as JP Daughton, Andreas Daum, Claudia Koonz, and Johannes Paulmann. Thanks too to our editor Deborah Gershenowitz for her enthusiastic advocacy of the project and her sage advice. We acknowledge with appreciation the efforts of archivists, librarians, and administrators at the numerous libraries and institutions for assisting us to secure high-resolution images and permission to publish them. We also thank Laurel Kirk for her conscientious work on the bibliography; Ian Burns for his judicious work on the index; and Patterson Lamb, Ramesh Karunakaran, and Jeanie Lee for their expertise in turning the manuscript into a book.

Last, but not least, we affectionately acknowledge our families: forbearing spouses, cuddly children, prickly teenagers (you know who you are) with whom we have had the great good fortune to share a secure existence. We also recognize those who have not enjoyed such essential privileges. It is to them, young and old, past and present, that this book is dedicated.

Introduction

The Morality of Sight: Humanitarian Photography in History

Heide Fehrenbach and Davide Rodogno

For well over a century, humanitarians and their organizations have used photographic imagery and the latest media technologies to raise public awareness and funds to alleviate human suffering. This volume examines the historical genealogies, evolution, and epistemologies of what today we call "humanitarian photography": the mobilization of photography in the service of humanitarian initiatives across state boundaries. The term itself is of recent origin, in use only since the 1990s. Yet over the last two decades, prizes and fellowships – such as the Care International Award for Humanitarian Photojournalism, the Luis Valtueña International Humanitarian Photography Award, UNICEF's Photo of the Year Award, and the Photocrati Fellowships – have been endowed in its name.[1]

What accounts for the historical shift from the fitful and debated use of photography for humanitarian purposes in the late nineteenth century to our current situation in which photographers market themselves as "humanitarian photographers"? This book is the first to investigate how humanitarian photography emerged and has functioned historically in diverse political, institutional, and social contexts. It brings together more than a dozen scholars working on the history of humanitarianism, international organizations or nongovernmental organizations (NGOs), and visual culture in Africa, Asia, the Middle East, Europe, and the United States. Based on original archival research and informed by current historical and theoretical debates, their chapters explore the historical mobilization of images and emotions in the globalization of humanitarian agendas from the late nineteenth century through the present.

This volume sits at the intersection of two distinct scholarly trends, one of which is focused on visual culture and media studies, the other on humanitarianism and human rights. There is now a well-developed scholarship concerned with the aesthetic and institutional development of photography and photojournalism, global and new media, and the circulation of images of violence and suffering, war and genocide; however, most of it is not written by historians or motivated by historical questions.[2] In 2003, shortly before her death, American writer and public intellectual Susan Sontag published her famous meditation on our "camera-mediated knowledge of war," in which she declared "being a spectator to distant calamities" a "quintessential modern experience." Although widely cited, her work was not the first word, nor the last, on how photos depicting "the pain of others" address viewers, incite voyeurism, touch emotion, convey knowledge, fix memories, or position privileged spectators in relation to human misery. Media scholars too have explored and debated photography's power as a medium as well as the ways that photography is implicated in structures of power, particularly the modern visual economy in which "we," in the industrial West, watch as "others," elsewhere, suffer.[3]

Historians, on the other hand, have begun to write the social, institutional, and legal histories of humanitarianism and human rights. They have focused, for example, on missionary work; the relationship between the imperialism and the humanitarian impulse; the growth of international law, international organizations, and NGOs; instances of ethnic cleansing, crimes against humanity, and genocide; natural disasters; the development of wartime refugee and relief work; and the values driving foreign policy and military intervention.[4] In addition, cultural and intellectual historians of North America, Britain, and France have investigated the emergence of humanitarian sensibilities since the late eighteenth century, which they have attributed to the spread of capitalist markets, empires, and technologies; shifting notions of pain (from unavoidable and God-given to "unacceptable and eradicable"); and the rise of sentimental literature, which engaged readers' emotions by acquainting them with the dramatic interior and social lives of sentient others.[5] In general, scholars agree that by 1850, "something changed."[6] There was a greater sense of interconnectivity and felt responsibility for distant human suffering among cosmopolitan publics in Western capitalist nations and empires. Through the international Red Cross movement, the humanitarian impulse spread to Asian countries as well, mixing with longer standing native traditions of charity and philanthropy.[7] Thomas Laqueur has suggested that humanitarian narratives "demanded new ways of seeing": "exact, slow, active, engaged seeing" in order to keep distant others "within ethical range."[8] Yet to date, historians have done very little to examine the visual histories of humanitarianism and, in particular, the question of what role photography has played in shaping and disseminating humanitarian agendas and values.[9] This is likely due to the relative youth of the field: the scholarly study of humanitarianism and internationalism is recent, and historians are still engaged in excavating their institutional, political, and social histories from the archives. Many of the chapters in our volume contribute to this project of archival excavation while refocusing attention on the use and significance of visual media and strategies.

Although the mobilization of photographic images has become so crucial in raising both awareness and funds for humanitarian and human rights agendas, historians have not yet studied it in a systematic way. As a result, scholars have too liberally claimed "first-time" status for their object or period of study: that this was the "first time" a certain photographic technology was used to a particular effect, that this was the first time certain visual narrative conventions were mobilized or that celebrities fronted humanitarian appeals.[10] This volume, in effect, tests such assertions and fills a gap in our historical understanding: first, by establishing humanitarian photography as a historical problematic, and second, by indicating key moments in humanitarianism's long visual history.

A critical word is in order regarding the geographical scope of our volume. The scholarship on photography and humanitarianism has had a strongly Eurocentric and North American orientation. Photography and humanitarianism have been treated as Western inventions and, more problematically, as peculiarly Western practices. While our volume is necessarily informed by this literature, it also aspires to unsettle these assumptions, particularly concerning humanitarian and photographic practice, and to present a somewhat more diverse perspective.[11] Our volume's overall contribution in this area is admittedly modest; it nonetheless reflects the current state of the research.[12] As a result, while the chapters offer geographical breadth, most of the humanitarian organizations, image-makers, and image-purveyors discussed come from Europe and North America. To date, we have little empirical knowledge of "how visuality and humanitarianism might intersect" in the great cultural and political expanses outside of the West.[13]

Historically, humanitarianism emerged and evolved in tandem with photographic technologies.[14] By the second half of the nineteenth century, photography was increasingly used to generate empirical knowledge of previously unseen worlds: from the spiritual to the material, from the microscopic to the cosmic, from the sociological to the anthropological.[15] Missionaries, reformers, and journalists began to employ photos in illustrated books and lantern-slide lectures to focus public attention on select examples of human misery in the world – from the local slum to the distant famine – transforming specific episodes of privation and suffering into humanitarian crises and campaigns. Humanitarian imagery gave form and meaning to human suffering, rendering it comprehensible, urgent, and actionable for European and American audiences.[16] Such photographic "evidence" was necessarily interpretative.[17] It commanded viewers' attention via specific narratives and moral framings. It articulated a duty and distinct worldview: *Here is a problem that requires redress: here are those who suffer, this is how and why they suffer, this is why we are responsible and what we need to do about it.* Photo-centered appeals forged communities of emotion and action, fleeting or otherwise, of like-minded viewers around specific "causes."[18]

Photographic imagery, narratives, and technologies helped to craft and disseminate humanitarian values via compelling content – both specific and symbolic. The chapters in this volume explore the special relationship between photography and humanitarianism. Nonetheless, we recognize that photography is part of a larger visual and cultural landscape. For more than a century and a half, photographs have co-habited with other existing and emerging visual media: drawings, etchings, cartoons, posters, prints, films, and later television, videos, the Internet, and social media. While photography assumed an important place in humanitarian campaigns, photography did not completely eclipse its visual forerunners. Nor has photography been displaced by its technological successors. The visual economy has remained diverse.

Since the mid-nineteenth century, visual media of various types have accompanied and supplemented each other in humanitarian appeals. Early on, this was due to limitations of photo-mechanical technologies. Some early photographic techniques, like the daguerreotype, did not enable reproduction. For those that did, development processes made it difficult to create photographs in tropical and other challenging natural environments. Even with the invention of dry-plate photography in the 1870s, exposing, developing, and storing glass negatives remained cumbersome. Photography became simple and widely popularized only in 1888 with the introduction and mass marketing of the Kodak camera: a point-and-shoot convenience that came loaded with film and was returned to the manufacturer for film development and reloading.[19]

Printing technologies too played a role. The half-tone process that allowed for the direct reproduction of photographs in print media was invented in the 1880s but became economical only in the 1890s. Prior to that, engravings of photographs were reproduced in print.[20] In addition, aesthetic and visual conventions, pedagogical choices, and other cultural factors came into play. Crucially, the juxtapositions of photographs with other visual media, as well as written text and captions, have shaped meanings of individual images and of humanitarian appeals. In the process, such strategies of representation and communication gave rise to a recognizable, if not unitary, "humanitarian imaginary" that not only reflects, but has also influenced, the historical evolution of humanitarianism.[21]

Even in the nineteenth century, contemporaries were hardly naïve consumers of photographs. Initially, photography was celebrated, or derided, as automatic "sun writing" (heliography): a chemical and optical process that rendered "neutral" and "natural" images, compared to paintings or drawing created by the hand of the artist.[22] Photography was understood to have a certain technical truth-value: each photo froze a distinct slice of time and space, fixing for posterity whatever appeared before the camera's lens. In the 1840s and 1850s, Europeans and Americans began to use photography to study and document the bodies of nonwhite humans at home and abroad in order to construct and legitimize racial typologies; in the process they pioneered the visual conventions of ethnographic and anthropological photography.[23] By the 1870s, photography was embraced by professionalizing scientists who established, through photographic evidence, for example, that lightning's actual form differed greatly from the geometrically perfect zig-zags of artists' renderings and that a world of microbes and bacteria existed, invisible to the human eye yet hazardous to human health. Photography was used and circulated – in scientific conferences, laboratories, publications, and the mainstream press – to both train "the scientific eye" and popularize advances in scientific knowledge.[24]

Yet scientists also found it prudent to rely on supplemental drawings or engravings to "paraphrase" the photograph in order to "see what was there" and "show scientific meanings." This was especially the case for photomicrography, since cellular and subcellular objects often appeared "poorly delineated" and did not reproduce well in textbooks.[25] So even as photography was employed to produce "evidence" and publicize scientific progress, it was simultaneously recognized as a malleable and unstable medium due to technical limitations and the vagaries of human intervention and interpretation.[26]

Nineteenth-century photographers, photographic subjects, and viewers noted that the medium could distort or misrepresent subjects, whether as a result of intentional artifice, technical incompetence, the angle, framing or duration of exposure, the processes of development, or some other choice or error of visual or narrative framing. Indeed, the mere presence of a camera could influence the action before its lens. In 1859, prominent American doctor and philosopher Oliver Wendell Holmes proclaimed himself "smitten" with the powerful new medium whose "*appearance of reality* ... cheats the senses with its seeming truth."[27] In sum, while Americans and Europeans were astounded by the medium's "uncanny" powers of representation, they did not necessarily accept photographic images as presenting an undisputed or indisputable truth. Substantial cultural work was required for photographs to acquire authority as "fact" or evidence.[28] Perhaps especially in humanitarian campaigns, photographic representations had to be authenticated in some way to be accepted as "truth": their value as evidence rested on convincing viewers of what, precisely, they were evidence *of*. Even then, as we shall see, political or ethical concerns could be – and often were – raised regarding the content, meanings, proper use, and display of photography, particularly in the case of photography depicting suffering bodies.[29]

Humanitarian activity and imagery are highly selective. Not all natural catastrophes or episodes of manmade violence are turned into humanitarian causes by humanitarian organizations or the news media.[30] But once a cause is identified, a depiction of human suffering is expected – and probably necessary – to rally the desired response.[31] Since the late nineteenth century, humanitarians, journalists, and missionaries have used visual props and narratives to summon attention and funds. These visual props – often photos – were not just "evidence"; they were *rhetoric*. In focusing the viewers' attention on individual cases of suffering (typically, individual cases were used to connote a larger group of victims), photographs made an argument that such suffering was undeserved and that it should be mitigated. Yet humanitarian imagery only rarely gestured at political causation. And if it did, it would not – likely could not – convey political and social complexities. Indeed, the effectiveness of humanitarian rhetoric appears to depend on its apparent simplicity and directness of emotional address. It focuses viewer attention on suffering, framing it as unjust yet amenable to remedy. It erases distracting political or social detail that would complicate the duty to act. In this sense, humanitarian imagery is *moral rhetoric* masquerading as visual evidence.[32] As such, humanitarian photography was, and is, politically and morally charged terrain. It was certainly not uncontroversial, whether among viewing publics or even, in some cases, among the individuals or organizations that created and distributed it.

Humanitarian imagery has been produced and disseminated by individuals and organizations concerned with aid, relief, rescue, reform, rehabilitation, and development: religious, moral, social, and political goals tied to organizational missions, agendas, and identities (in contemporary parlance, this has come to be called the organizational "brand"). Like modern humanitarianism proper, humanitarian organizations, campaigns, and imagery have never existed apart from the political world; they have been fraught with ideology and competing interests.[33] The term "humanitarian" is a case in point. First used in 1844 England – just five years after the invention of photography was formally announced[34] – it denoted "all that is concerned with benevolence toward humanity as a whole, with human welfare as a primary good" and was used to "designate someone who advocates action for such ends." Initially, the term was frequently employed in a pejorative sense to deride "do-gooders" or would-be reformers thought to be driven by an excess of sentimentality or irrationality and "an appetite for applause" – particularly if their efforts appeared unguided by political pragmatism or were inattentive to state, diplomatic, or economic interests and effects.[35] Only by the late nineteenth century was it used as self-ascription by organizations.[36]

Humanitarian organizations were, and are, rooted in national contexts. The majority of the international or transnational aid operations undertaken by humanitarian agencies took place in the age of nationalism.[37] Leaders of humanitarian organizations came from specific cultural, political, and religious milieus, which affected their humanitarian politics. In this volume, contributors focus on a specific variety of humanitarian actions: those undertaken by individuals, associations, and organizations beyond national frontiers. Nonetheless, the distinction between humanitarian aid taking place within *versus* beyond the nation is an artificial and, to some extent, a misleading one. It overlooks the range of actions that characterized humanitarianism – in its Western and non-Western variants[38] – from the mid-nineteenth century to the post-1945 era. During this period, humanitarians' mental geography – certainly for those from North America and Western Europe – did not necessarily coincide with state frontiers. In fact, many humanitarians undertook aid or rescue operations close to their headquarters, within national frontiers, and simultaneously operated in various colonial or imperial territories as well as beyond national and imperial borders. Examples include the American

Red Cross, the Quakers, and the American Board for Foreign Missions, three U.S. institutions active at three levels: domestically, in occupied (colonial) territories from Cuba to the Philippines, and internationally. In practice, humanitarian efforts directed outside the nation-state – whether within imperial holdings or beyond – were not completely distinct from more local acts of charity and philanthropy. Historically, humanitarian actors have moved rather fluidly between aid, relief, or reform efforts targeting domestic and distant unfortunates. Similarly, beginning in the mid-nineteenth century, professional journalists and photographers, on their own initiative or on behalf of organizations, moved fluidly between domestic, imperial, and broader international settings in their efforts to capture, document, and publicize instances of human misery.[39]

In this volume, we start with the assumption that humanitarian aid meant different things to different individual actors and to different organizations at different times. Despite its moniker, humanitarianism is not a singular -*ism*. In practice, it took various forms during the period covered in this volume, the 1870s to 2010. Humanitarians, sometimes within the same organization, disagreed – and still disagree today – on plausible categorizations of "needy" and on who should be recipients of aid. At its inception in 1863, the International Committee of the Red Cross (ICRC) focused on mitigating the worst effects of war and sought to aid only wounded soldiers on the battlefield. In ensuing decades, some humanitarians, for practical, political, or strategic reasons, specialized in relief for women and children; others – most famously, the Save the Children Fund – focused on feeding, housing, and educating children exclusively. Even the category "needy children" was hardly straightforward. Some humanitarians included children of all ages while others focused their action on behalf of orphaned children only. Historically, other key terms – such as "victim," "refugee," "crisis," or "emergency" – have emerged as foci for relief efforts and have been defined in various ways by humanitarian actors and organizations. Humanitarians disagreed on why, how, when, and for how long individuals, communities, or entire nations were worthy of aid or assistance.[40] Our goal is to examine the meaning and definitions that the protagonists of the time gave to humanitarianism.

Part of the backdrop to this study is the changing structures of humanitarianism and its organizations. The chapters in this volume examine humanitarian action and representation by a wide range of organizations, institutions, and actors: British and American *missionary groups*; *international organizations*, such as the International Committee of the

Red Cross (founded 1863), the United Nations Relief and Rehabilitation Administration (UNRRA, 1943) and the World Health Organization (WHO, 1948); *nongovernmental organizations*, such as Near East Relief and the Save the Children Fund, founded during or just after the First World War; *hybrid organizations* that fuse international and national goals, such as the Chinese Red Cross; and *development organizations*, such as Christian Aid. In addition, some chapters consider humanitarian imagery produced by *journalists* and *photojournalists* since the news media played, and continues to play, an important role in informing publics about large-scale episodes of human suffering and disaster, focusing public attention on and shaping perceptions of such events, and thereby motivating the perceived need for humanitarian intervention.

The chapters in this volume contextualize the efforts of select yet significant actors that made use of photography for a variety of purposes, assuming that the politics of humanitarianism are multiple, that various strands of humanitarianism can coexist within a single organization, and that expressions of humanitarianism can change over time. Given this historical diversity, what assumptions can be made regarding the role and use of photography? Is it plausible to imagine categories of humanitarian photography cutting across multiple humanitarianisms?

We seek to identify trends and threads, continuities and ruptures, similarities and differences related to cultural and representational practices and politics of humanitarian photography. Humanitarianism is not a monolith, it was – and is – a complex and fragmented system of individuals, organizations, and ideas, which coexisted, cooperated, and clashed. Still, since the late nineteenth century something similar to a system, with a gravitational force, emerged. The system expanded and shrank over time, with notable growth spurts accompanying and following the First World War and the Russian Civil War, as well as the Nazi seizure of power and war of aggression in Europe, and Allied victory over Germany and Japan in 1945. Since the late 1970s, humanitarian and human rights organizations have proliferated; after the turn of the 1990s, they multiplied at a historically unprecedented rate.[41] As far as Western humanitarianism is concerned, a heterogeneous group of individuals and organizational actors – as well as the publics they have communicated with – came to share some basic ideas about the desirability of compassion and aiding other human beings in distress. Since the late nineteenth century, this "ethics of care," Michael Barnett notes, has been "institutionalized" and "internationalized," yet nonetheless remains dynamic. "Humanitarians project their moral imaginations in ways that reshape the world," he argues, but "what is imaginable, desirable and possible" changes over time.[42]

In Britain, France, and the United States, one can identify common threads, or even ideological pillars, upon which humanitarian practices were erected. Liberalism and capitalism – in their diverse declinations – were two of them. To many humanitarians, these seemed to represent the only models able to ensure peace and prosperity. This in turn might explain why so many humanitarians, secular and religious, became agents of Western empires and of colonization and why they genuinely adopted a civilizational posture. Humanitarians active in domestic, imperial, and transnational contexts carried with them their profound belief that they were capable of "enlightening" and "elevating" the allegedly ignorant, needy, or less civilized.[43] Humanitarians presumed they knew how to solve what they had designated as a humanitarian problem, emergency, or crisis; they were confident in their abilities to transform the world – or at least the slice of it on which they were at work. Humanitarianism, in its Western variety, has been consistently asymmetrical in its power relations and ripe with paternalism.[44]

Christianity too has been pervasive in Western humanitarianism. Certainly up to the 1940s, Christian precepts, morality, and values informed the actions of humanitarians. Indeed, in Western humanitarianisms, it is often difficult to distinguish between secular and religious motivations, even when an organization explicitly claimed to be secular, as in the case of the International Committee of the Red Cross. Can we accept at face value this organization's claims to universalism and secularism and utterly ignore both its Swiss origins and the Calvinist background of all of its Committee members from the inception of the institution to the late twentieth century? Most humanitarian organizations, even if they were not explicitly Christian or religious, had "transcendental elements": a belief in "humanity" or some similar category that is greater than us, as individuals, and that lends moral gloss and meaning to our actions.[45] What is more, one's willingness to engage in humanitarian action, donate money, or shed a tear on behalf of suffering human beings abroad has been understood, since the nineteenth century, as a mark of *our* elevated humanity – as individuals who embody and express particular strands of Western political and cultural heritage. Over time, this has been reinforced as the emotionally, morally, and ideologically "correct" position to assume – at least in relation to successful humanitarian appeals and campaigns.[46]

Finally, the intimate relation of humanitarianism with modernity and notions of progress bears mentioning. By the turn of the twentieth century, humanitarians – particularly those operating within international organizations like the ICRC and national Red Cross societies – were increasingly convinced that science, technique, and professionalization would help solve the problems of those identified as in need. The rise of internationalism was accompanied by faith in "the expert."[47] Humanitarian aid has often been an opportunity to showcase efficient administration, logistics, professional training, and the use of new technology, photography included. Humanitarian organizations began to establish publicity departments in order to advance fundraising efforts and position themselves to advantage in relation to the expanding media and advertising landscapes.[48]

By the first decades of the twentieth century, photographic appeals shaped the public face of humanitarianism, popularizing it among diverse classes in Europe, the United States, and Asia. By the First World War, humanitarians increasingly claimed media attention and made savvy use of media outlets to acquire mass, cross-class support. This was a gradual process, reaching back to the mid-nineteenth century, as humanitarianism was shaped and promoted through the narrative techniques and visual strategies of the "new journalism," with its eyewitness and investigative reporting, exposés, and human interest stories, as well as the pictorial press and motion pictures, which increasingly dished out sensationalism to increase circulation numbers and box-office receipts.[49] Kevin Rozario has argued provocatively that instead of viewing "sensationalism and humanitarianism as distinct and competing cultural developments," we should recognize modern humanitarianism as a *creation* of a sensationalist mass culture" since, by the 1910s, donors were increasingly "treated as consumers who had to be entertained."[50] Humanitarian imagery competed for attention in a diverse visual economy produced by commercial, religious, and state-affiliated interests. This raises questions not only about the distinctiveness of humanitarian imagery but also about its reliance, and reciprocal effects, on the visual and narrative strategies of commercialized mass culture and political propaganda, which were rapidly becoming ubiquitous on the street, in publications, and in movie theaters by the early twentieth century in Europe and the United States.

The chapters in this volume consider a series of prominent humanitarian responses, since the late nineteenth century, to natural disasters, imperial brutality, wartime violence, and postwar crises in diverse regions spanning Africa and Europe, to the Middle East, India, and China. Each case study examines the particulars of when, where, why, how, and to what effect

individuals and organizations have used photography for humanitarian
causes: which subjects were featured, which audiences were addressed,
what were the politics informing each campaign? Each chapter responds
in some way to the cluster of the interpretative questions that motivate
our common project. None addresses all of the following questions, but
each is informed by reference to some of them:

- What visual presentation, strategies, and narratives have been
  employed? What visual conventions have been established? How have
  these changed – or persisted – over time and place? How have visual
  strategies been shaped, or altered, by distribution venues and visual
  technologies? How have they been informed by broader photographic
  and cultural practices?
- How does humanitarian photography relate to the media representation of war and atrocity, the Holocaust, and other genocides? How
  does it intersect with the histories of colonialism and imperialism,
  decolonization and post-colonialism, hot wars and the Cold War?
- What evidence do we have regarding the reception and impact of
  humanitarian imagery? What accounts for the "success" of humanitarian campaigns – as defined in terms of touching a nerve and raising
  public awareness and funds?[51]
- What attempts have been made to regulate humanitarian imagery?
  What can be said about humanitarian photography's *ethics of practice*
  over time?

Our goal is not to provide definitive answers to these questions but to
introduce these issues to historical scrutiny and open an important scholarly agenda in relation to the visual histories of humanitarianism and
human rights.

The chapters proceed in roughly chronological fashion, beginning
in the closing decades of the nineteenth century, in order to trace the
distinctive practitioners, institutional practices, narrative and pictorial conventions as well as the debates, disputes, and ethics informing
humanitarian photography. *Heather Curtis* explores the visual culture of
late nineteenth-century humanitarianism on display in American evangelical print journalism, arguing that evangelicals were "at the forefront
of pictorial humanitarianism." Her primary focus is the contested nature
of Christian humanitarianism and the proper use of imagery. Curtis
uncovers conflicts among American evangelicals regarding both the ethics of sensationalist journalism and the probity of American imperial
expansion. Her chapter shows that ethical debates about humanitarian

imagery – whether it aids identification with victims or results in feelings of difference and disgust – is well over a century old. *Christina Twomey* examines the historical emergence of the language of atrocity in the late nineteenth century, its use by humanitarian movements, and the subsequent linking of languages and images of atrocity. She focuses on three formative historical moments: the Bulgarian "atrocities" of the late 1870s; the Indian Famine of 1876–78; and the Congo Reform Campaign of 1903–13 to consider the emergence, evolution, and humanitarian use of "atrocity" narratives and photos.

Kevin Grant explores the gendered conventions of photographic display, narration, and exhibition of atrocity by British missionaries active in the Congo Reform Campaign, the largest sustained humanitarian initiative prior to the First World War. Grant examines how these humanitarians apprehended and structured their use of print media and public lantern-slide lectures to publicize and condemn the mutilation of Congolese men, women, and children who labored in the rubber trade in the Congo Free State under the rule of Belgian King Leopold II. Atrocity photos and horror narratives constituted the centerpiece of public meetings of the Congo Reform movement yet presented the greatest challenge: how could British humanitarians use them to stimulate "constructive provocation" yet avoid the "destructive alienation" of their audiences?

In "Photography, Visual Culture, and the Armenian Genocide," *Peter Balakian* analyzes two sets of images produced during and after the First World War: atrocity images taken by amateur photographers showing the deportation and destruction of Armenians by Turkish forces between 1915 and 1918 and humanitarian images generated after the war by the American Protestant organization, Near East Relief, to aid Armenian survivors and suffering Greeks, Syrians, and Arabs in Turkey, Transcaucasia, Syria, and Iran. In addition to providing historical context, Balakian seeks to understand these two strands of visual culture –"the raw and the cooked" – in relation to one another, probing how the graphic wartime shots of suffering and death, forbidden by the Turkish government, and the widely disseminated graphic poster art of Near East Relief campaigns, featuring sentimentalized depictions of women and children, have contributed to distinct political, historical and humanitarian projects.

The chapters by *Caroline Reeves* and *Francesca Piana* analyze the visual politics and practices of the Red Cross movement. Reeves sketches the history of the Chinese Red Cross from its founding in 1904 during the Russo-Japanese War through its rapid expansion in the Republican period (1911–37), examining how it intersected with earlier philanthropic and representational traditions, and how it served populations-in-need and promoted its work, at home and abroad. Reeves argues that the Chinese Red Cross departed from the conventions of both earlier Chinese philanthropic iconography and the images of suffering generated in the West, yet nonetheless developed visual tropes that remained useful under the subsequent Maoist regime.

Francesca Piana explores the International Committee of the Red Cross and its determined adoption of modern communications techniques after the "watershed" of the First World War. She argues that the ICRC increasingly used photographs and film to justify its expanding humanitarian mandate and to legitimize its leadership role in the rapidly professionalizing and highly competitive sphere of interwar international humanitarianism. Piana examines ICRC decision-making in Geneva as well as the ICRC's visual production and collaboration in the field, comparing its use of photographic media to that of other organizations, such as the American Red Cross and the Save the Children Fund.

Heide Fehrenbach explores the question of when humanitarian campaigns came to be dominated by a focus on the symbolic figure of the child. Focusing on a diverse set of actors in Britain, Europe, and the United States from the late nineteenth century through the Second World War, she traces emerging conventions of child-centered humanitarian photography in relation to other photographic genres and practices – such as family portraiture, ethnographic photography, advertising, and photojournalism. Her chapter examines the political valences of child-centered imagery and the extent to which it became a shared cultural strategy across media formats and political-ideological camps.

Silvia Salvatici analyzes the rich photographic collection of the United Nations Relief and Rehabilitation Administration, the United Nations (UN) agency in charge of assisting victims of "German barbarism" in the aftermath of World War II. In providing an account of UNRRA's international humanitarian activities, its Public Information Division relied heavily on images and on the services of professional photojournalists active during the war. Salvatici explores the pictorial recurrence of certain types of recipients such as children, mothers, and refugees, as well as strategies of self-depiction by the organization. Her analysis of UNRRA suggests both continuities with earlier iconographic practices as well as innovative departures after 1945. *Davide Rodogno* and *Thomas David* examine the visual politics of the World Health Organization through the lens of its magazine *W.H.O. Newsletter*, which began publication in 1949 and was rechristened *World Health* after 1958. Although the politics of the organization were not, strictly speaking, humanitarian, the narratives presented in its magazine were. This tension, and the rationale for editorial choices, are a central consideration. The authors examine how technological and technical assistance narratives interacted with humanitarian narratives and how photography – and prominent photojournalists – were employed to legitimize the WHO and its activities, render them a topic of public interest, and corroborate its successes.

Lasse Heerten examines how European and American media representations of starving "Biafran children" turned the Nigerian Civil War of the late 1960s into a "genocide" and an international "media event." Heerten explores the ways representations of the conflict in print and televised media constructed narrative and visual connections with the Nazi extermination of the Jews: a strategy that simultaneously established the meaning of the Nigerian conflict and the historical centrality of "the Holocaust" for contemporaries while reinforcing the repetitive visual tropes of genocide.

The final two chapters in the volume examine developments in the ethical practice of humanitarian photography since the 1970s. *Henrietta Lidchi* focuses on the period from the late 1970s through the early 1990s, when the promiscuous use of Third World images of human suffering, particularly in response to the Ethiopian Famine in the early 1980s, provoked criticism and calls to abandon such "negative" imagery, giving rise to a new voluntary code of conduct among humanitarian and development NGOs in Europe. After establishing the historical and theoretical context, she examines in detail an ad campaign by the British NGO Christian Aid from the turn of the 1990s, an early attempt to produce "positive" imagery. *Sanna Nissinen* considers the effects of such ethical mandates through the first decade of the 2000s, examining their institutionalization via the directives that NGOs provide their photographers as well as the unintended homogenizing effects the rules have had on the types of images taken and mobilized in publicity campaigns. Nissinen's discussion is based upon fieldwork in Bangladesh in 2010 during which she accompanied and interviewed indigenous photographers and observed their interactions with their subjects. Moving beyond characterizations of the "positive" and "negative" effects of photographic power, Nissinen posits a more complex collaboration between photographer and subject that recognizes volition, interests, and intelligence on both sides of the camera.

Since the nineteenth century, a central element of humanitarian photography has been a focus on visualizing the human body as vulnerable, under threat, in pain, or in recovery. So too is the mandate – expressed via image, framing, caption, and text – for viewers to respond: to recognize their moral "duty," whether as Christians, imperial subjects, democratic, or, most recently, global citizens, to address human suffering. In setting the photographic image and its relation to humanitarianisms in historical context, we aspire to move beyond the tendency– among scholars and cultural critics alike– to rely too heavily on the writings of Susan Sontag and a small coterie of her supporters and critics, to theorize photography's role in representing, publicizing, and ameliorating "the pain of others."[52] While our volume is shaped by an engagement with such literature, our purpose is to enrich it by exploring in detail actual practices, appeals, debates, ethics, technologies, distribution venues, and effects of humanitarian image campaigns across time and space.

There is a paradox at the heart of the history of humanitarian imagery. On the one hand, humanitarian imagery over the past century conveys a static quality, even though its meanings, and social and political functions, do change over time and space. Nonetheless, the visual repertoire of humanitarian photography has remained relatively constrained with its focus on suffering bodies and the effective work of humanitarian organizations, appended only in recent decades by images of resilient and self-reliant recipients of aid. On the other hand, these tried-and-true tropes – but particularly representations of human suffering that pervade our print and electronic news media – have been surprisingly effective over the long run in engaging the emotions and opening the purse strings of their viewing publics. For this reason alone, the historical trajectories of humanitarian photography merit analysis. Although they make no claims to comprehensive coverage, the chapters in this volume represent a start. They aim to chart, with historical specificity, how humanitarianism, the photographic image, and modern media technologies came of age together, informed each other, and evolved in tandem over the course of the twentieth century and beyond, shaping, in the process, the visual imaginary of our ethical worlds.

Notes

1   The authors thank Kevin Grant, Samuel Moyn, Silvia Salvatici, Deborah Gershenowitz, and Ian Burns for their useful comments and suggestions. Any errors of fact or judgment remain our own.
2   Such as Roland Barthes, Susan Sontag, Barbie Zelizer, Susie Linfield, Allen Sekula, Ulrich Baer, Geoffrey Batchen, Luc Boltanski, Cornelia Brink, Elizabeth Edwards, Vicki Goldberg, Robert Hariman and Jon Louis Lucaites,

Elizabeth Hight, Ulrich Keller, Susan Moeller, John Taylor, Caroline Brothers, Shawn Michelle Smith, and Sharon Sliwinski.

3 Sontag, *Regarding the Pain of Others*, 18, 24; see also Linfield's critical response to Sontag in *The Cruel Radiance*.

4 See recent notable work by Michael Barnett, Kevin Grant, Stefan-Ludwig Hoffmann, Samuel Moyn, Davide Rodogno, Silvia Salvatici, Peter Walker and Daniel Maxwell, and Jenny Martinez, among others.

5 See the important work of Thomas Haskell, Karen Halttunen, Thomas Laqueur, Lynn Hunt, Lynn Festa, Elizabeth Clark, Margaret Abruzzo. Quotation is from Halttunen, "Humanitarianism," 310.

6 Haskell ("Capitalism") notes a "spurt" of humanitarian reform activity between 1750 and 1850; Walker and Maxwell (*Shaping the Humanitarian World*) discuss humanitarianism as an "international system" and note that the first "modern principles of relief" (public works, food distribution, soup kitchens) were applied to famines in India (1837–8) and Ireland (1845–7) and involved government support, 17–22, quotation from 17; Barnett (*Empire of Humanity*) dates humanitarianism to the early nineteenth century and emphasizes its imperial context.

7 See Caroline Reeves's chapter in this volume.

8 Laqueur, "Mourning," 40.

9 Notable exceptions include Christina Twomey and Heather Curtis; see also Kevin Rozario, Julia Irwin, Mary Niall Mitchell, and T. Jack Thompson. Julia Adeney Thomas ("The Evidence of Sight") has written insightfully on the use of photos as historical evidence.

10 See, for example, Sliwinski, "The Childhood of Human Rights." In the well-received book *The Ironic Spectator*, media scholar Lilie Chouliaraki cites actress Audrey Hepburn's work with UNICEF (UN Children's Rights and Emergency Relief Organization) in the 1980s as corresponding to the "emergence" of "celebrity humanitarianism" (90), although celebrities have been used since the 1910 to front fundraising campaigns. Child actor Jackie Coogan was involved with *Near East Relief* in the First World War era. The American and Chinese Red Cross showcased celebrities and prominent people in publications to publicize relief drives in that period. See Reeves in this volume; also Irwin (*Making the World Safe*).

11 See the chapters by Caroline Reeves on the Chinese Red Cross in the early twentieth century and by Sanna Nissinen on Bangladeshi photographers working for international NGOs in the early twenty-first century.

12 The history of photography is perhaps the most developed scholarship in terms of a focus on diverse practices outside of Europe and North America; see the important work of Christopher Pinney, Rosalind Morris, Zahid Chaudhary, Deborah Poole, and Julia Adeney Thomas, among others. Our thanks to Kevin Grant for his useful comments on this issue.

13 Samuel Moyn, personal e-mail communication with Fehrenbach, 16 April 2014.

14 Scholars date the undisputed start of organized humanitarian action to the first third of the nineteenth century; see note 4 this chapter. The invention of photography was formally announced in France in 1839, and patents were filed that year in France and England. Marien, *Photography*, 6–32.

15 Tucker, *Nature Exposed*; Corey Keller, ed., *Brought to Light: Photography and the Invisible, 1840–1900* (New Haven, CT: Yale University Press, 2008); Robert A. Sobieszek, *Ghost in the Shell: Photography and the Human Soul, 1850–2000* (Cambridge, MA and Los Angeles: MIT Press and Los Angeles County Museum of Art, 1999); Louis Kaplan, *The Strange Case of William Mumler, Spirit Photographer* (Minneapolis: University of Minnesota Press, 2008); Edwards, ed., *Anthropology and Photography*; Pinney, *Photography and Anthropology*; Grimshaw, *The Ethnographer's Eye*; Hight, ed., *Colonialist Photography*; Maxwell, *Colonial Photography and Exhibitions*; Bank, "Anthropology and Portrait Photography"; Banks and Ruby, *Made to Be Seen*; Koven, *Slumming*; Smith, *American Archives*; Willis and Krauthamer, *Envisioning Emancipation*.

16 Laqueur, "Bodies" and "Mourning"; Haltunnen, "Humanitarianism"; Festa, "Humanity without Feathers."

17 Alan Trachtenberg has argued that photography and the process of photographing "lends a special kind of presence to what it depicts," *Lincoln's Smile and Other Enigmas* (New York: Hill and Wang, 2007), 110. Photographer and critic John Szarkowski called photography "a process of selection" noting that the "factuality of pictures" differs from "reality" itself: "much … is filtered out" while other elements are "exhibited with an unnatural clarity, an exaggerated importance." When we confront photos, he reminds us, "what we think about and act upon is the symbolic report and not the concrete event," *The Photographer's Eye*, 8.

18 On emotional communities, see Rosenwein ("Worrying about Emotions"); also Tagg (*The Burden of Representation*), 12, on the "moralism" of documentary photography. The humanitarian impulse was not "natural" – it was a product of specific geopolitical, economic, technological, intellectual, social, and cultural relations and formations. Yet humanitarian sentiment – and humanitarian reform – sometimes acquired a natural gloss: it could be conflated with the innate goodness of human beings – especially human beings who considered themselves civilized, of religious or moral disposition, and otherwise elevated in social and spiritual terms.

19 Even then, many photographers, such as missionary Alice Harris in the Congo, continued to use glass plates. See Grant in this volume; also Thompson, *Light on Darkness*, 18–61; on Kodak mania, see Robert Mensel, "Kodakers Lying in Wait: Photography and the Right to Privacy, 1885–1915," *American Quarterly* 43, no. 1 (March 1989): 24–45.

20 Prior to the 1890s, photographs would be rendered as engravings to be published, which meant that the engraver or editor could alter the image to emphasize or omit certain characteristics of the original image.

21 On contemporary humanitarian communications strategies, see Boltanski, *Distant Suffering*; Calain, "Ethics and Images"; Chouliaraki, *The Ironic Spectator*; Malkki, "Children" and "Speechless Emissaries"; and Manzo, "Imagining Humanitarianism."

22 Marien, *Photography*, 11, 23.

23 Well-known examples are the work of French photographer E. Thiésson's work on the "natives" of Sofala in 1840s Mozambique and J. T. Zealy's

photographs of North Carolina slaves in 1850 for naturalist Louis Agassiz, founder of Harvard's museum of comparative zoology. Marien (*Photography*), 37–42; see also Bank ("Anthropology"), Hight (*Colonialist Photography*), Maxwell (*Colonial Photography and Exhibitions*).

24 Tucker, *Nature Exposed*, esp. 126–233.

25 Ibid., quotations from 126, 221, 160, 181. Tucker also explores debates about life on Mars, based on 1905 photos of the planet that some interpreted as showing a system of canals; this also fueled concerns about how best to render the planet-scape in drawings, *Nature Exposed*, 194–233.

26 Trachtenberg, *Lincoln's Smile*, xx, and Tucker, *Nature Exposed*.

27 Trachtenberg, *Lincoln's Smile*, 86, emphasis added.

28 Trachtenberg, *Lincoln's Smile*, 86–122; also Szarkowski, *The Photographer's Eye*, Tucker, *Nature Exposed*, and Marien, *Photography*. This cultural work also included the "testimonial narrative" – an individual account of suffering and injustice experienced by slaves or other oppressed groups of people.

29 As Alan Trachtenberg argued, there is a distinction between "what's in a picture" and the "social function of pictures," 112–13. See also Twomey, Grant, and Curtis in this volume.

30 Haskell, "Capitalism," made this point early in the historical scholarship.

31 See Laqueur, "Bodies"; Halttunen, "Humanitarianism"; Boltanski, "Distant Suffering," among others.

32 Sontag makes a similar point and proclaims photographs of victims of war "rhetoric," *Regarding*, 6; also Manzo, "Imagining," and Malkki, "Children." On contemporary humanitarianism's communicative strategy, see Calain, "Ethics and Images," and Chouliaraki, *The Ironic Spectator*.

33 Barnett, *Empire of Humanity*; Hoffmann, ed., *Human Rights in the Twentieth Century*.

34 On recent rethinking of how we define photography and date its origins, see Marien, *Photography*, 1–23 and Geoffrey Batchen, *Burning with Desire: The Conception of Photography* (Cambridge, MA: MIT Press, 1999).

35 See Rodogno, *Against Massacre*, for a discussion of British military interventions in the nineteenth-century Ottoman Empire, which were portrayed as humanitarian and fueled by political and diplomatic interests.

36 One of the first was socialist Henry Stephens Salt's "Humanitarian League," devoted to the social and educational propagation of "humane-ness" in word, deed, and legislation. Katherine Davies, "Continuity, Change and Contest: Meanings of 'Humanitarianism' from the 'Religion of Humanity' to the Kosovo War." HPG Working Paper, August 2012. London: Humanitarian Policy Group/Overseas Development Institute, 2012, 3–4; also *Chambers Dictionary of Etymology* (New York: H. H. Wilson, 2003), 496; and Calhoun, "The Imperative to Reduce Suffering."

37 This includes post-1945 operations and the nationalisms of previously colonized African and Asian countries.

38 On the latter, see Caroline Reeves's chapter in this volume.

39 Examples are British "new journalism" coverage of the Irish and Indian famines, although photos exist only for the latter; Lewis Hine's photography on behalf of U.S. child labor reform and for the American Red Cross in postwar

Europe; the Save the Children Fund coverage of relief work in Europe and
at home in England in the 1920s; see Vernon, *Hunger*; Kaplan, *Photostory*;
Marshall, "Construction of Children"; Mahood, *Feminism*; also Reeves on
the Chinese Red Cross in this volume.

40 Because we are interested in examining historical varieties of humanitarianism and their use of photography, we avoid sweeping generalizations and
definitions. They are of limited value for understanding the historical development of humanitarianisms and their organizational cultures, representational
practices, and public information or fundraising campaigns. We do not label
humanitarian organizations as focused on either "triage" or "transformational agendas." We do not understand short-term, emergency aid humanitarianism to be systematically opposed to or distinguishable from "alchemical"
humanitarianism, that is, one that purportedly goes beyond immediate provisioning of aid to address structural or root causes of human suffering. In
many instances, in fact, supposedly "triage" organizations, such as the Save
the Children Fund or the ICRC, went beyond short-term relief operations; in
other circumstances, allegedly "transformational" organizations, such as the
Near East Relief, abruptly terminated long-term humanitarian operations.

41 For a schematic chronological overview, see Barnet, *Empire of Humanity*; on
the post-1945 humanitarian order, see Cohen, *In War's Wake*; for an interpretative argument about the human rights revolution of the Carter years and
beyond, see Moyn, *The Last Utopia*.

42 Barnett, *Empire of Humanity*, 8, 15, 11, 9.

43 See the work of Alice Conklin, *A Mission to Civilize*, Kevin Grant, *Civilized
Savagery*, and J. P. Daughton, *An Empire Divided*, among others.

44 Boltanski, *Distant Suffering*; Fassin, *Humanitarian Reason*. Barnett suggests
that "a world without paternalism might be a world without the ethics of
care" in *Empire of Humanity*, 12.

45 Barnett, *Empire of Humanity*, 20, quotation from 18; Barnett notes that religious "allegories, concepts, metaphors ... and iconography" pervade descriptions of humanitarianism, 17–18.

46 After all, successful campaigns are those that have persuaded viewers of their
moral duty to give or act. See Festa's perceptive discussion of "sentimental
sympathy" and "sentimental humanity": "Feelings of sympathy create the
humanity of the feeling subject, not the humanity of the object felt for.... Some
people have humanity; others are it," "Humanity without Feathers," 7–8.

47 See Laqua, *Internationalism Reconfigured*; Sluga, *Internationalism*; also
Irwin, *Making the World Safe*.

48 Near East Relief, the American Red Cross, and the League of Nations are
examples from the early twentieth century.

49 See Vernon, *Hunger*, on how hunger became news in nineteenth-century
Britain; on sensationalism in print and other media, Vanessa Schwartz,
Spectacular Realities: Early Mass Culture in Fin-de-Siecle Paris (Berkeley:
University of California Press, 1999); Judy Walkowitz, *City of Dreadful
Delight* (Chicago: University of Chicago Press, 1992); Koven, *Slumming*.

50 Rozario,"DeliciousHorrors,"418–19;seealsoHaltunnen,"Humanitarianism," on the nineteenth century.

51 Rather than the more intractable issue of resolving specific conditions or crises on the ground and thereby "solving" the problem of human suffering due to natural and manmade disasters.

52 Sontag, *Regarding;* also Linfield, *The Cruel Radiance.*

I

Picturing Pain

Evangelicals and the Politics of Pictorial Humanitarianism in an Imperial Age[*]

Heather D. Curtis

After months of anticipation, the July 1897 edition of *Cosmopolitan* illustrated monthly, one of the most popular general-interest periodicals in the United States, printed the first installment of a report by the magazine's "special commissioner to India," Julian Hawthorne. Hired to "seriously investigate … rumors of famine and plague" in the British colony from the perspective of an impartial eye-witness, the journalist departed on "this dangerous mission" in early February. During his three-month sojourn in the subcontinent, Hawthorne encountered "the saddest and grimmest spectacles known to modern times" – ghastly sights of starvation and disease that defied adequate description. "I can never bring home livingly to others the truth and horror of them," he confessed.[1] While editor John Brisben Walker had hoped Hawthorne's "clever literary style" would "enable readers of *The Cosmopolitan* to see through his eyes," he agreed in his prefatory note to the series that the author's words alone were not enough to convey the "inconceivable conditions" of famine-stricken India. Fortunately, Walker wrote, Hawthorne had documented his account with images that brought the dreadful realities of pestilence and pain "vividly to our understandings." In the photographs illustrating Hawthorne's reports, the editor averred, "there is told a story of human misery and suffering beyond which nothing more terrible can be pictured."[2]

[*] This chapter was originally published in the journal *Material Religion* 8, no. 2 (2012): 154–83. The editors thank Heather Curtis and Berg, a division of Bloomsbury Publishing, for permission to reprint an edited and condensed version of the original essay.

The images of plague victims, corpses ready for cremation, destitute families at the poorhouse, and "half-naked, wasted creatures" consisting of nothing but "bone and sinew" that supplemented Hawthorne's articles moved viewers to send "many letters of generous appreciation, accompanied often by contributions of money for the immediate relief of suffering." This outpouring of "truly Christian" charity surprised Hawthorne. Although he deduced that "fancy pictures" might arouse the feelings of his readers, the writer remained skeptical that images could fully bridge the expanses of space and cultural difference separating starving India from prosperous America. Throughout his report, Hawthorne expressed doubts about his fellow citizens' ability to grasp "the immensity of [the] disaster" unfolding on the other side of the globe, let alone to respond with heartfelt empathy and financial aid. "It is easy to pity and help the disaster of your neighbor across the street," he observed, "but to pity with something more than words the calamities of those whom we shall never see; whose ways and habitation are alien and remote; to come with tears in the eyes and purse in hand to succor them – there is something divine in that."[3]

Hawthorne's musings on the challenges of cultivating compassion across geographic, social, and religious divides offer an entrée into late nineteenth-century debates about the role of images in the expanding enterprise of American humanitarianism. During the 1890s, a number of overlapping factors – including the development of travel and communication technologies, the ongoing extension of international trade markets, the burgeoning of transnational reform networks, the exponential growth of the foreign missionary movement, and the intensification of imperialism – contributed to "the flowering of international humanitarianism in the United States," particularly although not exclusively among evangelical Protestants. Alongside ostensibly secular organizations such as the American Red Cross, which claimed to uphold the principle of neutrality enshrined in the first Geneva Convention (1864), religious internationalists belonging to a diverse array of Jewish, Catholic, and Protestant groups actively participated in "promoting a collective culture of humanitarianism." Although Americans had often aided victims of natural disaster and political upheaval in other nations prior to the 1890s, these earlier charitable efforts were "more episodic and less religiously based" than the organized humanitarian campaigns to assuage the afflictions of distant strangers that emerged during the latter decades of the nineteenth century.[4]

As Hawthorne's exposé reveals, photography played an integral part in the extension of American philanthropy abroad. When missionaries, moral reformers, and investigative journalists traveled overseas in these years, they carried cameras with them – a feat made easier after George Eastman introduced the first portable Kodak in 1888. By the early 1890s, advances in halftone printing techniques made possible the mass reproduction of original photographs in popular periodicals like the *Cosmopolitan*. While daily and weekly newspapers were slower to integrate photography into their pages, they increasingly included illustrations, engravings, and cartoons in their efforts to attract readers amid the intensifying competition provoked by the advent of "yellow journalism." As Americans encountered the horrors of plague, pestilence, and oppression during their perambulations in India and elsewhere, they took advantage of these developments in visual culture to document humanitarian crises in distant lands. By combining images of suffering people with graphic narratives of misery, publicists sought to stimulate American spectators to engage in benevolent action on behalf of their fellow beings around the world.

But the proliferation of pictures in print media during the "humanitarian upsurge" of the 1890s also posed problems for aspiring almoners. The sensationalism associated with the yellow press created a climate of suspicion about the credibility of images that undermined attempts to present photographs as incontrovertible evidence of catastrophe in remote regions. Rather than fostering faith, Hawthorne inferred, pictures often provoked doubt. "Photographs are incredible – we don't believe them," he remarked. Harrowing scenes of human torment, he also implied, stimulated viewers' emotions in ways that some found disquieting. Was titillation an effective and moral means of stirring up sympathy for sufferers in far-off places? Did photographs of "utterly destitute and helpless" people cultivate condescension rather than compassion for a "common humanity"?[5]

Hawthorne only hinted at some of these questions in his reports for the *Cosmopolitan*, but a number of his contemporaries raised similar queries more explicitly. Throughout the 1890s, and especially during the devastating India famines of 1896–7 and 1899–1900, the practical imperatives and ethical ambiguities of depicting distant suffering for humanitarian purposes were the subject of frequent comment and sometimes anxious deliberation, especially among American evangelicals actively engaged in relief efforts both at home and abroad. While secular publications such as William Randolph Heart's *New York Journal* and illustrated monthlies like the *Cosmopolitan* occasionally included articles on India's "starving millions" supplemented by images of famine victims, religious periodicals were replete with graphic appeals for help. Pictures of the ongoing crisis were particularly prevalent in interdenominational weeklies like the *Christian and Missionary Alliance* and the *Christian Herald* – the latter by some accounts "the most influential religious paper in America" during the 1890s.[6]

This chapter analyzes the visual culture of American humanitarianism displayed and debated in these evangelical journals. Probing how publications such as the *Christian Herald* and the *Christian and Missionary Alliance* used images to promote American participation in India famine relief campaigns confirms that evangelicals were at the forefront of pictorial humanitarianism in this period. Although Hawthorne's reports in the *Cosmopolitan* garnered a great deal of publicity during the summer of 1897, articles and photographs depicting India's affliction had appeared months earlier in both the *Christian Herald* and the *Christian and Missionary Alliance*. Examining the commonalities and contrasts between these two pioneering periodicals advances scholarship on imagery and the development of international philanthropy in several ways.

First, while a growing cadre of historians has recently explored the emergence of the "humanitarian sensibility" in the modern West, most have concentrated on the importance of philosophical ideals associated with the Enlightenment, or on the centrality of attitudes connected with the rise of market capitalism, largely neglecting the influence of evangelical visual culture in "imagining Humanity."[7] The few studies that do consider the connections between evangelical pictorial practices and humanitarianism show that antebellum abolitionists employed graphic images of horrific bodily distress in their attempts to establish "slaves as fully sentient beings" who deserved compassion.[8] The opening section of this essay traces the links between this ethics of "spectatorial sympathy" and late nineteenth-century relief campaigns.[9] When faced with the "dreadful scourge" of famine in India during the 1890s, contributors to both the *Christian Herald* and the *Christian and Missionary Alliance* exploited innovations in print journalism and photography to arouse sympathy for suffering strangers in ways that evoked the visual strategies of evangelical abolitionism.

Second, assessing the specific ways evangelicals employed images to promote empathetic engagement across racial, social, and even religious boundaries in an increasingly modern, "sensationalist," and imperialist age uncovers substantial tensions underlying attempts to unite American

Protestants in the common cause of international benevolence. While evangelicals associated with the *Christian Herald* and the *Christian and Missionary Alliance* were unified in their conviction that photographs and illustrations could encourage compassion for far-off and culturally different others, their conflicting perspectives on the ethics of yellow journalism, diverging views on the spiritual integrity of American culture, and contrary opinions about the probity of American expansionism produced subtle but significant differences in attitudes toward almsgiving. Careful analysis of how these two evangelical periodicals pictured "humanity" and portrayed the distress of strangers during the India famines exposes incongruent visions and contested definitions of humanitarianism. The "collective culture" of international philanthropy that emerged during the 1890s was, I contend, shot through with tensions and fissures made visible in the diverse ways evangelicals dealt with the challenges of depicting distant suffering.

Pioneers in Pictorial Journalism: Evangelicals and the Role of Images in Humanitarianism

Several weeks before Julian Hawthorne set sail for India, the New York–based *Christian Herald* printed a letter from correspondent Benjamin Aitken describing the "appalling destitution" he had witnessed as he traveled through the famine districts at the behest of the periodical's proprietor. Accompanying Aitken's report were "photographs taken by his order on the spot specially for THE CHRISTIAN HERALD." The two pictures of "starving natives" were, the editor claimed, "the first authentic photographs of the suffering people that have ever been published" (Figure 1.1). Similar images of the horrors unfolding throughout the subcontinent appeared in almost every succeeding issue for the next few months alongside impassioned appeals for financial contributions to the *Christian Herald* India Relief Fund. These vivid pictures of "appalling figures" whose "shocking ghastliness" told the "pathetic story of [their] urgent need" for succor from "the Christian people of America," the paper's publishers proposed, would induce readers to open their "hearts … hands … purses … and granaries" to "feed the hungry, to send or carry aid to the sick, and to spread the Gospel message everywhere."[10]

Since his purchase of the *Christian Herald* in 1890, the evangelical philanthropist Louis Klopsch had worked to make the periodical "a chosen channel of individual and collective benevolence for the Lord's people of all denominations."[11] As pioneers in the practice of "pictorial journalism,"

JAN. 20, 1897 THE CHRISTIAN HERALD AND SIGNS OF OUR TIMES. 45

INDIA'S STARVING MILLIONS.

"The Christian Herald's" Correspondent Describes the Scenes of Suffering, the People, and the Measures being taken for their Relief.

TWO months ago, when the reports of the appalling destitution in India indicated the widespread extent of the calamity, THE CHRISTIAN HERALD, desiring to lay the exact facts before its readers, cabled to Mr. Benjamin Aitken, a Christian journalist in Calcutta, commissioning him to visit the districts affected, and write the facts as he saw them. He accepted the commission and has personally visited the famine-stricken region. The first of a series of letters from him we give here, with photographs taken by his order on the spot specially for THE CHRISTIAN HERALD. These are the first authentic photographs of the suffering people that have ever been published.

Our Correspondent's Letter.

In the Vicinity of Bhopal.—A rough idea of the part of India affected by the present famine may be formed by beginning in the northwest, the Punjab, and running a band about one-third of the width of the country right down to about one-fourth of the distance from Cape Comorin. About the middle of India this band should bend and by keeping straight down it will avoid the whole west coast. Owing to several circumstances which would be tedious to go into, all parts of the area indicated are not equally affected; while certain parts outside of the area are suffering, conspicuously the great indigo region of Behar and parts of south Assam.

The course of the famine, which is only beginning, has been this: There are, in the main, two harvests in India: the autumn harvest, grown under the heavy monsoon rains of June to September; and the spring harvest, grown under the lighter rains of December and January. The cultivator watches each fall of rain with daily anxiety. For it is not enough that the rain be abundant; it must be properly distributed. If the first fall be too long deferred, the grain cannot be sown; if there be a drought of some weeks after the grain is sown, the young plants die; and if rains cease too early, the crop does not ripen. Well, the monsoon rains of the present year were very scanty in some parts, and while exceedingly abundant in others, failed altogether a month before the usual time. The result was that prices went up, people in moderate circumstances began to feel the pinch, and the mass whose means just suffice to sustain life in ordinary years, began to starve. The government was on the alert, and received weekly reports by telegraph from every part of the country, of the state of the crops and the rise of prices. Extensive schemes for making new roads, excavating tanks, filling up marshes, clearing away jungle, and breaking stones for road metal, all to give employment to the people were got ready, and orders went forth not to consider the cost, but to start the works one after another as soon as the scarcity made itself felt. Orders were also issued and funds allotted for the opening of poor-houses at suitable points throughout the affected area, to feed gratuitously those too weak for any kind of work, and especially the children, thousands of whom are losing their parents by death or desertion. Special European officers were appointed to have charge of both these measures of relief, with a perfect army of native supervisors and servants under them.

But it is one thing to organize relief measures, and a very different thing to induce the people to take advantage of them. When we have to deal with a population six times that of the United States, and crowded into a country no larger than the United States east of the Mississippi, it is surprising how quickly a few thousands can die without producing more than a ripple on the surface of life. The stupid stubbornness of the people passes belief, and is only accepted as a fact by Europeans who are here to see the way they act. Fatalism, superstition, prejudice, and indolence combined make multitudes of them take their chances of begging rather than leave their place of abode to go on a relief work; and at the poor-houses the starving people have such a mania for wandering all over the country that they do not get back for a second meal till they have gone perhaps two days without food; and their condition is then such that half of them die in a few days. So many people died on the roadsides and in the fields in August and September, that an imperative rule has been made requiring paupers to remain at the poor-houses if they are to be fed at all. This beneficent rule, although it looks like imprisonment, has practically stopped the people dying all over the country. They continue to die at the poor-houses, but that is the result of previous starvation, or of diseases—sometimes gangrene of the intestines—produced by long want of food. Quite often the first meal causes dysentery and death.

I do not say that all the poor-houses are managed as well as they ought to be. Of the hundreds of employes paid for looking after them, all are not honest; all the honest are not compassionate; and all the compassionate are not clever or diligent. But I am convinced that the best is being done for the starving population that it is possible to do. Besides, it is rare to find a native concerning himself about another native who is not of his own caste. As for the educated natives, who form a separate class by themselves, many of them are earnestly co-operating in measures of relief with the European officers, who are distracted with overwork and anxiety.

What renders the prospect now most serious is the threatened failure of the spring harvest. The first rain fell about ten days ago, very copiously in some parts. But it is found that over a full half of those parts the people had either eaten their grain for sowing, or had failed to sow it from mistrust that there would be any rain. In other parts there has been either no rain at all or an insignificant fall; so that even where the people had grain to sow and had sown it, no plants have come up. Thus the prospect for February and March, and then straight on till June, is truly awful. Much interest has been excited in India by the export of several ship loads of wheat from San Francisco for this market, purely as a mercantile operation. It will certainly bring local prices down a little.

Bhopal, where I am writing, is the capital of a Mohammedan State, independent of the British Government. The population is Hindoo, but the government is Mohammedan. It is the ninth centre I have visited since setting out from Calcutta; and I am working northward. Of these nine places, I have found the severest distress in Jabalpur (also spelled Jubbulpore). It is a large city and an important railroad junction, a little to the northeast of the centre of India. Sixteen hundred people are daily fed at the poor-house, and the accompanying photographs show two groups of the worst specimens of the inmates. They were specially taken to my order last week, and were sent to me after I left Jabalpur. I wished to have a third picture of the more pleasing sight of the paupers at their food; but the photographer had a long way to go to the poor-house, and it did not then happen to be the dinner hour.* BENJAMIN AITKEN.

* * *

Our correspondent's letter was written from an up-country district where the famine was likely to be severely felt. The premonitions he expresses in his letter of the large fatality have proved true. The cable brings the shocking news that in the Jabalpur district ninety thousand persons have died of want. It is evident that food ought to be sent there immediately to save the other inhabitants of the district of whom there are two millions. It is gratifying to learn that the English Government is doing so much for the sufferers, and we are glad to see that private subscriptions headed by the Queen with a gift of twenty-five hundred dollars, are being raised. But the need is so stupendous; and the men and women and children are dying. Christianity ought to be distinctively represented in the work of relief. These Hindoos and Mohammedans should know that when Christian people heard of their extremity they would not wait for the Government to act, but out of their own pockets contributed to provide the hungry with bread. This is an opportunity to give them practical proof of the love and kindness of the Christian religion, which should not be missed. Every Christian missionary in India ought to have the means in his hand to feed every starving creature whom he sees. Such help rendered now will be the most effective sermon he has ever preached. It will be a proof of love that will never be forgotten in India, a practical evidence that Christians are followers of him who commanded that the hungry should be fed in his name. Many a starving native who thus receives food will bless the name of Jesus for giving the command, and will be prepared to listen to the Gospel of the Being in whose name they have been fed. From men of their own faith the sufferers are little likely to receive substantial help, but they look hopefully to the missionaries who have come to them from America to preach to them of the Bread of Life. One missionary writes that he has had children brought to him in baskets, so weak from starvation that they could not stand, begging that he would give them food to save them from dying. Grown men and women have come, so thin that their bones almost protruded from the skin. It is heart-rending to resist the piteous appeals for food from such sufferers; but to enable the missionaries to give this relief a large sum of money must be put in their hands without a day's delay. Happily there is food to be had if the missionaries had the money to buy it. This they can have speedily if the Christian people of America will subscribe as they have done for other suffering peoples. THE CHRISTIAN HERALD will be glad to forward all sums sent for the purpose.

*Some of the people in the picture have tickets round their necks; all receive them, but all do not wear them.

A STARVING FAMILY AT JABALPUR.
From a Photograph taken specially for "The Christian Herald."

A GROUP OF STARVING NATIVES OF THE FAMINE-STRICKEN DISTRICT OF JABALPUR, INDIA.
From a Photograph forwarded by our own Correspondent in India.

FIGURE 1.1. The "first authentic photographs" of India's famine sufferers "ever published." From the *Christian Herald*, 20 January 1897. Courtesy of the Christian Herald Association, New York.

Klopsch and his editorial partner, the charismatic Brooklyn preacher Thomas de Witt Talmage, took advantage of new photographic and printing processes to publicize humanitarian crises such as the Russian famine of 1892 and the ongoing massacres of Armenians in the Ottoman Empire. When news of the dire food shortages in India first reached Klopsch and Talmage in November of 1896, they quickly acted to obtain visual evidence of the catastrophe. The photographs and reports Aitken supplied provided them with the "glimpses of suffering" they needed to "make the pressing need known to the Christians of America" and to enlist their "sympathy and help."[12]

From the perspective of these evangelicals, vision was a compelling vehicle for provoking Christian compassion. "Dr. Klopsch believed that there was no greater educating influence than good pictures," his biographer wrote, and throughout his career in journalism, he relied on illustrations as a means of eliciting empathetic engagement with sufferers around the world who were, as one contributor to the *Christian Herald* put it, "part of that human family which Jesus taught us to love."[13] As several historians have demonstrated, the "concept of spectatorial sympathy" first articulated by late eighteenth-century moral philosophers "steadily broadened the arena within which humanitarian feeling was encouraged to operate, extending compassion to animals and to previously despised types of persons including slaves, criminals, and the insane." During the abolitionist agitations of the antebellum era, antislavery advocates drew on this visual ethic in their attempts to demonstrate the shared humanity of enslaved Africans.[14]

By the 1890s, evangelicals such as Klopsch and Talmage had fully embraced the assumption that sympathy "was a sentiment stirred primarily through sight" and eagerly employed emerging technologies of visual representation in their efforts to further expand how American Christians imagined humanity. Like their forerunners in the antislavery movement, these crusaders believed that barraging the public with "pictorials" was an effective tactic for compelling viewers "to 'compassionate' across barriers of status and race."[15] Klopsch and Talmage were also confident that images could bridge territorial divides. Newspapers, Talmage preached, were "full of optic nerves" that enabled readers to "look far away" and near, to "take in the next street and the next hemisphere."[16] The woodcuts, engravings, and photographs published in the *Christian Herald* collapsed the physical distances that separated the victims of floods, earthquakes, plagues, famines, and wars on other parts of the planet from those in the United States who could come to their relief.

Visual depictions also transcended the particularities of place and dialect. "The human race is divided into almost as many languages as there are nations, but the pictures may speak to people of all tongues," Talmage declared."[17] Americans who could neither hear nor interpret the cries and groans of the afflicted in Russia or Armenia or India could see the sufferings of distant others vividly displayed in the pages of the periodical that also offered a way to respond.

Finally, evangelical proponents of pictorial humanitarianism claimed that images could help overcome what contemporary theorist Elaine Scarry has called "pain's inexpressibility" and resistance to "verbal objectification."[18] Missionaries and other observers of India's "terrible distress" frequently bemoaned the insufficiency of language to convey the horrors they were encountering firsthand. "I have no faculties for describing the awful sufferings of the poor people," one witness wrote.[19] During his own investigative tour of the famine fields in 1900, Klopsch repeatedly lamented his inability to depict the "scenes of desolation, of pain, of suffering, of hopeless despair, of heart anguish, of death" with which he came into contact. "Famine in India! How I dread to write about it! What pen can adequately portray the scenes which my eyes have witnessed?" he wondered. "How to describe it, so as to bring it within the grasp of the human mind, I know not." Despite many attempts to communicate the "abject misery" through detailed and vivid narratives that reported the sensory assaults he experienced ("the heat was intense ... the all-pervading stench from putrefying bodies impregnated clothes, hair and skin") and his emotional anguish ("my heart almost sank within me"), Klopsch felt that words had failed him. "I was painfully conscious of the paucity of my vocabulary to do justice to the subject, and after I have written the worst, I shall feel that even then I have only faintly indicated the real condition of affairs." Convinced that no pen could exaggerate the suffering and "word pictures" could only hint at the reality of India's tragedy, Klopsch and other eyewitnesses hoped that images might more adequately portray the "shocking and revolting" situation and motivate viewers to action.[20]

While Klopsch and Talmage were on the cutting edge of pictorial humanitarianism, other evangelical groups also used images to encourage international almsgiving. During the late 1890s, participants in the Christian and Missionary Alliance (C&MA) responded to frequent and fervent pleas for famine relief included in the organization's weekly illustrated magazine. Founded in 1887 through the leadership of the Reverend A. B. Simpson, the C&MA was an interdenominational association that

aimed to supplement the work of existing churches and mission boards
by concentrating primarily on evangelizing "the destitute and unoccu-
pied fields of the heathen world."[21] Like Klopsch, Simpson was a pioneer
in pictorial journalism, publishing the "first illustrated missionary magazine on the American continent" and continuing to edit the *Christian
and Missionary Alliance* until his death in 1919.[22] Although the *Christian
Herald* and the *Christian and Missionary Alliance* were both produced
in Manhattan and appealed to similar constituencies, the periodicals
were mutually supportive rather than competitive. When famine struck
in India in 1896 and again in 1900, C&MA missionaries under the leadership of India field superintendent Marcus Fuller were instrumental in
coordinating the distribution of aid raised through the *Christian Herald*.
In 1900, Fuller was appointed to serve as an executive member of the
Christian Herald's Interdenominational Missionary Committee, which
was charged with the task of apportioning and dispensing the grain car-
goes and sizable financial contributions collected through the periodical's
vigorous humanitarian campaign.[23]

In addition to cooperating closely with Klopsch and the *Christian
Herald*, C&MA workers also actively sought to stimulate compassion
for famine sufferers among their own supporters through regular reports
illustrating the affliction they faced. The front page of the *Christian and
Missionary Alliance* for May 12, 1900, for example, featured a display
titled "Famine's Ravages in India" by Marcus Fuller that included photographs of emaciated children, a pile of dead "bodies ready for burning,"
and (on the second page) a skeletal form stretched out on a pallet "starved
to death." Accompanying these images was a caption that explained their
purpose: "These pictures just received from Mr. Fuller present the awful
need of famine stricken India as no words could plead" (Figure 1.2).
Photographs, the editor indicated, served as a most effective medium for
revealing the realities of distant suffering to Americans who, once they
saw the "great and urgent need of these starving millions" would sympathize with them in their affliction and "surely do something for their
relief."[24] Marcus Fuller's wife Jennie expressed a similar confidence in
the power of sight in a letter to Louis Klopsch. "If your readers could
see the things we see daily," she asserted, "there would be no need for
appeals."[25]

Like Klopsch and Talmage, participants in the C&MA saw images
of suffering as powerful tools for the production of sympathetic feelings that would generate a concrete, compassionate response. Having
studied at Oberlin College – a center of abolitionist sentiment – both

CHRISTIAN AND MISSIONARY ALLIANCE

FOR THE FULNESS OF JESUS AND THE EVANGELIZATION OF THE WORLD

Vol. XXIV   NYACK AND NEW YORK, MAY 12, 1900   No. 19

FAMINE'S RAVAGES IN INDIA

REV. MARK B. FULLER.

It seems a pity that intelligent people should need to have their feelings stirred by pictures when the fact of sixty millions of people in the famine districts, with thousands already dead and thousands dying by inches, walking, crawling, lying by the roadside never to rise again, dying with cries of agony, or unconscious through the agony already suffered, when these facts are plainly put, sometimes vividly put in word pictures. If these facts do not stir people, I am afraid that pictures will fail too, yet I am willing to do anything not positively wrong to make the awful sufferings of India real to the thousands of happy, comfortable homes of God's children in America, where there is not only plenty, but abundance in many of them, not only luxury, but awful waste.

Many a Christian (?) man's tobacco bill would feed several starving men; many a Christian (?) woman's superfluous dress and finery for one season would save the lives of several of her sisters in India. The cost of one dinner party would feed scores of children for a month; and the cost of one church festival, where four-fifths of the whole cost is often eaten on the spot, would feed fifty orphans (at three cents a day per head) for a month.

May God pity the starving millions of heathen India, and may He have mercy upon the indifferent millions of Christians (?) in America. A few have come to the rescue and have done exceedingly well. A larger number have done well. A still larger number have done a little, so to speak, have tossed their penny or nickel, and gone complacently on, while the most of the churchmembers of America have done nothing, not even given the price of a single meal to save the perishing millions of India! It is hard to look a starving man or woman or child in the face and tell them of what Christ has done for the people of America. If these people knew of the wealth and luxury and waste in America as I know it, it would be harder still to preach the

A GROUP OF FAMINE CHILDREN.

FAMINES' AWFUL EFFECTS.

These pictures just received from Mr. Fuller present the awful need of famine stricken India as no words could plead. Contributions for the Relief Fund may be sent to this Office, or the Board of the CHRISTIAN AND MISSIONARY ALLIANCE.

BODIES READY FOR BURNING.

FIGURE 1.2. "Famine's Ravages in India." Cover page of the *Christian and Missionary Alliance* for 12 May 1900. Courtesy of the Christian and Missionary Alliance National Archives, Colorado Springs, CO.

Marcus and Jennie Fuller absorbed the ethical sensibilities that stirred their evangelical predecessors to engage in vigorous and visually vivid crusades to assuage the bodily afflictions of their fellow human beings.[26] Even as they acknowledged the spectatorial nature of sympathy, however, these C&MA workers also expressed some hesitancy about the ethics of pictorial humanitarianism that distinguished them from their colleagues at the *Christian Herald*. Attending to these differences among late nineteenth-century advocates of international almsgiving will show how the emerging visual culture of humanitarianism was beginning to fracture under the pressure of an increasingly sensationalist culture.

The Camera Cannot Lie? The Integrity of Images in a Sensationalist Age

Five months after the *Christian Herald* began publishing weekly reports of the suffering in India, a reader posed a profoundly disquieting question: "Are the pictures of emaciated men and children, which from time to time have appeared on the Famine Fund pages of THE CHRISTIAN HERALD, overdrawn?" The editors' reply was concise and clear-cut: "They are not." Klopsch and Talmage went on to explain that most of the images printed in their periodical were reproduced from photographs sent by missionaries or by the journal's special correspondent. Unlike wood engravings, lithographs, and illustrations that necessarily involved artistic representation, the editors implied, the invention of halftone technology allowed for the direct and accurate transcription of images captured by the truthful lens. "The camera cannot lie," they contended. "It will not reduce a well-fed man to a skeleton, any more than it will clothe a skeleton with flesh." For those who wanted confirmation of this claim, the original exposures were available for viewing at the *Christian Herald* office.[27]

During the 1890s, skepticism about the reliability of images intensified as rivalry among newspaper publishers such as William Randolph Hearst and Joseph Pulitzer II fueled the practice of "yellow journalism" – a term coined in 1897 to impugn the increasingly sensationalistic stories, dramatic and "imaginative" pictures, and "self-promoting" style that characterized publications like Hearst's *New York Journal* and Pulitzer's *The World*. Although critics employed the epithet to censure practitioners of the "new journalism," the ever-aggressive Hearst "took the insult as a compliment," asserting that his paper promoted a "journalism of action" which gave readers a way to participate in "solving crime, extending charity, influencing foreign policy, and thwarting what it deemed abuses of municipal government."[28] While Hearst suggested that his publication was at the forefront of this activist mode, the *Christian Herald* had embraced many of the techniques eventually associated with the "new journalism" several years before Hearst acquired the *New York Journal*. From the early 1890s on, Klopsch and Talmage never hesitated to include gripping headlines or images of "famine-stricken" sufferers in the service of their explicitly humanitarian agenda. "Dr. Klopsch himself did not object to being called sensational," his biographer avowed, and considered the "pictorial" press an indispensable instrument for exposing "wrongs that ought be righted" both at home and abroad.[29]

By 1900, however, the furor over sensationalism in the yellow papers prompted some evangelicals to question whether publishing photographs of famine horrors was warranted or wise. Even as Klopsch and Talmage continued to insist that "realistic productions of the camera" provided "ghastly evidence of the fearful pressure of the famine" and "incontrovertible proof" of "the terrible character of the suffering," others worried that uncertainty about the authenticity of photographs and illustrations would ultimately undermine efforts to cultivate concern for India's abysmal affliction.[30] As the credibility of pictures within the context of sensationalist journalism became increasingly suspect, commentators also began to express doubts about the ethical implications of pictorial humanitarianism. Participants in the C&MA were particularly ambivalent about the sensory strategies they felt compelled to employ in order to evoke empathy for famine sufferers. "It seems a pity that intelligent people should need to have their feelings stirred by pictures," Marcus Fuller lamented in the May 1900 article accompanying his photographs of "famine's awful effects." Although he did resort to publishing photographs of people "lying by the roadside never to rise again, dying with cries of agony" in order "to make the awful sufferings of India real to ... God's children in America," Fuller suggested that something was wrong with this method of encouraging almsgiving.[31]

The fact that American Christians appeared to require visual stimulation as a catalyst for compassion troubled Fuller for several reasons. First, the Protestant tradition in which he participated had long harbored a profound antipathy toward images and spectacle. As a missionary working among a people whose religions he described as "grossly idolatrous," Fuller was constantly confronted with sights that he and his C&MA coworkers found deeply disturbing. "The eye is brought continually in contact with the vilest things," one C&MA official remarked during a visit to the India mission field. "In the Nepaulese temple we saw a picture so vile we could not contemplate it, and yet the priest went on to explain it to us as though our salvation depended upon the filthy knowledge contained in the picture." While the "indecent and obscene" character of "heathen" iconography, devotional practices, and religious festivals was a common complaint among Protestant missionaries, the idea that images should serve as channels of spiritual transformation was especially problematic for evangelicals who exalted preaching above all other means of grace. C&MA missionaries were charged with the decidedly aural task of *proclaiming* "the whole Gospel to the whole world": a difficult assignment in contexts that valued ocular, tactile, and even olfactory forms of religious expression. As they struggled to persuade their Indian audiences to listen to "the Word of God alone," evangelists like Fuller worried when words failed to resonate with their American supporters and stir them to action on behalf of suffering others.[32]

This insensitivity, Fuller insinuated, was indicative of a serious spiritual problem: a self-indulgent and morally debilitating materialism that undermined the ethical sensibilities required for the practice of Christian charity. Surrounded by plenty and abundance, most Americans had become captives of their own comfort capable of ignoring the "cries of agony … of the perishing millions of India," he charged. While a few had heeded the call and "come to the rescue … most of the churchmembers of America have done nothing." Rather than giving even "the price of a single meal," Fuller lamented, "they go on using the money for the transitory things of this world, its pleasures, its follies, its carnal, soul-destroying indulgences, and leave the heathen to starve and die without Christ."[33] Fuller's anxieties about American apathy and extravagance were relatively common among his C&MA associates. Jeremiads bewailing the sins of "this so-called Christian country" featured regularly in the *Christian and Missionary Alliance*. Many of these complaints focused on the gluttonous and greedy spending habits that prevented Americans from adequately funding missionary efforts or extending "practical sympathy" to their suffering fellow-beings.

While C&MA workers like Fuller ultimately concluded that "photographs of living skeletons" might be required to shock selfish Americans out of their indifference, they remained uncomfortable with this tactic of persuasion. Appealing to the public's appetite for pictures, in this view, was at best a necessary evil that exposed the sorry condition of spirituality in the United States. Unlike Klopsch and Talmage, who commissioned a photographer and eagerly reproduced images depicting "the pinched faces, the bare bones, and the distended stomachs" that told "their sad story with a force beyond the possibility of contradiction," editors of the *Christian and Missionary Alliance* hoped to avoid publishing such "vivid and terrible pictures."[34] When photographs of "famine-stricken" sufferers did appear in the pages of the *Christian and Missionary Alliance*, the editors insisted that they would "offer no apology for calling attention" to the situation in India – revealing a defensiveness about their decision to include depictions of the "terrible distress" ravaging the region.[35]

The angst C&MA participants expressed about the practice of pictorial humanitarianism arose in part from their aversion to "sensational journalism." Publishing images of "ghastly scenes" they worried, might expose them to charges of exaggeration like the accusations Klopsch and Talmage were facing.[36] Even more troublesome was the possibility that appealing to the public's proclivity for images would stimulate, rather than challenge, the sensual decadence they found so unsettling. Recent studies that highlight the intrinsic connection between sensationalism and the development of "the compassionate sensibility" suggest that this fear was not unfounded. Historians such as Karen Haltunnen and Kevin Rozario have persuasively argued that nineteenth-century humanitarianism was "complicit in creating the sensational appetites that sustained the growth of the new mass culture" emerging in this period.[37] During the 1890s, very few observers recognized this reciprocal relationship and the handful of subtle protests from perceptive critics like Marcus Fuller went largely unheeded. As the United States pursued new forms of economic and territorial power during and after the Spanish-American War, criticisms of sensationalism and the spiritual decay of American culture became increasingly entangled in broader contests over the probity of colonial expansion. Exploring the intersections among the "new journalism," pictorial humanitarianism, and the escalation of United States imperialism that intensified in and beyond 1898 will help explain why so few American evangelicals had ears to hear dissenting voices like Fuller's, or eyes to see the ethically distressing implications of spectatorial sympathy.

Competing Visions of Humanitarianism in an Imperial Era

By early October of 1900, "India's famine cloud" had lifted. Rains had fallen and all were now "looking hopefully for a harvest."[38] During the preceding three and a half years, the relief campaigns conducted through the *Christian and Missionary Alliance* and the *Christian Herald* had been extraordinarily successful in raising funds and material aid for India's suffering people. "Never before in the history of religious journalism have the readers of a periodical proved so conclusively the power of the religion of Christ over the heart and life as have the readers of the *Christian Herald*," Klopsch declared with exuberance.[39] The harrowing accounts of physical affliction coupled with dramatic photographs of "living skeletons" had produced their desired effect: "Christian America" had become "the almoner of the world."[40]

The image bearing this caption that appeared on the cover of the *Christian Herald* on June 26, 1901, exemplified the editors' convictions about the United States' relationship to the needy of all nations (Figure 1.3). Surrounded by ragged children, veiled women, and poorly or half-clothed men of varying hues, the regally clad figure of America towers above her pitiable petitioners. In one hand, the solemn lady holds a book (a Bible?) while with the other she drops a measure of grain into the empty baskets at her feet. Sitting there on the ground are a naked child and a gaunt, turbaned man representing the starving people of India. The burlap sacks that fill in the space under America's outstretched arm are clearly labeled "Christian Herald India Famine Relief Work," making the source of the nation's generosity unambiguously apparent.

As historians of visual culture have argued, illustrations like "America, the Almoner of the World" reified the social and racial hierarchies that helped justify the United States' emergence as an imperial power in the late nineteenth century. While some cartoonists satirized the concept of "the white man's burden," many graphic artists and photographers produced pictures that validated American military and cultural expansion as the righteous exercise of Christian moral responsibility on behalf of "inferior" or "uncivilized" races. Throughout the 1890s, the pages of the *Christian Herald* were replete with images that celebrated the United States' superintending relationship to "destitute," "persecuted," and "helpless" people around the globe. Although Klopsch and Talmage preferred famine relief campaigns to armed combat, they did countenance "righteous" wars of "liberation" – such as the Spanish-American War of 1898 and the ensuing conflicts in the Philippines – as expressions of "humanitarianism."[41] These interventions, they proclaimed, were "God's way of ... giving us what he intends to be our share in the enlightenment and enfranchisement of the whole world." In addition to the "work of feeding the hungry, clothing the naked, and saving the dying from death," the editors insisted, the United States was now called to

FIGURE 1.3. "America, the Almoner of the World." Cover page of the *Christian Herald* for 26 June 1901. Courtesy of the Christian Herald Association, New York.

"redeem," "civilize," and "Christianize" the people "brought under [its] protection."[42] In the months and years following the acquisition of the island territories of Puerto Rico, Guam, Samoa, and the Philippines, the *Christian Herald* published numerous photographic essays documenting America's "progress" in its "new colonial possessions."[43]

For some evangelicals, this vision of American humanitarianism was deeply disconcerting. Missionaries struggling to nurture a sense of compassion for distant sufferers that spanned geographic, social, and ethnic separations were among the most distraught. Jennie Fuller, for example, condemned the notion that God had entrusted the United States with the "trusteeship" of "dependent nations and races." Although she saw the conflict with Spain as a valiant fight for freedom that "broke forever the yoke of oppression that had so long rested upon the necks of the people," Fuller criticized the United States' ongoing intervention in the Philippines. "The world, now that the strain of sympathy is broken, says that [the Filipinos] are not ready for freedom and are only children," she observed. By contrast, Fuller insisted that the Filipinos had a right to autonomy. Rather than acting as their protectors or stewards, "it is our duty to let time work out their problems for them," she averred. "Better the mistakes of freedom, a thousand times over, than the cruel wrongs of oppression and degradation." In keeping with her abolitionist forebears, Fuller believed that authentic Christianity required the ability to exercise moral agency. Subjugating the Filipinos to the rule of the United States against their will was, from this perspective, a form of slavery that violated both American political and Christian theological precepts. By denying the Filipinos' fitness for self-governance, Fuller implied, the United States forced them into a position of dependency that was unjust and degrading. Images that portrayed America as the protector of an "ignorant" people, as the parent of "misguided" children, or even as the "almoner of the world," in this view, exacerbated disparities and constituted difference, rather than cultivating the "strain of sympathy" that affirmed the common aspirations and "established rights of humanity."[44]

Throughout the 1890s and the early years of the twentieth century, missionary critics of American military imperialism engaged in a visual campaign to counteract the hierarchies and subordinations inherent in the practices, rhetoric, and pictorial representations of colonial expansion. Pictures that portrayed indigenous churches as self-reliant, independent, self-propagating entities were particularly popular. The photograph most frequently reproduced in the *Christian and Missionary Alliance* during this period, for example, celebrated the opening of a new chapel at the C&MA's Akola mission station built "almost entirely" through the monetary contributions and physical labor of local believers.[45] While C&MA missionaries were certainly not alone in their attempts to foster a self-supporting, self-governing, and self-extending "native church," the Fullers and their co-workers were "among the pioneers of Industrial mission work" that provided training in "good trades" such as "carpentry, tinsmithing and weaving" so that converts would "be able to support themselves as Christians."[46] During the famine years, C&MA missionaries regularly reiterated their commitment to upholding the self-sufficiency of the Christian community and to preserving the autonomy of all sufferers who sought their assistance. Rather than pressuring petitioners to convert or linking aid with spiritual performance, Marcus Fuller explained that C&MA missionaries were "slow to baptize during the famine for fear of getting 'rice Christians,'" preferring to wait until "the pressure of hunger is past" and thus allowing people to choose Christ "freely."[47] By providing employment through building and irrigation programs, and selling the grains distributed through the *Christian Herald* at "cheap rates," C&MA workers also aimed to relieve the hungry "without taking away their independence, and making paupers of them."[48] "We wish to give as little gratuitous help as possible," Jennie Fuller explained. Instead, missionaries would "Help the People to Help Themselves."[49]

Images highlighting this approach to relief work appeared in evangelical periodicals on a regular basis around the turn of the century. In June of 1901, for example, the *Christian and Missionary Alliance* reproduced a photograph of the "sewing class" at the Kaira orphanage. The following May, missionary J. P. Rogers contributed an article entitled "Industrial Training of Orphans" which included several pictures of the C&MA's workshop at Akola and a portrait of the foreman, Kanwadi Mudra Levarni, and his family. This young man had come to the mission as an orphan in 1884 and was now a government-certified mechanic and "steam engineer … of exemplary Christian character." He was also, Marcus Fuller noted elsewhere, "one of our best preachers."[50] Photographs of orphans and other famine sufferers who embodied the hopes of their missionary sponsors by converting to Christianity, learning a trade, and contributing their talents to the building up of the local church community were especially compelling for evangelicals of the Fullers' ilk. Early in 1902, C&MA missionaries sent home a picture of "A Native Convention" which took place at the recently opened Akola chapel (Figure 1.4). Indian preachers featured prominently on the program of this gathering, presiding over several sessions and offering

FIGURE 1.4. Marathi Convention held at the Alliance's new chapel at Akola. From the *Christian and Missionary Alliance*, 26 April 1902. Courtesy of the Christian and Missionary Alliance National Archives, Colorado Springs, CO.

"very fine" teaching to converts and missionaries alike. Kanwadi Mudra Levarni gave "a most remarkable clear and instructive address" which was, the missionaries reported, "the best of the whole convention."[51]

Through images and articles that focused on the abilities and agency of indigenous Christians, evangelical missionaries underscored their efforts to bind all tribes and nations into a universal spiritual fellowship in which distinctions of race and status were irrelevant. In the "Lord Jesus Christ," Jennie Fuller reminded her supporters, "'there is neither Jew nor Greek, there is neither bond nor free, there is neither male nor female' ... but all are one."[52] In order to impress this scriptural principle on their constituents in the United States, Fuller and her co-workers frequently stressed the similarities between American Christians and their "brothers and sisters" and "cousins across the sea" in India.[53] "These children are very much like yourself," Fuller wrote to members of the Junior Missionary Alliance. Referring to an accompanying photograph, Fuller added this exhortation: "Remember no child in America is any better than these dear children.... In Romans it says, 'There is no difference; all have sinned.'"[54] In fact, Indian children might even prove an inspiration to their American peers. The picture of "little Taji," a young

FIGURE 1.5. Taji and the blind man. From the *Christian and Missionary Alliance*, 2 November 1901. Courtesy of the Christian and Missionary Alliance National Archives, Colorado Springs, CO.

girl who came to the C&MA's India Berachah Orphanage during the famine of 1897 and was baptized in October of 1900, provided children in the United States with a model for how they could "serve the Savior" and proof that the "mites" they donated to famine relief were bearing fruit (Figure 1.5). "We call her the Little Missionary and she really is," proclaimed orphanage superintendent Alice Yoder in the letter accompanying Taji's photograph. Although Yoder worried that the picture did not adequately reflect the "brightness" of Taji's disposition, she was confident that the image of the young girl holding her Bible would clearly communicate her status as an exemplary proselyte who persistently and patiently preached the Gospel to "the old blind beggar" sitting at her feet.[55]

Unlike "America, the Almoner of the World," which placed a dominant United States at the epicenter of the "work of a great international benevolence," the photograph of "Little Taji and the Blind Man" affirmed the active and prominent role of Indian Christians in assuaging the spiritual and physical suffering plaguing their people.[56] These two images, which appeared just months apart in their respective publications, illustrate the differences between the *Christian Herald's* vision of American humanitarianism and the form of evangelical relief work favored by missionaries like Marcus and Jennie Fuller. "Christian America," Klopsch and Talmage confidently proclaimed, was "the hope of the nations of the whole earth."[57] The extension of the United States' imperial power, they concluded, would help further the reach of its "magnificent generosity" to "the afflicted and suffering throughout the world."[58] While the Fullers and their missionary associates never disavowed the benefits of American charity, they harbored doubts about the country's status as an unequivocally Christian nation and worried that its expanding colonial empire threatened the values of self-reliance, independence, and spiritual equality that they believed were essential to the establishment of an authentic, universal community of faith.

Conclusion: The Lure and Legacy of Pictorial Humanitarianism

During the 1890s and the early years of the twentieth century, the illustrations and photographs printed in evangelical periodicals introduced Americans to the "sore plight" of distant others whose distress was "beyond description." These images offered "glimpses of suffering" that would, their purveyors hoped, "enlist the Christian sympathy, and the response of readers" on behalf of their fellow beings on the other side of the globe.[59] "Let the pages of religious journalism spread out the stories of all such woes, and collect relief, and disburse alms all around our suffering world ... until there is no more hunger to be fed, and no more ignorance to be educated, and no more nakedness to be clothed, and no more suffering to assuage," the editors of the *Christian Herald* exhorted.[60] According to unabashed almoners like Klopsch and Talmage, "dreadful, shocking" pictures of people "in constant agony" played a vital role in the developing enterprise of American humanitarianism.

Others were uneasy about humanitarian campaigns that relied so heavily on harrowing depictions of horrible affliction. Authors like Julian Hawthorne worried that images had become "incredible" within the increasingly sensationalistic context of yellow journalism. He and other cultural critics, including missionaries such as Marcus Fuller, also suggested that graphic portrayals of gruesome sights might arouse viewers' appetites for spectacles of suffering – a prospect they found morally and spiritually troubling. As the United States enlarged its territorial empire through acquisition of the Philippines and other island "possessions," some evangelicals sensed that disseminating images of "living skeletons" reinforced the racial hierarchies and social dependencies they ultimately hoped to subvert.

During the past several decades, critical theorists from a variety of disciplines have affirmed this supposition. Pictures of bodies in pain, political scientist Denis Kennedy has recently shown, often present their subjects as "powerless, helpless" objects "defined not by agency or ability but rather by vulnerability and deficiency." Rather than eliciting empathy – a form of engagement involving imaginative identification with one's fellows – these photographs risk promoting pity – a response that entails "the feeling of difference" and perhaps even "antipathy" or "appalling disgust." Although such sensational images of suffering have succeeded in generating support for humanitarian relief efforts such as those undertaken by the *Christian Herald*, they have accomplished this goal, some scholars have argued, at the expense of exoticizing distant others, fetishizing affliction, and perpetuating "a set of power relations where the 'victim' is a passive recipient of aid from the heroic aid organization."[61]

In their ardent enthusiasm for America's emerging role as "the almoner of the world," evangelical crusaders such as Klopsch and Talmage seem to have been oblivious to this "darker side of humanitarian imagery." Missionaries who sought to safeguard the autonomy and agency of famine sufferers were more attuned to the moral hazards of American military and moral imperialism, but even the most ambivalent found the persuasive power of pictures hard to resist. Despite his suspicion that spectacles of suffering might damage attempts to establish solidarity, Marcus Fuller sent in the photographs of "famine's ravages." By framing these images with a critique of American sensationalism, decadence, and imperial expansion, Fuller hoped to cultivate compassion untainted by condescension, to stimulate sympathy without suggesting superiority, to promote a humble humanitarianism free from haughtiness.

The history of American humanitarianism in the years following the India famines of the 1890s suggests that Fuller's effort was largely unsuccessful. Over the course of the twentieth and twenty-first centuries, the United States' emergence as a world power has often been premised on the idea of the nation's responsibility to liberate the oppressed and advance the rights of humanity. While some American Christians have questioned this ethics of empire and intervention, many evangelicals have embraced the image of the United States as a Christian nation divinely commissioned to uplift and protect the world's oppressed and needy people. Within this context, pictures of human misery and affliction designed to stir up sympathy for distant and dependent sufferers have proliferated. The growth of the "aid industry" and the concomitant development of new mass media technologies have fueled the ever-increasing production and circulation of image-based appeals. Recent debates about the "ethics of representation" and the entanglement of humanitarian intervention with American imperialism show that many of the disquieting questions that vexed late nineteenth-century evangelicals like Marcus and Jennie Fuller remain relevant – and unresolved.[62] Shedding light on the tensions that characterized earlier efforts to extend American philanthropy abroad will, I hope, help place the issues that bedevil contemporary humanitarianism in broader historical perspective and provide a wider frame for current deliberations about the politics of depicting distant suffering.

Notes

1 Julian Hawthorne, "Report of the Cosmopolitan's Special Commissioner to India: The Horrors of the Plague in India," *The Cosmopolitan; a Monthly Illustrated Magazine* (hereafter, *Cosmopolitan*) (July 1897): 231–46; "Report of the Cosmopolitan's Special Commissioner to India: India Starving," *Cosmopolitan* (August 1897): 369–84; "The Real India: What Is England Going to Do about It?" *Cosmopolitan* (September 1897): 512–22; "England in India," *Cosmopolitan* (October 1897): 653–8; "Beauty and Charm in India," *Cosmopolitan* (November 1897): 3–15.

2 John Brisben Walker, note by the editor to Hawthorne, "Report: Horrors of Plague," 231–2.

3 Hawthorne, "Report: India Starving," 370, 377, 372; Hawthorne, "Beauty and Charm," 3–4.

4 Tyrrell, *Reforming the World*, 118 and 99.

5 Hawthorne, "The Real India," 519; Hawthorne, "Report: India Starving," 381.

6 "Our Corn Ship in India," *Christian Herald* (hereafter *CH*), 29 September 1897, cover, 723. Curti, *American Philanthropy Abroad* refers to the *CH* as "the most widely read religious newspaper in the world," 620.

7 Hunt, *Inventing Human Rights*; Mazlish, *The Idea of Humanity in a Global Era*, 21, 22.

8 Clark, "'The Sacred Rights of the Weak.'"

9 Halttunen, "Humanitarianism and the Pornography of Pain."

10 "India's Starving Millions," *CH*, 20 January 1897, 45; "India's Bitter Cry," *CH*, 3 March 97, 167; "Starving India's Pitiful Cry for Bread," *CH*, 4 April 1900, 286.

11 Louis Klopsch, "Seven Fruitful Years," *CH*, 1 December 1897, 912.

12 "India's Crisis," *CH*, 7 July 1897, 531–2.

13 Charles M. Pepper, *Life-Work of Louis Klopsch: Romance of a Modern Knight of Mercy* (New York: Christian Herald Association, 1910), 317; "Pastor Sheldon's Editorial Experiences," *CH*, 27 March 1900, 230.

14 Halttunen, "Humanitarianism," 303–8; Clark, "Sacred Rights."

15 Halttunen, "Humanitarianism," 303–8; Clark, "Sacred Rights," 484.

16 T. DeWitt Talmage, "Divine Mission of Newspapers," *CH*, 25 March 1896, 242–3.

17 T. DeWitt Talmage, "Pictures Good and Bad," *CH*, 21 June 1899, 492–3.

18 Scarry, *The Body in Pain*, 1–23, 5.

19 "India Famine Scenes," *CMA*, 9 June 1900, 378.

20 Louis Klopsch, "My Tour through Famine-Stricken India," parts 1–4, *CH*, 25 July 1900, 610–11; 1 August 1900, 633–4; 15 August 1900, 672–3; 29 August 1900, 706–7; "Famine Pictures," *CMA*, 19 May 1900, 337.

21 *Constitution of the Evangelical Missionary Alliance*, 1887, http://www.cmalliance.org/resources/archives/downloads/miscellaneous/1887-constitution-evang-miss-alliance.pdf (accessed 9 September 2010).

22 Albert Edward Thomson, *The Life of A. B. Simpson* (New York: Christian Alliance Publishing, 1920), 152.

23 "Pioneer of the Famine Fleet," *CH*, 18 April 1900, 329.

24 "India Famine Scenes," *Christian Missionary Alliance* (hereafter *CMA*), 9 June 1900, 378.

25 "Pioneer of the Famine Fleet," *CH*, 329.

26 On the Fullers, see Helen S. Dyer, *A Life for God in India: Memorials of Mrs. Jennie Fuller of Akola and Bombay* (New York: Fleming H. Revell, 1903), 151; "Independent Foreign Missions," *Missionary Review of the World* 5:1 (January–February 1882): 266–9.

27 "Famine Inquiries Answered," *CH*, 16 June 1897, 477.

28 W. Joseph Campbell, "1897: American Journalism's Exceptional Year," *Journalism History* 29, no. 4 (Winter 2004): 190–200.

29 Pepper, *Louis Klopsch*, 321–2, 4.

30 "India's Crisis," *CH*, 531–2; "Our Grain in Calcutta," *CH*, 18 August 1897, 643; "Famine Inquiries Answered," *CH*, 477.

31 Fuller, "Famine's Ravages," 12 May 1900, *CMA*, 303–4; M[ark] B. Fuller, "Famine Prospects in Gujerat," *CMA*, 25 November 1899, 407 and 419.

32 M[ark] B. Fuller, "What Has Buddhism Done for India?" *CMA*, 17 August 1901, 91; D. W. LeLacheur, "A Tour of Our Principal Mission Fields," *CMA*, 13 April 1901, 197–8.

33 Fuller, "Famine's Ravages," *CMA*, 303.

34 "India's Starving Millions," *CH*, 45; "India's Crisis," *CH*, 531–2; "Famine Horrors," *CMA*, 23 June 1900, 411–2.

35 "Poor Famine Stricken India," *CMA*, 31 March 1900, 195–7.

36 "Editorial," *CMA*, 18 June 1897, 588.

37 Halttunen, "Humanitarianism," 304; Rozario, "'Delicious Horrors.'"

38 "India's Famine Cloud Lifted," *CH*, 3 October 1900, 808; "India Looking Hopefully for a Harvest," *CH*, 12 September 1900, 751.

39 "Feeding India's Famishing Million," *CH*, 9 May 1900, 393, 398.

40 "America, the Almoner of the World," *CH*, 26 June 1901, cover.

41 "A Righteous War," *CH*, 4 May 1898, 392; "What Next after War," *CH*, 3 August 1898, 624.

42 T. DeWitt Talmage, "Face to Face with Our Destiny," *CH*, 25 May 1898, 448; "America's New Responsibility," *CH*, 19 October 1898, 808.

43 See, for example, "American Progress in the Philippines," *CH*, 26 July 1899; 580–1.

44 Mrs. Marcus B. (Jennie) Fuller, *The Wrongs of Indian Womanhood* (New York: Fleming H. Revell, 1900), 17–21, 200, 292–3. It is important to note that not all participants in the C&MA shared Fuller's anti-imperialist views. Many were not immune to the pretensions of "Anglo-Saxon" cultural superiority or impervious to the temptations of a United States' empire. When hostilities broke out with Spain in the spring of 1898, A. B. Simpson welcomed the conflict as a clear part of God's providential plan: Simpson, "Missionary Outlook of the War," *CMA*, 4 May 1898, 411.

45 W[illiam] Mosier, "Our Chapel in Akola," *CMA*, 7 April 1900, 214–15; the picture is reprinted in the *CMA*, 2 February 1901; 26 April 1902; 31 May 1902.

46 Dyer, *A Life for God in India*, 64–65; "Field Notes," *CMA*, 20 July 1901, 41; "A Journey to India," *CMA*, 3 March 1900, 142.

47 M[arcus] B. Fuller, "The Outlook for India," *CMA*, 22 September 1897, 289–93.

48 R. D. Bannister, "Needy Khandesh," *CMA*, 23 June 1900, 412–13;

49 Jennie Fuller, "Suffering India," *Triumphs of Faith* (January 1900): 18.

50 Mark B. Fuller, "Our Orphanage Work in India," *CMA*, 19 October 1901, 211–12.

51 Mr. and Mrs. Moyser, "A Native Convention in India," *CMA*, 26 April 1902, 228–9.

52 Fuller, *Wrongs of Indian Womanhood*, dedication.

53 Fuller, "What Has Buddhism Done for India?" *CMA*, 91.

54 Jennie Fuller, "A Needy Field," *CMA*, 11 December 1896, 531–2.

55 "Our Children's Bible School," *CMA*, 2 November 1901, 247.

56 "Our Famine Ship on the Ocean," *CH*, 16 May 1900, cover.

57 "Corn for Starving India," *CH*, 14 April 1897, 294.

58 "To Fill the Famine Relief Ships," *CH*, 12 May 1897, 386–7; Klopsch, "Seven Fruitful Years," *CH*, 912.

59 "Feeding India's Famishing Millions," 398.

60 Talmage, "Religious Journalism," 908.

61 Kennedy, "Selling the Distant Other"; Morgan, "The Look of Sympathy."

62 Barnett and Weiss, eds., *Humanitarianism in Question*. See also the chapters by Henrietta Lidchi and Sanna Nissinen in this volume.

2

Framing Atrocity

Photography and Humanitarianism[*]

Christina Twomey

It is widely acknowledged that photographic evidence is now central to our view of what constitutes atrocity.[1] The media attention generated by the photographs of emaciated Muslim inmates of Bosnian-run camps during the conflict in the former Yugoslavia in the early 1990s and the scandal caused in 2004 by the photographs of American military personnel torturing and humiliating prisoners at Abu Ghraib in Iraq are but two of the most famous instances of the contemporary link between photographic evidence and narratives of human rights abuses, which are now routinely constructed as "atrocities." The images of Bosnian "death camps," in particular, prompted overt comparison with what is often considered the point of origin for atrocity images: photographs of the liberation of Nazi-run concentration camps in Eastern Europe at the end of World War II.

Our understanding of the antecedents and development of this genre of photography prior to the Holocaust remains slight and is complicated further by a lack of scholarship on the etymology and cultural purchase of the concept of "atrocity." To fully appreciate the development of atrocity photography, we need to understand both sides of that formulation: the production, reception and circulation of images (photographs), and the meanings, inferences, and shared assumptions about the language employed to describe them (in this case, "atrocity"). It is also important not to confuse the concept of atrocity with the language of "human

---

[*] This chapter was originally published in the journal *History of Photography* 36, no. 3 (August 2012): 255–64. The editors thank Christina Twomey and Taylor & Francis for permission to reprint a slightly condensed version here.

rights abuses" with which it is frequently coupled. The late nineteenth century was the point at which the language of "atrocity" came to dominate discussion of the violation of the human body in the context of war and colonialism. This was also a period of renewed humanitarian concern and a wave of humanitarian interventions, even if the language of "human rights" with which we are most familiar was not commonplace until the mid-twentieth century. While the history of human rights has inspired a dynamic and still evolving historiographical debate, there is less attention to the ways in which photographic representations of human suffering might have contributed, from the late nineteenth century, to the new wave of humanitarian action that was the predecessor of concern about human rights in the twentieth century.[2] This chapter examines the links between humanitarian concern, photography, and atrocity at three key moments in the evolution of the relationship between them: the Bulgarian atrocities of the late 1870s; contemporaneous concern about a devastating famine in India; and, from 1903, another campaign about atrocities, this time in the Belgian Congo. The agitation around Bulgaria introduced the language of atrocity to public narratives about suffering, relief efforts for the Indian famine pioneered the use of photography in a humanitarian campaign, and the Congo reform effort brought these two concepts – atrocity and photography – together for the first time in an orchestrated, public campaign.

The Language of Atrocity and Humanitarian Sentiment

The *Oxford English Dictionary* defines the noun atrocity as "an atrocious deed; an act of extreme cruelty and heinousness." It attributes the first use of this meaning of atrocity to Thomas Jefferson, who referred in 1793 to the "atrocities" committed by a Native American tribe.[3] That year also saw the execution of the French King Louis XVI and the beginning of the Reign of Terror under the command of Maximilien Robespierre, which led to the execution of tens of thousands of people for counter-revolutionary activity in France. English pamphlet literature in relation to these events of the French revolution sometimes referred to these events as atrocities.[4] Yet it was not until almost a century later, in the 1870s, that atrocity in the sense we are most familiar with – as "an act of extreme cruelty and heinousness" – entered public narratives about armed conflict and colonial exploitation with full force.

In the mid-1870s, as the Ottoman Empire responded to the rise of ethnic nationalism and Christian dissent within its borders, Turkish authorities violently suppressed uprisings against their rule in Bulgaria and Serbia. Reprisals against nationalists and Christians gained considerable attention in the British press and aroused the interest of Liberal and religious nonconformist circles. The massacre of thousands of Christians as part of the Turkish reprisals against dissidents as well as further allegations about the mutilation of babies and children and the violation of women made for gruesome reading in the daily newspapers. William Gladstone, a former Liberal prime minister then in retirement, was inspired to publish a pamphlet in 1876 entitled *Bulgarian Horrors and the Question of the East*, which was an instant bestseller and generated further coverage of what came to be called "Bulgarian atrocities."[5]

The issue had sufficient purchase to restart Gladstone's political career and, despite the opposition of moderate Liberals and the Conservative Party (who were disinclined to criticize Turkey, then considered an ally), concern about "Bulgarian atrocities" inspired a new form of evangelical mass politics and prompted a wave of moral outrage in Britain.[6] After decades of pressure about reform in British politics, culminating in the significant expansion of the male franchise with the Reform Act 1867, by the 1870s the ground for the articulation of moral purpose in politics had moved offshore. The timing coincided with a broader shift in aesthetics that saw melodrama increasingly replaced by an emphasis on realism, a development both driven and expressed by the expansion of the press and its predilection for eyewitness accounts. As Patrick Joyce has argued, the "weight" and "awful reality" of the powerful term "atrocity" "demanded expression in the press, the new guardian of the real."[7] The suffering of remote others was back on the agenda in ways that had been in relative abeyance since the abolition movement of the 1830s.

There is, then, a link between the concept of atrocity, public concern about it, and periods of intensified humanitarian sentiment. Atrocity first emerged as a focus of public discourse at the end of the eighteenth century, an era scholars have associated with cultures of sentimentalism that articulated new understandings of suffering and the body and thereby prompted a wave of humanitarian action and a new fascination with pain (hence an increase in sensational crime reporting, particularly of murder, in this period). Historian Karen Halttunen has argued that eighteenth-century moral philosophers thought that sympathy was a sentiment prompted mainly through sight. She has described this as the "spectatorial nature of sympathy" and cites in support of her argument the flourishing of sentimental art in this period, which portrayed all manner of victims in distress, from children to animals, whose depicted plight implicitly beckoned the viewer to sympathize with their fate.[8]

The period of humanitarian activism that followed in the wake of these new cultures of sentimentalism has received quite extensive treatment by historians, concerned as it was with the abolition of slavery and the protection of indigenous peoples in the colonies.[9] Similarly, there is important scholarly work arguing that empathy developed new characteristics in the post-Holocaust era.[10] Scholarship on humanitarianism for the late nineteenth and early twentieth centuries, a period in which new forms of humanitarianism flourished, is a developing enterprise. The campaign in relation to the Bulgarian atrocities was typical of the new humanitarianism, which tended to be motivated at some level by religious interests but was also transnational in its concern with the human condition. Campaigns to assist starving famine victims in India and China, attention to the "new slaveries" attendant upon European imperialism in Africa, and concern with the ongoing oppression of indigenous people in settler colonies were all international in focus.[11] Rebecca Gill refers to the era as typified by a "rationalisation of compassion," which saw a new emphasis on quantifying, assessing, and fairly distributing humanitarian aid.[12] The developing aesthetic of realism and the emphasis on rationalization begs the question of what role the camera played in providing evidence as the basis for action. Abigail Green, who has researched the philanthropic work of prominent Jewish financier Moses Montefiore, emphasizes the transnational and religious dimensions of the new humanitarianism and also its use of "new communications."[13] The earlier work on the spectatorial nature of sympathy in the late eighteenth century would suggest that new visual cultures contributed to the evolution of new forms of humanitarianism in the later period.

This raises the issue of whether being able to see abuse or atrocity, via a photographic image of it, bore any relationship to the reemergence of a humanitarian movement in the late nineteenth century. These campaigns coincided with a period in which new visual cultures emerged in the form of press photography, moving images, and magic lantern slides, all of which had been illuminating photographs since the 1850s but enjoyed broader use in the last quarter of the nineteenth century owing to technological improvements.[14] Humanitarians made extensive use of such media to arouse the sympathy of British and American audiences. Indeed, human rights campaigns in the twenty-first century also make use of images of atrocity, suffering, and abuse to inspire giving and encourage action. Yet in the late nineteenth and early twentieth centuries "visual economies" were different from the way they are today, and they bear closer inspection.[15]

The significance of the Bulgarian campaign lay not in its use of photographic images but in the way it established a discourse about atrocity. In the 1870s, technology did not allow for the reproduction of photographs in newspapers. Reports about the violence in Bulgaria were rich in graphic textual description, particularly in those published by Irish American correspondent Januarius Aloysius MacGahan in the *Daily News*. One interpretation of the Bulgarian atrocities agitation is that it especially appealed to evangelical nonconformists, who responded to the strongly moral call for action. Nonconformity was a religion that valued the written word above all else, and a notable feature of the Bulgarian atrocities agitation was the lack of visual material, in the form of illustrations and photographs, to accompany verbal evidence of the terrible harm.[16] Gladstone's pamphlet contained no illustrations, and indeed, one of the few photographs (or more correctly, an engraving based on a photograph) that appeared in the pamphlet literature accompanying the scandal was used to prove that Christians too perpetrated atrocities.

"Turkish soldiers with faces mutilated by Christians" shows five Turkish soldiers with their noses and lips cut off, framed by two men (one in European dress, the other in a fez carrying a saber) symbolically cast as Christian and Muslim. Taken on the grounds of the hospital at Seutari, allegedly at the insistence of a doctor, the accompanying text states: "These 'atrocities' committed by Christians on Turks from the commencement of the insurrection naturally led to retaliation."[17] The pamphlet was written by a Conservative British MP (Member of Parliament), Bedford Pim, a former naval officer and barrister who argued that Turkey was an important ally to Britain and should not be painted into a corner as a brutal and vicious overlord.

"Their Bones Speak": The Indian Famine, 1876–1878

Contemporaneous with the agitation over conditions in Bulgaria, another cause celebre emerged in Britain, centered around a catastrophic famine in southern India during the years 1876–8, in which four million people perished. Indeed, the issues were so proximate that Florence Nightingale, when imploring people to donate on behalf of the starving, compared British inaction as morally equivalent to the brutal behavior of the Turks:

If English people know what an Indian famine is – worse than a battlefield, worse even than a retreat; and this famine too, in its second year – there is not an

English man, woman or child, who would not give out of their abundance, or out of their economy.

If we do not, we are the Turks who put an end to the wounded, and worse than they, for they put an end to the enemy's wounded; but we, by neglect to our own fellow starving subjects; and there is not a more industrious being on the face of the earth than the ryot.[18]

In relief campaigns for Indian famine victims of the mid-1870s, in which Indians were constructed as "fellow subjects" in dire need of assistance, photographic evidence was coupled with eyewitness accounts to emphasize the reality of the famine and the suffering it caused. The victims of the "Bulgarian atrocities" were Christians, whereas the Indian famine sufferers were not, which meant that despite the links of empire, there were differences of race and religion to be negotiated in the relief effort. Although the famine was not constructed as an "atrocity," it did introduce the practice of displaying shocking images of bodily suffering and deprivation as truth claims in order to prompt humanitarian action.

In 1877 a network of Indian Famine Relief Committees was established throughout cities in England, Scotland, and Australasia and raised a total of just under £700,000. One aspect of the Indian famine relief effort of the 1870s, which has passed virtually without comment by historians (as has, largely, the relief campaign itself), was its use of stark photographic images of famine victims. Willoughby Wallace Hooper, a British military officer stationed in India, had taken a series of photographs of the famine camps and more strikingly, of extremely emaciated men, women, and children.[19] Hooper's motivation for taking these particular images remains unclear, although he had previously produced portraits for the ethnographic survey *The People of India* (1868–75) and later attracted controversy for his graphic photographs of the execution of Burmese prisoners during the Third Burmese War in the 1880s.[20]

The famine photographs were sent back to Britain and to the colonies through a series of military and religious networks, and informal imperial connections ensured their circulation and entry into public discussions about the famine.[21] It is worth noting that the photographs did not have the official sanction of the British government, nor did they ever receive it. Even though they do not appear to have been created with the relief effort in mind and were not distributed through official channels in the Australian colonies, photographs were reproduced on small cards that were sold as fundraising devices and displayed on the walls during famine relief meetings.[22] In both Britain and the colonies, in light of the inability to reproduce photographs in daily newspapers, missionary magazines and illustrated journals reproduced the photographs as engravings and sketches.[23] In its final report, the main committee thanked the editors of these publications, which had "by a correct reproduction of sketches and of photographs of famine scenes ... greatly assisted in bringing home to the public some of the terrible scenes.... [T]he hearts of men were moved to their very depths.... [T]he photographs from Madras told effectively their own tale of sorrow and of suffering"[24] (Figures 2.1, 2.2, 2.3).

One of the most interesting aspects of the campaign was the ways in which those working on its behalf began to think about photographic images as tools that might assist their efforts or aid metropolitan comprehension of the extent of suffering. One visitor to the relief camps that had been established in southern India to distribute food to the starving thought the publication of photographs might help the British public understand the "native expression": their "bones speak."[25] Dr. William Cornish, surgeon-general of Madras, publicly challenged the extent of assistance and rations given by the colonial government and lamented that he did not have "a photographer temporarily attached to my office while moving about amongst the famine-stricken people of this Presidency." Words could only "feebly represent the actual facts," but a photograph would help members of the government "see the living skeletons assembled at feeding houses as I see them." He concluded: "Children of all ages [are] in such a condition of emaciation that nothing but a photographic picture could convey an adequate representation of their state."[26] Another correspondent to the *Friend of India* wrote about his "irresistible longing" to send home photographs of "the living skeletons" because "words convey a poor idea of the appearance of a human being for some days before he dies of starvation." "If the London Illustrated or the Graphic had an artist here for a week," the letter concluded, "he could create a sensation all over England that would surpass the stir that was made about the Bulgarian atrocities."[27]

In these estimations a photograph becomes an object of desire, of longing, one that might carry experience from one part of the empire to another. In that sense, the photograph was perceived to breach distance. There is continuity here with the eighteenth-century philosophers who considered sight essential to the creation of sympathy. As a technology capable of collapsing the perception of distance, of seeing metaphorically with the same eye, photography could take the place of and indeed offer a better picture of suffering than could words. Famine relief provided an opportunity to enact Christian principles, but it also enabled members of the extended British world to demonstrate a particular kind of empire

FIGURES 2.1, 2.2, 2.3. Famine victims. Photographer: Willoughby Wallace Hooper, c. 1876–1877. Images reproduced in souvenir album presented to the members of the Indian Famine Relief Fund Committee, Victoria. A copy of the album can be found in the City of Melbourne, Art and Heritage Collection.

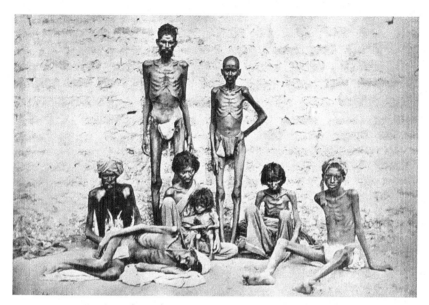

FIGURES 2.1, 2.2, 2.3. (*cont.*)

loyalty that distinguished them as a civilized, white community from a vulnerable, racial other: "their wretchedness," as one editorial put it, "is our opportunity."[28] Sympathy in this sense required distance: these people are so wretched, so distant from us that we are prompted to act – yet paradoxically, that distance was most effectively created by a technology that was seen to bridge distance by providing photographic evidence, by seeing, as Dr. Cornish put it, "the living skeletons … as I see them."

The Congo Reform Association, 1903–1913

It would be some years before there was another humanitarian crusade to stir the British public, but when it arrived, in the form of the Congo Reform Association, the language of atrocity and photographic images of the suffering body were combined to powerful effect. Like the photographs of Indian famine sufferers, again the bodies were black and frequently they were swathed in plain white cloth. The cloth covered nakedness, but its contrasting color also threw the black skin and bodies of the photographic subjects into stark relief. In the case of starving Indians, the emaciation of the body was highlighted. For the exploited indigenous workers in Belgian King Leopold's Congo Free State, the white cloth served to emphasize the mutilation and amputation of their

FIGURE 2.4. Mola and Yoka, victims of atrocities committed in the Belgian Congo, c. 1905. Courtesy of Antislavery International.

black limbs. Both the Indian famine photographs and the Congo atrocity images emphasized the distance between the white viewer and the mutilated black body, an essential precondition for the construction of empathy (Figures 2.4 and 2.5).

The abuses perpetrated by the regime associated with Congo Free State, run as a personal fiefdom of King Leopold, had been cause for concern among missionaries since the late nineteenth century.[29] Each village in the Congo was required to harvest a certain amount of rubber

FROM PHOTOGRAPHS, CONGO STATE

"The pictures get sneaked around everywhere."— *Page 40.*

FIGURE 2.5. From Mark Twain, *King Leopold's Soliloquy* (Boston: F. R. Warren, 1905).

for Belgian concession companies. Failure to meet this target meant that sentries from the companies would visit the site and massacre, torture, and harass the villagers. In some cases, the sentries would amputate the hand of a victim, either as a form of torture or to prove to their overseers that a bullet had killed its target. When Reverend Sjöblom of the American Baptist Mission visited London in 1897, he met with humanitarian groups in England and described the events he had witnessed. When informing the American public of Sjöblom's activities, the headline in the *New York Times* declared "Terrible Atrocities Committed in the Upper Congo Country."[30]

It would be several more years before thousands of people attended public meetings across Britain and the United States to protest against the administration of King Leopold. The groundwork had been laid by missionaries like Sjöblom and representations in the British House of Commons by members of the Aborigines' Protection Society and its members' authorship of pamphlets and books.[31] A key factor for the emergence of a popular movement was the influence of Edmund Dene Morel, an energetic journalist with long-standing trade ties to Africa, who established the Congo Reform Association in 1903 and helped transform the issue into a mass movement of moral outrage. That same year the growing controversy had encouraged the British government to request a report from Roger Casement, the British consul on the Upper Congo, who duly confirmed the loss of life, extortion, and mutilation that had occurred there.[32] Morel was also canny in drawing missionary organizations within his orbit, and he persuaded Dr. Grattan Guinness, head of one of the Congo's largest missions, the Regions Beyond Missionary Union, to join him on the platform. Ultimately Congo missionaries John and Alice Harris left their missionary union to join the Congo Reform Association. When seeking publicity for their cause, missionaries invoked the language of the Bulgarian agitation to galvanize attention. One British missionary, the Reverend A. E. Scrivener, declared: "The Bulgarian atrocities might be considered as mildness itself when compared with what was done here."[33] Meetings were held throughout the country "to protest against the atrocities perpetuated on the Congo."[34] Kevin Grant argues that it was the moral imprimatur bestowed upon the cause by missionary involvement that facilitated its transformation into a popular protest movement attracting thousands of people to its meetings in Britain and North America.[35]

The role of atrocity photographs, as several scholars including Grant have pointed out, was critical in engaging the attention of a popular audience.[36] Alice Harris was a skilled photographer and had provided photographs to Casement during his visit to the Congo. Her work was used as the basis of a lantern-slide lecture entitled "The Congo Atrocities." The lantern slides and lecture were copied for use by missionaries around the world, with performances as far away as New Zealand. A report of a meeting there described how "except for the focus on the sheet, the church was pitch dark," and the slides and their accompanying narrative created a "tense listening silence ... being occasionally broken by exclamations of wonder, indignation and horror."[37] E. D. Morel used the photographs Casement brought back to Britain as the basis of plates in his book *King Leopold's Rule* (1904) and also published photo-essays in his newspaper, *West African Mail*. The case for Congo reform attracted the attention of key public intellectuals and writers such as Mark Twain (Samuel Clemens), whose *King Leopold's Soliloquy* (1905) included a woodcut rendition of some of the Harris photographs. Twain's fictional King Leopold cursed "the incorruptible Kodak" as "The most powerful enemy that has confronted us [and] ... the only witness I have encountered in my long experience that I couldn't bribe."[38]

The atrocity photographs in the Congo campaign, like the famine images before them, entered the public domain through imperial, missionary, and charitable circles. The Congo images were circulated to metropolitan audiences via the agency of nonstate actors: they were not produced by the state, did not receive its official sanction, and circulated via informal imperial networks and personal connections. Indeed, the British government had passed up the opportunity to circulate the images Alice Harris had given to Roger Casement during his tour of the Congo. The photographs became prominent in the campaign after there was a questioning of the "evidence" upon which the reformers relied. Certainly, King Leopold of Belgium and his supporters attempted to discredit the evidence of missionaries and others as hearsay from the disgruntled few. Coming in a period when, thanks to the expansion of the education system, literacy rates in the British population had soared, there were new levels of sophistication about texts and authorship. Although photography was not an uncontroversial medium, and also attracted claims that its images might be fabricated, there was a less sophisticated discourse around the visual medium of the photograph. The photographic images therefore entered the campaign as evidentiary claims, although as Robert Burroughs has recently argued, it is important not to overstate their impact, to examine their role in the broader missionary project, and to give at least equal credence to the influence of textual accounts of atrocity.[39]

This chapter has opened up a series of questions about the relationship between photography, atrocity, and the growth of the "new humanitarianism" of the late nineteenth and early twentieth centuries. First is a question about the creation and circulation of images of suffering, atrocity, and abuse. It was only when "atrocity" became politicized in a situation of armed conflict between states – and this received its first flowering during the First World War – that the state committed its own resources to producing and circulating images of atrocity. Roger Casement's report on the Congo, prepared for the British government and published as a parliamentary paper, contained no visual images. A short time later, during World War I, a report on the treatment of "natives" in German South West Africa, written with the explicit purposes of arguing that German treatment of Africans was so beyond the pale that it would be immoral to restore Germany's empire at the conclusion of the war, included graphic photographs of the mutilated and executed bodies of Africans. Second, there is the question of the complicated relationship between text, visual culture, and history. Although it is tempting to see the Congo Reform Association campaign as a point of origin in the use of atrocity images, it relied on several precedents that made its campaign strategies possible. There was an extant language of atrocity and moral outrage available to Congo reformers that amplified the resonance of their claims. Images of the suffering black body had been previously used to great effect in the relief efforts centered on sufferers in the Indian famine of 1876–8. Finally, there is the issue of distance, and the apparently concomitant process by which new technologies of photography both collapsed distance between the subject of suffering and the viewer, and also created greater space between them – a sense of difference – that was essential to the empathetic or sympathetic response.

Notes

1 Sontag, *Regarding the Pain of Others*; Linfield, *The Cruel Radiance*.
2 On the origins and trajectory of "human rights," see Moyn, *The Last Utopia*; Hunt, *Inventing Human Rights*; Cmiel, "The Recent History of Human Rights."
3 Thomas Jefferson to William Carmichael and William Short, 30 June 1793, Thomas Jefferson Papers, Library of Congress, available online at http://jeffersonswest.unl.edu/archive/view_doc.php?id=jef.00062.

4 See, for example, *A View of the Relative State of Great Britain and France* (London: J. Debett, 1796), 16.

5 William E. Gladstone, *Bulgarian Horrors and the Question of the East* (London: J. Murray, 1876).

6 Richard Millman, *Britain and the Eastern Question, 1875–1878* (New York: Clarendon Press, 1979); Milos Kovic, *Disraeli and the Eastern Question* (Oxford: Oxford University Press, 2011), 117–65; R. T. Shannon, *Gladstone and the Bulgarian Agitation 1876* (London: Nelson, 1963).

7 Patrick Joyce, "The Narrative Structure of Victorian Politics," in James Vernon, ed., *Re-Reading the Constitution: New Narratives in the Political History of England's Long Nineteenth Century* (Cambridge: Cambridge University Press, 1996), 202 and 194–201.

8 Haltunnen, "Humanitarianism and the Pornography of Pain," 307. See also Laqueur, "Bodies, Details and the Humanitarian Narrative."

9 Thomas Haskell, "Capitalism and the Origins of Humanitarian Sensibility," Parts 1 and 2; David Turley, *The Culture of English Antislavery 1780–1860* (London: Routledge, 1991).

10 La Capra, *Writing History, Writing Trauma*; Dean, *The Fragility of Empathy after the Holocaust.*

11 Grant, *A Civilised Savagery.*

12 Gill, "The Rational Administration of Compassion."

13 Abigail Green, "Rethinking Sir Moses Montefiore: Religion, Nationhood, and International Philanthropy in the Nineteenth Century," *American Historical Review* 110, no. 3 (2005): 631–58.

14 Robinson et al., eds., *Encyclopedia of the Magic Lantern.*

15 Poole, *Race and Modernity.*

16 Goldsworthy, "English Noncomformity and the Pioneering of the Modern Newspaper Campaign." There were cartoons, but they were focused on the domestic politics of response to the situation.

17 Bedford Pim, *The Eastern Question Past Present and Future* (London: Effingham Wilson, 1877), "Turkish Soldiers with Faces Mutilated by Christians," 45.

18 A ryot is a peasant or cultivating tenant in South Asia. Florence Nightingale to Lord Mayor, London, 17 August 1877, repr. *Times*, 20 August 1877.

19 W. W. Hooper images of the Madras famine are in the Picture Library of the Royal Geographical Society, London, numbered S0001994-S0002012. The Museum Ludwig in Cologne, Germany, holds an album, *Hungersnot in Indien* in its Lebeck Collection containing W. W. Hooper's famine photography, with many photos captioned in English. See Peter Mesenhöller, "Störende Fenster: W. W. Hoopers Photgraphien der Hungersnot in Madras 1876–78," in Dewitz and Scotti, eds., *Alles Wahrheit! Alles Lüge!*, 373–9.

20 John Falconer, ""A Pure Labour of Love": A Publishing History of *The People of India*," in Hight and Sampson, eds., *Colonialist Photography*, 51–83; Kathleen Howe, "Hooper, Colonel Willoughby Wallace (1837–1913)," in John Hannavy, ed., *Encyclopedia of Nineteenth-Century Photography*, Vol. 1, A-I (New York: Routledge, 2008), 713–14; John Falconer, "Willoughby

Wallace Hooper: 'A Craze about Photography,'" *Photographic Collector* 4, no. 3 (Winter 1983): 258–86.

21 On the arrival of the photographs in Australia, see Thomas Lidbetter to Robert Wallen, repr. in *Argus*, 15 October 1877, 7. Lidbetter's copies were later circulated to relief committees in other Australian cities; see *Brisbane Courier*, 3 November 1877, p. 4.

22 *Argus*, 17 October 1877, p. 5. One of the reproduced photographs printed on a small card is now held in the collection of the State Library of Victoria, Accession No. H2005.34/458, Image no. je000608. Call number PIC LTA 2204.

23 See, for example, *Illustrated Australian News*, 31 October 1877.

24 William Digby, *The Famine Campaign in Southern India (Madras and Bombay Presidencies and Province of Mysore), 1876–78*, Vol. 2 (London: Longman, Green, 1878), 467.

25 Digby, *The Famine Campaign in Southern India*, Vol. 2, 162.

26 Dr. Cornish quoted in Digby, *The Famine Campaign in Southern India*, Vol. 1, 112–13.

27 Special correspondent of *Friend of India*, writing from Kalastri, North Arcot, on 16 March 1877, repr. in Digby, *The Famine Campaign in Southern India*, Vol. 1, 95.

28 *Argus*, 18 October 1877, p. 5.

29 For a sample of the extensive literature on the Congo, see Hochschild, *King Leopold's Ghost*; Martin Ewans, *European Atrocity, African Catastrophe: Leopold II, the Congo Free State and Its Aftermath* (London: Routledge, 1992); Robert Benedetto, ed., *Presbyterian Reformers in Central Africa: A Documentary Account of the American Presbyterian Congo Mission and the Human Rights Struggle in the Congo, 1890–1918* (New York: E. J. Brill, 1996).

30 *New York Times*, 14 May 1897, p. 7.

31 Aborigines Protection Society, *The Treatment of Natives in the Congo: A Statement Submitted to His Majesty's Government on Behalf of the Aborigines Protection Society* (London: Aborigines Protection Society, 1902); H. R. Fox Bourne, *Civilisation in Congoland: A Story of International Wrong Doing* (London: P. S. King, 1902).

32 1904 [Cd. 2097], Africa. No. 7 (1904), Further Correspondence respecting the Administration of the Independent State of the Congo in *20th Century House of Commons Sessional Papers* (Cambridge, U.K.: Chadwyck-Healey, 1980–83), Microfiche No. 110.563.

33 Reverend Scrivener, Report of a "Journey made in July, August and September, 1903," cited in Mark Twain, *King Leopold's Soliloquy: A Defense of His Congo Rule* (Boston: F. R. Warren, 1905), 15.

34 *Times*, 10 January 1906, p. 4.

35 Kevin Grant, "Christian Critics of Empire: Missionaries, Lantern Lectures and the Congo Reform Campaign in Britain," *Journal of Imperial and Commonwealth History* 29, no. 2 (2001): 27–58.

36 Sliwinski, "The Childhood of Human Rights"; Peffer, "Snap of the Whip."
37 *Otago Witness*, 18 March 1908, 17.
38 Twain, *King Leopold's Soliloquy*, 38.
39 For an insightful discussion, see Burroughs, *Travel Writing and Atrocities*, 87–91.

3

The Limits of Exposure

Atrocity Photographs in the Congo Reform Campaign

Kevin Grant

"Admission Free. Adults Only." So stated the advertisement for a lantern-slide lecture to be given by the humanitarian activist, E. D. Morel, in Hawarden, England, in April 1907 on the subject of the Congo atrocities.[1] "Adults only" was not, and is not, a phrase commonly associated with atrocity. However, this peculiar combination is telling of a broader, moral danger. Humanitarians have long run the risk that their narration and display of photographs of atrocity, such as those featured in Morel's lantern slides, might bring public condemnation upon not only the alleged perpetrators but also those showing the photographs. It is not just a question of whether photographs are authentic, doctored, or falsely staged.[2] A more subtle problem is that the humanitarian can tell the truth, offer photographic evidence of atrocity, and thus overstep the bounds of propriety and lose his or her moral authority in the public eye. The representation of atrocity must be tolerably shocking. The desired visceral effect must be balanced with an analytical, even clinical explanation that affords the audience safe emotional distance from an image of chaos brought to life.[3] Atrocity must also be framed in accordance with the culturally specific and historically contingent mores of strangers, if one is to enlist those strangers in bringing atrocities to an end. In Hawarden in 1907, Morel was especially concerned about observing sexual mores in his allegation that Congolese women had been raped by soldiers and employees of the Congo Free State and its concessionaire companies. This essay examines how participants in the Congo reform

I wish particularly to thank Heide Fehrenbach, Davide Rodogno, Dean Pavlakis, and Lisa Trivedi for their comments on drafts of this chapter.

campaign in the early twentieth century negotiated social mores in order to present atrocity to different audiences in Britain and the United States in ways that were variously appropriate. It specifically examines the narration and display of atrocity photographs, in conjunction with accounts of sexual violence, in the literature and lantern-slide lectures of this campaign, the first nongovernmental, humanitarian campaign to use atrocity photographs to mobilize sustained, international protest.[4]

The Congo reformers defined the significance of their atrocity photographs with words secular and precise, religious and allusive. Their words conformed in some respects to the modern humanitarian narrative described by Thomas Laqueur. Developing after the eighteenth century, this narrative was distinguished by extraordinarily detailed description of the suffering body and the causes of this suffering, which engendered compassionate empathy in readers and inspired them to take humanitarian action. The suffering body had previously been the object of Christian morality; "the universal body of the risen God ... [had mediated] ... between sufferer and those performing acts of mercy." Laqueur argues that in the modern, secular humanitarian narrative, by contrast, "the individual body, alive or dead, came to have a power of its own" in forging a "common bond between those who suffer and those who would help."[5] The Congo atrocity photographs and their attendant "horror narratives" depicted with terrible, still precision mutilated children and adults who proffered limbs that lacked hands and feet. Following the modern narrative described by Laqueur, scholars have commonly interpreted these photographs in secular terms as visual testimonies to the violation of human rights.[6] However, it was Protestant missionaries who established the basic narrative structure in which the photographs were situated, and these missionaries initially spoke not of rights but of Christian duties.[7] The humanitarian narrative of the Congo reform campaign developed into a synergy of the religious and the secular, produced through the cooperation of missionaries and humanitarians, such as Morel, who advocated the "elementary rights of humanity." These dual emphases proved compatible, versatile, and inspirational, within limits. Beyond the boundaries of propriety, there was suffering to which humanitarian narrators could only allude, or risk their moral outrage becoming profane.

The greatest threats to the narrators' moral authority were atrocities unseen. Nancy Rose Hunt observes, "The mutilation photographs, in particular, have directed interest away from what was more hidden, tactile, and out of sight, and away from another modality of violence, the sexual. And this modality of violence was intrinsically more reproductive and transgressive in its nature."[8] British activists in humanitarian causes ranging from child poverty to prostitution and sex trafficking had previously been tainted by charges of sexual impropriety in publicizing their work.[9] Thomas Barnardo, a prominent evangelist working among the poor of East London, was almost ruined by accusations that he had promoted his mission with falsely staged photographs of poor children that lewdly exposed the children's bodies through torn garments.[10] Examining humanitarian reform literature about subjects ranging from slavery to wife beating in nineteenth-century Britain and the United States, Karen Halttunen discerns "a new cultural linkage of violence and sex, a linkage whose primary purpose was to establish the obscenity of pain."[11] Humanitarians who testified to violence were self-conscious of appearing to engage in titillating spectacle, forsaking empathy for prurience. Halttunen suggests that by the turn of the century, in recognition of what she calls the "pornography of pain," civil society and the government cooperated in removing institutional cruelty from public view and fostered an illicit subculture of violent suffering accessible through the expanding practice of solitary reading.[12] Yet, at this same time, the Congo reformers were displaying atrocity photographs not only in books and pamphlets but also in lantern-slide lectures before audiences that ranged in size from dozens to thousands. In an attempt to control the double-edged power of atrocity, and, above all, the atrocity of rape, the reformers carefully gendered their display of atrocity in terms of its authentication and in the composition of its audiences.

King Leopold II of Belgium established the Congo Free State in the wake of the Berlin Conference (1884–5), with the tacit support of the great powers, declaring his commitment to the moral and material improvement of the Congolese through free trade and Christian conversion. Initially, the state's main task was to subjugate both the Congolese and Zanzibari slave traders, who dominated much of the upper river. Reports of "new slaveries" and atrocities perpetrated by the state itself began to circulate publicly in Britain after the mid-1890s, first in missionary and humanitarian circles, then through the *Times* and other newspapers. Protestant missionaries became increasingly vocal in their criticism of the state as its brutalities inhibited their evangelical work and after the state proved reluctant to authorize more Protestant mission stations while it permitted Catholic missions to expand.[13] After the publication of a scathing British consular report on the Congo Free State in 1904, a coalition of missionaries, humanitarians, and merchants formed the Congo Reform Association (CRA), under the leadership of Morel, then known as an advocate of commercial development in west and central Africa. The CRA lobbied the British government to exert diplomatic pressure on Leopold to reform his regime. Morel, the CRA's secretary and main publicist, argued that the welfare of the Congolese depended upon respecting the "elementary rights of humanity," and particularly rights to land and the fruits of one's own labor that would enable the Congolese and Europeans to benefit mutually in the imperial economy. Morel employed standard pressure-group tactics, publishing articles and lobbying members of parliament. These tactics initially failed, and by 1905 the CRA was on the brink of collapse. The campaign was then revived by two married missionaries, the Reverend John and Alice Harris, brethren of the Congo Balolo Mission, who returned to England after working in the Congo for most of the previous seven years. The Harrises reached out to British nonconformist churches, which exercised significant political power at this time, and developed a nationwide series of lantern-slide lectures and a network of CRA auxiliaries that established a solid base of public support for the organization and stabilized its finances. At the center of the campaign, in lantern lectures and numerous publications, was the photographic image of atrocity.[14]

The evidential force of the photograph was used to expose suffering under a variety of imperial regimes in the late nineteenth and early twentieth centuries.[15] Missionaries participated in turning photography to protest, applying their decades of experience in creating photographic ethnographies of foreign peoples and, above all, chronicling the progress of their evangelization with a photographic record of improvements in peoples' health, material cultures, and built environments.[16] Like many other missionaries, Alice Harris brought a camera to the Congo. She had a dry plate box camera, along with numerous glass plates in light-tight boxes and the requisite collection of chemicals for printing in the field (Figure 3.1). Dry plate photographic technology was more cumbersome than photography with the new Kodak cameras, which became popular after the first one was released in 1888. The Kodak cameras captured images not on plates but on sensitized rolls of film, which photographers then mailed to the Eastman Kodak Company for printing. Kodak's slogan, "You press the button, and we do the rest," did not appeal to Alice Harris, however. Perhaps she did not want to wait for months to evaluate and use her photographs, or perhaps she simply enjoyed a hands-on process that was decidedly challenging in the tropical African environment. As John Harris later wrote regarding a collection of one hundred photographs sent from west Africa to a colleague in London: "They are some

FIGURE 3.1. Alice Harris photographing in the forest on the upper Congo, c. 1903–1905. Reprinted with permission of the Bodleian Library, Oxford University. Collection reference, Rhodes House, Mss. Brit. Emp. s. 24 J/46.

68

of them a little stained but what with shortage of good water, excessive heat and chemicals affected by the elements we find it very difficult to get good prints. Fortunately the plates are keeping very well. Therefore there will be no difficulty in producing good copies when we can get good materials."[17]

Missionaries publicly displayed their photographs in multiple media, including missionary publications, newspapers and magazines, exhibitions, and lantern-slide lectures that followed the networks of missionary auxiliaries throughout Britain. The formulaic missionary narrative that defined the significance of these photographs pivoted on the experience of conversion and the newfound benefits of Christian civilization. The narrative began with a geographical overview of the given land and an introduction to the ethnography of its people. There was next an account of the people's savage practices, followed by an account of the missionaries' tireless proselytization and the benefits of reform. Finally, the narrator solicited support for the mission on the proven strength of its performance. After the mid-nineteenth century, photographs were integral to this narrative and could, in fact, visually abridge it for more concise proof and publicity. Missionaries displayed what one might call "before and after" photographs. The first photograph portrayed a person before missionary intervention and the second photograph portrayed the same person saved, with his or her improvement marked by new clothing and evident good health.[18] It was into this narrative framework that a founding member of the CRA, Dr. Harry Guinness, director of the Congo Balolo Mission, incorporated atrocity photographs.

Since the late 1880s, Guinness had presented missionary lantern-slide lectures to tens of thousands of people in Britain. Jack Thompson characterizes him as "the doyen of the missionary lantern show."[19] In 1903, Guinness began to deliver a lantern-slide lecture entitled "A Reign of Terror on the Congo" with the goals of promoting his mission and building public pressure upon the British government to take action against the Congo Free State. Although a transcript and the specific set of slides used in Guinness's lecture have not survived, one can deduce from Guinness's correspondence with Morel that he modified the standard missionary narrative in two ways. First, after an introductory overview of the Congo, he recounted the moral promises of the Berlin Act, which Britain had endorsed. Second, he broke from the normal narrative by displaying not the improvement of the Congolese people but their greater suffering under the Congo Free State. The pivotal moment of salvation in the standard lecture was thus replaced by betrayal and a prospective

moment of redemption for the British public, should they support the
efforts of missionaries on behalf of the Congolese and fulfill their own
Christian duty to force the state to rectify its sinful practices. Morel, who
preferred to speak in terms of commercial development and rights, was
initially repelled by Guinness's evangelical representation of the Congo
crisis, replete with hymns and prayers. Morel confided to a friend, "I
am so constituted that the very talk of religion in a matter of this kind
sets my teeth on edge."[20] Nonetheless, faced with the impending collapse of his campaign in 1905, he readily cooperated with the Harrises in
reviving the CRA through missionary methods. Morel and the Harrises
agreed to combine their secular and religious principles and goals in a
single humanitarian narrative in the hope of reaching a wider spectrum
of British society. John Harris explained to Morel, "You appeal to the
more educated classes and politicians, what I want to do is to appeal to
the popular mind." Having agreed to advocate property rights and free
trade for the Congolese, Harris added, "the ordinary Englishman is quite
in ignorance of this subject and therefore we want to be careful to hit his
intellect on the right spot."[21] The right spot for which the Harrises and
Morel subsequently aimed was Britain's Christian conscience. In advo-
cating both human rights and Christian duty through a combination of
publications and lantern-slide lectures, the Congo reformers successfully
sustained the largest, popular British protest against imperialism in the
decades before the first world war. As the main narrators of the CRA's
lantern-slide lectures, the Harrises and other missionaries brought strong,
moral authority to bear on their representations of atrocity, but they still
took precautions against shame.

Authenticating atrocity was the purview of both women and men. The
experience of the Harrises, as they first went public with their protests
against the Congo Free State, usefully demonstrates distinctions between
their gender roles in this campaign. It furthermore shows that the gen-
dering of authentication was to a great extent determined not only by
narrative structure and convention but also by institutional practices and
personal choices.[22] It was Alice Harris who took some of the best-known
atrocity photographs of the Congo reform campaign, but her authorship
of these photographs was initially obscured. This is apparent in the production and publication of her photograph of a Congolese man, Nsala,
sitting on the veranda of the Harrises' home at Baringa, gazing at the
hand and foot of his daughter, who, along with his wife and son, had been
allegedly killed and eaten by sentries of the local concessionaire company
(Figure 3.2). Alice Harris and another missionary, the Reverend Edgar

NSALA OF WALA IN THE NSONGO DISTRICT (ABIR CONCESSION)

(Photographed by Mr. John H. Harris in May, 1904, with the hand and foot of his little girl of five years old—all that remained of a cannibal feast by armed rubber sentries. The sentries killed his wife, his daughter, and a son, cutting up the bodies, cocking and eating them. See letter from Mr. Stannard in the Appendix.)

FIGURE 3.2. Nsala of Wala. Reprinted from E. D. Morel, *King Leopold's Rule in Africa* (London: Heinemann, 1904).

71

Stannard, encountered Nsala on 14 May 1904, while John Harris was out of station at a missionary committee meeting downriver. Private correspondence between Alice Harris and a company official, and between John Harris and Stannard and Guinness, indicates that Alice Harris staged and took the picture.[23] She promptly developed the photograph and showed the image to her husband when he returned on the following day. They quickly grasped the potential propaganda value of this image in making a case against the Congo Free State before the British public. John Harris wrote to Guinness four days later, "The photograph is most telling, and as a slide will rouse any audience to an outburst of rage, the expression on the father's face, the horror of the by-standers, the mute appeal of the hand and foot will speak to the most skeptical."[24]

Later in 1904, Morel included this photograph in his book, *King Leopold's Rule in Africa*, which offered a comprehensive indictment of the Congo Free State for atrocities and new slaveries.[25] The subcaption of the photograph attributes authorship to "Mr. John H. Harris."[26] This misattribution is contradicted by an account of the incident that Stannard provided in a letter to Guinness, dated 21 May 1904, which was reprinted in the appendix of the same book.[27] Stannard further recounts in this letter that on 19 May he and John Harris were approached by three men who presented them with two severed hands as further proof of atrocities committed by the company sentries. Alice Harris took a photograph of the men displaying the hands, with John Harris and Stannard looking on.[28] Stannard explained, "Mr. Harris and I stood in the group, as we thought it would be additional testimony" (Figure 3.3).[29]

In this photograph, also published in Morel's book, the authenticating gaze is masculine, though the photograph represents the view of a woman behind the camera. Roland Barthes observes that to see beyond the reality effect of a photograph one must engage in a secondary action of reflection and recognize the photograph itself as an object. Without this reflection, the photograph as an object and the photographer go unacknowledged; only the subject exists, as drawn by the pencil of nature.[30] Even if a reader in 1904 recognized this photograph as an object and a mediated representation, he or she would find no attribution of authorship in the subcaption, so there would be nothing to break the masculine gaze. It appears that this was an editorial choice, not an oversight, given that Morel's book also features two images of chained African "hostages" at Baringa in 1903 that are attributed to the Reverend Herbert Frost.[31] The aversion to connecting Alice Harris to the visual evidence of atrocity extended, moreover, to the public narration of atrocity. Despite the

NATIVES OF THE NSONGO DISTRICT (ABIR CONCESSION)

(With hands of two of their countrymen, Lingomo and Bolengo, murdered by rubber sentries in May, 1904. The white men are Mr. Stannard and Mr. Harris, of the Congo Balolo Mission at Baringa. See letter from Mr. Stannard in the Appendix.)

FIGURE 3.3. Natives of the Nsongo District. Reprinted from E. D. Morel, *King Leopold's Rule in Africa* (London: Heinemann, 1904).

fact that Alice Harris wrote and retained copies of her correspondence with a company official about the case of Nsala, the appendix of Morel's book includes only accounts of events at Baringa written by John Harris, Stannard, and Frost. Alice Harris authored the atrocity photographs, but she did not, initially, author the narrative that defined the significance of the photographs for the British public.

There are a few explanations of why Alice Harris's authorship of the atrocity photographs was initially obscured, and why the authenticity of the atrocities was sealed by a masculine gaze. The decision may have reflected, to some extent, the patriarchal structures of authority so common in British overseas missions. While approximately half of British missionaries in Africa were women, virtually all of the positions of leadership in these missions were held by men. The Harrises lived and worked together on the Congo, but John Harris customarily spoke for their mission station in committee meetings and conducted correspondence with the mission director or state officials. Alice Harris's direct correspondence with the company official in this case was unusual. It is probably attributable to the urgency of the moment. Also, the correspondence was in French, a language in which Alice Harris was proficient, while her husband probably was not.[32]

The attribution of authorship and the authentication of these photographs may also have been influenced by well-defined gender roles within the standard missionary narrative discussed earlier. Female missionaries embodied dutiful maternalism, while men were to embody the ideal of "muscular Christianity," identified with bravery and tenacity in the spirit of the legendary Victorian missionary, David Livingstone. Alice Harris certainly fulfilled her gender role at Baringa, serving as a helpmeet to her husband and, on at least one occasion, becoming the very image of civilized, moral maternalism in Africa (Figure 3.4).

Christina Twomey observes of the photograph in Figure 3.4, "Her symbolic presence in this image, dressed in white in an elevated and central position, constructs Alice Harris as a potential saviour and guiding light for the children of the Congo."[33] This maternalistic image, typical of missionary representations of the white woman's role in Africa, posed the visual antithesis of an atrocity photograph of a Congolese father gazing at his daughter's remains, or of three Congolese men displaying severed hands as two male missionaries look on. To step into the frame of an atrocity photograph may have been visually and morally appropriate for men, who were expected to come to grips with savagery, but it would have tainted Alice Harris, not necessarily as an individual, but as

FIGURE 3.4. Alice Harris with Congolese children. Reprinted with permission of Antislavery International.

a symbol of Christian civilization devoted to uplifting, educating, and healing, not interacting with the civilized savagery of imperialism.

The most clear-cut explanation of authorship and authentication in this photograph is based on gender roles, but not of the discursive kind. Alice and John Harris were still living in the Congo Free State when Morel published these atrocity photographs. Both had been threatened with murder by the local company official and his sentries for reporting atrocities to Guinness and Morel. In the small world of Baringa, everyone must have known that Alice Harris was the photographer, but her authorship was probably obscured in Morel's book so as not to strengthen the motive for reprisal against her. It is probable that the Harrises themselves decided to misattribute the atrocity photograph to John Harris for the simple reason that Alice Harris was the mother of two small children, who were then being raised in England by friends. For all the importance of patriarchal authority and maternal devotion in British missions, the Harrises probably chose to risk sacrificing a father in order to spare a mother for the sake of children of their own. Not long after the Harrises returned to England on furlough in 1905, the CRA published a brochure entitled "Camera and the Congo Crime," which included twenty-four atrocity photographs attributed to Alice Harris, now out of harm's way. By April 1907, the organization had sold 10,000 copies.[34] If in fact these atrocity photographs represented a pornography of pain, it is remarkable that a female missionary would put her name to them, and that photographs from this brochure would be featured in lantern lectures narrated by both John and Alice Harris, as well as other men and women. A female missionary putting her name to these atrocity photographs and narrating their significance before the public perhaps suggests that the images were not perceived as obscene. Susie Linfield argues persuasively that the moral or immoral connotations of a humanitarian photograph depend on the use to which the photograph is put.[35] If so, it seems in this case that the usage as humanitarian testimony was validated by a female missionary's moral authority. Be that as it may, the unseen atrocity of rape apparently gave every narrator pause.

Missionaries and humanitarians generally protested against the maltreatment of Congolese women on the grounds that this resulted in the neglect of children and a decline in population.[36] They seldom referred publicly to sexual violence, although in private correspondence they discussed among themselves and with state officials atrocious sexual violence in graphic detail.[37] Alice Harris observed that in order to find sexual violence against women in the official language of consular reports one had to "see it between the lines."[38] When missionaries or humanitarians themselves publicly referred to sexual violence against women, this violence was most often located in the "hostage house," where officers and sentries held women until their husbands redeemed them with rubber or other goods demanded by the regime. They published descriptions of women of the hostage house being flogged, or, "with babies at their breast," working as slaves.[39] They avoided making more than implicit or euphemistic reference to rape.[40] Some accounts of coercion, reminiscent of the humanitarian narratives examined by Halttunen, evoked sexual sadism. For example, in *King Leopold's Rule in Africa*, Morel condemns sentries for "dragging women away from their homes for forced labour requisitions – seizing them as 'hostages,' and 'tying them up,' whether virgins, wives, mothers, or those about to become mothers."[41] According to Morel, "[Congolese women] are imprisoned, flogged, left at the mercy of the soldiery, taxed beyond endurance, regarded as lower than the beasts."[42] Undoubtedly, British readers recognized that women "left at the mercy of the soldiery" were raped. Perhaps this particular outrage was easier to acknowledge, as Morel does here, in passing, followed by reference to the relatively mundane burden of taxation and situated in a larger, dizzying montage of abuses.

In the booklet *Rubber Is Death* John Harris offers numerous testimonies to theft, murder, and mutilation in the village of Bongwonga. He recounts "amongst other printable tortures" the case of a man named Akumugon: "[He] was first made to eat excrement and then tied to a post, his upper and lower lips were cut off thus leaving his mouth gaping. After being left to suffer in terrible agony for some time, he was mercifully shot."[43] In view of this account, and others comparably atrocious, Harris still observes, "Common decency forbids my giving scores of other horrible tortures."[44] It appears that only sexual violence transgressed this common, public decency. But there were advantages in shying away from sexual violence. Harris thus maintained his moral high ground and employed the power of suggestion to spur the audience's imagination. "It is impossible to print details of all tortures perpetrated on Congo natives," he explains.

No journal would publish them for they reek with unheard-of filthiness and inhumanity; the mind must imagine them. No opium-haunted brain could ever conjure up a more horrible nightmare. The poor Bongonga women have suffered as possibly no other women in history have done. Again I must ask the reader to picture those sentries at work as they rush into a village, seize any of these defenceless women, and after subjecting them to the most brutal and bestial treatment, tied them to trees until the husbands out of pity for their wives bring forward the price of ransom.[45]

In only one case did missionaries and humanitarians consistently put names to sexual violence. The victim of the violence was originally identified as a woman named Boali, though in subsequent publications she was sometimes referred to as Boaji, and the perpetrator was identified as a sentry named Ikelonda, sometimes referred to as Ekolonda. The notable inconsistency of the representations of this case in the literature and lantern lectures of the Congo reform campaign conveys the uncertainty and maybe even trepidation with which missionaries and humanitarians discussed Boali's experience in public. They attempted to place Boali, themselves, and their audiences within a stable, moral framework of gender roles in order to mitigate the potentially destructive threat of rape to their own moral authority and the efficacy of their narratives in inspiring humanitarian sympathy and support.

Boali was one of 258 Congolese, including thirteen women, who testified before a state-sponsored commission of inquiry that traveled in the Congo to investigate reports of atrocity and slavery in 1905. She testified at Baringa, in the presence of Alice and John Harris, who had persuaded her and many others to address the commission. According to the transcript of her testimony, translated and reproduced by Hunt from records in the African Archives in Brussels, Boali stated,

> One day when my husband went into the forest to gather rubber, the sentry Ikelonda came, finding me in my hut where I stayed, and asked me to give myself to him. I rejected his proposition. Furious Ikelonda fired a gun shot at me, which gave me the wound whose trace you can still see. I fell on my back; Ikelonda thought I was dead, and to get hold of the brass bracelet that I wore at the base of my right leg, he cut off my right foot.[46]

The final report of the commission generally substantiated the charges that British missionaries and the CRA had leveled at the Congo Free State.[47] In the meantime, however, missionaries and humanitarians had been skeptical that the commission would report truthfully and fairly upon the many Congolese testimonies that missionaries, including the Harrises, had witnessed. In a preemptive measure, the Harrises and Guinness cooperated with Morel in publishing a booklet, *Evidence Laid before the Congo Commission of Inquiry*, in the summer of 1905, as the Harrises were returning to England. In this booklet one finds a rare usage of the word "rape." John Harris declares, "Every witness tells of floggings, rape, mutilations, murders, and of imprisonments of men, women and children, and of illegal fines and irregular taxes, etc., etc."[48] Alice

Harris asserts, "Whilst the men were in the forest trying to get rubber, their wives were outraged, ill-treated, and stolen from them by the sentries."[49] She specifically recalls Boali's testimony:

Then Boali, a woman of Ekorongo, appeared before the commissioners, and her maimed body itself was a protest against the iniquitous rubber system. Because she wanted to remain faithful to her husband, who was away collecting rubber, and would not submit to be outraged by a brute of a sentry called Ekolonda, she was shot in the abdomen, which made an awful wound.... She fell down insensible, and the wretches were not yet satisfied, for they then hacked off her foot to get the anklet she was wearing. And yet she has survived it all, and to-day comes to bear her testimony. It is a pity that woman's mutilated body cannot be seen at home as we have seen it, and her pitiful story reach the ears of all those who feel for their fellow-beings.[50]

Harris already had a photograph of Boali, probably taken in anticipation of publicizing the woman's story in Britain. The photograph was first published later in the year, in Samuel Clemens's satire, *King Leopold's Soliloquy* (Figure 3.5).

The photograph is not referenced in Clemens's text, nor does it have a subcaption, apart from the attribution to "Mrs. Harris." It appears to have been subsequently published in only one CRA pamphlet, "The Indictment against the Congo Government," and in an article published in the *Penny Pictorial* in August 1907 under the title, "Murderland! New Series of Congo Articles by E. D. Morel."[51] This photograph was featured regularly, however, in lantern lectures of the Congo reform campaign that were attended by tens of thousands of men and women in Britain after 1906.

These lantern lectures were so successful that by late 1906 the Harrises, who lectured on almost a daily basis and oversaw other speakers, found themselves overwhelmed by requests from all over Britain. Unable to provide speakers to meet the demand, they worked with Morel to create a standard set of sixty lantern slides, accompanied by a descriptive lecture, which they rented to churches, philanthropic societies, workingmen's clubs, and any other organizations that wished to attend a lantern lecture on the Congo atrocities. The text of the lecture was methodically structured, its slides enumerated and narrated, so that any competent speaker could deliver it before an audience that the Harrises could not otherwise reach.

Slide number 34 was the photograph of Boali, captioned, "Boaji: Mutilated for her constancy." The text that accompanied the photograph reads as follows:

Amongst the mutilated was a woman named Boaji, who was so treated because she wished to remain faithful to her husband. You must understand that when the soldiers drive men into the forest for rubber, a sentry is left behind to "guard" the

FIGURE 3.5. Photograph of Boali. Reprinted from Mark Twain, *King Leopold's Soliloquy* (London: T. Fisher Unwin, 1907).

women. The women are at his mercy. In this case he asked the woman for food, but she had none. He therefore struck her down on the left side with the butt of his gun – you see the permanent deformity it left – then assaulted her; and cut off her foot to secure the valuable anklet she wore. When her husband protested a little later, he was cruelly beaten with a *chicotte* [whip] for his interference.[52]

In emphasizing Boali's constancy and faithfulness to her husband, the Harrises not only attempted to portray this Congolese woman as properly moral by British standards; they refuted the stereotype of Africans as an essentially savage race possessed by unrestrained sexuality. They suggested that British women could find in Boali, despite her race and her nakedness, a woman worthy of compassionate empathy. Missionaries and humanitarians returned repeatedly to the claim that there was no difference between the fundamental humanity of blacks and whites, a point brought home by this example of a Congolese woman suffering atrocious violence for marital fidelity, which was a foundation of a moral, Christian home (although the nature of this marriage between unbaptized Congolese was never explicitly defined).[53] Beyond this assertion of common moral ground, the Harrises blurred not only Boali's original testimony that they had heard at Baringa but also Alice Harris's previous account of this testimony in 1905. Following their initial emphasis on Boali's constancy as a proper wife, they suggest that Boali was first attacked because she refused to give the sentry food, not sex, and that she was struck with a gun, not shot. The account is muddled, reflecting perhaps the Harrises' hesitancy in writing for an unseen audience whose response they would not be able to measure and, if necessary, assuage. There is, furthermore, an addition to this narrative that does not appear in other accounts but which completes the representation of moral Congolese gender roles. There is the husband who reciprocates Boali's faithfulness, and whose honor is marked with a whip.

The text of the standardized, descriptive lecture on the Congo atrocities makes no particular allowances for the composition of the prospective audience. Taking a broader view of the Congo atrocity lectures, one finds sporadic evidence that different audiences rendered the narratives that accompanied atrocity photographs anything but standard. This lecture should not be treated as a universal script, but as one version among many produced by a group of reformers who struggled to appeal to the public without alienating or offending different parts of this public in the face of atrocity. These lectures were not equivalent to solitary readings of "horror narratives" of Congo atrocities; they were social events in which the audience was conscious of not only the speaker's words but also the speaker's gender and the presence of other audience members and their judgments regarding their appropriate, gendered relationships to atrocity and, especially, sexual violence. Lantern lectures were most morally problematic in the presence of "mixed audiences" of men, women, and sometimes children. In a speech in New York City during a U.S. tour in December 1906, Guinness stated, "The natives [of the Congo] are now compelled to bring the King of Belgium in rubber and ivory about $10,000,000 worth of goods a year. And if they don't? Ah, my friends, now comes a story which I cannot tell here. This is a mixed audience." It was an audience, the *New York Times* reported, of men and women. Guinness proceeded to talk about sentries cutting off the hands and feet of their victims. Turning to the case of Boali, he continued,

Women as well as men are compelled to do the bidding of these sentinels with guns in their hands. I will cite you only one instance, that of a woman who refused to do the bidding of one of these sentinels. He struck her in the abdomen with the butt of his rifle so that she was maimed for life. Then he cut off one of her feet.[54]

In the context of this specific lecture, the sentinel's "bidding" referred clearly to previously mentioned demands for rubber and ivory. Guinness did not provide information that might have led his audience to infer the threat of rape, though some may have interpreted the sentinel's "bidding" in this way; nor did Guinness offer a reason for the severing of the woman's foot, thus representing the act as a heinous caprice. He implies that had the audience not been mixed, he might have told a different, more explicit, story.

As early as January 1904, Guinness presented a lantern-slide lecture on Congo atrocities to a mass "men's meeting" in London.[55] Only occasionally in the records of the early lantern-slide lectures of the Congo reform campaign is a gathering described as a "men's meeting" or a "woman's meeting," but these segregated meetings nonetheless offer critical insight into the representation and reception of atrocity in terms of sexuality and gender. On 20 November 1905, for example, there was a "protest meeting" held at St. Peter's Mission Church in Heeley, Sheffield, chaired by Sir Charles Skelton. Later that afternoon, there was a separate "ladies' meeting" held at the same location.[56] The CRA records do not indicate whether the first meeting was "mixed" or restricted to men, but it was likely the latter, because the purpose of the "ladies' meeting" was most likely to enable women to hear about atrocities and hold discussions that would be unseemly in the presence of men. In June 1907, in anticipation of a protest meeting in Hull, Morel wrote to the local organizer, "There should be no attempt to restrict the evening meeting to men. In my speeches I deal far less with the atrocities than with the system which is responsible for them, our historical relations, and the general international outlook with regard to action at the present time."[57]

After 1907, the year in which Morel lectured for "adults only" at Hawarden, he and the Harrises undoubtedly perceived that the "horror narratives" and atrocity photographs of their lantern lectures were so morally problematic that they needed to begin segregating their audiences on at least some occasions. When Alice Harris published a pamphlet entitled, "Enslaved Womanhood of the Congo. An Appeal to British Women," she or Morel stipulated on the cover, "FOR ADULT READERS ONLY."[58] Inside, without photographic illustration, Harris recounts many aspects of the abuse of Congolese women by the state and concessionaire companies. She refers to female hostages who endured "constant subjection to the ungoverned passions of a brutalized soldiery – (too often diseased)." She explains that every white man who works for the state has a menagerie of Congolese women and girls, presumably for his sexual pleasure. She asserts that "the immense Congo army is made attractive by reason of the abundant opportunities for securing 'wives'"; she decries the "vast horde of soldiery numbering many thousands, possessing a good knowledge of European weapons, which for years has been given licence to loot, rape and outrage." She reports that Congolese women are openly sold as slaves. "Nothing can escape: – Tribal custom; family life; chastity; motherhood; childhood; all become engulfed in the ruinous flood of avarice, lust and passion, which is surging through the Congo Valley."[59]

While Harris or Morel attempted to restrict the readers of this pamphlet by age, Harris and other female supporters of the Congo reform campaign became concerned with segregating lantern lectures by gender. Toward this end, they established the women's branch of the CRA in April 1909. At their inaugural meeting, Harris declared that their principles and goals were the same as those of the CRA executive committee, and that they would dutifully support the committee's policies. The purpose of the branch, she explained, was to facilitate the exchange of information about atrocities perpetrated against women on the Congo by segregating women's meetings from men's meetings. According to Harris, "The condition of the [Congolese] women was such that the matter could scarcely be dealt with in a mixed audience, the effects could only be appreciated by women. Therefore meetings for women were necessary to disseminate facts concerning their treatment."[60] Recognizing both the moral imperative of Congo reform and the moral danger of atrocity photographs and sexual violence, female reformers thus sought to enhance both their understanding of Congolese women's suffering and their political influence on the women's behalf by carefully staging the gendered boundaries of the moral display and sight of atrocity. Harris later proposed to take one step more on behalf of the women's branch. She indicated that she had "written to ladies at work on the Congo for recent information, and if possible for photographs wherewith to make lantern slides."[61] Unfortunately, we do not know whether Harris received and displayed such photographs before exclusively female audiences. Yet we can surmise that Harris had come to believe that women's representation of atrocity was distinctive from that of men and more attuned to the interests, sensibilities, and moral integrity of female viewers.

On 6 November 1906, Alice Harris gave an address to six hundred people in the village of Crosshills, with the Reverend George Armitt presiding. The audience subsequently passed a resolution, which stated at the outset: "That this meeting expresses its deep sense of indignation at the barbarities inflicted upon the natives of the Congo, and denounces, as contrary to the elementary rights of humanity and as a violation of the Berlin Act, the principles introduced and enforced by the Congo Free State..."[62] The same language is found in the "suggested form of Resolution for Public Meetings" that concludes the text of the standard, published lecture on the Congo atrocities. There is no mention of Christian duty in the full text of this resolution. It was to be forwarded to the British Foreign Office, so the reformers might have employed the discourse of rights to make their case against the Congo Free State in terms that more closely corresponded to and challenged the sovereign rights of nations under international law. Preceding and framing this assertion of rights, however, the standard lecture invokes Christian duty at its end. "Are the Churches of Christ to remain silent?" asks the speaker. "Will the heart of civilization remain unmoved? Surely not." The speaker then testifies to hearing "a great cry for Justice and Mercy" from the Congo forests, and implicitly calls upon the British nation to fulfill its historical role in leading the fight for emancipation in the Christian tradition of leading evangelical figures in the abolition of the British slave trade in 1807 and the emancipation of slaves in the British Empire in 1833. Quoting from Morel's book, *Red Rubber*, published in 1906, the speaker finally declares,

Let us prove to them that the heart of the nation still beats soundly as of yore, by the performance of our plain and simple duty, by saving the races of Central Africa from the grip of the modern slavers.[63]

The lantern-slide lectures, for all their differences in the treatment of atrocity, suggest that the humanitarian narrative of the Congo reform campaign derived consistent power from its declaration of a Christian duty to enforce human rights.

"Shame" was a word commonly shouted by members of the audiences who attended the lantern-slide lectures on the Congo atrocities. It was directed toward the representation of the atrocities of the Congo Free State, affirming a moral bond between the audience and the speaker. The reformers regarded this bond as both essential to the success of their cause and severable, should their treatment of atrocity and especially sexual violence offend their audiences and bring shame upon themselves. In differentiating their lectures in view of their audiences, and in segregating audiences by age and gender, the reformers acknowledged that lantern-slide lectures were social forums in which atrocity heightened the observance and volatility of moral propriety. The segregation of audiences enabled reformers to speak more explicitly about atrocity and sexual violence, woman to woman or man to man, which effectively broadened their margin for moral error. In the terms of the reformers' own narrative, their transgression of propriety might have rendered them guilty of a violation of the elementary rights of humanity. Within the predominant narrative framework of Christian duty, defined largely by missionaries, it is more likely that reformers feared their own transgression into sin.

Notes

1 E. D. Morel Collection, London School of Economics (hereafter Morel Collection), File I, Volume "1907–8, Congo and CRA."
2 For more on this critical issue, which lies outside the scope of this chapter, see Twomey, "Severed Hands," 39–50.
3 Thomas, "The Evidence of Sight," 151–68.
4 For a general discussion of the Congo reform campaign, photography, and lantern-slide lectures, see Kevin Grant, "Christian Critics of Empire," which is a reprint, with revisions, of an essay published in 2001 in the *Journal of Imperial and Commonwealth History*. Regarding the Congo reform campaign as a precedent in the deployment of photography in international humanitarian protest, see the chapter by Christina Twomey in this volume; also Linfield, *The Cruel Radiance,* 48–50.
5 Laqueur, "Bodies, Details, and the Humanitarian Narrative," 176–7.

6   Sliwinski, "The Childhood of Human Rights"; also see Hochschild, *King Leopold's Ghost*.

7   Óli Jacobsen, *Daniel J. Danielsen and the Congo: Missionary Campaigns and Atrocity Photographs* (Troon: BAHN, 2014).

8   Hunt, "An Acoustic Register," 223.

9   Walkowitz, *City of Dreadful Delight*.

10 Koven, *Slumming*, 91.

11 Halttunen, "Humanitarianism and the Pornography of Pain," 325.

12 Ibid., 334. For a treatment of the Congo reform campaign in similar terms, see Peffer, "Snap of the Whip."

13 Jean Stengers, "King Leopold's Congo, 1886–1908," in Roland Oliver and G. N. Sanderson, *The Cambridge History of Africa*, Vol. 6 (Cambridge: Cambridge University Press, 1985), 346.

14 For fine studies arguing that I have overstated the role of missionaries in the Congo reform campaign, and which place greater emphasis on the roles of Morel and the British Foreign Office, see Burroughs, *Travel Writing and Atrocities*, and Dean Pavlakis, *British Humanitarianism and the Congo Reform Movement, 1896–1913* (forthcoming from Ashgate).

15 Barthes, *Camera Lucida*, 88–9; Twomey, "Framing Atrocity"; Jane Lydon, "'Behold the Tears,'" 234–50; Lydon, *The Flash of Recognition: Photography and the Emergence of Indigenous Rights*; Godby, "Confronting Horror," 34–48.

16 Thompson, *Light on Darkness?*

17 Letter from John Harris to Travers Buxton, secretary of the British and Foreign Anti-Slavery and Aborigines' Protection Society, 23 December 1911, Collection of the British and Foreign Anti-slavery and Aborigines' Protection Society, Rhodes House, Oxford (hereafter Anti-Slavery Collection), Mss. Brit. Emp. S24, J/46.

18 Thompson, *Light on Darkness?*, 209.

19 Ibid., 213. Regarding missionaries and lantern-slide lectures, see ibid., 207–38; Simpson, "Missions and the Magic Lantern," 13–15.

20 Morel to Lady J. A. Chalmers, 10 March 1904, Morel Collection, Copybook, January–May 1904.

21 John Harris to Morel, 19 August 1905, Morel Collection, F8, file 75.

22 Martínez and Libal, "Introduction: The Gender of Humanitarian Narrative," 161–70. Regarding the knotty issue of establishing the authorship of other photographs in the Congo reform campaign, see Óli Jacobsen, "Daniel J. Danielson (1871–1916): The Faeroese Who Changed History in the Congo," *Brethren Historical Review* 8 (2012): 5–37.

23 See Grant, 117, endnote 1, for relevant correspondence.

24 John Harris to Dr. Harry Guinness, 19 May 1904, Anti-Slavery Collection, Mss. Brit. Emp. S19, D5/9.

25 E. D. Morel, *King Leopold's Rule in Africa* (London: William Heinemann, 1904).

26 Ibid., photograph facing page 144.

27 Ibid., 445.

28 Ibid., photograph facing page 48.

29 Ibid., 447.

30 Barthes, *Camera Lucida*, 5–6.

31 Morel, *King Leopold's Rule*, photographs facing page 224.

32 See John Harris's many letters in the Anti-Slavery Collection.

33 Twomey, "Severed Hands," 44.

34 "Annual Report of the London Auxiliary of the Congo Reform Association, April 1907," Morel Collection, Section A.

35 Linfield, 60.

36 For example, Morel, *King Leopold's Rule*, 247–8. Also see Hunt, 225–9.

37 For example, in a letter from John Harris to the vice governor general on 17 January 1905, Harris states, "Bolumba another woman wishing to remain faithful to her husband had a pointed stake forced into her womb, through the vagina, as this did not kill her she was shot." Morel Collection, F8/75.

38 Alice Seeley Harris, "*Enslaved Womanhood of the Congo. An Appeal to British Women*" (London: Congo Reform Association (London Branch), c.1908–9), 2.

39 Morel, *King Leopold's Rule*, 244–5.

40 Ibid.

41 Ibid., 247.

42 Ibid., 242.

43 John Harris, "'*Botofe Bo Le Iwa.' Rubber Is Death*" (London: Regions Beyond Missionary Union Publication Department, c.1905), 19.

44 Ibid., 21.

45 Ibid.

46 Hunt, 225.

47 *The Congo: A Report of the Commission of Enquiry Appointed by the Congo Free State Government* (New York: G.P. Putnam's Sons, 1906).

48 "Evidence Laid before the Congo Commission of Inquiry" (Liverpool: CRA, 1905), 24.

49 Ibid., 28.

50 Ibid., 30.

51 Hunt, 247, footnote 8.

52 "The Congo Atrocities. A lecture to accompany a series of 60 photographic slides for the optical lantern" (n.d.), Morel Collection, 19.

53 Also see E. D. Morel, "*The Treatment of Women and Children in the Congo Free State*" (Liverpool: Congo Reform Association, c.1905), 4.

54 "3,000,000 Natives Slain to Get Congo Rubber," *New York Times*, 19 December 1906, 11.

55 *Official Organ of the Congo Reform Association*, May 1904, 26.

56 *Official Organ of the Congo Reform Association*, December 1905, 19.

57 Morel to R. Shields, 6 June 1907, Morel Collection, Copybook, January–October 1907.

58 Harris, "*Enslaved Womanhood.*"

59 Ibid.

60 *Official Organ of the Congo Reform Association*, April 1909, 275.

61 Ibid., 276.

62 *Official Organ of the Congo Reform Association*, December 1906, 25.

63 "The Congo Atrocities," 32; E. D. Morel, *Red Rubber* (New York: Nassau Press, 1906), 200. In the preceding text of *Red Rubber*, Morel refers by name to leading evangelical figures in the legendary abolitionist campaign.

4

Photography, Visual Culture, and the Armenian Genocide

Peter Balakian

I

In the evolution of photographs of atrocity and war, Roger Fenton's images of the Crimean War of 1852–5 and Matthew Brady's images of the American Civil War of 1861–5 marked dramatic uses of the camera to locate and situate a visual encounter with war and its encompassing human realities of suffering and survival. Images of the brutality done to the Congolese in the Belgian Congo of the 1890s and of the Abdulhammit Massacres of the Armenians in Turkey in 1894–6 also mark historically important visual records of mass violence.[1]

However, by 1915 two connected and simultaneous events of atrocity gave rise to images of unprecedented kinds. They were images of trench warfare in northern France, Belgium, and Germany: photographs of gouged-out earth, miles of trenches in which men were living and dying amid the corpses of their comrades, as they were killing their enemies with rifles, machine guns, grenades, and chemical weapons. Photographs of heaped and conjoined human bodies, weapons, and ruined earth gave a vivid perspective on the new age of technological warfare. Those images appeared in newspapers and magazines throughout the second half of the twentieth century's second decade.

In the same arena of war, on the eastern front, in Ottoman Turkey – from the western littoral to the eastern provinces and the deserts of northern Syria – images of the Armenian genocide were being taken and would surface after the war in various publications and forums. And after World War I, more images were taken – by Protestant and Catholic missionaries and Near East Relief workers – of survivors, mostly orphans and destitute women. These images would become important in post–World War I international politics, as the Allies and President Wilson tried to create peace settlements and new nations out of the ruins of the war and post-empire restructuring; and they were valuable for the nongovernmental organization Near East Relief that was engaged in a major humanitarian campaign for survivors and refugees in the Middle East.

The eradication of the Armenians by the Ottoman Turkish government behind the screen of World War I affords an interesting perspective on a particular kind of visual culture that evolved from what is widely regarded as the first genocide of the twentieth century to be implemented with modern techniques, national ideology, and state and bureaucratic apparatus: in short, the first *modern* genocide. The arc of events that began in 1915 with the deportation and mass killing of the Armenian Christian minority population of Turkey and continued into the postwar period of humanitarian relief was the setting for historically significant images of genocide and its aftermath – in what became a defining moment of modernity.

One can see in the unfolding events of this history two distinct strands of visual culture. In the first, the photographs of the genocide of the 1915–18 period present images that capture aspects of the process of deportation, mass killing, and atrocity. These include images of forced marches, lynchings, and refugee camps as well as images of corpses and human remains. The photographs were taken almost entirely by nonprofessional photographers, apparently snapped on the spot in impromptu moments by bystanders and missionaries, Foreign Service officers, or others who might have been passing through the region.

The photographs of the postwar period, mostly taken between 1918 and the early 1920s, were taken for humanitarian relief efforts by Near East Relief (NER), a Protestant missionary NGO that implemented the largest international humanitarian drive to that date in U.S. history. NER served thousands of marooned refugees and orphans, not only Armenians, but also Greeks, Syrians, and Arabs who were still living in conditions of famine, disease, and destitution in various pockets of Turkey, Transcaucasia, Syria, and Iran. These images, taken by NER workers or professional photographers hired by NER, became crucial for the fundraising drives across the United States that in the end raised more than $100 million ($1.3 billion today) in an age when a loaf of bread cost a nickel. The photographs taken during the period of genocide (1915–18), and the photographs and constructed images (mostly posters) produced in its aftermath and following World War I during a time of urgent humanitarian appeal, make an interesting comparison and offer insights into the forms and formations of atrocity images, their roles and functions, and the visual cultures from which they emerged.

2

Much of the recent photography of genocide, human rights atrocities, and war has been produced within the boundaries of performative conventions and ethical commitments. Photojournalism is a profession with a set of assumptions, conventions, and personal motivations. Photographers who go to war or into regions of human rights catastrophe often bring with them moral perspectives and goals. They enter their arenas of conflict with their training as photographers, and often as artists, and they are self-aware about how they shoot images and frame scenes. There are always levels of performative gestures in their work. In certain dramatic cases, photojournalists have worked hard to stage images of war and heroism for political and even commercial purposes.

Susan Sontag has noted that some of the most famous images of war were highly staged. Roger Fenton made his official photographs of the Crimean War for the British government and created soothing landscapes out of terrains of mass slaughter. Some of the famous and self-consciously created image-history of the American Civil War by Matthew Brady and his team Alexander Gardner and Timothy O'Sullivan were shaped and packaged for Brady's thriving commercial business in New York City. Two of the most famous triumphalist war photographs of the twentieth century were staged with directional care. The image of the American flag on Iwo Jima on 23 February 1945 was a careful construction of the Associated Press photographer Joe Rosenthal, who "captured" the image after the capture-event was over and used a larger flag in his photo shoot. Yvegeny Khaldei's iconic image of Russian soldiers hoisting the Soviet flag on top of the Reichstag as Berlin burns was also staged for the camera.[2]

In recent decades, as Susie Linfield has pointed out, photojournalists such as Robert Capa, James Natchwey, and Gilles Peress have taken their craft and artistic and professional talents into atrocity and war zones with moral missions to capture human suffering and the criminal behavior of the perpetrators.[3] In different ways, their work is shaped by a highly professional context and a self-awareness about social and political performance.

In assessing the first chapter of Armenian genocide images, the atrocity images of 1915–18, we are confronted with photographs that did not emerge from self-conscious photojournalism nor were taken as performative acts of image construction. The Armenian atrocity images were taken by bystanders who found themselves in unforeseen circumstances. They were missionaries who had been working in Turkey among the Christians of the Ottoman Empire for decades, Foreign Service officers from the United States who had been stationed in the interior provinces of Turkey, or military officers of Turkey's wartime ally Germany, such as Armin T. Wegner.

The images compel us to ask questions about how we read photographs that were not taken by professionals situating themselves in an atrocity-event as self-conscious artists or journalists. How do we understand photographs taken by bystanders who snapped them spontaneously in unexpected situations of mass violence; or by bystanders who were compelled to record what they could, in a given moment, because of their sense of horror or curiosity? Are such images – taken without professional ego, assumptions, and techniques – different in form and content? What are the differences between these images and those packaged by a highly professional humanitarian movement for the purpose of raising relief funds for survivors and refugees, mostly women and children marooned thousands of miles away?

Both chapters of the visual culture of the Armenian genocide were lost, along with the largely forgotten history of the event, until the genocide became the subject of intensified scholarly work over the past forty years. In part, the obscurity of the Armenian genocide was due to an ongoing campaign by the Turkish government to falsify the events of 1915 in a campaign of denial for the purpose of absolving Turkey of responsibility. As the international legal scholar Richard Falk has noted, Turkey's campaign "is a major, proactive deliberate government effort to use every possible instrument of persuasion at its disposal to keep the truth about the Armenian genocide from general acknowledgement, especially by elites in the United States and Western Europe."[4] Holocaust historian Deborah Lipstadt has written:

Denial of genocide whether that of the Turks against the Armenians, or the Nazis against the Jews, is not an act of historical reinterpretation. Rather, the deniers sow confusion by appearing to be engaged in a genuine scholarly effort. The abundance of documents and testimonies that confirm the genocide are dismissed as contrived, coerced, or forgeries and falsehoods.[5]

For this reason, as well, the photographic evidence of the Armenian genocide continues to accrue weight and significance as it presents a visual record of an event that the perpetrator and its legacy still aggressively attempts to falsify.

3

Susie Linfield, among others, has argued that photographs have been essential to moral progress and to the history of human rights in the twentieth century. Photographs bring us "close to those experiences of suffering in ways that no other form of art or journalism can," and "they illuminate the unbridgeable chasm that separates ordinary life from extraordinary experiences of political trauma."[6] If there is some validity to her assertion, how might we situate the photographs of the Armenian genocide? There are dozens of images of the Armenian event in motion: deportations, refugees in camps, lynchings, corpses and remains in the aftermath of mass killing.[7] In selecting several images for this essay, I'm interested in how the images situate us in the texture of the event, how they allow us a particular kind of knowledge about the process of genocide.

While each photograph has a context, photographs taken by amateur photographers who were bystanders make issues of authorship often unknowable. Thus, situating the photographs in place and time becomes crucial to understanding more about each image's provenance, and of course its meaning, in the larger history of the event. One of the Armenian genocide's most reproduced images in recent decades is a photograph of men being marched out of Kharpert (Turkish Harpoot), today Elizag (Figure 4.1). The provenance is the diary of the Danish missionary nurse Maria Jacobsen who was stationed in Kharpert from 1907 until 1919. Having lived through the entire period of killings and forced marches as a foreign missionary worker from a neutral wartime country, Jacobsen witnessed the events as a bystander who had a stake in helping to save Armenians. Her own photograph bears her handwritten caption in Danish "Armenenske Maend fores ud af Byen for at draebes 1915" (Armenian men being led out of the city to be killed, 1915). According to Matthias Bjornlund, the earliest publication of the photograph appears to have been in a 1920 pamphlet by Amalia Lange, *A Page from Armenia's History: K.M.A (Women Missionary Workers) 1910–1920*.[8] The photograph later appeared in *Maria Jacobsen's Diaries, 1907–1919 Harpoot*, which was published in 1979 and reissued in 2001. In the last decades of the twentieth century the photograph has become almost iconic in its presence and use.

It is clear from the photograph's perspective that it was taken from an elevated place, most likely from a window of the U.S. Consulate in

FIGURE 4.1. Armenian men being marched out of Kharpert. Anonymous donor, Project SAVE, Armenian Photograph Archives.

Mezre, the connecting twin city of Kharpert (though the mailing address was listed as Kharpert, hence the caption). While the photographer remains unknown, Abraham Krikorian and Eugene Taylor, among others, have conjectured that the photo may have been taken by the U.S. Consul Leslie A. Davis, his wife, the German pastor Ehmann, or even by Maria Jacobsen.[9]

What does the image tell us about the larger event? The punctum for me – to use Roland Barthes's term for the point of the viewer's most intense contact – is the gendarme midway in the line of the deportees. He is in a light-colored uniform carrying what appears to be a rifle, which makes a diagonal form against the linear column of deportees: it creates a visual tension that draws us into the drama. Because a good deal of killing was done with rifles and bayonets (numerous witness accounts describe this), the rifle and the bayonet are indexical images. Even though there is no killing in view, the weapon signifies an important aspect of the killing process and an object of power that defined the perpetrator's control of life and death. The line of men being marched through the town is an ur, or quintessential image – a representation of a large infrastructural dimension of the mass killing program.

Furthermore, the Armenian men are dressed formally, in dark jackets and coats; they are cultural leaders of this mid-sized Anatolian city that was a significant center for Armenians, in part because it was the home of Euphrates College, an important American Protestant missionary college where Armenians were prominent in both the faculty and student body. Since we know that the cultural leaders of the city, especially the Armenian professors at Euphrates College, were imprisoned, tortured, and killed, it is not difficult to conclude that these formally dressed men are those leaders being marched to prison.[10]

I find the mis-en-scène particularly revealing. The white, mostly flat-roofed buildings of the city with their mullioned windows convey the solidity of this small provincial city of eastern Turkey. Then the scene intrudes: several dozen men who are formally dressed are being marched out of a town that otherwise looks normal. No smoke, no flames, no ruins. The gendarmes along the inner perimeter with their rifles mark the other side of the motion the image captures. The photograph captures the tension between the city as a structure of civilization and the chaos and impending destruction of the deportation that will result in imprisonment, torture, and death.

A significant group of photographs of the genocide in motion comes from the collection of Armin T. Wegner, the German nurse and second lieutenant in Field Marshall Von der Goltz's retinue, who spent time, against orders, in the Armenian refugee camps at Ras-el-Ain (as well as Rakka, Meskene, Aleppo, and Deir el-Zor). From Ras-el-Ain in November 1915, he wrote:

> I have just returned from a round of inspection of the camps: hunger, death, disease, desperation on all sides. You would smell the odour of feces and decay. From a tent came the laments of a dying woman. A mother identifying the dark violet badges on my uniform as those of the Sanitary Corps, came towards me with outstretched hands.
>
> Taking me for a doctor, she clung on to me with all her might, I who had neither medicines, nor bandages, for it was forbidden to help her. But all this is nothing compared to the frightful sights of the swarms of orphans which increase daily. At the sides of the camp, a row of holes in the ground covered with rags, had been prepared for them. Girls and boys of all ages were sitting in these holes, heads together, abandoned and reduced to animals starved, without food or bread, deprived of the most basic human aid, packed tightly against the other and trembling from the night cold, holding pieces of still smoldering wood to try and get warm.[11]

Wegner defied Turkish and German orders by taking photographs, which was forbidden, and collected others from missionaries and other eyewitnesses. His collection comprises a major source of Armenian genocide images. He made notes, wrote letters about what he saw, and even carried letters from deported Armenians to Constantinople, where he gave them to Ambassador Morgenthau to send to the United States. When a letter to his mother describing the Armenian atrocities was intercepted by the authorities, he was expelled from the Armenian camp zone and forced to work in the cholera wards, where he fell ill, was sent back to Constantinople, and then to Germany. In the end, he risked his life hiding in his belt the negatives of the photographs he had collected and taken.[12]

To understand the Wegner images it is essential to understand the Ottoman government's use of the northern Syrian desert for the mass killing of Armenians. Since it was acknowledged in testimony by high-ranking Ottoman officials during the 1919–20 courts-martial trials that *deportation meant massacre*,[13] the concept of herding Armenians from their villages, towns, and cities toward northern Syria was designed to leave those who managed to survive the forced marches marooned in a desolate desert where famine, disease, and exposure would take care of most of them. In this way, Der Zor soon became the epicenter of death.

"Everybody knew by now," the priest Grigoris Balakian wrote in his memoir, *Armenian Golgotha*, "that being exiled to Der Zor was synonymous with death." A man who survived Der Zor told Balakian as they met in hiding in the Amanos mountains:

It is impossible for human language to be able to describe what those who went to Der Zor experienced.... We came across thousands of corpses which were naked as the day they were born and whose eyes had been gouged out; all their limbs had been cut off for sport and their bodies were swollen; their entrails were spilled out; during the daytime, the vultures would descend on these corpses and have a feast, while it was the wild animals' turn at night. Reverend Father, where is the God of the Armenians? ... [W]here is the Jesus you preach about?

In the summer of 1916, Minister of the Interior Talaat Pasha, the primary architect of the Armenian killing plan, was disturbed to discover that, notwithstanding the deaths of more than 250,000 Armenians in the Der Zor region in the summer and fall of 1915, the survivors were beginning to show signs of life, and in certain encampments, they were trading their skills and artisan knowledge with the local Bedouins for goods and food. Thus, he ordered another spree of mass killings in the summer of 1916.[14] And by the end of the summer of 1916, another 160,000–200,000 Armenians died in the Der Zor region, increasing the death toll in and around Der Zor to over 400,000.

To get a further sense of the conditions of that moment, the reports of Auguste Berneau, a German businessman, are among various witness accounts that depict the conditions of mass death. In the summer of 1916, U.S. Consul Jesse B. Jackson, stationed in Aleppo, worked hard to get relief to the Armenians of the outlying regions. In August, he sent his part-time employee, Bernau, on a secret relief mission to the refugee camps in the Der Zor region. Bernau's report of his mission was forwarded by Jackson to Secretary of State Lansing in Washington, DC, stamped "Very Confidential."[15] He rendered what he saw vividly.

"It is impossible to give an account of the impression of horror which my journey across the Armenian encampments scattered all along the Euphrates has given me," Bernau wrote Jackson. "Brutally dragged out of their native land," naked, starving, robbed of everything, he found them "penned up in the open like cattle." A few of the survivors had made makeshift tents out of cloth and had found watermelon or a sick goat for food, but "everywhere," he reported "you see emaciated and wan faces, wandering skeletons, lurking for all kinds of diseases, and victims moreover to hunger."[16] And "the young girls, often even very young ones have become the booty of the Musulmans." If they weren't killed, he noted, they were raped and sold into slavery or harems.[17]

"As on the gates of 'Hell' of Dante," Bernau wrote, "the following should be written at the entrance of these accursed encampments: 'You who enter, leave all hopes.'" Feeling that what he "had seen and heard surpasses all imagination," he underscored: "I thought I was passing through a part of hell.... Everywhere it is the same Governmental barbarism which aims at the systematic annihilation through starvation of the survivors of the Armenian nation in Turkey," Bernau explained; "everywhere the same bestial inhumanity on the part of these executioners and the same tortures undergone by these victims all along the Euphrates from Meskene to Der-i-Zor. " In Meskene alone, Bernau reported, there were 60,000 Armenians buried, and "as far as the eye can reach mounds are seen containing 200 to 300 corpses."[18]

The Wegner photographs invite us into this historical moment. Photo text and context create a kind of depth that is compounded by the relationship between the image and the knowledge of the historical moment and event that context affords. Tessa Hoffmann and Gerayer Koutcharian in their seminal essay "Images That Horrify and Indict"[19] present various groups of Armenian genocide photographs, among them a group from Wegner's collection of the Syrian desert camps taken in the 1915–16 period. Figure 46 in the essay is an image of Armenians in a camp in the desert region; Hoffmann and Koutcharian note that "there were no preparations" for the surviving Armenians who were dumped here.

For me, the photograph is defined by the complex perspective created by foreground, midground, and distant ground. The emaciated body of what appears to be a women leaning over a bundle of blankets in the lower right foreground is my punctum. Her tousled dense head of hair leads me to her shoulder and arm which are grotesquely distended like an elastic band from shoulder to elbow. It's impossible to know whether there is a child or objects under the bundle of blankets, which sends me into the midground to another pile of blankets, and there a child's head appears – quite normal looking. Behind the child several feet away a woman looks on from the ground where she is shawled by a blanket. There's a propped pile of sticks and branches in midground and more makeshift tents that show the camp as an ad hoc creation of available materials. The two men standing are in dark clothes; one appears to be wearing a fez, suggesting that he may be a gendarme patrolling the refugees.

It is a raw image of survivors in the middle of nowhere: a glimpse of the conditions of minimal survival – and the ragtag closeness to death on

FIGURE 4.2. Armenian deportees, 1915. Photographer: Armin T. Wegner, Wallstein Verlag, German.

arid gouged ground in summer temperatures of 100 to 120 degrees F. The words of Bernau and Wegner help deepen the context and reality of the Syrian desert concentration camps, as they were referred to.[20]

While this camp photograph has not been reproduced often, other Wegner images have become iconic. The photograph of a woman walking with a bundle on a dirt road (Figure 4.2) was probably taken, as Tessa Hoffmann notes, in 1915 when Wegner was on his way to Baghdad as a soldier in the German-Ottoman Sanitation Mission. In his diary entry of 19 October 1916, while in Aleppo on his way to Constantinople, he wrote:

In the last few days I have taken numerous photographs. They tell me that Jemal Pasha, the hangman of Syria, has forbidden the photographing of the refugee camps on the pain of death. I carry these images that horrify and indict hidden under my cummerbund. In the camps of Meskene and Aleppo I collected many petitions, which I have hidden in my knapsack, in order to bring them to the American embassy in Constantinople, since the postal service will not deliver them. I do not doubt for a moment that I am thereby committing an act of high treason and yet the knowledge of having helped these most wretched people at least in a slight respect fills me with a feeling of greater fortune than could any other deed.[21]

Wegner presented this image and others in two slide-show lectures he gave after the war. In the first, of 26 January 1918, at Breslau for the German-

Turkish society, he was under pressure from the German government to
frame the images to appease the Ottoman government and so presented
the Armenians as seditious in the wake of "treasonous" behavior at Van.
A year later in a slide show he presented in March 1919 in Berlin, Wegner
called his lecture "Expulsion of Armenians into the Desert," and spoke
openly about "Armenian atrocities," and criticized Germany for its complicity in the Armenian extermination plan. This second lecture was given
after the German military censorship had been lifted and affirms Wegner's
original perspective on the atrocities.[22]

The image of the woman in the foreground walking with a bundle in
her arms brings us into motion. We are caught up in the movement of
people on a dirt road in arid desolation. There are trees on a sloping hill
in the midground and mountains rising from left to right. I'm jolted by
the vast terrain in which deported women whom we see close up, walk
toward famine, disease, abduction, or death. The tension in the image is
heightened because viewers, then as now, know from the reportage and
testimony that sexual violence was ubiquitous and women were continually subject to rape, abduction, and other sexual tortures.[23]

The women are dressed in traditional village garb of long dresses and
head covering, and the children with them appear to be between the ages
of three and perhaps six or seven. The one figure on the left, dressed in a
dark jacket, appears to be a man, and the long object hanging from his
right hand appears to be a rifle. Thus, we are looking at a ragged end of a
deportation of remaining women and children. We are catching a glimpse
of a larger process that was happening all over Turkey – a freeze-frame
of a moving picture. For all the vivid candor of this image, a mystery
stares at us. What is wrapped in the bundle? A child, supplies, personal
items? The striped blanket or cloth is for me the punctum because it is a
traditional textile, an Armenian artifact – an image that embodies culture
and normative village life. But now, it is a remnant of life that's been terminated, and so the textile shocks the photograph into another layer of
signifying what is lost in the genocidal event.

4

While the atrocity photographs were taken under cover, smuggled or
quietly carried out of Turkey, and had slow journeys into public view,
another visual culture emerged from the Armenian genocide after the War
and was centered around relief and rescue. The Armenian relief movement began in October 1915 in New York City. After the urging of U.S.

Ambassador to Turkey Henry Morgenthau, a group of philanthropists led by Protestant missionary figures came together in the offices of Cleveland R. Dodge on Park Avenue South in New York City in early October 1915. Among them were James Barton, former secretary of the American Board of Commissioners of Foreign Missions, and Dodge, a philanthropist and trustee of Robert College, the Protestant missionary college in Constantinople.

Morgenthau had been receiving dispatches, witness accounts, reports, and other testimonials since the summer of 1915 from his consuls who were stationed in the Armenian provinces of Turkey. Many of these reports also emanated from American Protestant missionaries who had a vast network of schools, colleges, and churches across Turkey and for whom the Armenians were among their most avid students, fellow teachers and professors, and congregants. As early as July 1915, Ambassador Morgenthau wrote to Secretary of State Bryan: "Deportations of and excesses against peaceful Armenians [are] increasing and from harrowing reports of eye witnesses it appears that a campaign of race extermination is in progress under a pretext of reprisal against rebellion."[24] His perceptive view of how the Ottoman government was setting up the extermination plan would be borne out throughout the year.

The American Committee on Armenian Atrocities, as it was first called, still bore some connections to the self-styled activists and philanthropists of the 1890s like Julia Ward Howe, Alice Stone Blackwell, and Spenser Trask, to name a few who created a national movement for relief and rescue during the Armenian Massacres of the Sultan Abdulhammit period. But the new philanthropists who founded the American Committee on Armenian Atrocities were shaped by the emergent Progressive era's orientation toward bureaucratic specialists and public relations and by the relatively new Social Gospel movement with its commitment to bringing together Christianity and social engagement.[25]

The Committee helped to spawn press coverage of the Armenian atrocities and, in 1915, the *New York Times*, for example, ran 145 articles – though without images– on the massacres, some of them with front page headlines, during a time when the coverage of World War I in Europe dominated all popular media. Some *New York Times* headlines read: TELL OF HORRORS DONE IN ARMENIA: REPORT OF EMINENT AMERICANS SAYS THEY ARE UNEQUALED IN A THOUSAND YEARS; A POLICY OF EXTERMINATION PUT INTO EFFECT AGAINST A HELPLESS PEOPLE. As early as 7 October a headline read: 800,000 ARMENIANS COUNTED DESTROYED: VICOUNT BRYCE TELLS HOUSE OF LORDS.[26] Money appeared quickly as the Rockefeller Foundation, the

Guggenheim Funds, local civic organizations from Rotary to Lions Clubs, and church organizations across the country contributed to the cause.

By July 1916, Congress passed a resolution requesting President Wilson to designate a special day for Armenian relief, and Wilson responded by declaring 20–21 October Armenian and Syrian relief days. Civic fundraising events continued to cut across a variety of popular venues including New York City's Amsterdam Opera House, the Philadelphia Stadium, Billy Sunday's Tabernacle in Detroit, and the Harvard-Yale football game. By the end of 1916, the American Committee on Armenian Atrocities, which had now become the Committee on Armenian and Syrian Relief as the killing of Syrian Christians escalated, had raised $20 million – an astounding sum for the time.[27]

With this kind of humanitarian infrastructure in place, the post–World War I relief movement for the Armenians widened under the new name, Near East Relief. For both political and humanitarian reasons, the directors changed the name in order not to rankle the Turkish government by focusing on the Armenians, and also because the needs of many minority groups – Arabs, Greeks as well as Armenians, and Assyrian and Syrian Christians – were severe.

But after the War, the appeal for Armenian relief, rescue, and justice took on a new focus as the hope for an independent Armenia emerged in the wake of the Paris Peace Conference and President Wilson's commitment in his Fourteen Points to the self-determination of small nations. The European Powers had awarded Armenia a significant piece of historic Armenian territory in eastern and northeastern Turkey.

By 1919, the possibility that the United States might make a fledgling Armenian republic its mandate became part of President Wilson's agenda, but an independent state without aid and protection from a major power would most likely fail. In the end, President Wilson's appeal for an American mandate for Armenia failed, largely due to the Republican Party's emergent isolationist stance following the war and its general disdain for Wilson's new American internationalism with its interventionist proclivities. And by the early 1920s, the new Turkish republic under the leadership of Mustafa Kemal was committed to a denialist policy on the eradication of the Armenians and a refusal to entertain any reparations for them, and thus brokered its position aggressively with its client states.

In this historical moment – the dovetailing of the pursuit of postwar justice for the Armenians and the urgent need for relief for the orphans and refugee survivors in Turkey, Syria, the Levant, and Transcaucasia – a visual culture of relief posters and photographs emerged in American popular culture. These images – that in various ways were new, as NER was new – allow us to see some of the ideological and cultural dimensions of a vanguard humanitarian movement configured to aid destitute survivors thousands of miles away. These images were the TV and computer screens of the era, and they brought into popular culture perspectives on human suffering in a modern context.

But in the 1918–20 period, in this complex matrix of political events, images of "the starving Armenians" (the epithet that had been coined by Clara Barton in 1896 when she took the first Red Cross mission out of the United States to the Turkish interior on a relief mission for the Armenian survivors of the Abdulhammit massacres of the mid-1890s) populated American culture. They were taken by Near East Relief workers and professional photographers, or illustrated by artists hired by NER with its Progressive-era professionalism.

So defined was NER by an ideal of Christian philanthropy and its American sense of moral mission that President Calvin Coolidge wrote in his introduction to James L. Barton's history of the organization, *Story of Near East Relief*: "No private enterprise ever undertaken by Americans and in the name of America has accomplished more to arouse in the minds and hearts of all the peoples of the countries in which this organization has carried on its operations, a sincere regard and even affection for America." President Coolidge saw in NER a vanguard Christian movement that brought "new methods in child welfare, in public health and in practical education," and "a new sense of the value of the child, a new conception of religion in action and a new hope for a better social order."[28]

Barton called *Story of Near East Relief* "a narrative of American philanthropy" and the most "heroic" chapter of American philanthropy of the Great War.[29] "The effort to heal and comfort actual millions of desperate people, and to rescue and feed and train 132,000 orphan children, has revived hope and inspired new ideals in two generations, in eleven countries, on three continents."[30] Barton believed in NER as a force of Christian progress and as an exemplary Christian American vision of international humanitarian enterprise.

Furthermore, bound up in the humanitarian drive for the Armenians was NER's focus on the Armenians as ancient Christians of the Holy Land. Christian Americans found something heroic about Armenia being the first nation to make Christianity its national religion in 301 CE. For Protestant evangelicals, Armenians were slightly mythic because they

were associated with the Holy Land terrain including Mount Ararat and
the imagined place of the Garden of Eden. So embedded was this notion
for Western Christians that Lord Byron wrote that "it was in Armenia
that Paradise was placed, and it was in Armenia that the flood first abated
and the dove first alighted."[31] Now, in the hands of Muslim killers, the
Armenians were not only victims of unprecedented atrocities, but part of
a Christian narrative of martyrdom for their faith. That "Christ is still
being crucified in the plains of Armenia" was a compelling idea to the
NER mission.[32]

Out of this institutional vision emerged a campaign that raised more
money from Americans than any such NGO in U.S. history, in large part
with the appeal of images of suffering that were essential to its success.
The relief work involved the establishment and maintenance of orphan-
ages in Turkey, the Caucasus, and other parts of the Middle East; the
resettlement of refugees and the maintenance of staff in dozens of towns
and cities throughout those regions; and, of course, the administrative
staff in the United States.

The image of children huddled on the ground near a wall or building,
which appeared on the cover of *Save a Life*, a publication of NER, in May
1920, depicts an essential representation of the relief campaign.[33] The
photograph is of Armenian child survivors marooned somewhere in one
of the refugee zones. It's an image of the suffering of children, of vulnerable innocence, the human crime that severed Ivan Karamazov's faith in
God in Dostoevsky's *Brothers Karamazov*. The children are depicted here
with the cover text "Will You Help Supply Food for These Children?"
The photograph shows the bodies of children huddled and strewn on a
mound of arid ground. The several children in fetal positions in the center of the photo are my punctum, and their emaciated bodies, some half
naked, others under cloth, push close to a stone wall. Are they that close
to sanctuary? Is the figure with his or her back to us a relief worker? In
their fetal positions, the children linger between death and life. The message is clear: your donation can save them from certain death.

The NER posters were distinctive signatures of the fundraising campaigns, and they appeared in storefront windows, subway and street cars,
railway cars, and on highway billboards throughout the United States
during the postwar decade. Images of women in need were central to
NER poster iconography, and the viewer's knowledge of the realities of
sexual violence that Armenian women endured or perished from was part
of the subtext of all of these visual presentations. However, the NER
poster images transformed women from conditions of emaciation and

destitution to pop culture figures who appear more as damsels in distress from pulp fiction or silent films. In one of the most well-known posters, a young woman stands against a white backdrop with her arms reaching out to us (Figure 4.3). She's an alluring figure who dominates the poster. Although her red kerchief falling over her floral dress has an ethnic touch about it, her flowing hair is black, and with her porcelain white skin and deep-set eyes and beautiful mouth, she looks more like a movie actress than a supplicating refugee.

As Kevin Rozario has noted in his study of the Red Cross relief campaigns during this period, the whole operation appealed to the new mass media of sensationalism as a way of "turning philanthropy into a consumerist activity."[34] Rozario sees the Red Cross campaigns as oriented toward Gothic-like pulp fiction and popular movie sensationalism as a sales strategy for fundraising. Although NER's approach to images of suffering refugees seems less gothically sensational, their poster images of women are media-savvy constructions of women in distress, aimed at a mass market audience that is used to reading about tragic heroines in Dreiser or Hardy novels, or seeing women in distress in the new silent films of the day. And they are a long way from looking like emaciated figures in a famine-ravaged part of the world.

While children, women, and girls were prominent images in the NER philanthropic campaigns, the image of mother and child also brought another trope of Victorian and Christian culture together in the modern form of humanitarian sales culture. In a well-known relief poster of a mother-child image under those familiar words "Lest They Perish" (a phrase of biblical high rhetoric, evocative in the way President Lincoln used it at the end of the Gettysburg Address), NER presents a mother in traditional village garb – her head covered and a child carried on her back, papoose style, and her hands clasped prayer-like (Figure 4.4). Her face has a look of muted anguish: she is clearly in great need, and the life of her child is at stake. Mother and child are set against a backdrop of collapsed antiquity buildings, a stream of smoke clouding the sky and a burning building in the far distance. And the poster text reads: CAMPAIGN FOR $30,000,000. AMERICAN COMMITTEE FOR RELIEF IN THE NEAR EAST Armenia – Greece – Syria – Persia. Beneath that: One Madison Ave. New York. Cleveland H. Dodge Treasurer.

The image evokes the sanctity of mother and child who are captive in a land of woe. The poster offers a Gomorrah-like image of fire and smoke and toppled Classical columns and stones; here is an Orientalist image of the Middle East that is exploding while a mother prayerfully perseveres

FIGURE 4.3. Near East Relief poster, "Lest We Perish," c. 1918. Artist: Ethel Franklin Betts. Library of Congress, Prints and Photographs Division, Washington, DC.

FIGURE 4.4. Near East Relief poster, "Lest They Perish," 1917. Artist: W. B. King. Library of Congress, Prints and Photographs Division, Washington, DC.

with her child. But the words "One Madison Avenue. New York" at the bottom of the poster make a semiotic jolt, pushing the viewer back to the center of power – Madison Avenue– suggesting that American philanthropy is at hand. The number $30,000,000 looms on the poster as a vast idea at a time when the average annual American salary was about $1,200. Because the Dodge family were noted industrialists, and Cleveland Dodge was now in the center of Protestant philanthropy, his name on the poster signifies the stature of the old Protestant elite. The poster's configuration of images, symbols, and meta-meanings work the viewer into a central American narrative of Protestant moral sanctity and American power; and the image is packaged in a slick movie poster form in which epic history with Orientalist inflections and human struggle are rendered with rich (American) colors – blue, red, and white – by the American graphic artist W. B. King.[35]

As M. Kelechian has pointed out, this poster image is based on a photograph of unmistakable likeness.[36] The photo shows a woman in her own indigenous dress, head wrapped, and a child on her back in a carrier. She stands in what looks like a narrow street that is crowded with elderly women and mostly children, many of whom are wearing head coverings and all of whom look forlorn. It could be a refugee street scene in Aleppo. The writing along the side of the photo reads "Armenian Woman," and below – the Near East Relief logo. The transformation of this sober refugee image into a modern movie poster with mythic appeal tells us something about the modern making of NER images for a mass audience.

If an NER poster could transform a mother-and-child image into a movie poster image with its Victorian Christian significations, this image of a mother and two children, from Wegner's collection, may be the earliest, most publicized atrocity photograph. The photograph is centered on the fresh corpses of an Armenian woman and (according to the caption) her two children (Figure 4.5). It was first shown most likely in Wegner's slide show of 26 January 1918. It then appeared in the American edition of *Ambassador Morgenthau's Story*, which was published in 1918 to acclaim, and also in the most comprehensive early memoir of the genocide – Grigoris Balakian's *Armenian Golgotha*, published in Vienna in 1922. Two years later the image appeared in the groundbreaking book *War against War* by the German peace activist Ernst Friedrich.

The image came to embody something fundamental about the death of innocence. This mother and her two children appear to have expired on the ground where they lie near to something made of stone which appears in the backdrop; is it a street wall or a building? The corpses of

FIGURE 4.5. Starved woman and two children. Courtesy of Sybil Stevens, Wegner Collection, Deutsches Literarturarchiv, Marbach.

the woman and the children are fresh; the mouth of the woman seems arrested in a cry, and for me this is the punctum—the mouth frozen in its last gesture of life, an expression of the ineffable in a moment of the unthinkable: the death of the two children with her; there is still flesh on the corpses; their hands and feet are caught in gestures. The image is both sensational and horrific, yet plain and unadorned, and it evokes the mother and child topos, and in doing so signifies various Christian meanings evoking and signifying both the Madonna and child and the sacredness of mother and child extolled by middle-class late Victorian culture.

Conclusion

In the widening discourse on humanitarianism, scholars continue to raise questions about the manipulative impact of the cultural and ideological dimensions of humanitarian campaign images for the purpose of arousing sympathy, compassion, and philanthropic outreach.[37] Do such images generate feelings of compassion, empathy, sympathy? Or revulsion, alienating horror, pity, condescension, and imperious white man's burden attitudes? Do the campaigns of visual culture activate our moral faculties? Or do they factually deaden our responses and create oversaturated numbed-out audiences, as Susan Sontag has suggested.

Any attempt to generalize about American humanitarian campaigns is inadequate, I think, because any humanitarian organization, in any given historical moment, will create and use visual culture differently. Any assessment of humanitarian visual culture in this case lies in assessing the images of a particular historical event and an organization's particular identity and its relationship to that historical event. As a Protestant missionary philanthropic organization, NER's vision was grounded in what I would call a social gospel version of Protestant evangelicalism, and the visual culture that emerged from its campaign was shaped by Victorian Christian notions of moral duty and human emotion. In a Victorian sense, the appeal to emotion was an affirmation of sentimentalism, which was not then a suspect emotion, as it would become in later twentieth-century thinking, but a moral orientation that was noble and humane and an emanation of our deeper spiritual natures. With its emphasis on emotion and the cult of feeling, Victorian Christianity had also absorbed Romanticism's belief in personal emotion as a deeper kind of knowledge, and for Christians that meant compassion and moral duty.

Near East Relief's pictorial representation of Armenian suffering, especially the poster images of women and children, appropriated sentimental Christian notions of mothers and children, suffering innocence, and martyrdom. These images embodied encoded meanings and metonyms for Victorian and Christian moral values. In both Victorian and Christian contexts, mother, woman, child were the basis of family and civilization. A mother walking into the wilderness on a death march, a mother with a child on her back with the world crumbling behind her, and many other images appealed to the mainstream American viewer who encountered such symbols of innocence in captivity and death through a deeply emotive Victorian Christian lens.

The Victorian cult of motherhood, which idealized and pietized the mother and the sanctity of mother as foundation of the family, source of life, and keeper of virtue, was also a presiding moral assumption of the viewer.[38] Perhaps Walt Whitman underscored the era's perspective in exclaiming: "there is nothing greater than the mother of men."[39] Furthermore, mother as embodiment of virtue was encoded with another meaning. Most viewers would have read accounts in the press of women being raped ("outraged" in Victorian nomenclature), abducted, tortured, and such images of woman in distress called Christian virtue into action.

Similarly the presentation of suffering children invoked a particular kind of nineteenth-century feeling for children. Not only did the teachings of Jesus invoke the purity of the child as a spiritual ideal, but Victorian Christianity's particular appropriation of the Romantic veneration of the child added another dimension to the semiosis of child images in the visual culture of NER and Armenian atrocity images. The ideal of the child was an emanation of Christian purity as Jesus's words in the Gospel of Matthew note, "unless you are converted and become like children, you will not enter the kingdom of heaven." And the Wordsworthian notion that the "child is father to the man" and that humans come into the world "trailing clouds of glory" helped give further sustenance to Victorian Christianity's ideal of the child. Whether seeing gritty photographic images of dead children or emaciated, skeletal ones, or the faces of poster-made children begging for help, the Christian viewer would have had deeply felt notions of the child as innocence endangered, defiled by evil, in need of rescue from the heathen.

The sense of moral urgency that the NER posters elicited also stemmed from the nationalist narrative that was embedded in the text of the posters. The narrative was not only Christian philanthropic but American humanitarian, and so each poster read not simply Near East Relief but *American Committee for Relief in the Near East*. In this way NER was calling on the idea of American exceptionalism that President Wilson had popularized with his slogan of U.S. entry into World War I: America was "making the world safe for democracy." The combination of an American moral mission and Protestant humanitarian charity focused on Armenian Christians of the Holy Land region created a powerful ideological pull.

Images of atrocity taken in ad hoc ways during the time of massacre, and images constructed for a humanitarian relief campaign primarily in the aftermath of genocide suggest some interesting contrasts and insights about visual culture and histories of historical extremity – in this case the Armenian genocide.

The atrocity images emerged out of a political climate of extremity and perpetrator taboo. Taking photographs of the Armenian arrests, forced marches, massacres, and the remains of the dead was forbidden by the Ottoman government and by Turkey's wartime ally Germany. Thus, there were no professional photographers or photojournalists coming to the sites of killing to frame atrocity images for the press or humanitarian relief campaigns. And although we know little about the precise moments the atrocity photographs were taken, and in most cases, little about the photographers, we know enough about the conditions in which they were taken to know these were images accrued quickly, spontaneously, on the spot, with little time for framing or staging. Their rawness gives us a glimpse, a view, an insight into certain aspects of the genocide as it was happening. Although the images would be used as evidentiary texts, primarily in scholarly books or in commemorative texts and pamphlets, and then on TV and in film in the ensuing decades, they were not a public part of the commerce of publicity and relief efforts during the major period of atrocities, 1915–16.

Their value as evidentiary texts has become increasingly important in the wake of the Turkish government's continued denialist campaign. The images have become both iconic and indexical in their impacts and meanings. The men being force-marched out of Kharpert, a woman being marched with a few other stragglers on a dirt road, survivors in chaos in a refugee camp in the Syrian desert, the fresh corpses of a young mother and her children on arid ground near a wall – all embody representative dimensions of the genocidal process. And like almost all atrocity images, they do not fully emerge as informing texts of evidence without well-situated contextual knowledge: place, time, and a historical understanding of the political machinations.

By comparison, the wrenching images of women, orphans, and other survivors in crisis – derelict, deported, or in places of crowded squalor – became sources for other image constructions, often on posters, that played to mass-audience appeal. The post–World War I Near East Relief images allow us to see the complexity of image construction and the strange brew and intersection of cultural and ideological forces and aesthetic figurations that make up their visual and graphic meanings and presentations. Unlike, say, the more secular humanitarian projects driven by the Red Cross or the League of Nations, as both Kevin Rozario and Keith Watenpaugh have noted, NER was defined by its Protestant evangelical ethos and an American national moral appeal, and this resulted in a complex blend of cultural and semiotic structures. James Barton, Cleveland Dodge, and others brought to their Christian mission a new Progressivist entrepreneurialism in which specialists in public relations and advertising became essential to the selling of Christian charity for those suffering thousands of miles away, and notably Christian Armenians associated with the Holy Land. The two segments of visual culture might be said to move from the raw to the cooked, and in doing so show us how the commercialism of a religious humanitarian movement articulates its visual project in relation to the raw images taken of that same historical event under different conditions.

Notes

1 See the chapters by Grant and Twomey in this volume.

2 Sontag, *Regarding the Pain of Others*, 49–56.

3 Linfield, *Cruel Radiance*, chapters 8–9.

4 Richard Falk, "The Armenian Genocide in Official Turkish Records," *Journal of Political and Military Sociology* 22, no. 1 (Spring 1997).

5 Deborah Lipstadt, 12 September 2000, Letter to Honorable Chris Smith, House International, Operations Subcommittee, Washington, DC, 20515.

6 Linfield, *Cruel Radiance*, xv.

7 Important Armenian genocide images can be found at http://www.genocide-museum.am/eng/photos_of_armenian_genocide.php; http://www.armenian-genocide.org/photo_wegner.html; http://www.armenian-genocide.org/photo-intro.html; http://www.loc.gov/pictures/search/?q=armenian+relief&sp=2&sg=true.

8 Matthias Bjornlund in *The Genocide of the Ottoman Greeks: Studies on the State-Sponsored Campaigns of the Christians of Asia Minor, 1912–1922 and Its Aftermath: History, Law, Memory*, edited by Tessa Hofmann, Matthias Bjornlund, and Vasileios Meichanetsidis (Scarsdale, NY: Aristide D. Caratzsas, 2011), 397.

9 Ibid. Also Krikorian and Taylor, "Achieving Ever-Greater Precision in Attestation and Attribution of Genocide Photographs," 394–6.

10 Ibid., 395–8; see also Balakian, *The Burning Tigris*, chapter 18.

11 *Armin T. Wegner and the Armenians in Anatolia, 1915* (Milan: Guerini e Associati, 1996), 61–3.

12 Ibid., 35–6, 51.

13 Vahakn Dadrian, "The Armenian Genocide in Official Turkish Records," *Journal of Political and Military Sociology* 22, no. 1 (Summer 1994), reprinted with corrections, Spring 1995, 53–92. See also Vahakn Dadrian, "The Turkish Military Tribunal's Prosecution of the Authors of the Armenian Genocide: Four Major Court-Martial Series," *Holocaust and Genocide Studies* 7 (Spring 1997): 28–59.

14 This was made possible, in part, by the lenient treatment they received from Der Zor's Governor, Ali Suad. When Talaat realized what was happening, he replaced Ali Suad with the anti-Armenian zealot, Zeki, whom he had brought in from Kayseri, and whose job it was to see that the remaining Armenians of the region that stretched from Aleppo to Der Zor were killed. Taner Akcam, *The Young Turks' Crimes against Humanity: The Armenian Genocide and Ethnic Cleansing in the Ottoman Empire* (Princeton, NJ: Princeton University Press, 2012), 268.

15 Hoffman Philip to Secretary of State, 15 September 1916, US State Department Record Group 59, 867.4016/301.

16 August Bernau to Jesse B. Jackson, Aleppo, 10 September 1916. US State Department Record Group 59, 867.4016/302, pp. 1–2.

17 Ibid., 2.

18 Bernau to Jesse Jackson, Aleppo, Syria, 10 September 1916, 3–4.

19 Tessa Hoffmann and Gerayer Koutcharian, "Images that Horrify and Indict": Pictorial Documents of the Persecution and Extermination of the Armenians

from 1877 to 1922," *Armenian Review* 45, no. 1–2 (Spring/Summer 1992): 53–184.

20 Ibid., 109.

21 Hoffmann and Koutcharian, 54, quoting Armin T. Wegner, *Der Weg ohne Heimkehr: ein Martyrium in Briefen* (Berlin: Fleischel, 1919), 169ff, and idem, *Fallst du, umarme auch die Erde oder Der Mann, der an das Wort glaubt: Prosa, Lyrki, Dokumente* (Wuppertal: Peter Hammer Verlag, 1974), 53ff.

22 Hoffmann and Koutcharian, 57–8.

23 For an extraordinary view of sexual violence in the Armenian genocide, see Aurora Mardiganian's memoir *Ravished Armenia*, ed. Anthony Slide (Lantham, MD: Scarecrow Press, 1997).

24 Henry Morgenthau to Secretary of State, 16 July 1915, US National Archives, State Department Record Group 59. 867.4106/76, College Park, MD.

25 Balakian, *The Burning Tigris*, chapters 6–8, 10.

26 Richard D. Kloian, ed., *The Armenian Genocide: News Accounts from the American Press 1915–22* (Berkeley: University of California Press, 1987).

27 Balakian, *The Burning Tigris*, 287–8.

28 James L. Barton, *Story of Near East Relief* (New York: Macmillan, 1930), viii–ix.

29 Ibid., xi.

30 Ibid.

31 Balakian, *The Burning Tigris*, 32.

32 Sarah Miglio, "America's Sacred Duty: Near East Relief and the Armenian Crisis, 1915–1930," www.rockarch.org/publications/resrep/miglio.pdf, p. 6.

33 Center for Holocaust and Genocide Studies, University of Minnesota www.chgs.umn.edu/histories/armenian/theArmenians/nearEast.html.

34 Rozario, "Delicious Horrors," 49.

35 Not to be confused with the British artist of the same name.

36 www.google.com/url?q=http://www.armenews.com/IMG/Revised_NER_POSTER_The_University_Of_Minnesota_Light_1_.doc&sa=U&ei=_r4UUp2hGOSqiAK71YBI&ved=0CA4QFjAD&client=internal-uds-cse&usg=AFQjCNGLgTbvgKEuF7e70YytRXStujLLZw.

37 See Heather Curtis's chapter in this volume; also Watenpaugh, "The League of Nations' Rescue of Armenian Genocide Survivors."

38 For example, William G. McLoughlin, *The Meaning of Henry Ward Beecher* (New York: Alfred A. Knopf, 1970), chapter 4.

39 Walt Whitman, *Leaves of Grass* (New York: Holt, Rinehart, Winston, 1949).

5

Developing the Humanitarian Image in Late Nineteenth- and Early Twentieth-Century China

Caroline Reeves

Introduction

On 19 November 1912, Japanese jurist and Red Cross authority Ariga Nagao spoke to a crowded hall of Chinese philanthropists in Shanghai. To encourage charitable donations, he urged, the Chinese should follow the Japanese model: publish photographs of flesh flying about. These photos, he told his audience, "inspire benevolence."[1]

This model of visual humanitarianism was already widespread in international humanitarian circles. Sensationalism, the fetishization of suffering, and the presentation of the needy as powerless victims were becoming well-established tropes in the Euro-American humanitarian sphere.[2] As in print journalism, where the mantra of the day was "if it bleeds, it reads," the spectacle of suffering seemed to be the most effective way to move Western – and Japanese – audiences to compassion and to generate funds for worthy causes. How did China's philanthropists fit in with this visual convention?

Photography – from portraiture to commercial pieces – was widespread in China by 1912. By the 1920s, vivid photographs from China's battlefields and disaster zones were indeed animating Chinese charitable appeals and publications. Were these images the same or different from other humanitarian photography of the period? This chapter examines the development of the use of early twentieth-century photography to encourage China's citizens to see, to feel, and to take action to help victims of war, disaster, and poverty.[3]

Moving away from the better-known story of foreign photography in and about China,[4] my work focuses on the profoundly transnational – yet no less indigenous – development of the relationship between image, photography, and humanitarianism within China, tracing indigenous and Japanese as well as Western influences. Investigating the visual record of the Chinese Red Cross Society, one of China's foremost charities of the Republican-era (1912–37) as a case study, this chapter elucidates the confluence of philanthropy and photography, modernity and humanitarianism in pre-Communist China.

In the early twentieth century, newly minted Chinese citizens were in the process of enlarging their charitable range. Their new sphere of concern embraced not only local Chinese whose faces, language, and customs they shared, but also distant Chinese newly conceived as *tongbao* (literally, "of the same womb") whose appearances, worlds, and cultures were far from their own.[5] The Chinese nation was being created, and social relief provision extended to encompass all those whom the new technologies now rendered reachable. Chinese Red Cross philanthropists called what they did *rendaozhuyi* – humanitarianism.[6] This extension of philanthropy from China's southerner to northerner, easterner to exotic westerner, problematizes the idea that humanitarianism is a special form of philanthropy. For the Chinese, humanitarianism could be practiced both at home, within the boundaries of their fledgling nation, *and* on individuals civilizationally and /or "racially" different from the practitioners.[7]

The Chinese Context

At the start of the twentieth century, China's natural and political landscapes were in flux. Natural disasters – floods and droughts, famines and other catastrophes – occurred with alarming frequency. Between 1876 and 1879, nine million to thirteen million Chinese died in the deadliest drought-induced famine in China's history.[8] Within twenty years, famine hit again, and twenty years later, China would lose another half million people in yet another North China Famine.[9] This dire situation was exacerbated by round upon round of civil violence as China's leaders and common people experimented with alternatives to the ancient dynastic system. The quasi-religious Taiping Rebellion (1850–65) left twenty to thirty million Chinese dead in history's most lethal civil war.[10] Internal unrest did not stop there. Uprisings – religious, political, and economic – continued across the centuries' divide. China's 1911 Revolution brought down the Qing Dynasty (1644–1911) but did not end the struggle for political power in China. Imperialism and geopolitics encroached on China, and these escalating external threats worsened domestic volatility. Poverty, political instability, social conflict, and increased mortality became the norm for many Chinese, over 90 percent of whom were rural peasants.

This litany of catastrophe and death was highlighted in vivid portrayals in China's print media, usually through words, and, increasingly, in images. These were produced to warn, to inform, to memorialize, and to solicit aid, mostly among China's elite, an educated minority who comprised less than 10 percent of China's population. China's print culture went back to the eighth century CE, fostering the circulation of printed material, including official news gazettes, novels, histories, genealogies, letters, poetry, pornography, classical literature, and exhortatory pamphlets. Paper had been invented in China in the Later Han Dynasty (25–220 CE), and woodblock printing in the Sui (589–618) and Tang (618–907).[11]

Traditionally, Chinese print technologies had been used in the service of philanthropy, and vivid imagery played a significant role. As early as 1594, a Confucian official submitted a report to the emperor about a famine in his province, illustrated by fourteen woodblock pictures of his constituents' suffering. The pictures – successful in their mission – were meant to move the Wanli emperor and his court women to open their purses for famine relief.[12] This use of illustration to move hearts surfaced repeatedly in China's elite circles. Another famous example came in 1864 at the end of the Taiping Rebellion. Confucian scholar Yu Zhi produced a pamphlet called *A Man of Iron's Tears for Jiangnan*, featuring forty-two images directed at raising money for refugee relief in the southern Yangtze area. These illustrations ranged from scenes of decapitation and cannibalism to utopian images of southeast China rebuilt and Confucian order restored.[13] Yu Zhi's influential work became an inspiration for future philanthropists, and in the Great North China Famine of 1876, philanthropists intentionally cribbed both the name of his pamphlet and many of his illustrative tropes for a deliberately similar charitable appeal.[14] The 1878 version, "Henanqihuang tieleitu" [The Incredible Famine in Henan: Pictures to Draw Tears from Iron], inspired a front-page article in the Chinese-language, Chinese circulation newspaper *Shenbao*, particularly for its use of images. "Why use [these images] to encourage donations for each province afflicted with flood and drought? Because, though there have been many articles written to encourage relief, only the literate can understand them."[15] The power of the image was apparent to all, whether they were reading the accompanying prose or simply viewing the pictures. Thus well before the spread of photography in China, the image was already in service to humanitarian goals.

Helping Others, Chinese Style

Charitable activity in China did not arrive with Western missionaries. The Chinese tradition of philanthropy was as old and as well established in China as its print culture. If Alexis de Tocqueville had arrived in early nineteenth-century China instead of in America, he would have found a society even more vibrant with associational activity than his beloved United States.[16] Charities in China were formed for the burial of the dead, the care of widows and orphans, the founding of schools for indigent children, the provision of medicines and medical care for the poor, and the distribution of winter clothing to peasants and refugees, as well as for saving animals' lives, preserving sacred texts, providing life boats at dangerous river crossings, caring for ancient sites, and spreading the words of Confucius, Buddha, and the emperor.[17]

China had boasted mutual aid societies from the Han Dynasty on (206 BCE–220 CE). By the fifth century CE, voluntary associations composed of common people were formed to pool resources in the face of crises. By the Ming Dynasty (1368–1644), China's intellectual elite, a Confucian-trained oligarchy connected intellectually and practically to government service, appropriated the idea of such voluntary associations, and "resituated [them] in … an elite milieu."[18] Claiming philanthropy as an expression of elite culture, scholars, officials, and merchants aspiring to social status used involvement in charitable enterprises and societies to garner social capital and acquire merit – both religious (according to Buddhist tenets) and official (in line with Confucian strictures).[19] These philanthropic institutions and the myriad societies that were formed in the next 250-plus years of the Qing Dynasty were encouraged by and reinforced the Imperial government, but were privately run, despite the fact that they acted as an arm of the government. They provided Max Weber's informal "liturgical governance,"[20] where "local elites were called upon to perform important public services on the state's behalf, at their own expense."[21]

At the end of the nineteenth century, with the slow and grinding demise of the Qing Dynasty and its state welfare systems, China's social actors did not wait for the establishment of a new, operational government to tackle the country's many social ills. From the early 1900s, the suffering of China's populace weighed increasingly heavily on the minds of China's elite, who – although buffered from the actual suffering of war, catastrophe, and dislocation – wanted a better situation for China domestically and in the world comity. Inspired by Social Darwinist rhetoric translated from the West,[22] and fearing for the "extinction" (*miewang*) of the Chinese polity,[23] Chinese of all classes were moved to act. Rooting their solutions in long-standing traditions of state-sanctioned, community-based social welfare action, China's concerned elite began to develop new modes of philanthropy, supported and funded by popular participation. Although the traditional elite remained in the vanguard, newly politicized and engaged members of China's lower classes and peasantry were empowered to take part in the changing society, contributing time and money to social welfare initiatives.

As China became more technologically sophisticated and the national elite were better able to extend their charitable reach, China's charitable institutions became first nationally linked, and then internationally involved, creating new spheres of social welfare engagement within and beyond China.[24] The new technologies of imagery were intricately involved in this expansion of the charitable realm.

Founding of the Chinese Red Cross

In 1904 the Russo-Japanese War broke out. The Japanese, intent on becoming a major power in the region, had beaten the Chinese ten years earlier in the Sino-Japanese War. Now, audaciously (according to many), they set their sights on a European power: the Russians. Much of the war was fought in Manchuria, on Chinese territory. As the conflict became deadly, foreign nationals were quickly evacuated.[25] Russia, however, refused Chinese entry into the Manchurian ports to help distressed Chinese refugees. Afraid of being drawn into hostilities, and too weak to hold its own if forced into war, the Qing Imperial government would not challenge the blockade, even to rescue its own people.[26] Responding to the crisis, Chinese community leaders in Shanghai met to pledge their financial support if some way could be found to help "repatriate" their Chinese countrymen trapped in northeastern China.[27]

The civic rescue initiative was led by Shen Dunhe, a prominent Shanghai tea merchant, philanthropist, modernizer, and aspiring government official who had studied international law at Cambridge University.[28] Shen's exposure to Western organizations and his knowledge of international law alerted him to the existence of a unique organizational vehicle that could cross closed "borders": the Red Cross Society. The Red Cross organization had become internationally well known after Henri Dunant, founder of the group, won the Nobel Peace Prize in 1901.[29] In the east, Japanese were also extensively publicizing their adherence to the Red Cross movement, promoting their national Red Cross activity in newspapers, journals of international law, and other domestic and international publications, including a series of postcards based on vivid woodblock prints picturing the Japanese Red Cross Society in action on the battlefields[30] (Figure 5.1). These images were intended to demonstrate Japan's "civilized" (to use the parlance of the day) adherence to humanitarian norms, impartially caring for war wounded according to the Geneva Conventions of 1864. Rather than demonstrating the horrors of war, these images celebrated the conduct of war in accordance with international law. Their bright colors and dramatic scenes were often more engaging than black-and-white photographs of similar material.[31] Widely distributed, these advertisements for the Red Cross may have crossed Shen's path.

In China, Shen's familiarity with the Red Cross might also have developed through his close contact with Western missionaries, who had flown the Red Cross banner unofficially over their medical relief activities in the Sino-Japanese War of 1894–5.[32] In 1904, Shen saw and utilized the potential of the Red Cross organization to solve the prevailing crisis.

As Shen knew, the Red Cross organization offered a well-publicized political neutrality that would allow Chinese philanthropists unchallenged access to sensitive international war zones.[33] In 1904, armed with this knowledge, Shen moved quickly to contact Shanghai's Chinese and foreign community leaders to form such a group. Anticipating a negative reaction from the Japanese and Russian belligerents to a solely Chinese organization, Shen crafted an *international* Red Cross group to represent China, composed of prominent men from neutral Western countries living in Shanghai (Great Britain, France, Germany, the Netherlands, and the United States) as well as Chinese elites. He named this new group the International Red Cross of Shanghai.[34] This impetus to help fellow Chinese was not new; China's tradition of philanthropy was long established, and the elite Shanghai community was often at its forefront.[35] What *was* new here was the adoption of the Red Cross aegis, a practical and astute co-optation of a transnational symbol and the savvy adaptation of a Western organization to the Chinese milieu.

Through Shen's efforts, China's first indigenous Red Cross group was born. The International Red Cross Society of Shanghai began operations in April 1904. Thanks to donations from the Chinese Railway authorities and the Telegraph Administration, elites from Shanghai were able to travel by train to the northeast and communicate by telegraph free of charge, facilitating relief efforts and drumming up local Chinese patronage.[36] Magazines, newly emerging on the Chinese scene, published articles

FIGURE 5.1. Japanese woodblock print of humanitarian activity during the 1904–1905 Russo-Japanese War. From the Jean S. and Frederic A. Sharf Collection at the Museum of Fine Arts, Boston, reproduced in "Throwing Off Asia III" by John W. Dower – chapter 2, "Old Media, New Enemy," 2–2. Massachusetts Institute of Technology © 2008 Visualizing Cultures http:/visualizingcultures.mit.edu.

about Chinese Red Cross work.[37] These new technologies helped spread the word about the Red Cross organization and improve its effectiveness across the country.[38]

By the close of the Russo-Japanese War in 1905, the new Red Cross group had evacuated over 130,000 refugees from Manchuria and coordinated more than twenty relief centers and hospitals across the area, aiding more than a quarter million people. They had raised well over half a million Shanghai taels of silver through public subscription drives, 120,000 taels more than they actually spent.[39] By the end of the war, the Society's work was so popular that rather than disbanding, the Red Cross organization in China continued to grow. Increasingly staffed by the Chinese themselves, displacing Western missionary organizers and medical men, the organization built on its initial successes to become the Red Cross Society of China.

The Institutionalization of the Chinese Red Cross Society

After the war, the balance of the initial fund drive went to starting a Red Cross medical school and building a Red Cross hospital in Shanghai.[40] The predominantly medical and relief activities of the Society continued through the end of the Qing and into the Republican period (1911–37), expanding in reach and sophistication, caring for Chinese across the entire country in war and disaster, working with governments as they emerged, and working despite them as they fell. Buffeted by constant political change and loose central control of everything from the government to the cultural orthodoxy, the Republican interregnum – although marred by political violence – allowed a period of intellectual and cultural opening and efflorescence. These years were marked by the richness of new ideas, experiments, and foreign implants grafted onto (or less often, replacing) China's traditional systems.

The success of China's Red Cross association during this time could be measured by its national growth: by 1924 it boasted over 40,000 members and 286 chapters[41] and by 1934, almost 120,000 members and 500 chapters.[42] It also had a profound influence on other philanthropic groups within China, inspiring the formation of other internationally oriented charities, including the Red Swastika Society.[43] The initial growth and establishment of the Society after the fall of the Dynasty indicates the expansion of China's national philanthropic network, China's increasingly optimistic international position, and the success of a citizen-run social welfare organization in China.

The Chinese Society also reached out to the international Red Cross organization and to other national Societies around the world. Through its new Society, China became a full participant in the international Red Cross movement. In 1904, the Qing adhered to the international Geneva Convention, paving the way for international recognition of China's Red Cross group.[44] In 1912, sponsored by the Japanese empress, China's Red Cross was officially recognized by the International Committee of the Red Cross (ICRC) in Switzerland and became a full-fledged member.[45] This gradual progression toward official recognition was consonant with the trajectory of other emerging national Red Cross Societies.[46]

The Chinese Society was affiliated with the ICRC from 1912 and with the League of Red Cross Societies from its establishment in 1919. These connections entitled the Chinese Red Cross to receive publications from other groups as well as to send their own materials to Paris and Geneva, where many printed pieces from the early 1920s survive. In fact, some of these publications were clearly made for Western audiences, specifically prepared for international gatherings of Red Cross Societies or for dissemination in the West. This target is clear from the English language text in some of the materials.

The Chinese Society also donated significant funds to Red Cross disaster relief in other countries. After earthquakes in San Francisco in 1906, in Kagoshima in 1914, and in Tokyo and Yokohama in 1923, the Society sent money to aid the relief efforts. In addition, it worked to help overseas Chinese outside the Red Cross network. For example, in 1919, the Society put forward $20,000 to repatriate Chinese workers who were stranded in Germany and Austria-Hungary after World War I. In turn, China's Red Cross was also a recipient of internationally coordinated Red Cross aid.[47] In one instance, during record-breaking floods in Zhili in 1917, Japan's Red Cross sent the Chinese Society a donation of 5,000 yen.[48] This international interaction familiarized the Chinese headquarters with international practices.

Imagery in Red Cross Publications

With the expansion and institutionalization of China's Red Cross Society after the fall of the dynasty came a flurry of publishing activity. In its periodicals, the newly reorganized Society mobilized images to publicize and fund its activities, to attract members and donors, and to inform the world community about its work. These visual representations appeared most frequently in publications produced by the Red Cross itself, although photographs of Red Cross work also appeared in local newspapers and magazines.[49] The introduction of modern printing presses imported by missionary groups in the 1870s, the technology of half-tone printing, and the development of the portable camera (George Eastman's Kodak, available after 1888 in the West and shortly thereafter in Asia) had made the expansion of photography increasingly possible and affordable in China.[50] China's new Red Cross Society used these technologies and their resultant images to establish its own credibility as a charitable organization and to create an identity for itself as a modern and national organization, as modern and national as the newly formed Republic was intended to be.[51]

Right from the start, Red Cross imagery in China took its antecedents from the world of photography rather than from earlier Chinese or Japanese woodblock prints. Although there was some backsliding into traditional formats, for the most part the Chinese Society blazed a new visual path, departing from earlier humanitarian iconography in China. Instead of depicting dramatic scenes of human trauma or the pitiful plight of victims as in the earlier *Tears from Iron* pamphlets or in Japanese images, the Chinese Red Cross Society launched its pictorial debut with portraits of its celebrity principals: high officials, presidents, and diplomats serving as honorary and actual officers of the Chinese Red Cross Society. Their photographs became a staple of Red Cross periodicals. Red Cross publications also sported group portraits taken at Society gatherings as it institutionalized its new operational bases after the founding of the Republic.

The use of cameo portraits, which preface all Chinese Red Cross publications after 1912, reveals the designers' connection to the bourgeoning field of photography in China. These cameos owe their presence and power to the popularity of photographic portraiture and *cartes de visite* sweeping across Asia. *Cartes de visite*, offspring of the earlier phenomenon of calling cards, had become a global trend by 1853 as "the first mass-produced portrait photographs."[52] In England, Queen Victoria herself collected these *cartes* and was said to have more than a hundred albums filled with portraits of fellow nobility and the social elite.[53] This craze was not confined to the West. Queen Victoria's collection held Asian *cartes,* including portraits of King Rama IV (Mongkut) of Siam, taken in Siam in the late 1860s by John Thomson. Thomson was a Scottish photographer who traveled throughout Asia, bringing his portraiture and "cardomania" to China as well (King Rama IV also became a fan).[54] This innovation took the world by storm. Ultimately, the popularity of portrait photographs would be harnessed to the cause of philanthropy, a connection that remains strong today.[55]

Originally meant as personal tokens to be exchanged in elite social circles, by the turn of the twentieth century, photographic portraits of dignitaries became wildly fashionable and widely available in China, too.[56] Portraiture, particularly ancestor portraits intended for family altars, had a long history in late nineteenth-century China, and the transition to photographic portraiture was an easy one.[57] Often opening in ateliers previously producing painted portraits, by the 1860s portrait photography studios had proliferated in Hong Kong and southern China and further spread to north China by the 1870s.[58] Chinese photographers adopted the new art form and ran their own commercial studios, where they hung their work in their storefronts to publicize their craft.[59] By 1906, photographic portraits of even the Empress Dowager Cixi, previously proscribed from general viewing due to her imperial status, had become publicly available.[60]

Photographic portraits of Red Cross dignitaries in Red Cross periodicals – captioned boldly with their names and titles – picked up on the *carte-de-visite* fad. Their faces gave an elite imprimatur to the Red Cross organization and its publications as well as a distinctive modern cast, marking the group as a new-style organization. In turn, the participants' involvement in the Red Cross Society was made even more visible and the scope of that visibility enlarged through the photos' publication. This publicity conferred significant social capital on the men pictured.[61] Celebrity sponsorship of good works communicated through imagery thus began early in China and remains a worldwide hallmark of humanitarian organizations today.[62]

In 1913, the Society produced a number of publications, all featuring photographic portraits. A slim pamphlet, *A Guide to Humanitarianism* (Rendao Zhinan) came out in March 1913, followed by the *Chinese Red Cross Magazine* in May. Both periodicals sport portraits on the cover. The *Guide* presents cameos of new Republican president Yuan Shikai (1859–1916) and Vice President Li Yuanhong (1864–1928), honorary president and vice president of the Society. Prominent on the cover, their images bestow official sanction and endorsement on the Red Cross group. The vice president appears in formal dress, wearing Western military garb and a cap, smart and crisp in a three-quarters view. In contrast, President Yuan looks right into the camera, bareheaded and wearing a rumpled, padded coat like a common soldier. The visual difference between these men and the Manchu rulers they replace could not be more striking, highlighting the bold new nature of the Red Cross Society – and, at the same time, of the new Chinese nation (Figure 5.2).

FIGURE 5.2. *A Guide to Humanitarianism* (Rendao Zhinan) from March 1913 included cameos of new Republican president Yuan Shikai and Vice President Li Yuanhong, honorary president and vice president of the Red Cross Society.

The *Chinese Red Cross Magazine* was another early post-1911 Red Cross publication, ultimately producing only two editions (the first of which included Ariga Nagao's speech, cited at the start of this chapter). Photography also figured prominently in its pages. Group photographs picturing crowds of Red Cross participants broadcast the organization's wide support as well as its national scope, using the camera to emphasize the charitable organization's broad popular base. Group photos include a shot of the hall where the Red Cross's first general meeting was held, packed with delegates from across China, men *and* women (although physically segregated), representing the more than one thousand supporters attending the meeting.[63] These photographs helped define and affirm the delegates' – and the Society's – identity as active, dedicated, modern philanthropists. Furthermore, the gathering of delegates from all over China to one central national headquarters concretely strengthened the abstract notion of a national organization and a national identity, as did the group photo itself, commemorating the event and codifying it in a tangible image.

Another group photo showcases the newly built, state-of-the-art Red Cross hospital in Shanghai.[64] Against the Western-style building crowd Chinese men in long Confucian gowns, with dignitaries and Westerners prominent in the center of the photo. Chinese women in traditional pants and jackets are sprinkled throughout the crowd, and just off center, three Western women in large hats cluster, with a small Chinese boy (one of a number of children in the picture) next to them. There are at least two hundred people visible in the photograph. The imposing Western architecture of the building conveys stability and modernity. Despite the very traditional outfits worn by the majority of the participants, the presence of Westerners, and of Chinese and non-Chinese women and children in the scene, as well as the size of the crowd and *the very fact of the photograph itself* reveal the Red Cross organization to be a progressive, international, modern association, attracting a large number of progressive, modern citizens of the new China.

The new prominence of the image emanated not only from Red Cross headquarters but also from the chapter level in Red Cross branches across the country. For example, at the close of the Red Cross General Meeting and the subsequent Unification Conference in Shanghai in 1912, the Red Cross delegate from the northern city of Tianjin presented the Red Cross Central Committee with a copy of the *Red Cross Tianjin Branch Society Pictorial Magazine*, and distributed it to all other branch representatives at the conference and also to Shanghai's newspaper offices.[65] These locally produced photographs often found their way into nationally published Red Cross periodicals.

By 1913, illustrated publications were being produced, and images proliferated within their pages. One such publication, the 1914 pamphlet *The Morality of Caring for the Living* (Haoshengzhide) makes its distribution method part of its text. The cover is decorated with photographic portraits of national leaders: President Yuan, Vice President Li, Red Cross president and former Qing official Lu Haihuan, and executive director and Red Cross founder Shen Dunhe. Scrolling around the edges (since Chinese can be written left to right, right to left, as well as up and down) are the words: "Free of Charge. This is a booklet that every Chinese citizen (*tongbao*) should read. Please read this carefully, give us your feedback, and donate in any amount you can.... If you don't want this booklet, give it to someone else who might donate to us: Please don't just leave it somewhere!"[66] The text on the pamphlet's cover makes the purpose of this publication (as well as the Society's other printed matter) explicit. This booklet was meant as a money raiser, and if the viewer wasn't interested, he or she should pass it on.

While celebrity portraits and group photographs remained a mainstay of Red Cross publications for the next two decades,[67] a new type of photo began to dominate the visual landscape of the Society: photos from the field. These were photographs taken of Chinese Red Cross operations or sites of operations (hospitals, ambulances, field stations) that highlighted the activities of the Chinese Red Cross Society and its achievements.

A Call to Arms: Imagery and Action in Red Cross Photography

Interestingly enough, despite encouragement from Japanese Red Cross advisor Ariga Nagao and China's own tradition of using dramatic images in fundraising, the new Red Cross photos did not focus on blood and gore, although these elements are certainly present. Instead, the images consistently highlight Red Cross workers in action: doctors working with the wounded, the Red Cross Burial Corps picking up bodies for burial, Red Cross workers shown with victims of disasters preparing to rescue or feed the needy. The focus in these shots is unswervingly on the actions and efficacy of the Chinese Red Cross Society in service to its constituents, alive and dead, rather than on the pathos of the scene. Red Cross uniformed personnel, in their white coats marked with Red Crosses, or traditionally dressed Chinese in long gowns carrying a white flag emblazoned with the Red Cross symbol dominate the photographs. Rather than emphasizing suffering, these images visually stress the actors and actions being taken to remediate disaster and relieve distress.[68]

These photographs fit with a more general cultural call for action then resounding across China. According to a growing cadre of public intellectuals voicing their opinions stridently in China's public forums, the Chinese people needed to "wake up," to shake off their moribund natures, to embrace a new world, to become more active in determining their own fates.[69] In *A Call to Arms* (Na Han), famous writer and public intellectual Lu Xun likened China's nascent citizenry to a group of sleeping people trapped in an iron house that had just caught fire. He suggests that while waking the inhabitants in an attempt to save them from death might prove futile, those who could do so had a responsibility to try to rouse them. This "call to arms" was felt across the polity and would give rise to various political movements, including the Chinese Communist Party. It also strengthened a national commitment to social welfare provision for all of China's people. The Chinese Red Cross leaders were part of this wave, and the visual humanitarianism they promoted reflected the appeal for action galvanizing Chinese citizens across the fledgling Chinese nation.

Thus the directors of the Society saw images of relief work as a powerful tool for producing nationalist feelings that would generate a concrete, participatory reaction to the Society and to relief work in general. The evocation of compassion, of sympathy, of feelings of noblesse oblige was not the primary goal of these photos, unlike the contemporary photographic repertoire of the international community.[70] In Chinese images, the viewer was to become a participant in the relief action, not a bystanding spectator of suffering. Partaking of the image, the viewer was to identify with the active provision of aid to fellow Chinese rather than to identify with the victims or to remain a passive audience, witnessing suffering with all the compromises inherent in that act of viewing pain. The provision of relief was a nationalistic act. Red Cross volunteers – and donors – could actively join in saving the nation, viewing Red Cross images and then donating money to the Red Cross cause.

The experience of writer Lu Xun himself sums up this stance. In discussing the imperative to act in his preface to *A Call to Arms*, Lu Xun recounts his own encounter with images of suffering during his medical studies in Japan.[71]

At the time, I hadn't seen any of my fellow Chinese in a long time, but one day some of them showed up in a [lantern] slide. One, with his hands tied behind him, was in the middle of the picture; the others were gathered around him. Physically, they were as strong and healthy as anyone could ask, but their expressions revealed all too clearly that spiritually they were calloused and numb. According to the caption, the Chinese whose hands were bound had been spying on the Japanese military for the Russians. He was about to be decapitated as a "public example." The other Chinese gathered around him had come to enjoy the spectacle.[72]

Lu Xun's extremely popular story stresses that it is not enough to view suffering in order to be moved to cure suffering. This outspoken recognition that witnessing death and horror is not necessarily enough to move people to action – particularly not people who have been surrounded by and perhaps inured to massive death and horror – helped inform the new Chinese approach to humanitarian photography.

From the 1920s on, the Chinese Red Cross Society began producing a monthly magazine. The *Red Cross Monthly* devoted a large section each month to photographs. This magazine was sent to subscribers within China as well as to overseas Chinese and other interested parties. The cost of the magazine was offset by the sale of advertising, which filled the last pages of the magazine. Where did the photos that complemented these pages come from?

Many local Red Cross chapters produced a rich archive of photos of their activities. One prominent chapter of the Red Cross, the Tianjin Branch mentioned earlier, kept detailed financial records that are still available today and which give a window on the chapter's photographic production. The records of a 1917 emergency relief operation clarify where some of these photos come from and how much they cost.[73] The bulk of the monies spent for a relief operation were spent on personnel (75%) and a quarter on supplies and miscellaneous expenses (528 yuan). Of the 25 percent spent on the latter, photographs of the Tianjin Emergency Relief Corps posed in front of the Beijing Renmin (People's) Hospital cost 25.35 yuan. To put this figure in perspective, stretcher bearers were paid 8 yuan for a month of work; twenty-nine pairs of shoes for the coolies cost 30 yuan. The importance of the photographs in documenting the chapter's work was enough to justify their relatively large expense, however. These photographs appeared in Tianjin's own fundraising and publicity materials and were sent to the Central Committee in Shanghai for inclusion in national publications.

The *Monthly*'s photographs focus unfailingly on Red Cross volunteers in action, on celebrity portraits, and, particularly in the earlier years, on images of trains, ambulances, and boats in the service of the Red Cross. This emphasis on the technology available to Red Cross participants, including the technology of biomedicine featured in photos of surgery being performed, or in close-ups of the interiors of the most up-to-date Red Cross hospitals located across China stresses the modernity of the Red Cross operations.[74] The focus on the uniforms – military, Western-style jackets and pants for men[75] and a Western, often military-style cap – highlights another aspect of modernity. This trope is also available in Western Red Cross photography from the same period.[76]

One iconic photo of the Red Cross hospital in Shanghai gathers all these cues together.[77] Doctors and nurses in crisp Western uniforms assemble on the hospital's rolling, very Western front lawn. The shot – men and women together, female nurses, their signature outfits, the architecture and size of the hospital in the background, the idea of the biomedicine being practiced within the walls, the very concept of a hospital staffed by such a team – is striking and exciting in its connotations of modernity (Figure 5.3). Photos like these put the Chinese Red Cross Society at the very forefront of modern humanitarianism in China.

Chinese Red Cross Images Abroad

Even beyond Chinese audiences, the usefulness of photographs in conveying the Society's accomplishments was clear to Chinese Red Cross humanitarians from the start. Through the late 1920s and the early 1930s, a number of pictorials were prepared for foreign audiences. Dr. B. Y. Wong, director general and senior medical officer of the Chinese Red Cross, put together the series *The Chinese Red Cross Activities Told in Pictures*, of which two are available in the Federation Archives in Geneva. The first is undated, but seems to be from 1928, and the second, labeled "Series No. III" (suggesting another, unseen piece, probably from 1929), is dated 1930.[78] Although the Chinese could and did present their activities to the international community in English texts, photographs eliminated the mediation of language and provided the "collapsing" of distance between foreign viewers and Chinese relief work. Besides functioning as a fundraising strategy, the visual presentation of China's Red Cross work to foreign audiences was also a consciousness-raising event, demonstrating to Western viewers the Chinese commitment to humanitarianism. In case the message of the photographs was not abundantly clear to the Western audience, the pictures were often enhanced by the addition of English-language (often counterfactual) captions.

Due to the Chinese convention of writing directly on pictures (an ancient practice dating back to hand scrolls and ink paintings and continuing onto photographs), the viewer today can see the discrepancy between the Chinese and the English captions and thus can see distinctly where meanings were manipulated for a foreign audience by attaching English-language text to the photo. Whereas Chinese photos were labeled with information usually consisting of the date, the name of the Red Cross chapter, the unit involved (flood relief unit; burial unit; relief corps; medical unit helping wounded soldiers), and sometimes the action pictured, in English these captions were embellished, rather than translated,

FIGURE 5.3. Doctors and nurses in front of the Red Cross hospital in Shanghai. From *The Chinese Red Cross Activities Told in Pictures, Series No. III* (1930), chapter 2, np.

for the pictorials sent overseas or circulated among China's large foreign community. For example, a photo appeared in the 20th Anniversary volume showing eleven relief workers, eight in white Red Cross uniforms, two in traditional gowns, and one in a coolie's outfit carrying a Red Cross Burial Corps placard and two Red Cross flags, standing over two corpses and a dead horse. In this publication, the photo is labeled on the picture in Chinese: "the 22nd of the third month of 1911. Photo of this chapter [Xindu] on the battlefield relieving the wounded." In the Western targeted *Chinese Red Cross Activities Told in Pictures*, the English-language caption inscribed on the edge of the photograph proclaims, "They give up Lives; We give out Peace!!!"[79] This type of dramatic caption was not uncommon in Western publications, such as the American Red Cross monthly magazine. As in many cases, here the primary emphasis of the English-language caption is the victims rather than the aid providers (Figure 5.4).

Other captions in the English-language pictorial similarly move the viewer's attention to the victims in the photographs. A striking piece features a derailed train as backdrop and shows eight corpses on the ground.[80] Two Red Cross workers, one smiling and holding a Red Cross flag, face the camera. Another worker walks with his back to the viewer toward the trains. The caption in Chinese reads: "Photo of Chinese Red Cross Pingyuan Chapter Relief Corps, in Wangyi Village, Rescuing Wounded Soldiers and Burying the Dead, 1926, 5 May." The English caption reads: "The sacred remains of the war heroes attended by our Burial Corps." The difference in focus and in language is not a linguistic difference between Chinese and English; Chinese Red Cross poetry about the work of the Burial Corps often surpasses English-language captions in flowery hyperbole, and poetry was not out of place inscribed on images in traditional China. But in viewing the photograph, the Chinese audience is directed to the workers in the frame and is left to its own devices to devise meaning from what it sees. Foreigners, on the other hand, were understood to need something more and different. Thus the photograph is (re)interpreted through the (melo)drama of the caption.

Conclusion

Denis Kennedy has written that "humanitarian fundraising appeals derive emotional force through their reliance on human misery." He calls this "the veritable commodification of suffering."[81] In Chinese humanitarian photography, the focus of the image was on the provision of aid – not on the wretchedness of the victims. In China, the thrust of the humanitarian

They give up Lives; We give out Peace!!!

FIGURE 5.4. "They give up Lives; We give out Peace!!!" *The Chinese Red Cross Activities Told in Pictures* (probably 1928), np.

visual message was identification with the aid providers, not with the victims of war and disaster. Who the victims were was less important than who the viewer could be: a modern, active humanitarian. The time/ space compression of the photograph allowed observers to participate in the relief of the needy with other Red Cross volunteers and thus share in the performance of both the traditional good deed of helping the destitute and the modern good deed of saving the nation. The photographic message of the Chinese Red Cross Society targeted a set of motivational emotions different from the visual humanitarianism that has become so familiar to us today. The trigger to action was not the image of the victim; rather, the dramatic and meaningful work of the Chinese Red Cross was to be the clarion call to arms.

This focus has endured in China. In the later 1930s and '40s, as World War II in the Pacific overtook China, international humanitarian groups began to dominate the relief community in China. These groups popularized images of war- and disaster-stricken Chinese victims in the international press, images intended to mobilize Western giving.[82] But with the installation of the Maoist regime in 1949, international groups were forced to leave China. Private domestic relief work also ceased operation as the Communist state became the sole social welfare provider.

Maoist ideology that emphasized the role of Party members as the vanguard of social action became paramount in post-1949 China. Consonant with this vision, the visual legacy of the early part of the century actually flourished. "Art in the service of politics" was the official line of the regime, and much of the photography that was displayed in the era followed this dictum.[83] In fact, in keeping with state dogma, China's official press now magnified the earlier focus on the aid provider – rather than on the aid recipients – emphasizing the Maoist inspiration and imperative to assist others. Photographs of happy People's Liberation Army soldiers helping grateful villagers in China and distributing aid overseas became a dominant visual trope of Chinese aid during this period.

In the post-Mao period, the government once more allows nonstate humanitarian work, and humanitarian photography and mass philanthropy flourish in China. As Chinese photos from the 2008 Sichuan earthquake demonstrate, images focusing on the provision of relief outnumber photographs focusing on the suffering of victims.[84] Political imperatives and the historical visual legacy dovetail to maintain this focus despite cultural pressures from abroad. As China's cultural influence expands in the twenty-first century, the tension between the visual tropes of East and West will be interesting to watch.

Notes

1 Ariga Nagao, speech to Chinese philanthropists, Shanghai, 19 November 1912. *Zhongguo Hongshizihui Zazhi* 1 (May 1913).

2 Cf. chapters by Twomey, Curtis, and Grant in this volume; also Rosario, "'Delicious Horrors,'" and Irwin, *Making the World Safe*, 87–8.

3 There is little written on indigenous Chinese photography. Roberts, *Photography and China*; Oliver Moore suggests he has work forthcoming; Carlos Rojas in Morris, ed., *Photographies East*; Cody and Terpak, eds., *Brush and Shutter*.

4 Lau, *Picturing the Chinese*; Thiriez, *Barbarian Lens*; James Hevia in Morris, ed., *Photographies East*.

5 Chinese homogeneity is mythical and apparent only to non-Chinese.

6 This term is different from the traditional term for "charity," *cishanshiye*.

7 The author does not believe in the empirical validity of the biological category "race."

8 Edgerton-Tarpley, *Tears from Iron*.

9 Pierre Fuller, "North China Famine Revisited: Unsung Native Relief in the Warlord Era, 1920–1921," *Modern Asian Studies* 47, part 3 (May 2013): 820–50.

10 Tobie Meyer-Fong, *What Remains: Coming to Terms with Civil War in 19th-Century China* (Stanford, CA: Stanford University Press, 2013).

11 Joan Judge, *Print and Politics* (Stanford, CA: Stanford University Press, 1996), 17–18.

12 Meyer-Fong, 52, 226.

13 Meyer-Fong, 51–63, for images and a detailed description of this pamphlet.

14 Edgerton-Tarpley, 132–41.

15 *Shenbao*, 15 March 1878, 1.

16 De Tocqueville, *Democracy in America*, Book II, chapter 5 from http://xroads. virginia.edu/~HYPER/DETOC/ch2_05.htm.

17 Smith, *The Art of Doing Good*; Tsu Yu Yue, *The Spirit of Chinese Philanthropy: A Study in Mutual Aid* (London: Forgotten Books, 2012, originally published 1912); Angela Leung (Liang Qizi), *Shishan yu jiaohua: Ming-Qing di cishan zuzhi* (Charity and Moral Transformation: Philanthropic Organizations of the Ming and Qing periods) (Taipei: Linking Publishers, 1997).

18 Smith, 50.

19 Cynthia Brokaw, *Ledgers of Merit and Demerit* (Princeton, NJ: Princeton University Press, 1991).

20 Susan Mann, *Local Merchants and the Chinese Bureaucracy, 1750–1950* (Stanford, CA: Stanford University Press) develops this idea, particularly in chapter 2.

21 Mann, 12–13.

22 Prominent Chinese intellectual Yan Fu translated Thomas Huxley's *Evolution and Ethics* into Chinese in the mid-1890s, popularizing these ideas. Jonathan Spence, *The Search for Modern China* (New York: Norton, 1990), 301.

23 Rebecca Karl, *Staging the World: Chinese Nationalism at the Turn of the 20th Century* (Durham, NC: Duke University Press, 2002) discusses this beautifully.

24 Reeves, "The Changing Nature of Chinese Philanthropy in Late Qing China."

25 *North China Herald*; *Zhongguo Hongshizihui ershi zhounian jiniance* (The Twentieth Anniversary Celebration of the Red Cross Society of China) (hereafter ZHEJ) (Shanghai: Red Cross Society of China, 1924), *dashi gangmu* section, 1.

26 *Zhongguo Hongshizihui zazhi* 1 (May 1913), 1.

27 *Beijing zazhi* (Peking Magazine) 2 (1904), 22–3.

28 Tiao Shui Waishi, *Shen Dunhe* (Shanghai: Jicheng Tushugongsi, 1911).

29 Moorehead, *Dunant's Dream*, 168.

30 Checkland, *Humanitarianism and the Emperor's Japan*.

31 From the Jean S. and Frederic A. Sharf Collection at the Museum of Fine Arts, Boston, reproduced in *Throwing Off Asia III* by John W. Dower – chapter 2, "Old Media, New Enemy," 2-2, Massachusetts Institute of Technology © 2008 Visualizing Cultures http://visualizingcultures.mit.edu.

32 See Reeves, "The Power of Mercy," chapter 1.

33 Shen's articles in the *Shenbao* trumpet the Red Cross's intrinsic neutrality; for example, he provides a translation of the Red Cross Treaty (the Geneva Convention) which discusses neutrality in *Shenbao*, 30 March 1904, 3.

34 K. Chimin Wong and Wu Lien-Teh, *History of Chinese Medicine*, 2nd. ed. (Taipei: Southern Materials Center, 1985), 571; also Timothy Richard, *Forty-Five Years in China* (New York: Frederick A. Stokes, 1916), 322, and *Shenbao*, 14 March 1904 and *passim* throughout late March and April.

35 Mary Backus Rankin, *Elite Activism and Political Transformation in China* (Stanford, CA: Stanford University Press, 1986); Edgerton-Tarpley, *Tears from Iron*.

36 *Shenbao* 29, 30 July 1904; *Beijing zazhi* 3 (1904): 32–7; *Red Cross Society Articles of Association*, Shanghai 1912; *Chinese Red Cross Society Central Committee Articles of Association*, Shanghai 1922.

37 *Beijing zazhi* 3 (1904): 32–7.

38 Reeves, "The Changing Nature of Chinese Philanthropy," discusses the marriage of technology and philanthropy.

39 *Shanghai International Red Cross News Bulletin* (1938), 2.

40 *Zhonghuaminguo Hongshizihui Bainianhuishi 1904–2003* (Taipei: Chinese Red Cross, 2004), 108–15.

41 ZHEJ 55; *Hongshizihui Lishiziliao Xuanpian, 1904–1949* (Selected Historical Materials of the Red Cross Society, 1904–1949) (Nanjing: Nanjing Daxue chubanshe, 1993) 155.

42 Zhang Yufa, ed., *Zhonghua Minguo Hongshizihui Bainian Huishi, 1904–2003* [An Organizational History of One Hundred Years of the Red Cross Society of the Republic of China 1904–2003] (Taibei: Red Cross Society of the Republic of China, 2004), 269, 279.

43 The Red Swastika Society (Hongwanzi Hui), founded in 1922, was explicitly modeled on the Red Cross pattern but took a Buddhist symbol as its namesake and the syncretic Dao Yuan (the Society of the Way) ideology as its creed. Thomas David DuBois, "The Salvation of Religion? Public Charity and the New Religions of the Early Republic," *Minsuquyi* 172 (June 2011):

73–126; also Rebecca Nedostup, *Superstitious Regimes* (Cambridge, MA: Harvard University Press, 2009), 60–6.

44 *Bulletin International des Sociétés de la Croix-Rouge* (Geneva: Comite International), 139 (July 1904), 190. There is much confusion over the actual date of China's adherence to this Convention and to the Geneva Convention of 1906.

45 *Bulletin International des Sociétés de la Croix-Rouge* (Geneva: Comite International), 169 (January 1912), 8–9.

46 Few of these stories have been documented except in Red Cross-sponsored hagiographies. The history of the Japanese Red Cross is an exception; see Checkland.

47 ZHEJ, 25–26.

48 ZHEJ, 20.

49 For example, in the *Dongfang Zazhi* 10, no. 2 (1 August 1913).

50 Roberts, *Photography and China*, 53.

51 For a revealing cross-cultural comparison of Red Cross societies' entry into publication, cf. Irwin, 83–90, which discusses the origins and rise of the American Red Cross magazine.

52 Roberts, *Photography and China*, 27.

53 "A Brief History of the carte de visite," http://www.photographymuseum. com/histsw.htm.

54 Morris, 124–6.

55 For an interesting and important analysis of the efficacy of celebrity portraiture in the advancement of philanthropic causes, see "Why Photos of One Direction Won't Save Us from Global Warming," *The Guardian*, 25 January 2013, http://www.guardian.co.uk/environment/blog/2013/jan/25/ one-direction-climate-comms.

56 Roberts, 42.

57 Regine Thiriez, "Photography and Portraiture in Nineteenth-Century China," *East Asian History* 17/18 (June/December 1999): 77–102.

58 Evelyn Rawski and Jan Stuart, *Worshiping the Ancestors* (Stanford, CA: Stanford University Press, 2001), 166–7.

59 Ibid.

60 Roberts, 56. Rawski and Stuart, 167. This mania for portraits of dignitaries would reach its apogee in China during the Mao years, when the Mao portrait became omnipresent.

61 Rarely women, except in group portraits of nurses.

62 See "Why Photos of One Direction Won't Save Us."

63 *Hongshizihui Zazhi*, 1.

64 *Hongshizihui Zazhi*, 1.

65 *Zhongguo Hongshizihui Tianjinfenhui dierci Baogao* (Chinese Red Cross Society Tianjin Chapter Report, #2) (Tianjin: Zhongguo Hongshizihui Tianjin fenhui, 1914) from Number Two Archives, (1001) (1872) (2). I have never seen the pictorial, although many of Tianjin's photographs are reproduced in national Red Cross publications.

66 *Haoshengzhide* (Shanghai, 1914) available in Number Two Archives and in Federation Archives.

67 In the 1924 *Twentieth Anniversary Commemorative Volume of the Chinese Red Cross Society* (ZHEJ), photographs command their own category in the table of contents, and the photography section is divided into three groups: Photographic Portraits, Photographs of Hospitals, and Photos of Relief Efforts. The portraits section is first and impressively populated with stars.

68 Cf. Silvia Salvatici's chapter in this volume.

69 John Fitzgerald discusses this trope brilliantly in his book *Awakening China: Politics, Culture and Class* (Stanford, CA: Stanford University Press, 1996).

70 Curtis in this volume; Rozario, "Delicious Horrors," particularly 435–9; and Irwin, 87–8.

71 Yomi Braester analyzes this event as photographic spectacle, applying the work of Sontag, Barthes, Rey Chow, et al., *Witness against History* (Stanford, CA: Stanford University Press, 2003), 36–40.

72 See http://mclc.osu.edu/rc/bios/lxbio.htm.

73 In 1917, violence erupted in Beijing when a northern general tried to restore the last Qing emperor, Puyi, to the throne. Tianjin's Red Cross chapter sent emergency workers to Beijing to help with victims of the carnage. Financial records from this event, dated 7 July–5 August 1917 come from the Number Two Archives in Nanjing (476) (3234). Records were submitted to the Red Cross Central Committee on 12 November 1917.

74 Leo Ou-fan Lee, *Shanghai Modern: The Flowering of a New Urban Culture in China, 1930–1945* (Cambridge, MA: Harvard University Press, 1999) offers a cogent discussion of what modernity meant in China in this period.

75 Traditionally, jackets and pants were women's or coolie's wear in China.

76 Francesca Piana's chapter in this volume discusses this phenomenon in the West.

77 *The Chinese Red Cross Activities Told in Pictures Series No. III* (1930), chapter 2, np.

78 B. Y. Wong, *The Chinese Red Cross Activities Told in Pictures,* published in English by the Chinese Red Cross Central Committee, Shanghai (probably 1928) (stamped by American Red Cross Library, acquired in Federation Archives).

79 *The Chinese Red Cross Activities Told in Pictures* (probably 1928), np.

80 *The Chinese Red Cross Activities Told in Pictures Series No. III.*

81 Kennedy, "Selling the Distant Other," 2.

82 The iconic photo "Bloody Saturday" of a Chinese infant stranded on railway tracks after a 1937 Japanese bomb attack on a Shanghai rail station is one such photo. Although taken by a Chinese photographer, this photo was explicitly intended for a Western audience. http://en.wikipedia.org/wiki/Bloody_Saturday_(photograph).

83 The film *Making Mao* (dir: Galen Yeo, produced by Moving Visual Co., 2009) about Maoist propaganda elucidates this visual history.

84 It is important to note the origins and destinations of the photos from this event. Photos for China's own audiences are well represented here: http://www.china-quake.com.

6

Photography, Cinema, and the Quest for Influence

The International Committee of the Red Cross in the Wake of the First World War

Francesca Piana

Chaque Suisse devrait considérer comme son devoir
d'être membre de la Croix-Rouge de son pays.[1]

Introduction

In late March 1921, members and delegates of the International Committee
of the Red Cross (ICRC) gathered in Geneva for the 10th Conference of
the Red Cross movement. In attendance were members of thirty-six Red
Cross and Red Crescent national societies, along with representatives
of thirty governments that had signed the Geneva Convention for the
Amelioration of the Condition of the Wounded in Armies in the Field,
and prominent international organizations.[2] As the supreme deliberative
body of the Red Cross movement, the conference was intended to confirm the ICRC's "influence and authority," support the extension of its
mandate in peacetime, and discuss financing.[3] The conference was anything but impromptu. Since the end of World War I, and especially following the creation in April 1919 of the League of Red Cross Societies
(LRCS), another organization within the Red Cross movement, the ICRC
had pushed for the conference to be convened.[4]

I would like to thank the editors of this volume, Heide Fehrenbach and Davide Rodogno, for
their comments on earlier drafts of this chapter. Gianni Haver, Julia Irwin, Andre Liebich,
Samuel Moyn, Daniel Palmieri, and Amalia Ribi Forclaz also provided useful insights.
Thanks also goes to Fania Khan Mohammad, Fabrizio Bensi, and Marina Meier of the
ICRC. This project was supported by the Swiss National Science Foundation.

At the suggestion of Giovanni Ciraolo, president of the Italian Red Cross, the ICRC frantically organized an exhibit for the paying public as a side activity to the conference.[5] The exhibit featured both photos and movies. At that time, the ICRC had already been using photographs, posters, and postcards to document its activities.[6] Filmmaking, in contrast, represented a complete innovation for the organization. While photos and movies provided evidence and information about the activities of the ICRC, movies were intended to show the reality on the ground in a more truthful and emotional way than photos and texts alone could.[7]

On the ground floor of the Bâtiment electoral,[8] situated in downtown Geneva, national societies displayed photographs, pamphlets, posters, and various field materials, such as huge tents that occupied the center of the room. The first floor of the building was mainly reserved for the ICRC, which used maps to show the expansion of the Red Cross movement around the world and illustrate the growing cooperation and interdependence of national societies and the ICRC over the decades.[9] On the same floor, a room was reserved for "propaganda movies." Four of them portrayed the activities of the ICRC in postwar humanitarianism; the Italian Red Cross sent one that depicted young Italian pupils having their classes outdoors; another was from the Swedish Red Cross showing the repatriation of wounded soldiers throughout northern Europe.[10] The LRCS also projected movies sent by the American Red Cross, the Rockefeller Foundation, and the Young Men's Christian Association (YMCA). At the time of the conference, the ICRC had made four movies, whereas the LRCS had collected sixty.[11]

The 10th Conference of the Red Cross movement is a historical laboratory in which various "forces, events, and structures" influenced the development and shape of the mandate of the ICRC, and which, in turn, were also influenced by the ICRC.[12] This chapter breaks new ground by combining a local, national, and transnational perspective on the visual culture of the ICRC at the end of the First World War. It frames the relationship between the ICRC's humanitarianism, photography, and cinema within the transnational emergence of Western civil society, modern humanitarianism, and mass culture.[13] Since the end of the nineteenth century, international humanitarianism has been rooted in middle-class cultures throughout the West. This chapter examines political, cultural, and religious spaces in which the ICRC operated, both in Geneva and, more broadly, throughout Switzerland.[14]

After sketching the challenges that the ICRC was facing in the aftermath of the First World War, this chapter moves to consider its Propaganda

Commission.[15] The chapter reviews the tools and methods that the ICRC used to raise public awareness among the Swiss people and to be accountable to its benefactors. It shows that despite its international mandate, the ICRC remained a Swiss organization in scope: it appealed to patriotic feelings and strove to convince the Swiss people of their responsibility to financially support the organization's actions abroad. The second part of the chapter considers technical issues concerning the ICRC's production and use of photos and movies as well as the impact of ICRC archival practices on historians' attempts to study these. The final section analyzes ICRC iconography by dividing photographic subjects into two categories: a primary focus on the organization and its agents, and a secondary, more fluid iconographic approach to victims and the recipients of its humanitarian assistance.

Compared to other textual sources, visual media represent a privileged point of access to further nuance the exceptionality of the ICRC and question the principles that are at the core of its mandate – namely, universality, neutrality, independence, and the equality of all its members – during a watershed moment for the organization and world politics.[16]

"Making War More Human"

The fundamental principles of the Red Cross movement are based on the ICRC's original mid-nineteenth-century mandate, according to which the organization aimed to assist wounded soldiers and neutralize medical personnel.[17] In legal terms, the ICRC is grounded on Swiss civil law and receives its mandate from the state-parties to the Geneva Conventions, which commit to respecting a code of conduct during war. It is not a proper intergovernmental organization, such as the United Nations, nor a nongovernmental organization.

The mandate of the ICRC evolved over time and space. The First World War represented a watershed for the organization. Besides sick and wounded combatants, delegates of the ICRC – who acted as the arm of the organization – assisted prisoners of war; in addition, the ICRC established the International Prisoner of War Agency. Operating until the end of 1919 from its headquarters in Geneva, the Agency collected lists of the wounded, dead, and prisoners of war from all sides and took charge of transmitting this information to governments and families.[18] For this work, the ICRC was awarded the Nobel Prize in 1917.

Immediately after the signing of the General Armistice on 27 November 1918, the ICRC announced that it would expand its mandate from "oeuvres de guerre" to "oeuvres de paix."[19] On one hand, this announcement responded to the dire humanitarian conditions of the European population at the end of the First World War. Faced with few or no governmental responses, international organizations, often supported by the military, helped save hundreds of thousands of adults and children from untimely deaths in the countries of Central, Eastern, and South-Eastern Europe, as well as Russia and the Near East. On the other hand, the ICRC justified its actions by framing former prisoners of war, civilians stricken by epidemics, those displaced by the war, and needy children as "victims of war."[20] Soon after, the ICRC shifted from focusing on international wars to including internal civil wars, such as those in mandate Syria, Hungary, and later Spain.

What accounts for these changes in the ICRC's mandate? Moving beyond the Red Cross motto "Inter Arma Caritas" [In war, charity] at the end of the First World War, many existing and newly created organizations were competing in the burgeoning field of humanitarianism in the United States, Britain, and Western Europe. The ICRC, whose prominent position had never been questioned until that time, felt threatened by this typically Western phenomenon. Moreover, the main concern came not from organizations external to the Red Cross movement but from within the movement itself. National Red Cross and Red Crescent societies had enlarged the scope of their activities during the war, funded in part by national governments concerned with addressing the humanitarian needs of their populations. The most powerful Red Cross and Red Crescent societies also provided relief beyond national boundaries, overlapping with the activities of the ICRC.[21] This perceived threat to the ICRC by national Red Cross societies was exemplified by the establishment of the League of Red Cross Societies (LRCS). Created on the initiative of the American Red Cross, the LRCS included only the Red Cross societies of the victors in the First World War. In one stroke, the establishment of the LRCS challenged both the status of the ICRC as the primary intermediary in humanitarian crises as well as the organization's principle of political impartiality.[22]

The LRCS proposed a humanitarianism that was professional, efficient, and scientific and criticized the ICRC for the amateur character of its approach. As historian John Hutchinson has demonstrated, from 1918 to 1923, relations between the ICRC and the LRCS passed from phases of cooperation to moments of open rivalry. Eventually, the 11th Conference of the Red Cross movement, held in Geneva in 1923, confirmed the leadership of the ICRC.[23] Despite these tensions within the

Red Cross movement, the ICRC played a central role in taking on post-war problems that governments deemed unworthy of diplomatic and financial resources. The Genevan Committee contributed to internationalizing postwar humanitarianism and to increasingly orienting non-governmental organizations to the intergovernmental sphere – as, for example, in the case of how to handle displaced Russians.[24] At the end of the First World War, the ICRC was composed of a Committee, which was the main decision-making body of the organization, a Secretariat, and the delegates working in the missions.[25] In 1920, according to the best estimates available, there were sixteen members of the Committee; all came from the Genevan middle class. From the end of World War I until 1923, "principal delegates" numbered 107, according to an official publication of the ICRC. This included delegates who went on long missions, mostly to Central, Eastern, and Southeastern Europe, as well as those who worked for the ICRC for only a few weeks.[26] Delegates were "where things happened": they knew what the needs were and who the other players were in the same area. By informing the organization of developments in the field through detailed reports and, inter alia, photographs and movies, delegates contributed to shaping and orienting the ICRC's agenda. After 1923, as the major postwar relief emergencies were addressed, the meager financial resources of the ICRC prevented it from engaging in medium-scale rehabilitation or state-building activities. Over the course of the following years, the ICRC would focus on the international negotiations that ended with the approval of the Genevan Convention for Prisoners of War in 1929.

The Propaganda Commission

The challenges presented by the silences and gaps in the archives of the ICRC force historians to take a creative approach to the question of the visual culture of the organization. From the sparse primary sources available on the topic, it is clear that the organization did not develop a comprehensive visual strategy and its decision-making process was informal, fragmented, and extemporary. In sum, it developed from postwar circumstances. The organization's precarious financial status, the necessity of re-acquiring the legitimacy that had been lost due to the inter-Red Cross fights, and the increasing number of humanitarian organizations acting transnationally were the elements that triggered the ICRC's visual turn.[27]

The ICRC's humanitarian policy attempted to position the organization nationally and internationally. In December 1919, its Propaganda

Commission was established.[28] It worked closely with French-speaking local Red Cross sections and authorities and also with the Swiss Red Cross and federal authorities in Berne. The Propaganda Commission was composed of some of the members of the organization's Committee. Due to the extension and articulation of propaganda activities, in the spring of 1922 the ICRC appointed Julien Lescaze as what we would today call a "communication officer." French, trained in law and social sciences, and hired through informal channels (as was the case for everybody working for the ICRC), Lescaze further met the expectations of the ICRC by being a Christian.[29]

In the months preceding the 1921 conference, the ICRC and the Swiss Red Cross set up a joint campaign, the first of many.[30] The ICRC was to organize and publicize conferences, while the Swiss Red Cross was to distribute material and proceed with fundraising. The money collected would be shared between the ICRC and the Swiss Red Cross, to be used for both national and international humanitarian purposes.[31] Different communication methods were simultaneously employed, both textual and nontextual.[32] Patriotic associations, such as Club Alpin Suisse, Sociétés militaires, and Nouvelle Société Helvétique, distributed 20,000 copies of a pamphlet called *The Appeal*, which contained no illustrations, in two of the four official Swiss languages (French and German).[33] ICRC's publications, such as the biography of Gustave Ador, its president, and an album of the International Agency for Prisoners of War, were distributed to federal authorities and presidents of Red Cross sections.[34] Articles were published in the local press, including *Le Genevois, L'Express,* and *Le Journal de Genève.* Public lectures were organized and posters were displayed in different cities in Switzerland.[35]

In 1918, 550 copies of the *Bulletin International des sociétés de la Croix-Rouge* (renamed *The International Review of the Red Cross* in 1919) were distributed mainly to national societies.[36] However, photographs of missions were absent from the *Review* until 1924. Before that year, the *Review* contained a few portraits of personalities and photographs of the exhibit organized on the occasion of the 10th Conference of the Red Cross movement.[37]

What explains the lack of images in the *Review*? This did not seem to rest on the principles underpinning the ICRC's mandate, such as neutrality and impartiality, since photos and movies were shown at public gatherings. Readership might have mattered. There may have been a bias that educated readers – the target audience for the *Review* – had less need for visuals than the general audience attending public conferences. Other reasons make the absence of visual material in the *Review* of the ICRC surprising. In Switzerland at the time, the printing of images had become a common practice for many newspapers (*presse illustrée*). Indeed, the First World War had triggered the inclusion of images in Swiss journals.[38] Moreover, printing was historically an important industrial activity in Geneva. The city had inherited Calvinism's evangelical mission, with a strong desire to spread the new Protestant faith through printed documents and images.[39] At the transnational level, during the second decade of the twentieth century, almost all of the other humanitarian organizations were already making use of images in their pamphlets and publications. In particular, the discrepancy between the resources of the ICRC and the American Red Cross is striking, as historian Julia Irwin suggests. From September 1917, the American Red Cross magazine increasingly incorporated more images, including some in color. More generally, the ICRC lagged behind in the resources, know-how in communication campaigns, and mobilization techniques of the American Red Cross both during and after the First World War.[40] The "visual language" of the ICRC was just beginning to be developed and the ICRC appears to have been unsure of how and where to most effectively mobilize it.[41] More than an exceptional player, the ICRC seemed to run against the tide of modernization.

The Technology

It is worth dwelling on some technical issues that affect any retrospective assessment of the ICRC's visual politics. First, it was not until 1946 – when Jean Pictet, one of the directors of the ICRC, suggested the creation of an iconographic service – that the organization began to catalogue its photographs.[42] At the time, the classification of photographs was entrusted to the voluntary work of a student from the Library Department of the École d'Études Sociales in Geneva, Ursula Stauffenegger.[43] In the introductory remark to her dissertation on the iconography of the ICRC, Stauffenegger wrote that "photography had *almost* the same value as texts."[44] In keeping with the word "almost," the ICRC made the inauspicious decision, a few years later, to remove most of the photographs from their original boxes – where they stood side-by-side with paper documents – to create what is the current photo library. This institutional decision severely compromised the work of historically reconstructing the ICRC's production and use of visual sources.

Second, when delegates commented on photographs portraying the work of the ICRC at public gatherings, they did not mention who took them. As a result, we know little about the authorship of the images. Clearly, what mattered to ICRC delegates were the message conveyed and the expected results. Despite the fact that delegates had not taken the photographs and, in most cases, were not involved in the processes concerned with the selection and inclusion or exclusion of subjects, by showing photographs the ICRC appropriated the images as its own. Even though cameras started being more widely used during the First World War, the ICRC did not provide delegates in the field with cameras or financial means to hire local photographers. One of the few exceptions was Maurice Gehri, who possessed his own camera, and as a result took impressive shots witnessing the atrocities committed by the Greek army in the occupation zone of Samanli Dag (Marmara Sea) against Armenian and Turkish civilians during the Greco-Turkish War.[45] Photographs that the ICRC exhibited came largely from national societies, the Save the Children Fund, and the Union Internationale de Secours aux Enfants, whose work was closely related to the ICRC. The photo library also contains photographs from other organizations, such as those of the Near East Relief.[46]

As far as movies are concerned, the Propaganda Commission exhorted delegates in the field to elaborate techniques that could be used for fundraising campaigns.[47] Prior to the 10th Red Cross Conference in 1921, Victor Gloor, the delegate of the ICRC in Poland, was contacted by the cinema section of the Young Men's Christian Association (YMCA), which proposed making a movie on the relief operations carried out by the ICRC in the country.[48] This example shows the dynamics – both from outside the ICRC and in the field – of how the ICRC began to use alternative forms of representation, in this case film. It shows that delegates rarely worked in isolation but were exposed to the ways in which other international organizations performed and promoted their humanitarianism(s). It is not a coincidence that this initiative came from Poland: at the end of the First World War, European and American organizations made their first step into postwar humanitarianism in Poland where they observed and learned from each other.[49]

In contrast to the ICRC's improvisational production of photographs, the organization maintained tighter control over movies. All of the scenes were staged. Film scripts were carefully negotiated between the organization and its delegates, even if the external circumstances (weather, conditions in the field, and the "turnover" of subjects) remained beyond their control.[50] Four movies were made between December 1920 and March 1921: the first one on the fight against epidemics in Poland; the second on the exchange of prisoners of war in the Baltic Sea, through the naval bridge connecting Narva and Stettin; the third on the conditions of Russian refugees in Istanbul; and the last on relief actions on behalf of Hungarian children in Budapest.[51]

It was left to ICRC delegates in the field to find local filmmakers and monitor the shooting. It was also their responsibility to raise part of the funding for the movies. For instance, the Hungarian government paid part of the expenses for the movie on needy children in Budapest.[52] Several months after the end of the filming in Istanbul, the ICRC asked its delegate to negotiate with the filmmaker, a Russian refugee himself, to reduce the cost of production, due to the dissatisfaction of the organization with the final result.[53] The ICRC invested some of its money into filmmaking, which it hoped to recuperate by influencing donors.

In keeping with the technology of the time, all of the ICRC films from this period are in black and white and without sound. Rather rudimentary images are separated from each other by brief intertitles that explain the scenes.[54] In the movies about Budapest and the repatriation plans for prisoners of war, intertitles were in both French and English, while in the movies on Istanbul and the fight against typhus in Poland they were only in French. Generally, intertitles were normally made of one sentence or title.[55] This would say something about the work of the ICRC, such as "another school supported by the ICRC," "the ICRC gave relief on behalf of the Save the Children Fund," or would introduce the situation depicted, such as "going to dinner," "the kitchen," "handing out the dinner," "children going to the workrooms of the Save the Children Fund," and "sewing rooms."[56]

The experience gained from this joint national campaign and efforts at filmmaking became the basis on which the Propaganda Commission would ground successive improved campaigns. Less than two years later, in the issue of the *Appeal to the Swiss People*, photographs accompanied the text. Interestingly, some brochures were translated into English to reach a larger international audience.[57] Moreover, in the spring of 1922, the ICRC also issued an appeal addressed to the Muslim "world" related to relief and reconstruction plans for Anatolia. Translated into Arab, Persian, and Urdu, the appeal was supposed to reach an "uncontaminated" market, one that no other international organization had previously targeted.[58] During the meeting of the Propaganda Commission in July 1922, the creation of what is now the museum of the International Red Cross and Red Crescent Movement was suggested, where synoptic tables would be displayed and foreigners passing through Geneva could be informed about the work of the organization.[59] By the end of the 1920s, the ICRC was also using the radio as a method of disseminating information about its work.

At the 10th Conference of the Red Cross movement the previous year, a suggestion had already been made to expand the use of movies. There was particular interest expressed in movies from American organizations, especially for those that were not simple documentaries but engaged audiences with a narrative. For instance, a film by the YMCA portrayed an orphan Polish girl, who, after being educated as a nurse, visited the zone where typhus was endemic in order to educate Polish people about health measures. The ICRC knew that American organizations were at the cutting edge of modern filmmaking. Already in 1918, the Near East Relief commissioned a Hollywood production, entitled *Ravished Armenia*, which told the story of Aurora Mardiganian, a survivor of the Armenian genocide.[60]

In 1922, the ICRC commissioned a movie on its postwar activities by Genevan filmmaker and engineer Jean Brocher.[61] A second film, supervised by the ICRC's delegate in Greece, Baron Rudolph de Reding-Biberegg, was made on the work of the ICRC after the Greco-Turkish War and was screened at the 11th Conference of the Red Cross movement in 1923.[62] It was common practice at the time for the ICRC to cut scenes and integrate them into other movies: this partially explains why Brocher's film contained images from 1921 movies.[63]

The Iconography of the ICRC

In the wake of the First World War, the ICRC's visual language was characterized by continuity and by rupture. A few elements remained unchanged, representing the ICRC in the decades before the war, such as the appearance of the organization's symbol on cars, ambulances, and the arms of humanitarians. Other images were shaped by postwar humanitarian needs and reflected the expanded mandate of the ICRC, such as a focus on children.

The ICRC's iconography had two main themes focused on the organization and those entitled to humanitarian assistance. At public lectures and charity dinners, delegates of the ICRC and, in some cases, Bernard Bouvier, the president of the Propaganda Commission, would provide commentary for projected slides (clichés).[64] The ICRC would give delegates a "script," where photographs were numbered, explained, smoothly connected, and contextualized. The script contained references to fifty-four photographs.

Among them, thirty-two depicted the traditional mandate of the ICRC in wartime, focusing on the wounded and prisoners of war, whereas the rest portrayed the organization's postwar activities, with particular attention to the work on behalf of children and refugees.[65]

The ICRC on Stage

Faced with tough competition in the humanitarian realm, the ICRC felt the need to increasingly advertise its activities. Not all of them were portrayed though: more attention was given to the operations in the field than to the work carried out at the Genevan headquarters. Therefore, the focus was mainly on the delegates and logistics. Geographically, not all of the missions were represented. The amount of time it took for mail to get to Geneva from Vladivostok, for instance, spared the ICRC's mission in loco from having to participate in the visual representation of its activities. It is also likely that the personalities of individual delegates, their workloads, and the technical means at their disposal played a role in the level of representation of their missions.

Through their work, delegates carried out the mandate of the organization and personified the principles underpinning ICRC operations.[66] This gave a concrete sense of the ICRC's humanitarian involvement and showed that the organization was, and is, a fair and competent international player that solves humanitarian emergencies provoked by absent or inattentive national and local authorities.[67] Delegates received their mandates from Genevan headquarters, responded to these directions as well as needs that arose in the field, and reported back to the organization.

Delegates came to the ICRC from the Swiss military, governmental institutions, and universities where they were trained in engineering and medicine. More generally, delegates were represented as highly skilled professionals carrying out their daily activities. They were meant to represent their brand of scientific, "modern," and accountable humanitarianism, in which the positivist norms of current relief culture are still rooted, in terms of reports, statistics, and food distributed on the basis of calories. Those coming from the military were portrayed checking lists of prisoners of war before repatriation; they controlled the distribution of food and clothes; they were in the same boats as former prisoners of war to supervise the treatment that they received from national authorities; and they negotiated with local authorities and international relief workers from other organizations. For instance, Rodolphe de Reding-Biberegg, delegate of the ICRC in Greece from September 1922 to July 1923, is represented controlling the embarkment of prisoners of war (Figure 6.1).

FIGURE 6.1. War between Greece and Turkey. Prisoners of war being repatriated under ICRC auspices. © Photothèque CICR (DR), *V-P-HIST-00981-65*, 1922.

ICRC iconography also tended to glorify doctors, a common visual trope in humanitarian representation.[68] For instance, showing the work of doctors was not only proof of the scientific nature of the work carried out by the ICRC but also of the neutrality of the organization. Science was considered ipso facto neutral and objective. Upon the express request of the Committee of the ICRC, much of the movie on Poland is centered on the activities of Dr. Alexis Tarassoff, a Polish doctor.[69] Tarassoff is shown conducting research with the microscope in his laboratory, using extremely modern and scientific methods, providing medical care to people in need, going to an orphanage, and interacting with prisoners of war and refugees.[70]

Only in the movie commissioned for the 11th Conference of the Red Cross movement were members of the Committee and its president, and former president of the Swiss Confederation, Ador, portrayed. In the movie, Ador is giving a speech on the role and importance of the Red Cross movement in the world. Vehemently, Ador bangs his fist on the table. His eyes and physical posture communicated strength and commitment. It should not be forgotten that only after the 11th Conference did the ICRC win the internal rivalry with the LRCS.

Images of delegates and doctors contributed to transforming the ICRC's public image of humanitarianism from nineteenth-century volunteerism, often fueled by religious impulses, to a more professional, secular, and technocratic endeavor. Logistics occupied a significant part of the ICRC's imagery, both in photographs and movies. Images portrayed boats and trains used to repatriate prisoners of war. This is the case for the German boat "Baghdad" that was used to transport prisoners of war in the Baltic Sea, who would later be exchanged in the camp of Narva, Estonia (Figure 6.2). Images also depicted camps where prisoners of war were hosted, with a particular focus on the infrastructure, namely, views of the tents and sanitary and delousing installations[71] (Figure 6.3).

Between War Victims and Beneficiaries of Humanitarian Assistance

The representation of individuals oscillates between war victims and dependents in need of help. Images of the "suffering body" were mainly contained in photographs, whereas movies almost exclusively showed images of rescued people, stressing the agency of beneficiaries to "help themselves." Documents do not explain why, despite the wartime toleration for violent images, the ICRC privileged a more "neutral" approach in movies. We can assume that a success story would bring the ICRC more financial contributions. However, we cannot exclude the possibility that the absence of extreme suffering reflected the ICRC's moral limits of what could or could not be shown.[72]

Photos exhibited at public conferences showed prisoners of war whose legs had been amputated, the bodies of those killed by typhus and famine, the corpses of those who were buried in mass graves, and abandoned orphans, all of which endorsed the narrative of traumatized victimhood. These were visually decontextualized and dehistoricized to become the universal and politically neutral representations of extreme distress. Moreover, since the photos were accompanied by limited captions, delegates became powerful voices speaking on behalf of silent victims.[73]

In some cases, the captions for the photographs provided viewers with some information. For instance, the caption of a picture showing two poorly clothed children locates them in a train station in Yerevan, Soviet Armenia, from 1921–2, and notes that they are orphans. Without this caption, one would be left to wonder where these children happened to be and what their social circumstances were (Figure 6.4).

We live in such a rich visual environment that it seems difficult to understand how the ICRC's photos and movies were received. In building

FIGURE 6.2. Post–World War I – Stettin. Arrival of the *Bagdad* transporting German prisoners of war repatriated from Russia. © Photothèque CICR (DR)/V-P-HIST-*01128*, 09/1920.

human emotional responses, the ICRC relied on both Swiss and Western cultures and morality. Christian symbols as well as a religious sense of "sin" underpinned images, which a virtuous and civilized audience was expected to respond to by giving money.[74] The immobility of victims, visual references to the crucifix, images evoking Madonna holding Jesus as well as of saints and martyrs were some of the elements characterizing the ICRC's iconography of victimhood. The aim of showing distant suffering was to prod those who had not experienced war to imagine the vulnerability of other human beings and experience feelings of solidarity, responsibility, empathy, and compassion.[75]

At the same time, the iconography of victimhood was likely rooted in images that the audience would not easily forget. Victims of war appeared to be reduced to objects of pity or revulsion, through which emotional responses were also built.[76] Viewers could feel repelled by the extent and violence of humanitarian catastrophes, which took place outside the borders of civilized Europe. This was also intermingled with national pride, where the superiority of Switzerland was heralded over the "hellish" places where catastrophes happened. Paternalism was evident toward the "half-civilized" Eastern Europeans (albeit still Christians) and barbarous Turks (Muslims), for whom the ICRC and its delegates were making decisions, largely dismissing the agency of the victims.

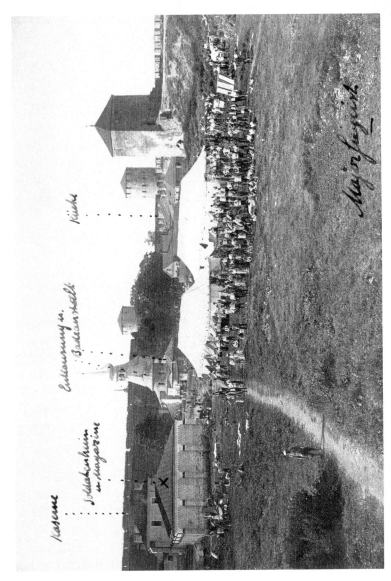

FIGURE 6.3. Post–World War I – Narva, Ivangorod fortress. ICRC transit point for Russian prisoners of war repatriated from Germany and German prisoners of war coming from Russia. © Photothèque CICR (DR)/*V-P-HIST-03054-06*, 1921.

FIGURE 6.4. Soviet Armenia 1921–1922, Eriwan. Orphans. © Photothèque CICR (DR)/s.n., *V-P-HIST-00387-11.*

Delegates also sold excitement and exoticism. They took the audience beyond European borders, showing faraway landscapes brimming with ethnographical interest. When presenting photos of prisoners of war in Algeria, delegates pointed out those in an Arab crowd wearing "bathrobes," meaning traditional clothing, for example.[77] In line with the spirit of the epoch, it should not be forgotten that the ICRC, as well as all of the other humanitarian organizations, operated in a broad ideological context, which was highly anti-Bolshevik. For instance, images show the devastated surroundings of Brest-Litovsk and the intertitle ascribed it to the Bolshevik invasion. Combating typhus in Poland, assisting White Russians in Istanbul, and helping settle Greek refugees were deemed essential actions in order to remove the Bolshevik "contagion" from Europe. At the same time, the ICRC also made clear that the same food ration was provided to both Polish soldiers and Bolshevik prisoners of war.

This leads to the second and main category of the ICRC's representation of the recipients, namely, beneficiaries of humanitarian assistance. In the repatriation of prisoners of war, images show Russian prisoners of war waiting to embark from the German port of Stettin under the control of the organization's delegates. Then, on the boat, they depict the joy of these men, who danced and played music in anticipation of their return home. A large number of images portray stories of food distribution and rehabilitated children. Images of newly clothed rescued Polish orphans, surrounding Tarassoff in the orphanage of Kowel, are reminiscent of the codes of missionary photography, colonial photography, and antislavery photography.[78] Some of the images show children involved in education and vocational programs (Figure 6.5).

Because of the recent expansion of the ICRC's mandate to children, the organization was particularly eager to represent them. The ICRC's approach, activities, and ambitions were in keeping with a specific trend of the period, in particular increased attention to youth as the basis for the reconstruction of postwar Europe. Children became the preferred targets of humanitarian organizations' visual campaigns, and the ICRC also followed this international trend. For instance, in 1921, in coincidence with the relief operations to fight hunger in the Volga region, the Save the Children Fund produced and directed a movie entitled *Famine: A Glimpse of the Misery in the Province of Saratov*. The movie, which portrayed images of deep suffering and dying children, would be largely shown in Europe and North America in the following months.[79] Besides the fact that European youth were in real danger of malnutrition and disease in the aftermath of the First World War, the focus of the ICRC reflected overlapping interests among institutions.[80]

Conclusion

This chapter has suggested that in the aftermath of the First World War, the ICRC was not as independent, impartial, and neutral as one would think. The postwar setting was a moment of transition, where pre-existing and new practices interacted. It was also a moment in which power relations among actors were renegotiated, reallocated, and redistributed. Against this changing context, the early 1920s witnessed the rise of international organizations and their increasing importance in world politics. The "survival" of the ICRC after the First World War required adaption to the evolving circumstances. Therefore, the expansion of the ICRC's mandate encompassed the necessity of using new forms of communication.

By analyzing the photographs and movies of the ICRC, this chapter has considered the distribution of power around humanitarianism. On one hand, visual materials were used to emphasize the apolitical nature of the

FIGURE 6.5. Après-guerre 1914–1918 – Kowel. Orphelinat fondé par le CICR. © Photothèque CICR (DR)/V-P-HIST-00382-41, 06/1919.

ICRC's mandate and practices. In other words, photography and movies were intended to depict humanitarianism in its purest form and to publicize the ICRC's engagement with people in need. On the other hand, the ICRC's use of photos and movies was markedly political and was oriented toward gaining influence in postwar humanitarian questions and increasing financial resources.[81] Moreover, the ICRC's visual humanitarianism communicated that the organization was moving from charity, volunteerism, activism, and social service to "modern" values of professionalization, science, and accountability. At the same time, these images and movies also communicated the "dark side" of humanitarianism, namely, ongoing paternalism, a sense of superiority, and the civilizing mission.

In the future, posters and postcards of the ICRC should also be analyzed in parallel with photographs and movies. More scholarly work should be done to compare the ICRC's historical visual humanitarianism with contemporary campaigns carried out by other organizations, both European and American. Attention should be devoted to the transfer of models, which seem to connect "modern" interwar humanitarianism with colonial photography, antislavery photography, and religious journals and pamphlets.[82] Culturally, the Swiss and Western aesthetics and symbolism, from the end of the nineteenth century to the beginning of the twentieth century, might be productively examined to contextualize the iconographical language of the ICRC at the end of the First World War.[83] These insights into the iconography of the ICRC would permit an in-depth reconstruction of human emotional communities and an examination of the understudied relationship between the donors and the victims/recipients. The ICRC's visual humanitarianism would also benefit from a gender analysis. Delegates and doctors depicted the male strength of the organization, while in other images the ICRC was portrayed as a caring mother.[84]

All in all, a focus on the visual representation of the ICRC shows that it was in the early 1920s that humanitarianism was transformed into a mass marketing venture, when current communication and fundraising practices were first formulated and implemented. The history of the visual representation of the ICRC is a useful lens through which to interpret the specific Swiss and international contexts in which the organization operated.

Notes

1 The quotation continues: "Nos concitoyens auraient-ils oublié que notre devise nationale est: tous pour un! Et que notre patrie est le berceau de la

plus noble institution qui soit au monde: la Croix Rouge." Archives of the International Committee of the Red Cross (AICRC), CR49, Procès-verbal des délégués de la direction de la Croix-Rouge suisse, des présidents des sections de la Croix-Rouge suisse et de la Commission de Propagande du Comité International de la Croix-Rouge, tenue à Berne, 12 septembre 1920.

2 AICRC, Commission mixte, vol.[II.5], Résumé de l'activité du CICR au cours de l'année 1921. Among the most important organizations that attended the conference we find the League of Nations, the International Labour Organization, the League of the Red Cross Societies, the Union Internationale de Secours aux Enfants, the Save the Children Fund, the Oeuvre des Chevaliers Italiens de Malte, the YMCA, and the International Council of Women.

3 ACICR, CR 76, 10th Conference of the Red Cross Movement. See also, article 9 of the Resolutions of the Geneva International Conference of 1863 states that "the committees and sections of different countries may meet in international assemblies to communicate the results of their experiences and to agree on measures to be taken in the interest of the work."

4 The Red Cross movement is composed of the ICRC, which plays the role of intermediary among the constituent parts; the International Federation of the Red Cross and Red Crescent Societies (renamed after the League of the Red Cross Societies in 1991); and national societies, of which there are more than 180 today.

5 Ciraolo attempted to create an organization to mobilize in the event of a natural disaster. Hutchinson, "Disasters and the International Order."

6 For an overview on the visual humanitarianism of the ICRC, see Moorehead, ed., *Humanity in War*. This volume followed an exhibit organized at the headquarters of the organization, entitled "Humanity in War. From the Mid-19th Century to the Conflicts of Today." Some of the postcards portraying the ICRC can be found in the Centre d'Iconographie Genevoise. See "série carte postale classe 46."

7 So far, the topic of the visual humanitarianism of the ICRC has received little attention. A few exceptions are International Review of the Red Cross (IRRC), Enrico Natale, "Quand l'humanitaire commençait à faire son cinema: les films du CICR des années 1920s," 854 (2004): 415–37; Sébastian Farré and Yan Schubert, "Le délegué du CICR Maurice Rossel et les photographies de Theresienstadt," *Le Mouvement Social* 227 (2009): 65–83; Marina Meier and Daniel Palmieri, "Les Équivoques du Cinéma Humanitaire. L'exemple d'Helft helfen (1948)," in *La Guerre après la Guerre. Images et Construction des Imaginaires de Guerre dans l'Europe du XXe siècle*, ed. Christian Delporte (Paris, Nouveau Monde Éditions, 2010), 65–80; Fania Khan Mohammad and Daniel Palmieri, "Des morts et des nus: le regard du CICR sur la malnutrition extrême en temps de guerre (1940–1950)," in *Mémoires croisées autour des deux Guerres mondiales*, ed. Renée Dickason (Paris, Mare & Martin, 2012), 85–104; IRRC, Valérie Gorin, "Looking Back over 150 Years of Humanitarian Action: The Photographic Archives of the ICRC," 888 (2012): 1–31. None of these studies have considered more than one visual tool, whereas this chapter adopts a comparative approach.

8 Documents also refer to it as Palais Electoral.

9 Pictures of the exhibit are contained in AICRC, CR89/II, Exposition de la 10ème conference, no. 302–446, du 26.3.1921 au 10.10.1922.

10 AICRC, CR89.353, Letter by Etienne Clouzot, secrétaire général de la Xème conférence internationale de la Croix Rouge to Monsieur le Consul Général de Suède, Geneva, 13 April 1921.

11 *Compte rendu de la 10e Conférence internationale de la Croix-Rouge tenue à Genève, du 30 mars au 7 avril 1921* (Genève : Imprimerie Albert Renaud, 1921), 8235–6.

12 Paulmann, "Conjunctures," 223.

13 Two of the most relevant works on transnationalism are Pierre-Yves Saunier, "Circulations, connexions et espaces transnationaux" *Genèses* 57 (2004): 110–26; Patricia Clavin, "Defining Transnationalism," *Contemporary European History* 14, no. 4 (2005): 421–39.

14 This chapter is based on published and unpublished material, written and visual sources from the ICRC, postcards held at the Centre d'Iconographie Genevoise, articles published in the French- and German-speaking Swiss press, as well as comparative knowledge of other contemporary humanitarian organizations.

15 During the 1920s, the term "propaganda" did not yet have the negative meaning that totalitarian regimes gave it during the following decade.

16 IRRC, Brigitte Troyon and Daniel Palmieri, "The ICRC Delegate: an Exceptional Humanitarian Player?" 865 (2007): 103.

17 For the history of the ICRC, see David P. Forsythe, *Humanitarian Politics, the International Committee of the Red Cross* (Baltimore, MD: Johns Hopkins University Press, 1977); André Durand, *De Sarajevo à Hiroshima* (Geneva: Institut Henry-Dunant, 1978); Pierre Boissier, *De Solférino à Tsoushima* (Geneva: Institut Henry-Dunant, 1987); Jean-Claude Favez, avec la collaboration de Geneviève Billeter, *Une Mission Impossible? Le CICR, les Déportations et les Camps de Concentration Nazis* (Lausanne: Éditions Payot, 1988); Moorehead, *Dunant's Dream*; David P. Forsythe, *The Humanitarians, the International Committee of the Red Cross* (Cambridge: Cambridge University Press, 2005); Rainer Baundendistel, *Between Bombs and Good Intentions: The Red Cross and the Italo-Ethiopian War, 1935–1936* (New York: Berghahn Books, 2006). Catherine Rey-Schirr, *De Yalta à Dien Bien Phu: histoire du Comité international de la Croix-Rouge, 1945–1955* (Geneva: CICR Georg, 2007). Françoise Perret, François Bugnion, *De Budapest à Saigon: histoire du Comité international de la Croix-Rouge, 1956–1965* (Geneva: CICR Georg, 2009). At present, the ICRC still lacks an in-depth study, or due to the extent and difficulty of the task, a series, on the history of the organization, conceived and written by historians. There is also the need for a study that engages critically with the historiography of the ICRC.

18 L'Agence internationale des prisonniers de guerre. Le CICR dans la Première Guerre mondiale, Genève, CICR, 2007. AICRC, Rapport général du Comité international de la Croix-Rouge sur son activité de 1912 à 1920, Geneva.

19 IRRC, "La mission du Comité International de la Croix-Rouge pendant et après la guerre," signé par Edouard Neville, Adolphe D'Espine, Dr. F. Ferrière, and Alfred Gauthier, Genève, 27 novembre 1918, 75.

20 Ibid.

21 Francesca Piana, "L'humanitaire d'après-guerre: prisonniers de guerre et réfugiés russes dans la politique du Comité international de la Croix-Rouge et de la Société des Nations," *Relations Internationales* 151 (2012): 64.

22 Irène Herrmann, "Décripter la concurrence humanitaire: le conflit entre Croix-Rouge(s) après 1918," *Relations Internationales* 151 (2012): 91–102.

23 Hutchinson, *Champions of Charity*.

24 Piana, "Towards the International Refugee Regime."

25 Daniel Palmieri, "An Institution Standing the Test of Time? A Review of 150 Years of the History of the International Committee of the Red Cross," *International Review of the Red Cross* 94, no. 888 (2012): 1273–98, here 1278. Accessed 8 September 2014. http://www.icrc.org/eng/assets/files/review/2013/irrc-888-palmieri.pdf.

26 *L'expérience du Comité International de la Croix-Rouge en matière de secours internationaux* (Geneva: ICRC, 1925), 54–60. This volume is significant since it is the only source containing biographical information on the delegates of the ICRC for the early 1920s.

27 Opposition to the work of the ICRC came not only from the LRCS but also from Swiss actors. For instance, socialist and communist circles criticized the organization's financial support for the counter-revolutionary forces fighting against the Bolsheviks. See "Die Aktion!" *Basler Vorwärts Offizielles Organ der Kommunistischen Partei der Schweiz*, 17 March 1921, 1.

28 Archival material on the Propaganda Commission is scarce. There is a gap between the meetings of December 1920 and July 1922. Some references to the work of propaganda can be found in the minutes of the Committee of the ICRC.

29 AICRC, CR49/IV, 1, Letter to Chenevière, 30 April 1922.

30 AICRC, CR49/V, 2, Letter from Chenevière to Swiss Red Cross, 26 September 1922.

31 In 1919, the expenses of the ICRC included paying for the Agency for Prisoners of War, the staff working in Geneva, the delegates and their missions in the field, and the publication of the *Review*. AICRC, CR49, letter from the ICRC to the president and members of the High Federal Council, 9 September 1919.

32 Walter Lippmann quoted by Susan Sontag, "Photographs have the kind of authority over imagination today, which the printed word had yesterday, and the spoken word before that. They seem utterly real." Sontag, *Regarding the Pain of Others*, 22.

33 AICRC, CR49/1.1, Appel au people suisse, Geneva, June 1919.

34 AICRC, CR49/11, Procès-verbal, séance de la commission de [propagande], 18 décembre 1920.

35 "La croix rouge au cinéma," *Le Genevois*, 15 January 1921.

36 The *Bulletin* was created in 1869 and became the *International Review of the Red Cross* in 1919. It was published only in French until 1961, then also in English. The format of the *Review* remained unchanged over the period under consideration. Each issue typically began with a long article that was signed by either a delegate, depicting the work in the field, or by a member

of the Committee, and then focused on matters discussed at ICRC headquarters. Sometimes the organization published the day-to-day work accounts of the delegates, unsigned summaries on topics ranging from precise financial accounts to communications with the national societies, and book reviews on relevant issues. The *Review* usually concluded with a list of operations in the field, occasionally accompanied by a map and arranged according to the names of the delegates and the countries of operation. AICRC, CR76, L'activité du Comité International depuis la Conférence de Washington de la Croix Rouge jusqu'à la Guerre Mondiale.

37 Some pictures were published in *L'expérience du Comité International de la Croix-Rouge en matière de secours internationaux*, published in 1925 with 500 copies made. Prior to this, pictures were also published in Comité international de la Croix-Rouge, *L'Agence internationale des prisonniers de guerre: Genève, 1914–1918* ed. album établi sous la dir. d'Etienne Clouzot; avec la collab. de K. de Watteville; photogr. de Fréd. Boissonnas (Geneva: Sadag, 1919).

38 Gianni Haver, "La Presse Illustrée en Suisse, 1893–1945," in *Photos de Presse: Usage et Pratique*, ed. Gianni Haver (Lausanne: Antipodes, 2009), 39–65.

39 See Morgan, *Protestants and Photos*. "Cinq siècles d'imprimerie genevoise," *BBF*, 1983, 4, 439–440, http://bbf.enssib.fr/, last consulted 31 October 2013 ; Paul Chaix, *Recherches sur l'imprimerie à Genève de 1550 à 1564. Étude bibliographique, économique et littéraire* (Genève: E. Droz, 1954).

40 Irwin, *Making the World Safe*, 78–90.

41 AICRC, CR76, Procès verbal de la 10ème séance du 19 mars 1920.

42 AICRC, CR230, iconographie, Letter by Pictet, M 1734, 17 May 1946.

43 In total, Stauffenegger tidied up 4,700 photos and 536 clichés.

44 AICRC, CR230, iconographie, "La Documentation iconographique du Comité International de la Croix-Rouge," février 1948. Translated from French. Emphasis added.

45 These photos are to be found in the boxes and not in the photo library. They are attached to binders and could not be removed from the boxes. Davide Rodogno, "L'enquête du délégué du CICR qui déjoua un mensonge historique," *La Cité*, numéro du 28 octobre au 11 novembre 2011, 14–17.

46 When photographs came to the ICRC, they were labeled as "© Photothèque CICR (DR)." For the number of photographs that belonged to the organization, one will find "© CICR."

47 AICRC, CR 49, Commission de propagande, 4 November 1922.

48 The copyright of the movie belonged to the ICRC, and the YMCA officially agreed not to show it. AICRC, CR89, Contract between the cinema department of the YMCA in Warsaw and the ICRC, 26 February 1921.

49 This was the case for the American Relief Administration, the American Red Cross, the League of the Red Cross Societies, the League of Nations, the ICRC, the Union Internationale de Secours aux Enfants, and the Save the Children Fund.

50 See annex 1, programme du film, AICRC, CR 89, 277. AICRC, CR89, Gallati to the ICRC, 19 March 1921. AICRC, CR89, Gallati to the ICRC, 8 March 1921. "Nous vous permettons de vous faire remarquer que la saison n'est guère

propice à la prise d'un tel Film et que depuis quelque temps presque tous les transports de Russie reviennent vides ou avec un très petit nombre de prisonniers. Pour un Film d'une telle importance, qui doit surtout, vu son but humanitaire, faire une grande impression sur les spectateurs, il serait peut-être nécessaire de choisir un jour de beau temps, et attendre un transport moins nombreux."

51 In the mid-1990s, preoccupied with the deterioration of the material, the ICRC restored some of the movies from the 1920s in collaboration with the Memoriav, an association aimed at preserving Swiss audiovisual heritage. Humanitaire et cinema: films CICR des années 1920 (Humanitarian Action and Cinema. ICRC films in the 1920s), Memoriav, J.-B. Junod, 2005. For information on memoriav, see the website: www.memoriav.ch.

52 AICRC, CR89, de Reding to the ICRC, 8 March 1921.

53 AICRC, CR89.11, Burnier to the ICRC, 4 August 1921.

54 Technically, these movies are shot on 35 millimeter film. From the 1950s onward, ICRC movies were shot on 16 millimeter film and, since the 1980s, they are on video support.

55 Sometimes, the English text was a simplified version of the French one.

56 These references come from the movie *Organization of Help in Favor of the Hungarian Children in Budapest*.

57 AICRC, CR 49/IV, 1, Commission de propagande, procès verbal de la séance du 20 juillet 1922. AICRC, CR 49/IV, 1, Commission de propagande, procès verbal de la séance du 4 novembre 1922.

58 ACICR, MIS 15, Mission at Constantinople, Lucien Brunel, General Secretary of the Mission service to Georges Burnier, 4 April 1922.

59 AICRC, CR 49/IV, 1, Commission de propagande, procès verbal de la séance du 28 juillet 1922. See also the article by Davide Rodogno, "The American Red Cross and the International Committee of the Red Cross' Humanitarian Politics and Policies in Asia Minor and Greece (1922–1923)" *First World War Studies* 5:1 (2014): 83–99, here 90.

60 "The frank story of Aurora Mardiganian who survived while four million perished in Ravished Armenia," production made from scenario by Nora Waln for the American Committee for Armenian and Syrian Relief. Also see chapter by Balakian in this volume.

61 Brocher was a member of the Romand Secretariat for Swiss popular cinema and was co-opted by Etienne Clouzot – the former chief of the French Service, then co-director of the Triple Entente service of the International Prisoners of War Agency, member of the Propaganda Commission, head of the ICRC's secretariat, editor of the Review of the ICRC – who was in contact with the French avant-garde milieu. Dumont Hervé, *Histoire du cinéma suisse, films de fiction, 1896–1965* (Lausanne: Cinémathèque Suisse, 1987).

62 AICRC, CR 49/IV,1, Commission de propagande, procès verbal de la séance du 9 juillet 1923.

63 Ibid.

64 *L'Express*, 11 February 1921.

65 AICRC, CR49/11, clichés (larger photos, normally used for exposition and light projections), undated and unsigned. This document is of exceptional value for the purpose of the chapter.

66 *Manuel du délégué* (Geneva : Comité international de la Croix Rouge, 1972): 145–146.
67 IRRC, Troyon and Palmieri, "The ICRC Delegate."
68 See the chapters by Reeves, and Rodogno and David in this volume.
69 The ICRC has included some excerpts of its movies on the organization's website. http://www.icrc.org/eng/resources/documents/film/fcd13.htm, accessed 31 August 2014.
70 AICRC, B MIS 5/5, Gloor to the ICRC, 7 December 1920; Natale, "Quand l'humanitaire commençait à faire son cinema," 428.
71 AICRC, B, MIS 33.5/5180, Journal de voyage d'inspection de Frick, délégué général du Comité international de la Croix-Rouge, août-septembre 1921.
72 Kennedy, "Selling the Distant Other."
73 Malkki, "Speechless Emissaries," 378.
74 Halttunen, "Humanitarianism and the Pornography of Pain," 307.
75 Rozario, "'Delicious Horrors.'" See also Kennedy, "Selling the Distant Other," 1.
76 Taylor, *Body Horror*, 2.
77 AICRC, CR49/11, clichés, undated and unsigned.
78 See chapter by Grant in this volume.
79 Roland Cosandey, *La famine en Russie 1921–1923. Une filmographie documentée* (Perpignan: Institut Jean Vigo, 1998).
80 See chapter by Fehrenbach in this volume.
81 Manzo, "Imagining Humanitarianism," 634.
82 See chapters by Curtis, Grant, and Fehrenbach in this volume.
83 See the exhibit "Mythes et Mystères. Le symbolisme et les artistes suisses," Kunstmuseum, Berne, 2013. An aesthetic approach might also fruitfully consider ICRC photographs and movies in relation to the Russian avant-garde photography of 1920s and 1930s. In the Soviet context, images were also used as a tool of communication and information, and aimed at a large audience. Professor Alexander Alberro suggested this research perspective while commenting on the ICRC's photographs and during the classes he taught on Russian avant-garde photography in the "Histories of Photography" course at Barnard College in spring 2014.
84 There were only four women working for the ICRC in the aftermath of the First World War: Marguerite Frick-Cramer, Pauline Chaponnière-Chaix, Suzanne Ferrière, and Lucie Odier. See Diego Fiscalini, *Des Elites aux service d'une cause humanitaire: le Comité International de la Croix-Rouge* (Geneva: University of Geneva masters' thesis, 1985).

7

Children and Other Civilians

Photography and the Politics of Humanitarian Image-Making

Heide Fehrenbach

For over a century, humanitarian appeals have increasing relied on images of children to raise public awareness and funds to alleviate human suffering. American photographer Thérèse Bonney's wartime image of an exhausted French boy fleeing Nazi bombardment is a case in point (Figure 7.1). Collapsed on an improvised bed of burlap bundles, the worldly goods of refugees-on-the-move, the boy's small hunched body dominates the frame. His head hangs heavily forward, drawing our eyes to his exposed legs and rounding his shoulders to provide us a peek at the scene beyond. Although mute, his image strains to tell us something about the undeserved effects of war and the vulnerability of the displaced. If only we could properly decipher it, it suggests, we could attend to its message and his needs.

In recent years, social scientists have noted, and probed, the prevalence of children in contemporary humanitarian imagery. Political scientist Kate Manzo has explored how development NGOs mobilize an "iconography" that draws on the cultural meanings of modern Western childhood to project institutional values and to cultivate a humanitarian identity via strategies of "innocence-based solidarity."[1] Anthropologist Liisa Malkki has examined "humanitarian modes of imagining world community" since 1945, arguing that "the moral figure of the child" has been used to manipulate emotion and to foster a "*self-conscious* globalism" grounded in notions of a depoliticized shared humanity."[2] Sociologist Laura Suski

I would like to thank Kevin Grant, Davide Rodogno, Silvia Salvatici, and graduate students Ian Burns, Nicole Dressler, Krista Albers, and Michael Hall for useful criticism and feedback on this essay.

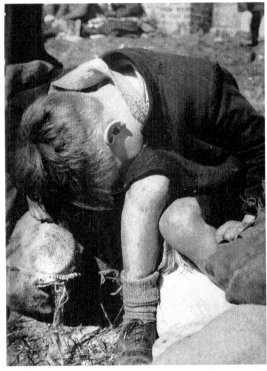

FIGURE 7.1. "… it seemed almost impossible to trudge on." Thérèse Bonney, *Europe's Children, 1939 to 1943* (New York: self-published, 1943).

has suggested, more bluntly, that humanitarianism might well "require a concept of childhood innocence to legitimate it."[3] To the extent that the scholars of humanitarianism have engaged these insights, they have tended to apply them, rather than interrogate them in historical terms. This chapter examines what are arguably the formative years of humanitarianism's "iconography of childhood" – the late nineteenth century through the two world wars – tracing aspects of its historical development in the visual and rhetorical practices of politically diverse actors in Britain, Europe, and the United States. It explores the emerging conventions of humanitarian photography in relation to a broader range of photographic genres and practices in order to speculate about how Western viewers' experience of, and familiarity with, other photographic forms may have affected their visual and emotional response to humanitarian images of suffering.

Due to its brevity, this chapter is an exploratory and highly selective attempt at historical excavation.[4] Its ambitions are modest, yet nonetheless essential: first, to establish a loose chronology of when humanitarian imagery came to be dominated by a focus on the symbolic figure of the child. Second, to chart some visual tropes that informed, or emerged from, this practice in a range of distribution venues, including illustrated books, organizational newsletters, and pictorial magazines. Third, to suggest the political valences of child-centered imagery as well as the extent to which it became a shared cultural strategy across media formats and political-ideological camps in an extended era of world war (1910s–40s). I conclude by raising the question of whether the "humanitarian eye" that developed in this period, based upon the moral training of vision through photography and other media, was a gendered one.

My chronological argument is straightforward and can be summarized up front: humanitarian photography emerged in the era of Western imperialism and was informed by the conventions of late nineteenth-century photography and journalism. At first, children appeared in photos in social and familial groupings. By the turn of the twentieth century, suffering children were increasingly pictured with mothers in variations of the well-known Christian tropes of Madonna and Child or the Pietà. Only after the First World War, as famine ravaged Central Europe and postrevolutionary Russia, did the images of the lone suffering child proliferate. This trend intensified, spreading through photo-stories and photojournalistic practice during World War II, and was employed by both sides in the European conflict. After 1945, images of children became ubiquitous in the official publications of UNESCO and UNICEF, in Western press coverage of conflict and crisis, and in the fundraising campaigns of religious and secular NGOs.

Children in Social Context

When children initially appeared in photographs used for humanitarian campaigns, they were typically located in European colonies and depicted in the company of indigenous adults. Early humanitarian photography had roots in ethnographic travel literature, missionary photography, and the internationalizing "new journalism" of the 1880s. As a result, humanitarian photography was shaped by the characteristics and conventions of those genres. All were grounded in the epistemological authority of the "eyewitness account." All employed photography to capture specific elements of social life deemed noteworthy or inadequately expressible in words. And all, if subsequently used for humanitarian purposes, included firsthand narratives of suffering.[5]

Not all of the photographs employed for humanitarian purposes were originally created with that aim in mind. As Christina Twomey has shown, British military officer Willoughby Wallace Hooper's specific motives for taking photographs of famine victims in southern India in 1876–8 are unclear, though they were part of a photographic study of India.[6] What is clear is that they were subsequently appropriated by Indian Famine Relief Committees in England, Scotland, and Australia and reproduced, circulated, and sold for fundraising purposes. Twenty years later, F. H. S. Merewether, Reuter's special famine correspondent, published his *Tour through the Famine Districts of India*. Despite its ostensible purpose to chronicle the Indian Famine of 1899–1901, the book reads like an ethnographic and architectural travelogue. While it includes photographic depictions and narrative descriptions of native suffering, these are interspersed with discussions of Merewether's own personal inconveniences and pleasures on the journey. In narrating his visit to "God-forsaken" Banda, for example, he frames his description of his visit to an orphanage of starving children, who had lost their parents and were reduced to "miserable relics of childhood … resembling apes rather than human beings," with complaints about the discomforts of local transport and reference to his subsequent dinner and "pleasant chat" with a British major who regaled him with an amusing tale of establishing British authority among the locals. The construction and flow of Merewether's narrative is jarring to the modern reader, in part because it is so closely aligned to the genre of ethnographic travel writing. His attention to the social and individual effects of starvation is infrequent and episodic: one of many foci rather than the moral heart of the narrative.[7]

Historian James Vernon has argued that photos like Hooper's and Merewether's were part of a larger trend in the print media of the period. By the mid-nineteenth century, journalists and correspondents increasingly used photographs, eyewitness accounts, and individualized narratives of suffering to report on "hunger" as "news."[8] In the process, they established it as a worrisome "discovery" and "pressing social problem" – in the Empire as well as urban slums at home – that required redress, whether through charitable private aid or state-sponsored action.[9] Hooper's and Merewether's photos helped to construct the visual trope of hunger we have come to recognize through its visible effect on the human body: jutting ribs, bloated bellies, stick-like arms and legs, listless poses, wan and pinched faces, blank direct gazes.[10]

Yet Hooper's and Merewether's photos share other attributes that distinguish them as early representations of hunger. They are posed group portraits, mostly a mix of adults and children, and ethnographic in their composition. The photographers favored long- to medium-long range shots, with subjects arranged against a local building; in some, there is a depth of field that gives the impression of a village backdrop (see Curtis, Figure 1.1).[11] In addition to organized groupings of starving villagers, we discern details of buildings and construction methods, evidence of social life. The children, that is to say, are represented as part of a distinctive culture and community. Although they might be orphans, they exist – and indeed are positioned – in a specific social context in relation to other individuals. Although they suffer, they are neither abandoned nor alone. In visual terms, they are socially and culturally embedded in their environs. Social relations, though not necessarily explicated, are nonetheless there to see.[12]

That does not mean that sentimental forms of visual address were absent. Perhaps Hooper's photos were attractive for humanitarian purposes, regardless of his original motives in taking them, because he posed his subjects to evoke family relationships.[13] We do not know whether the subjects in his photographs were related; but in some photos, starving individuals were grouped in ways that suggest the intimacy of family bonds. Compositionally, the figures evoke the conventions of a middle-class family portrait (see Twomey, Figure 2.2). The father figure centers the group and watches over it from his higher vantage point on a stool; the mother figure appears on his right, the daughter figures to his left, with the elder one posed as though stroking or tending to a younger sister. The composition of the photo evokes both a patriarchal family structure and the affective bonds that undergird it. By Western standards, the family unit is underdressed and in visible distress: the father's gaunt upper body is a geometric play of light and shadow as he holds himself upright between staff and pole; the mother and child are supine; none has the energy to confront the camera's lens with open eyes. The photo addressed its viewers in a dual manner: through the contemporary conventions of ethnographic photography and of family portraiture. Viewers likely moved back and forth between both modes, attending to signs of the distant exotic as well as the intimacy of the familial. The latter would have been the more powerful and familiar narrative: one middle-class viewers could identify with, the one they would find emotionally affecting.[14]

After all, by the last decades of the nineteenth century, middle-class families in Britain, Europe, the United States, and beyond were increasingly having their own likenesses fixed by professional photographers in order to frame and display them in their homes. Photographic portraits signaled and celebrated the family: its additions by birth and marriage, its subtractions by illness, accident, and death.[15] In the Victorian era, photos were paired with embroidery or a snippet of hair to memorialize a departed love one. More than mere images, such photos had "brute" physicality, a "comforting solidity" that served the grieving as visual and tactile talismans.[16] Even those of limited means found themselves summoning a new breed of photographer, on call twenty-four hours a day, to capture the final breath, or newly expired body, of an ailing child in order to claim a visible treasured remembrance of their loved one – often posed lifelike with surviving siblings – before consigning her to the grave.[17] Hooper's photo, and others like it, should be read in relation to these popular photographic practices that had already emerged by the 1850s; it likely resonated with Western viewers because of them. Hooper's photo situated starving Indians as a family unit, yet suggested its imminent demise.[18]

The social and familial framing of children extended beyond photographic depictions of famine in India. By the turn of the twentieth century, in fact, family tropes increasingly animated the emotional address of humanitarian photographs involving children. Western viewers, drawing on both sentimentalized notions of parent-child bonds as well as photographic practices that help to construct and express these, likely read such photos in terms of "love" and "loss," in large measure because they were encouraged to. Two examples will have to suffice.

British missionary Alice Harris's famous 1904 photograph of Nsala contemplating the remains of his five-year-old daughter on the porch of her Congo mission is a poignant case in point (see Grant, Figure 3.2). Harris's photo of Nsala is carefully composed as the intimate scene of a father's quiet grief as, head bowed, he gazes at the small severed hand and foot.[19] To his right stand two somber young men, facing the camera and observing the tragic scene. Their frontal stance and their body language (one stands with hands on hips, the other with arms crossed at chest) confront the viewer as if to say: "This man is suffering; his daughter has been slain. What will you do about this?" In the background, at a distance, stands an indistinct figure of a child, just barely legible, as if a phantom vision of Nsala's loss.[20] Reproduced in E. D. Morel's 1904 book *King Leopold's Rule in Africa*, the photo was accompanied by a caption noting that this awful scene connoted yet a larger horror: the murder of Nsala's wife and son, along with his daughter, all of whom were cannibalized by sentries serving the Anglo-Belgian Rubber Company. His gaze, viewers come to realize after reading the caption, was locked on all that remained of his family. The photo's actual, or at least anticipated, effect must have been substantial since it was one of the most widely circulated, exhibited and reproduced of the campaign.[21]

Although Harris's photo and Morel's caption were grounded in sentimental tropes of a father's familial and filial loss, it is important to note that the photo's out-of-door setting, natural panorama, and accompanying narrative of cannibalism also evoked conventions of ethnographic photography. Like the photos of famine in India, Harris's photo too mixed photographic conventions and modes of address. All of the Congo photos mobilized for humanitarian purposes condemned the brutal and exploitative practices of unfree labor under Belgian King Leopold. Yet most focused on the violence and injury perpetrated on *adult* bodies. Other photos featured individual portraits of young workers and children whose hands were hacked off as punishment for unmet quotas or insufficient productivity. And although these latter examples were in portrait form, many adhered to the classificatory photos of professional ethnographers and physical anthropologists, down to the use of white cloth as backdrop to allow physical features, in this case severed hands and arms, to register more crisply. So although the viewer is confronted with individual faces, the repeated instances of similar shots – and their mosaic arrangement in the case of Twain's book (see Twomey, Figure 2.5) – pioneered a new ethnographic type: "victims of colonial violence" and, in particular, of unfree labor practices.[22]

My second example is drawn from the same period and is again British in origin. Instead of spotlighting grieving fathers and dead families, these humanitarian photos emphasized grieving mothers and dying children. In December 1900, Quaker reformer and pacifist Emily Hobhouse traveled to South Africa to investigate and protest British treatment of Afrikaner women and children interned in concentration camps during the South African war (1899–1902). These were white families of Dutch origin in the Orange Free State and South African Republic whose farmsteads had been razed by British troops due to concerns they were surreptitiously supplying their menfolk-in-arms and, in effect, aiding Afrikaner guerrilla action against the British. British officials characterized such scorched-earth tactics and military actions against noncombatants as "necessities of war" and called camp inhabitants "refugees." Hobhouse toured the camps in the first months of 1901, filed an eyewitness unillustrated report with Parliament, and helped found the South African Women and Children Distress Fund. In 1902, she published a book titled *The Brunt of War and Where It Fell,* which included nine photographs collected, but not taken, by her.[23]

Hobhouse pressed British officials to improve camp conditions and provisioning in order to staunch the high mortality rate among inhabitants.[24] She took her quest public and was met by hostile criticism: her country, after all, was at war. Ultimately her campaign compelled officials to improve camp conditions, but not until tens of thousands of Afrikaner women and children, and their black African workers and servants, segregated into separate camps, had died of malnutrition, dysentery, and disease. Her book, released at the end of the war, serves as a detailed eyewitness account of life and death at the British camps, complete with statistics, and a polemic criticizing British conduct of war. The photos focus on white camp inhabitants only; no residents of the black camps were portrayed.

The most affecting photos and narratives appeared in the chapter titled "Women in 1901." Hobhouse opens it with a large group shot of nearly two dozen women and children lined up against a backdrop of "camp huts": an image that suggests the gendered and generational composition of the population as well as their rudimentary conditions of daily life.[25] The next photo, entitled "The Last of Seven," is a medium-long shot of two women in long, dark dresses confronting the camera directly, faces shadowed by the brims of their dark bonnets. Tents and onlookers are arrayed in the background. In front of the woman on the right stands a young boy; her hands rest on his shoulders and are lit, along with his face, by the bright sun. He, the reader is told, is her last surviving child; six others died in the camp. This bleak fact is underscored by the somber tone of the photo with its dark, indistinct figures set starkly against arid earth in the harsh midday sun. Subsequent photos continue the theme of maternal worry and loss, such as the grave-faced women kneeling next to a seated, malnourished child against a backdrop of tents and parched, littered landscape.

A compositional oddity in the volume is a medium-close shot of a placid, malnourished child sitting on the lap of a woman whose head is cropped by the top of the frame (Figure 7.2). Its caption, "Feeling the brunt of war," evokes the book's title and suggests the effects of British military policy on children, cared for by despairing mothers who could do little to save them. In this, as in the other photos, the bond between mother and child is visually represented as intimate and intact: the mother's presence is protective, holding or touching the child. The absence, or indistinctness, of the mothers' faces suggests that the photos illustrate

FEELING THE BRUNT OF THE WAR. 1901

FIGURE 7.2. Feeling the brunt of war (1901). Emily Hobhouse, *The Brunt of War and Where it Fell* (London: Methuen, 1902).

a specific experience as well as a general problem: individual fates are interchangeable. Here, the mother's body becomes backdrop and the moral center of the photo: her dark clothing – reminiscent of mourning dress – allows the viewer to better discern the starving body of her pale child. Her maternal presence fills the frame, giving the photo a static and monumental quality, effectively closing off the view of the background and training our eyes on the child-in-crisis and the mother-child bond.

Although funerary photos were taken in the camps for families' private use, Hobhouse did not publish any of these in her book. Nor did she use a now-famous shot of the severely emaciated Lizzie van Zyl, lying near naked and alone in a camp hospital bed shortly before she died.[26] Hobhouse had befriended the young girl and obtained the photo (likely taken by camp inhabitant and photographer Mr. De Klerk) "out of affection for the child." She did not circulate the photo publicly, although about a month after Lizzie's death in May 1901, it was published by *The New Age* in London as a depiction of wartime suffering. Six months later, the pro-government press, along with Arthur Conan Doyle, used it to denounce Hobhouse and to suggest that Lizzie's death was intentional: the result of maternal neglect, not camp conditions – a charge Hobhouse vigorously countered. At issue was who was to blame for child mortality: were Afrikaner women devoted and loving mothers, deserving of viewer concern, or something more unnatural and sinister? The photo of Lizzie showed a lone suffering child, with gaunt, empty gaze and no mother present. After its pro-government propagandistic use, Hobhouse chose to include it in her book but was blocked by her publishers who considered it "too painful for publication." In reporting this fact, Hobhouse asked readers whether "it is right to shrink from a typical representation, however distressing, of suffering which others have to endure, and which has been brought about by a sequence of events for which we are partly responsible."[27]

Hobhouse's humanitarian campaign targeted her own government and criticized its wartime behavior toward noncombatants. "Never before have women and children been so warred against," she wrote:

Is it to be a precedent for future wars, or is it to be denounced, … by every humane person of every creed and every tongue, denounced as a 'method of barbarism' which must never be resorted to again – the whole cruel sequence of the burning, eviction, the rendering destitute, the deporting and finally the re-concentrating all of the non-combatants of the country, with no previous preparation for their sustenance.[28]

Using photographs and narrating them with the experiences of individual women and children she met at the camps, as well as detailed reporting on failures of provisioning and medical care, Hobhouse skirted the question of the women's "innocence." Rather, she focused on the issue of "civilized" conduct in war – a concern that informed the 1899 Hague Convention.[29] Hobhouse, a woman, stressed that locked away in camps were mothers and their dying children rendered vulnerable by British military policy and a fatal lack of planning. Her book aimed to show that

Lizzie's and other children's deaths resulted not from maternal malice or "military necessity," as her critics claimed, but could have been avoided with more humane and "civilized" policy and planning.[30] As a result, she argued, the English public as a whole shared the responsibility for needless suffering and loss of life.[31]

Mothers and children became a common narrative and visual trope for relief efforts during the First World War, as evidenced by the posters and printed matter circulated by Near East Relief on behalf of Armenians and other Christians who survived massacres and mass deportations by Turkish forces or were subject to population exchanges following the war. As Peter Balakian has shown, the Near East Relief's public campaigns favored sanitized, sentimentalized depictions of mothers and children or young girls rendered in pastel tones by the hand of an artist (Balakian, Figures 4.3, 4.4) over the cold gray tones of the atrocity photograph. Atrocity photos, while not completely absent, were circulated in books and specialized newsletters that were viewed privately rather than in public.[32] Here too we see evidence of repeated use of the mother-child trope. Such photos sought to prick the viewer's heart and conscience by emphasizing the failure or insufficiency of a mother's protection through no fault of her own: she was depicted as a victim, along with her children, in death (Balakian, Figure 4.5) or in mourning over the bodies of massacred children.[33]

Atrocity photos were used to raise viewers' ire as well as their sympathy, and to make a broader political point. Henry Morgenthau, former U.S. Ambassador to Turkey, published an essay, "The Greatest Horror in History," in the *American Red Cross Magazine* in March 1918. Included among the illustrations was the photo of a mother with the sheathed corpses of her five sons, as well as a group shot of "starving children" with a caption explaining that they were "sold" to strangers by desperate mothers hoping to rescue them from certain death. In his essay, Morgenthau insisted that the German government shared responsibility for the Ottoman-authored atrocity since they *"could have prevented it."* He argued that it was now the duty of Christians of Europe and America to make certain that Armenians "be freed from the yoke of Turkish rule."[34] The atrocity images served a dual purpose as evidence and as emotional provocation: they were to provide the factual and visceral motivation for readers to respond to his political plea for the impending peace settlement and an altered postwar order. The "diabolical cruelties" against Armenian, Syrian and Greek Christians must be remembered and punished, he insisted; their perpetrators must be neutralized and prevented from victimizing "fine, old, civilized" Christian minorities ever again. Like Hobhouse's campaign against her own government, the photos in Morgenthau's essay were used to censure wartime behavior – in this case, the enemy's – by depicting it, through a sentimental lens, as the wanton destruction of the mother-child bond and the very possibility of maternal nurture. Such photographs sought to cultivate sympathy for noncombatants, summon viewers' moral indignation, and ignite a sense of moral duty to effect political reform or political action. The sentimental object was depoliticized; the purpose in displaying such images was not.

Mere Children: Save the Children Fund

A different type of politics was embraced by Save the Children Fund (SCF), which advertised itself as an "avowedly non-political fund" in the aftermath of the First World War.[35] Founded in London in May 1919 by sisters Eglantyne Jebb and Dorothy Buxton, its purpose was to provide relief for children living in famine-stricken areas of Central and Eastern Europe and the Near East, including former enemy nations such as Germany and Austria, whose food supplies were constricted by an ongoing British blockade.[36] Jebb is famous for having distributed a leaflet in Trafalgar Square in April 1919 featuring the image of a deformed Austrian girl, with a large head and withered body, whose physical development was stunted by severe malnutrition. In fact, the leaflet and image did not initially cause a stir; Jebb's subsequent arrest and trial did.[37] That experience encouraged Jebb and Buxton to develop an effective strategy for attracting public support for their otherwise unpopular cause of European famine relief. Already active in the Fight the Famine Council, an elite political pressure group composed of feminists, pacifists, and liberal internationalists, they resolved to found a separate organization devoted to the nurture and well-being of "the child."[38] This exclusive focus on children was fueled by principles, politics, and a quest for publicity and rhetorical persuasiveness: if "war stops" for "wounded soldiers," Jebb declared, it "must even more respect the innocent child."[39] Jebb conceived of the humanitarian focus on children as a way to build goodwill among former enemy nations and populations: feeding and socializing younger generations was a practical and symbolic investment in a better postwar future. Her vision was to use the common denominator of children to transcend national and ethnic hostilities, foster international cooperation, and secure lasting peace.[40]

Children had already become a focus for reformers and protection societies, medical professionals, social and child-welfare workers in the United States and Europe in the years leading up to the First World War. All understood the importance of childhood and advocated its recognition as a unique formative phase of human life marked by specific normative stages that required nurture, attention, and oversight. Children were identified as "objects of development" to be educated and fed in public schools, protected in, or from, work. They became a "site of investment" by parents and the state: a future resource for one's family, economy, and national polity. Eglantyne Jebb's innovation was to suggest children's utility beyond the nation: she recast them as universal symbols and the valued building blocks of a peaceful, internationalist future.[41]

Jebb's humanitarian work was initially at odds with British foreign policy and its protracted economic blockade of Germany and Austria. Her vision was a hard sell to the British press and public, which reacted with hostility to the suggestion that the suffering of their recent enemy – even in diminutive form– should attract Britons' concern or cash. Already during the war, Buxton had been informed and alarmed about the dire health of European children; evidence suggests that she, as a mother and a Quaker, genuinely believed the SCF to be engaged in nonpolitical work.[42] Her sister Eglantyne was substantially less sentimental about children but recognized a strategic tool when she saw one. Mounting her own defense at her trial on 15 May 1919, she argued that she should not be convicted for distributing leaflets under the 1914 Defense of the Realm Act since they were humanitarian materials, not "political propaganda." Although she was ultimately found guilty as charged, she scored a moral success, receiving the reduced sentence of a £5 fine along with a £5 donation to her fund from none other than the chief prosecutor. The formal foundation of the organization occurred just four days later in a well-attended famine relief meeting at Royal Albert Hall.[43]

Over course of the next two years, Jebb would experiment with modern fundraising methods, drawing charges of sensationalism from prominent supporters when she chose to place full-page ads in newspapers to attract donors. Such tactics nonetheless succeeded in securing cross-class support. Jebb's determined rhetorical and pictorial focus on children's "beautiful innocence" and shared humanity masked the radical political roots of the famine relief campaign; moreover, it assisted in rendering SCF's humanitarianism both an extension of Britons' imperial duty and an expression of their global influence.[44]

The *Record of the Save the Children Fund,* the organization's primary public face, published a range of photos.[45] Only one, early on, featured a disheveled mother and her children, squatting inside a bedframe sans mattress: "an *actual* photograph showing the condition of destitution and utter helplessness under which some families are living ... in parts of the Famine Area. All bedding has been sold to secure mere Fragments of food." In 1920, the first year of publication, reports from the field were punctuated by photographs that omitted mothers in favor of lone children: "Doomed!" read one headline over the head-shot of a "Russian boy" who "must die unless food is sent quickly."[46] Another, titled "Orphaned and Destitute," showed a pair of "little Armenians who might be saved" standing against a stone wall, the hand of the taller boy resting protectively on the shoulder of his younger brother. It was accompanied by a report on a children's camp in Cyprus housing 650 such children.[47]

By late 1921, images of the Volga famine took precedence. Save the Children had followed Herbert Hoover's American Relief Administration into Russia to address the worsening famine provoked by drought and exacerbated by disrupted agricultural production and food distribution accompanying World War I, the Bolshevik Revolution, and the subsequent civil war.[48] Multiple full-body shots of somber, malnourished individual children or groups of children, inadequately clothed or naked from the waist up, appeared from Saratov Province in the *Record* that fall. Just before Christmas 1921, a posed group photo of nine Tatar refugee children, likely between the ages of four and ten, accompanied a poem by the British pacifist writer Israel Zangwill:

> Alas! For the wizened infants
> > Sucking at stone-dry breasts;
> Alas! For the babies writhing
> > In the grip of plagues and pests.
> They are fever-stricken and famished,
> > They are rotten of skin and bone;
> Yet their mothers must die and leave them
> > To suffer and starve alone;
> And any one of these children
> > Might be your very own.[49]

Sentimental poetry and artwork that celebrated the middle-class ideal of childhood, or focused on its reprehensible absence, frequently accompanied famine images. The mix of literary and visual forms sought to disarm critics' refusal of relief for "Bolshevik babies" by invoking the natural (and therefore universal) vulnerability of the young sufferers and convincing readers of their own moral duty, as parents, to protect children wherever they may be.[50]

Early in 1921, a set of striking baby food advertisements appeared by London-based companies that were reprised in the *Record* over the course of the year. A full-paged Mellin's Foods ad (Figure 7.3) was prominently placed on the opening pages of the magazine and featured before and after images of a reclining baby – putatively the same child – depicted first in a severely malnourished state and then, some months later, as a thriving well-fed infant. The ad by Virol – which claimed that its product was used "in large quantities in more than 2,500 hospitals and public health institutions" – contained a similar set of before and after photos and cited a report from a University of Cambridge laboratory attributing Virol's "remarkable results" to the presence of "Vitamines [*sic*] essential to growth and development."[51] A subsequent issue of the *Record* published this scientific endorsement of Virol and vitamins as editorial content rather than advertising copy, blurring the lines between commercial and humanitarian enterprises.

The "before and after" presentation was already a long-standing photographic convention and rhetorical strategy employed by abolitionists, missionaries, and child reformers since at least the 1860s. For fundraising purposes, such groups would sell *cartes-de-visite* photos, printed on stiff paper, showing posed studio shots of slave children "as we found them" along with a post-liberation shot of the same children, now well-groomed and respectable, after having been redeemed and educated by the reformers. Similar before and after photos were sold in London in the 1870s to benefit Dr. Barnardo homes that reformed street children, training them to be productive members of the workforce.[52] Save the Children Fund also used the convention in the *Record* in early 1922 in a feature titled "The Deadly Contrast." In the first photo, the frozen body of a dead child sits upright, wrapped in rags with cap askew, tucked into the outdoor corner of a brick building. The second shot shows a small child, snug in a jacket with a fur-trimmed hood, sitting at a table and slurping soup from a pot with large spoon. Behind him loom two white SCF logos, framing the child and broadcasting the organization's life-saving relief work.[53] By the early twentieth century, before and after photography had become a shared rhetorical strategy used by nonprofit groups and for-profit businesses to advertise the effectiveness of their humanitarian missions and commercial products.

The Mellin's Food ad – and the Fund's editorial endorsement of Virol's vitamin-packed formula – linked the domestic and international projects

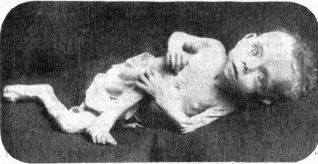
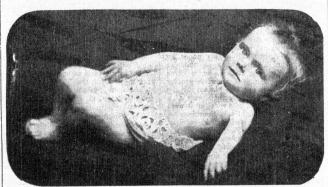
FIGURE 7.3. Mellin's Food ad. *The Record of Save the Children Fund*, June 1, 1921. Cadbury Research Library: Special Collections, SCF Box A670, University of Birmingham.

of postwar recovery, centering both on the proper nutrition and nurture of "the wasting child." The ad, with its savvy blend of sensationalism and scientific expertise, echoed Jebb's own strategy of combining shocking images with expert reports authored by the respected medical doctors and public health officials she recruited for fact-finding missions abroad.[54] Such reports convinced Jebb that while starving adults, once fed, could "recover vitality later on," children were a special case. If their normal physical and psychological development was interrupted, it could not be readily put right but would have negative lifelong individual and social effects. Emerging medical models of child development and welfare thus informed SCF's humanitarian mission and imagery.[55] The Mellin's Food ad – and its prominent placement in SCF's magazine – broadcast the message that child hunger and malnutrition were shared human problems that required scientific solutions and provoked maternal distress both domestically, within Britain, and beyond it. This message, which connected the experiences of underfed children at home and abroad, may help explain the organization's success in attracting donations from workers as well as the wealthy.[56] When it came to endangered infants the world over, Cambridge University scientists affirmed, there was but one universal cure: vitamin-rich baby food.[57]

The *Record*'s visual shift to lone and orphaned children was accompanied by a new fundraising initiative, perhaps SCF's most famous: the child-adoption subscription. In November 1920, donors could choose between making a one-time pledge to feed "suffering children in the Famine districts" or becoming a "godparent" by contributing to a child's in-country care abroad on a monthly basis. Initially no photos of children were published, but gradually "adopt a child" photos did appear scattered throughout the publication. Unlike the children-in-distress shots that accompanied reports from the field, these photos were respectable headshots of unnamed children, properly clothed and groomed. Sometimes they appeared individually; other times a number of individual portraits were artfully grouped together using a graphic frame. Usually, children were identified by nationality; only in the late 1920s was a first name supplied: "Juliska is a Hungarian child now in her fifth year suffering from rickets and chronic catarrh due to undernourishment."[58]

If SCF invoked the universal category of "the child" as a protracted stage of human development requiring protection and nurture, its adopt-a-child fundraising and individual portraits gestured to that other, more "priceless" child: the reader's own.[59] Since the photos appeared with vague captions and impersonal reports from the field rather than detailed stories of individual children's circumstances, their emotional pull was dependent on the strength of the beseeching child's portrait read against the reader's accumulated knowledge of conditions in the "famine district."[60] After the worst of the famine years had passed, the children's faces, unanimated by gripping narratives, remained but two-dimensional images on the page and contributions fell off. By the late 1920s, SCF addressed this issue by launching a "choose your child" campaign, which put donors "in direct touch" with children. After indicating a preferred sex and nationality for "their" child, contributors received the child's photo and the possibility of exchanging letters with her. "Very touching and interesting letters are frequently received," claimed the insert, dangling the promise of individual stories to bring the adorable faces to life.[61]

Feed the Children, Save the Revolution

In February 1922 the New York-based magazine *Soviet Russia*, published by Friends of Soviet Russia (FSR), ran this photo (Figure 7.4) of a starving child to publicize the Volga famine. The goal was to encourage reader donations for relief and thereby counter the efforts of "bourgeois" organizations like Herbert Hoover's American Relief Administration. In the ten months between late September 1921 and July 1922, the FSR fundraising drive collected over a half million dollars.[62] Donations poured in from individuals, families, and groups of workers from around the United States. Part of Internationale Arbeiterhilfe (IAH, International Worker's Relief) led by the prominent German communist Willi Münzenberg in Berlin, the American fund drive was wildly successful, especially compared to its German counterpart. Perhaps this was not surprising given the desperate straits of the postwar German economy following military defeat in 1918.[63] Yet even in the United States, public support for humanitarian causes abroad was beginning to wane after enthusiastic wartime support for the relief work of the American Red Cross.[64]

The photo was unique among the images in *Soviet Russia*: it was one of only a handful of photographs for famine relief published in the magazine over the course of the year, and the only one that featured a lone starving child. Although uncredited, the photo was taken on behalf of the International Committee of the Red Cross.[65] Why were so few famine photos published? Perhaps it was due to difficulty securing such shots; after all, Willi Münzenberg complained numerous times during the same period that his fundraising efforts in Germany were hampered by a lack

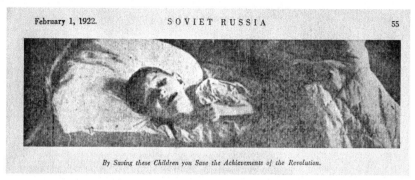

February 1, 1922.   SOVIET RUSSIA   55

By Saving these Children you Save the Achievements of the Revolution.

FIGURE 7.4. "Save the Children, Save the Revolution." *Soviet Russia* magazine, 1 February 1922, p. 55.

of photos, which he urged Soviet officials to send. In his case, when a packet of photos was finally dispatched in January 1922, it got lost in transit and never arrived in Berlin.[66] Yet *Soviet Russia* proved willing to publish shots taken by the ICRC. It also regularly published a range of non-famine-related photos. So the paucity of famine photos was likely the result of editorial choice rather than a consideration of access, cost, or aversion to the medium.[67] That does not mean that famine-related imagery was lacking. Both *Soviet Russia* magazine and the German branch of the IAH drew upon stark graphic imagery – in this case a dramatic woodcut of an anguished mother and dying child by the Berlin-based artist Käthe Kollwitz – to dramatize starvation and the need for response.[68] The magazine prominently displayed the work of a number of left-leaning artists on its covers from December 1921 until late 1922.[69] In every case, the artwork portrayed either a secular pietà of a starving mother and child (Figure 7.5), a mother slinging her babies into the Volga River, or groups of starving children. The famine, that is to say, was envisioned through the plight of mothers and children and of children alone. The graphic imagery provided a visceral and narrative punch. Yet the visual style of choice was not photographic realism, with its visual representation of *actual* individuals and their specific idiosyncratic physical and emotional states. Rather, the imagery showcased the revolutionary aesthetics of German Expressionism and Soviet Proletkult, already evident in the political posters and publications of workers' parties and organizations, to construct a generalized narrative of dying mothers and children.[70] In *Soviet Russia* magazine, short text periodically appeared noting that "the dying are eating their dead … mothers are drowning their children to silence their heartrending cries for bread," or that orphaned children were begging for

"*HUNGER*"

A striking poster designed by Käte Kollwitz, a well known German artist, who is no longer a stranger to readers of SOVIET RUSSIA. All over the world, not only in Russia, well-known artists and cartoonists have found in the Famine a stimulus to help in the work of appealing to the masses for aid. Volume VII of SOVIET RUSSIA contains many such artistic contributions. The front cover of our last issue (September 15), which was particularly effective, was the work of Lydia Gibson, an American artist.

FIGURE 7.5. Käthe Kollwitz, "Hunger." *Soviet Russia* magazine, 1 October 1922, p. 197.

money to bury their mother. Yet these descriptions typically stood alone: emotionally affecting words and images were segregated from one another, rather than used in concert.[71] Action was necessary to "save the children" and, with them, the revolution, the magazine instructed. Yet its editorial staff chose to minimize the use of famine photography, perhaps to avoid excessive pathos – or to preemptively deflect criticism regarding the social effects of the revolution and civil war. Either way, in the early 1920s, the preference for graphic art over photos differentiated the visual culture of this communist relief drive from that of liberal organizations like the Save the Children Fund.[72] Ultimately, however, they all relied on the shared sentimental themes of broken mother-child bonds and endangered children.

Wartime Disorder, Displacement, Destruction: Children as Civilians

The Spanish Civil War (1936–39) has been widely credited as the advent of modern war photography. This was the first conflict covered by an international corps of photographers whose work was immediately transmitted and published in the mass-circulation press. The innovation of the light-weight Leica camera, with its portability and fast shutter speed, allowed photographers to capture action shots and establish professional careers in the growing field of photojournalism. Photographers Robert Capa, David "Chim" Seymour, and until her early death, Gerda Taro, built their reputations, and those of European and American news magazines *Regards, VU, Match, Picture Post, Life,* and *Look,* among others, by supplying exciting wartime images starting in Spain and spanning out across the continent as Nazi Germany launched its war of aggression.[73]

Beyond the renown of their striking wartime images, Capa and Chim have been credited for their humanitarian focus on non-combatant refugees and especially children: those ultimate innocents who suffer disproportionately greatly from the violence of war. Yet if one reviews their wartime work –as opposed to their postwar commissions for UNESCO– it is puzzling how this reputation developed.[74] Although it included images of non-combatants, their wartime photography focused disproportionately on the destruction of the built environment and on soldiers readying for the fight, fighting or falling in battle, and relaxing afterwards. Capa's now-iconic photo, "The Death of the Republic Soldier," for example, appeared on the left of a two-page spread on "The Civil War in Spain" under the subtitle "How They Fell." The facing page contained a set of five smaller photos of women, carrying belongings or children, subtitled "How They Fled." The first photo, which captured 'the moment of death' in meaningfully heroic form, is the one that seized contemporaries' imagination, was reprinted widely on both sides of the Atlantic, and has been the object of endless critical fascination and debate since, effectively nudging his images of refugee women and children from view.[75] Similarly,

Chim's now-famous photo of a woman, with upturned face, nursing her child at an outdoor political meeting on land reform in Badajoz was an immediate hit among Republicans in 1936. But it became iconic only the next year when it was reprinted on a book cover, set against a sky and the vertical thrust of a falling bomb bearing a Nazi swastika. Now the emotional center of a photo montage, the politically engaged mother was thus subsequently re-cast as the victim of fascist bombing.[76]

A hint into how Capa acquired his child-friendly reputation can be found in the work of Gerda Taro, his romantic and professional partner during the Spanish Civil War. Taro, a German-born exile with socialist sympathies, met Capa in Paris in 1934 and shortly thereafter joined forces with him, marketing her photos under the names of "Capa" or "Capa and Taro," and less frequently "Photo Taro."[77] In early 1937, she commuted several times from the fighting front in Spain to shoot a series on children orphaned by the war and living in a home run by the Spanish Red Cross. Drawn to socially responsible reportage, she did the piece freelance. However, she found she could not interest mainstream news magazines in the story and had to resort to its less lucrative sale to the newsletter of the International Red Aid, the Communist International's version of the Red Cross.[78] After Taro's untimely death in July 1937 – she was crushed by a tank in the field – her photos were merged with Capa's and then attributed to him, first in his 1938 book on the Spanish Civil War, *Death in the Making,* and then in subsequent publications, magazines, and exhibitions. Only recently have scholars disentangled their work and credited her contributions.[79]

If photojournalism's coverage of the Spanish Civil War initiated the image-rich interpretation of war as a breakdown of civil society, photographic responses to World War II further developed this trope, using the innovative techniques developed by the pictorial press in Germany, France, Britain and the United States in the interwar period: the photo story. The photo story created meaning and narrative through conceptual and pictorial sequences of shots and text, rather than through single shots or cluster layouts.[80] A prominent example that narrated World War II through the lens of destroyed families and children alone was published in 1943 by Thérèse Bonney. Bonney, an American-born photographer, studied at the University of California, Berkeley, before becoming an expatriate in 1920s Paris and founding her own photo agency there. In the 1920s and '30s, she made her name in fashion photography and with a well-received coffee-table book offering an inside-look at the Vatican. In 1939, she began to document civilian wartime experience: "the story of human tragedy not in terms of soldiers, guns, tanks, ... and other weapons of war, but in their total and terrible effect on the little people of the earth who cannot fight back: the children, the old people, the mothers with babies, the wounded and the forever lost." Her wartime work appeared in prominent newspapers and magazines in the United States and Europe and was featured in one of the first exhibits devoted to photography at the Museum of Modern Art in New York.[81] In 1943, Bonney's self-published book, *Europe's Children, 1939–1943*, became an overnight success and media sensation. The first run immediately sold out, the book was reprinted by a commercial press, and its photos were turned into an exhibit that toured forty American cities.[82]

Bonney's book disseminated a shockingly intimate view of the ravages of war, capturing how it broke the bonds of family and destroyed the reassuring predictabilities of daily life. The full-page photos were offered with minimal commentary yet had a distinct narrative sweep, chronicling the destruction of the patterns and protections of "normal" childhood – school, home, family life, mealtime, bedtime. Terrified and exhausted children cling to traumatized mothers on the road during the invasion of France or are separated from parents due to death, illness, or flight. A young boy with bare legs on a chilly day, slumped over from fatigue at the side of a road (Figure 7.1); two young, solemn girls, likely sisters, peering through the barbed wire of a unnamed concentration camp; Finnish toddlers on a child transport to Sweden in search of safety; a premature newborn wrapped in paper rather than blankets; starving children and infants with bony limbs and distended stomachs, staring hollowly at the camera. All vulnerable, some of the verge of extinction, each an iconic child-in-need, silently pleading for care, nurture, rescue, and a compassionate maternal or parental response.

Bonney disavowed the distancing lens of ethnic or national distinctiveness. Her photos favored intimate, individual portraits of suffering that encouraged white American viewers to respond to these children-in-need viscerally and on the basis of shared humanity, even kinship.[83] Bonney drew on the visual vocabulary of social documentary photography developed over the previous three decades by American photographers like Lewis Hine (on child labor in the 1910s) and Dorothea Lange (on migrant labor and poverty in the 1930s) in an effort to document, expose, and reform domestic problems. Like Hine and Lange, she focused on children alone or with mothers to clarify and interpret social experience. Unlike those photographers, Bonney used an extended sequence of photos to visually narrate the continent-wide dissolution of community

and family. With each turn of the page, she depicted children released
into a wartime world: being rendered vulnerable, exhausted, and hungry; dislocated and disconnected from family; in jeopardy, orphaned.
Through its pictorial progression, her book constitutes readers as moral
witnesses of war, charting its devastating effects through the destruction
of mother-child bonds, and makes an emotional appeal for the children's
need for nurture and for humanitarian food aid abroad. Her book and
traveling exhibition helped popularize a particular moral vision based
on a specific *interpretative lens*, fixed on a foreign subject yet articulated
through the figure – and, as important, the as-yet unresolved future – of
the "imperiled ... helpless" child.[84] This lens shaped the way Americans
apprehended social problems "out there" and the ways they began to con-
ceive of involving themselves in the postwar solutions to those problems.
Visioning the European war as the continent-wide crisis of destroyed
families and vulnerable children-in-need combined with American social
trends to suggest particular humanitarian "solutions" to these problems
after 1945. One notable such solution was the innovation of international
adoption, and in particular the eager adoption of European children by
American couples at home in the United States or stationed abroad with
the American military, a postwar development avidly covered in various
sectors of the American media.[85]

The pictorial focus on children during the Second World War was not
the preserve of Allied nations alone. The Nazi Regime mobilized positive
images of children and the mother-child bond in its nationalist propaganda to celebrate Aryan supremacy and convince Germans of the need
to practice proper racial hygiene. Nazi publications also drew upon the
now popularized *conventions* of humanitarian photography for purposes
of ideological persuasion: to explain and justify the regime's sociopoliti-
cal and foreign policy goals in moral language.[86] The photo-story book,
Der Untermensch [The Subhuman], like Bonney's, uses the lens of family, mothers, and children to document the destruction of Europe and
European civilization. One page toward the middle of the book illustrates
the deplorable state of Soviet children under "Jewish-Bolshevik" leadership (Figure 7.6): "These ten-year-olds in the horrors of Soviet hell," reads
the caption of the shot at bottom-left, "are certainly the most frightful
indictment of this anathema of humanity."[87] Yet the Nazi publication
also employed the before- and- after convention to contrast "children
of the state" suffering in "Soviet hell" to the intact bonds of beaming,
rosy-cheeked children and eugenically healthy mothers in Switzerland,
the Netherlands, Germany, and Denmark. In this case, the paired pages

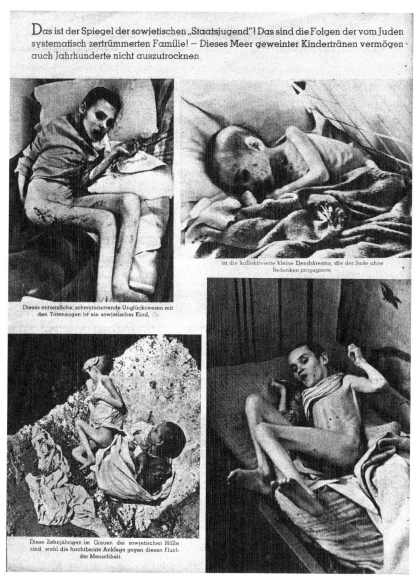

Das ist der Spiegel der sowjetischen „Staatsjugend"! Das sind die Folgen der vom Juden systematisch zertrümmerten Familie! – Dieses Meer geweinter Kindertränen vermögen · auch Jahrhunderte nicht auszutrocknen.

Dieses entsetzliche, schmutzstarrende Unglückswesen mit den Totenaugen ist ein sowjetisches Kind, ...

ist die kollektivierte kleine Elendskreatur, die der Jude ohne Bedenken propagierte.

Diese Zehnjährigen im Grauen der sowjetischen Hölle sind wohl die furchtbarste Anklage gegen diesen Fluch der Menschheit.

FIGURE 7.6. "This is the picture of youth under the Soviet state! These are the results of the systematic destruction of the family by Jews! Centuries will not suffice to dry this ocean of children's tears." *Der Untermensch* (Berlin: Nordland Verlag, 1943), p. 18.

of photos, left and right, connoted both social "problem" and "social solution," as well as "social threat" and "social ideal." The Nazi publication, unlike Bonney's, did not call upon its readers to aid or feed Soviet children. The photos of Soviet youth acknowledged – and played upon – reader sympathy for suffering children: after all, this was presented as powerful evidence for "indicting" the "Soviet-Jewish system." Yet the rallying call forsook humanitarian assistance for armed "defense." The book's moral message – and its instructions regarding readers' moral duty – was contained not in a single photo, or a set of photos, but in the narrative sweep of its full photographic sequence. The book concludes with a medium-close-up shot of the body of a prone boy, spread across the page, lying face-up on a bed of hay, his lifeless eyes half-open and his mouth ajar: "The children of Europe will be murdered just as this innocent boy was," exclaims the over-title. "The subhuman has risen up to conquer the world. Woe to you members of humanity who don't stand together! Defend Europe!"[88] The visual conventions of humanitarian photography, summoning viewer sympathy and moral outrage with its focus on the suffering child, gave way to the visual conventions of atrocity photography, with its moral denunciation and call for retribution for the *crime* of the murdered Aryan child.

The persuasive capacity of Nazi propaganda was limited, by design, to "Aryan" audiences and their affiliates. Hitler reviled humanitarianism as an ideology that aided the weak and inferior: those, in his eyes, who were unviable human beings. Nazi propaganda like *Der Untermensch* selectively employed the moral address of humanitarian photography but did not embrace its universalist values. The gritty, ugly, clinical quality of the photos of naked and soiled Soviet children contrasted sharply with the monumental individual portrait of the respectably clothed "murdered" boy with well-lit face and clean, graceful hands. In visual terms, these children – and their suffering – were represented as neither equal nor interchangeable.

In contrast, Thérèse Bonney's photos brought her readers into close proximity with her child subjects (Figure 7.1). Even naked, they are rendered sentimentally as more than clinical objects: they retain their individuality and a somber human dignity, leavened with childhood innocence (Figure 7.7). In formal terms, Bonney's photos evoke child portraits taken by commercial studios or doting parents: recognizable photographic practices of middle-class families that could have contributed to the call of moral duty. *This is like your child*, the photo's genre and form suggested to white Western viewers, *absent food, clothing, nurture, and a reason to smile*. Provided these things, this child would be like yours (Figure 7.8).[89]

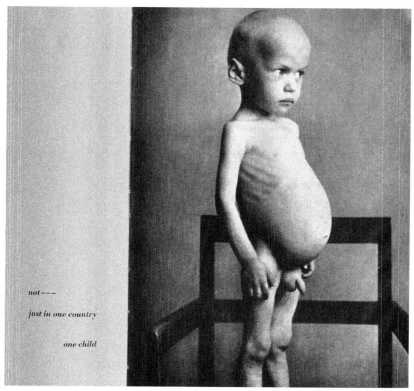

not – – –

just in one country

one child

FIGURE 7.7. "Not just in one country, one child …" Bonney, *Europe's Children* (New York: self-published, 1943).

By World War II, photos like Bonney's popularized the notion of "the civilian" as imagined through the figure of the innocent endangered child. This doubly depoliticized category – civilian as child – is a moral construct. Bonney's camera lens lent it geographical and cultural particularity: civilian as *European* child. Familiar photographic form – child portraiture – helped make the moral argument on the basis of recognition: "civilian as European child" deserved the protection of Western viewers. Violence against it was emotionally upsetting, worse than unjust, because it could imaginably be violence against one's own child.

Historically, then, humanitarian photos – even those that claimed to have a "global object" (the suffering child) – have addressed specific audiences that were necessarily narrower than global humanity. Strategies of emotional address were developed that played upon the emotional resonance of familiar, and sometimes familial, photographic genres and

FIGURE 7.8. Boy with telephone. American studio portrait, c. 1930s, subject and photographer unknown. From author's private collection.

practices. In addition, appeals to a viewer's moral duty were often cast in languages of national, imperial, religious, or civilizational responsibility. Unlike the "iconography of childhood" discussed by social scientists for the period after 1945, with its focus on the previously colonized regions of the "Third World," humanitarian imagery after the First World War focused predominantly on European environs and was informed by representational practices connected with family photography, social documentary photography, and photojournalism. Concerns about *European* families, societies, and civilization gave rise to the powerful trope of the "civilian" expressed through the image of the innocent imperiled child.[90]

This selective survey of pre-1945 humanitarian photography has shown that a significant number of humanitarian image-makers and image-purveyors of the period were women. This is not to suggest that humanitarian photography was propelled by maternal instinct, but to note that humanitarian photography and its visual and narrative expressions reflect a marked perception of, and sensitivity to, the peculiar experiences of women and children in war. After all, these were sectors of the population – whether living in nation-states or empires – who did not enjoy political representation or rights, or had only recently acquired them in the interwar period. Emily Hobhouse and Eglantyne Jebb advocated pacifism, internationalism, and women's suffrage; Käthe Kollwitz and Gerda Taro supported socialist causes, the decriminalization of abortion (Kollwitz), and antifacism (Taro). Their humanitarian efforts and imagery were informed by these political commitments, along with their recognition of the inadequacies, particularly in wartime, of the patriarchal protections of one's state, one's husband, and one's father. The historical question remains, then, of the extent to which the "humanitarian eye" that developed prior to 1945 – articulated through photography and other visual media and based upon the moral training of vision and emotion – has been shaped by specifically *female* politics, experiences, and sensibilities.[91]

Notes

1 Manzo, "Imaging Humanitarianism," 633, 635.
2 Malkki, "Children, Humanity," 58–9, 84. The "standardized, representational uses of children," Malkki argues, depoliticize children as a category, making it difficult to treat children as individualized historical and political subjects rather than timeless, innocent, passive objects of "charismatic suffering" (59–60, 63, 64, 70, 79); also Erica Burman, "Innocents Abroad."
3 Suski, "Children, Suffering, and the Humanitarian Appeal," 202.
4 This chapter is part of a book project on the history of child-centered humanitarian imagery.
5 See Bank "Anthropology and Portrait Photography"; Hight and Sampson, *Colonialist Photography*; Burroughs, *Travel Writing*; Vernon, *Hunger: A Modern History*; and Peffer, "Snap of the Whip"; also Curtis, Twomey, and Grant in this volume.
6 See Twomey in this volume; also Marien, *Photography*, 160, 162.
7 Merewether, *A Tour through the Famine Districts* (New Delhi: Usha, 1985, reprint; original publication 1898), 184–7. Fewer than two pages (of 304) were devoted to describing the state of the children in the orphanage. While noting high mortality rates, he assured readers that the orphans were "fed twice a day, and the dole received seemed sufficient" (186).
8 Vernon, *Hunger*, argues that government ministers in London relied on press reports for information on developments in colonial territories, making "the power of the special correspondents in the field ... considerable" (27).
9 Vernon, *Hunger*, chapter 2, quotation from 22. Reports on suffering in the Empire were paralleled by exposés of suffering at home, such as Krausse's *Starving London* (1887), serialized in the *Globe*, 27–30.

10 See Heerten's chapter in this volume for a discussion of Biafran imagery of the late 1960s.

11 The large photo in the middle of the page from the January 1897 issue of *Christian Herald* appeared the following year in Merewether, *A Tour through the Famine Districts*, 184.

12 This analysis is based on photos in F. H. S. Merewether, *A Tour through the Famine Districts* and those of Hooper and Scott in Twomey, this volume; Marien, *Photography;* and Vernon, *Hunger*, 36–9.

13 Hight and Sampson argue that "the Western visualization of native people and their environments as primitive or exotic was … often an attempt to make the unfamiliar or strange desirable in a traditionally legible way," *Colonialist Photography*, 4.

14 My reading differs from Chaudhary in *Afterimage of Empire* who suggests that the "reduction to the body and our physical limits" is the only common ground in these photos and suggests that such photos encouraged viewing relationships based on difference and emotional distance while allowing viewers to "practice one's civilizational or liberal drills," 85, 87. I argue that by using familiar photographic genres, like family portraiture, the photos opened space for recognition and notions of similarity as well.

15 Marien uses German photographer Gustav Oehme's work from the late 1840s as evidence of a shift from rigid and severe to "congenial" family portraiture, *Photography*, 64; see also her discussion of the composite photo by H. P. Robinson, "Fading Away" for sentimental family photography focused on a child's death, 93. Also Szarkowski, *The Photographer's Eye*, 19 and 28; and Smith, *American Archives*, 113–35, on baby photo albums and the practice of photographing one's own children by the 1890s. For examples of African American family portraits (c. 1860s), see Willis and Krauthamer, *Envisioning Emancipation*, 46, 81, 176–7; on Indian photos see Pinney, *Camera Indica*.

16 Photos could be framed or in jewelry, such as lockets, to be worn on the body. Geoffrey Batchen, "Vernacular Photographies," in idem., *Each Wild Idea: Writing, Photography, History* (Cambridge, MA: MIT Press, 2001), 57–80, here 60.

17 Jay Ruby, *Secure the Shadow: Death and Photography in America* (Cambridge, MA: MIT Press, 1995), 52–3; also Audrey Linkman, *Photography and Death* (London: Reaktion Books, 2011).

18 Along with the distant setting and other markers of cultural difference, the photo's emotional sting might have been mitigated by the likelihood that its subjects' deaths would be near simultaneous: no member would linger long enough to have to grieve the others.

19 Twomey, "Severed Hands," and Peffer, "Snap of the Whip."

20 Peffer mis-reads it as a "young man."

21 Twomey, "Severed Hands"; also Peffer, "Snap of the Whip," and Twomey and Grant in this volume. The image was also reproduced in Twain's *King Leopold's Soliloquy* (1905); Thompson, *Light on Darkness*, 186–8.

22 Quotation is from Peffer, "Snap of the Whip," 62; see Grant and Twomey, this volume; also Bank, "Anthropology and Portrait Photography," on distinctions between ethnographic and anthropological uses of photography

based on nineteenth-century German examples. Kevin Grant, in a personal communication, suggested that about half of the atrocity portraits of severed limbs had white backdrops.

23 Emily Hobhouse, *Report of a Visit to the Camps of Women and Children in the Cape and Orange River Colonies* (London: Friars Printing, n.d.); Godby, "Confronting Horror." For a useful analysis of women's involvement in, and contributions to, the British campaign against the Boer War that contextualizes Hobhouse's activities, see Eliza Riedi, "The Women Pro-Boers: Gender, Peace, and the Critique of Empire in the South African War" in *Historical Research* 86, no. 231 (February 2013): 92–115.

24 Some 26,370 Afrikaners, mostly women and children, died in the white camps. Black workers and servants of Afrikaner families were rounded up and placed in segregated camps where 14,000 to 20,000 died, over 80 percent of whom were children. War Museum of the Boer Republics 1899–1902, http://www.anglo-boer.co.za/concentration-camps, accessed 10 February 2014.

25 Although the composition of this photo is similar to ethnographic conventions, it does not claim to convey knowledge about native life or habitat. Since it depicts an intentionally displaced population corralled into a constructed camp environment, its purpose is to convey information about British-authored living conditions, not the practices of Afrikaner daily life.

26 The image is available online: http://en.wikipedia.org/wiki/File:LizzieVanZyl.jpg, accessed 10 February 2014.

27 Hobhouse, *The Brunt of War and Where It Fell* (London: Methuen, 1902), 215. Also Godby, "Confronting Horror," on the use of the van Zyl photo and on photography in the camps.

28 *Hobhouse, Brunt, 317–18.* The phrase "methods of barbarism" was used first by Sir Henry Campbell-Bannerman, Liberal Party leader, in a speech criticizing policies sanctioned by the Conservative government during the Boer War. My thanks to Kevin Grant for this information.

29 The preamble to Hague II (1899) stated: "Until a more complete code of the laws of war is issued, the High Contracting Parties think it right to declare that in cases not included in the Regulations ... populations and belligerents remain under the protection ... of the principles of international law, as they result from the usages established between civilized nations, from the laws of humanity, and the requirements of the public conscience." Hobhouse did not explicitly cite Hague II but her ethical position seems compatible with it, including the protection of private property and the humane provisioning of captured noncombatant belligerents.

30 Hobhouse also defended Afrikaner women as committed and caring mothers, an image Hobhouse's pro-government critics attempted to subvert by using Lizzie van Zyl's photo as putative evidence of maternal (rather than British) callousness.

31 On the politics of British maternalism at home and in the colonies, see the classic essay by Anna Davin, "Imperialism and Motherhood," *History Workshop* 5 (Spring 1978): 9–67; also Susan Pedersen, "The Maternalist Moment in British Colonial Policy: The Controversy over 'Child Slavery' in Hong Kong, 1917–1941," *Past and Present* 171 (2001): 161–202.

32 See Balakian's chapter; see Grant's chapter for a discussion of public viewing conventions in Britain prior to World War I, both this volume. The American Red Cross also used some mother-child imagery in World War I; see Irwin, *Making the World Safe.*

33 Wegner's photo of dead mother and children was published in 1918 in Henry Morgenthau's book, *Ambassador Morgenthau's Story*; in March 1918, Morgenthau published an essay, "The Greatest Horror in History: An Authentic Account of the Armenian Atrocities" with further photos in the *American Red Cross Magazine* 13, no. 3: 7–15. On Armenian child saving after the war, see Watenpaugh, "The League of Nations' Rescue."

34 Morgenthau, "Greatest Horror," 15; italics appear in the original. He urged that "definite steps be ... taken to rescue permanently the remnants of these fine, old, civilized Christian peoples from the fangs of the Turks."

35 Clare Mulley, *The Woman Who Saved Children* (Oxford: OneWorld, 2009), 246.

36 The blockade was lifted only after Germany signed the Versailles Peace treaty in late June 1919.

37 She was charged for failing to get government clearance for public distribution of the leaflets. Mulley, *The Woman Who Saved Children*, 239–41.

38 Founders of the Famine Council included members of the Women's International League for Peace and Freedom, suffragists, pacificists and "new liberal internationalists" J.A. Hobson, J. M. Keynes, and Leonard Hobhouse (Emily's brother). See Emily Baughan, "'Every Citizen of Empire is Implored to Save the Children': Empire, Internationalism, and the Save the Children Fund in Inter-War Britain" in *Historical Research* 86, no. 231 (February 2013): 116–37, here 120. Also Mulley, *The Woman Who Saved Children*, 227–9.

39 Jebb was referring to the Geneva Treaty of 1863 and its sponsoring organization the ICRC, quoted in Marshall, "Humanitarian Sympathy," 187.

40 Marshall, "Construction of Children"; also Cabanes, *The Great War.*

41 Quotations are from Stephen Lassonde, "Age, Schooling, and Development," in Paula Fass, ed., *The Routledge History of Childhood in the Western World* (New York, Routledge, 2013), 216, 220–1. In addition to the Paula Fass anthology, see, for example, Viviana Zelizer, *Pricing the Priceless Child: The Changing Social Value of Children* (Princeton, NJ: Princeton, 1994); Edward Dickinson, *The Politics of German Child Welfare from the Empire to the Federal Republic* (Cambridge, MA: Harvard University Press, 1996); James Schmidt, *Industrial Violence and the Legal Origins of Child Labor* (New York: Cambridge University Press, 2011); Tara Zahra, *Kidnapped Souls: National Difference and the Battle for Children in Bohemian Lands, 1900–1948* (Ithaca, NY: Cornell University Press, 2011).

42 Mulley, *The Woman Who Saved Children*, 246–7.

43 Mulley, *The Woman Who Saved Children*, 240–5 and 261–72.

44 SCF established a national propaganda office, hired a press secretary, and spent an "unprecedented 5 percent of its income on media appeals. Baughan, "'Every Citizen of Empire,'" 118, 123, 128–30; and Marshall, "Children's Rights," "The Construction of Children," "Humanitarian Sympathy." The

Fund hit a period of crisis in the mid-1920s, after famine relief for Central European and Russian children ended, and debate broke out about whether it should continue its international work or shift its focus to pressing domestic problems. Western Aid and the Global Economy: Series I: SCF Archives (New York: Thomson Gale, microfilm, 2004), Reel 13, "The Future of Save the Children Fund?" December 1926; Reel 34, "Miss Jebb's Memorandum on the Policy of S.C.F.," 9 July 1928.

45 The *Record* began as a monthly in October 1920 and appeared semi-monthly by 1921. In August 1922 it became *World's Children* and contained fewer photos and more professional articles on child welfare. In December 1926, *Save the Children Fund Pictorial* was launched and distributed free of charge to a broad readership.

46 The *Record,* January 1920, p. 64, and 15 August 1920, p. 325.

47 The *Record,* 1 January 1921, p. 52.

48 SCF, in its fundraising, emphasized the famine's natural, rather than political, causes in order to establish the children as worthy and innocent victims. Mahood and Satzewich, "The Save the Children Fund," 59–61. SCF's famine relief campaign in Russia was surpassed only by Hoover's organization; see Baughan, " 'Every Citizen of Empire,'" 122.

49 Zangwill was author of the play, and phrase, "The Melting Pot." See photos in the *Record,* 1 and 15 November, and 1 and 15 December 1921; poem appeared in 15 December issue. See also Mahood and Satzewich, "The Save the Children Fund."

50 Bruno Cabanes argues that Russian famine relief helped to establish the humanitarian "right to assistance" in calamities, *The Great War,* 189–299.

51 Virol ad in the *Record,* 1 January 1921, p. 2.

52 M. N. Mitchell, *Raising Freedom's Child*; Willis and Krauthamer, *Envisioning Emancipation,* 19; Koven, "Dr. Barnardo's." Mitchell and Koven note the constructed character of the shots, which were taken the same day in the same studio; Koven discusses controversy unleashed when critics realized the artificial quality of the children' improvement.

53 The *Record,* 15 March 1922; Mahood and Satzewich, "The Save the Children Fund," also discuss this item.

54 Such as Dr. Hector Munro and Dr. Frédéric Ferrière who were sent to Vienna; Mulley, *The Woman Who Saved Children,* 236–8.

55 Lassonde, "Age, Schooling, and Development," 216, 220–1.

56 Marshall essays "Children's Rights," "The Construction of Children," and "Humanitarian Sympathy."

57 Ad libbing during a speech at the 1919 founding of SCF, Dorothy Buxton held aloft a can of condensed milk and declared: "There is more morality in this tin than in all the creeds," Mulley, *The Woman Who Saved Children,* 245. On the scientific study of nutrition and the feeding of British school children, see Vernon, *Hunger.*

58 *SCF Pictorial,* Winter 1927, p. 2. In this case, the child was shown bare-chested. Adoption subscriptions for English children began after mid-decade when support for foreign children fell off and the SCF reassessed its purpose.

59 The phrase is from Zelizer, *Pricing the Priceless Child.*

60 An early announcement appeared in the *Record* in December 1920 with no photos included. The total number of SCF "adoptions" sponsored in Central and Eastern Europe then was 5,601.

61 In spring 1927, the *SCF Pictorial* magazine announced that "over 1,400 children were being helped" through subscription adoptions. "Choose Your Child, Direct-Help Giving" appeared in the *SCF Pictorial* (Spring 1928): 7.

62 The figures appear in *Soviet Russia* issues from May through August 1922. The magazine was published semi-monthly, as were the names and dollar amounts of all donations received.

63 Sean McMeekin, *The Red Millionaire* (New Haven, CT: Yale University Press, 2003), esp. 103–22.

64 Irwin, *Making the World Safe*; Cabanes, *The Great War*.

65 A similar photo of the child crying inconsolably, with mouth ajar, is printed in *Humanity at War*, 32 and credited to ICRC. Other photos included two macabre still-life shots of heaped, frozen human body parts, evidence of cannibalism that appeared to be carefully posed, and an unremarkable group shot of worker delegates touring the famine district. *Soviet Russia*, July and October 1922.

66 McMeekin, *The Red Millionaire*, 117.

67 The magazine frequently printed photos of prominent Soviet leaders, of construction and railroad projects, of Soviet political posters, and other such "positive" imagery.

68 Kollwitz also contributed lithograph poster of mothers and children for food relief drives for Berlin and Vienna.

69 Such as work by American Lydia Gibson and Armenian Kizil Zdanovich. In Berlin a portfolio of graphic works by sympathetic artists, including Kollwitz, was published and sold for famine fundraising.

70 Bärbel Schrader and Jürgen Schebera, *Die 'goldene' zwanzige Jahre. Kunst und Kultur der Weimarer Republik* (Vienna: Böhlau, 1987); also Lynn Malley, *Culture of the Future* (Berkeley: University of California Press, 1990).

71 *Soviet Russia*, December 1921, 238; 1 March 1922; December 1922, 294.

72 Since the Friends of Soviet Russia campaign was based in the United States, it is possible that the organization was aware that its readership would be familiar with the famine photos used in Hoover's ARA fundraising and therefore opted to run a more self-consciously political visual campaign.

73 Lebeck and Dewitz, *Kiosk*, 190–209; Young, *We Went Back*; and *Gerda Taro*, ed. Irme Schaber, Richard Whelan, and Kristen Lubben (New York: International Center of Photography/Steidl, 2007).

74 See Robert Capa, *Children of War, Children of Peace*, ed. Cornell Capa and Richard Whelan (Boston: Bullfinch, 1991); Young, *We Went Back*; Bernard Lebrun and Michel Lefebvre, *Robert Capa: The Paris Years, 1933–1954* (New York: Abrams, 2012); Robert Capa, *Death in the Making* (New York: Covici-Friede, 1938); Tom Beck, *David Seymour (Chim)* (New York: Pfaidon, 2005) on Chim's postwar work for the United Nations, see Salvatici and Rodogno and David in this volume. Seymour did the photos for the 1949 UNESCO book, *Children of Europe*.

75 Lebeck and Dewitz, *Kiosk*, 202; Brothers, *War and Photography*, 178–85. Brothers discusses other photos of civilians by Capa and Chim, along with Chim's shot of "politicized" Spanish children, 121–60.

76 Young, *We Went Back*, 36–7.

77 Capa, a Hungarian Jew, was born André Friedmann; Taro, a socialist from Stuttgart, was born Gerta Pohorylle.

78 It was published in Paris in French and German language versions of the newsletter. *Gerda Taro*, 41–51, 22–3, and 86–7.

79 Irme Schaber, "The Eye of Solidarity" in *Gerda Taro*, 9–37.

80 Young, *We Went Back*; and Brothers, *War and Photography*.

81 Bonney was the first female photographer exhibited there. The Museum of Modern Art (MoMA) in New York City exhibited her "War Comes to the People" in December 1940; a similar exhibit by Bonney, "To Whom the Wars Are Done," was shown at the Library of Congress. MOMA Archives, REG 119. Quotation is from the MoMA press release, 11 December 1940.

82 The book was also published in Europe. Thérèse Bonney, *Europe's Children, 1939 to 1943* (Self-published ed., 1943); letter from Bonney to Jane Lawson at Alfred A. Knopf, 28 October 1943 (in author's possession); *Publisher's Weekly* (23 October 1943): 1594–5.

83 The children were depicted as European and white; this held for other popular books that appeared during and after the war, such as Otto Zoff, *They Shall Inherit the Earth* (New York: John Day, 1943); Anne Barley, *Patrick Calls Me Mother* (New York: Harper, 1948); Irena Wasilewska, *Suffer Little Children* (New York: Maxlove, 1946), John P. Carroll-Abbing, *A Chance to Live: The Story of the Lost Children of the War* (New York: Longmans, Green, 1952); Robert Collis, *The Lost and Found: The Story of Eva and Laszlo, Two Children of War-Torn Europe*, intro by Margaret Mead (New York: Women's Press, 1953).

84 Bonney, *Europe's Children*; also Brothers, *War and Photography*, on the photo-story and the "open," or unresolved, ending, 149.

85 Including Christian and U.S. military publications, the African American press, and the mainstream commercial press. Fehrenbach, "From Aid to Intimacy"; also Fehrenbach, *Race after Hitler* (Princeton, NJ: Princeton University Press, 2005).

86 Claudia Koonz, *The Nazi Conscience* (Cambridge, MA: Harvard University Press, 2003).

87 *Der Untermensch* (Berlin: Nordland Verlag, 1943), 18.

88 Ibid., 51.

89 See Smith, *American Archives*, on vernacular practices of child portraiture and magazine articles, beginning in the 1890s, instructing mothers in taking such photos.

90 For a discussion of the evolution of the concept of "civilian," see Helen Kinsella, *The Image before the Weapon* (Ithaca, NY: Cornell University Press, 2011).

91 I explore this issue in my current book project, *The Humanitarian Eye*.

8

Sights of Benevolence

UNRRA's Recipients Portrayed

Silvia Salvatici

Introduction

The last years of World War II and its immediate aftermath offer
meaningful glimpses into the complex and uneven historical path of
humanitarianism. Initially, the United Nations Relief and Rehabilitation
Administration (UNRRA), and later the UN itself, were in charge of
rebooting humanitarian action in the new international order.[1] These
two intergovernmental organizations portrayed themselves as the champions of a "new humanitarianism" that was based on revived ideas of
internationalism and the modernization of relief practices. This chapter
concentrates on the case of UNRRA and analyzes the role played by
photography in representing the postwar years as the founding period
of modern humanitarianism. Photography also contributed to forging
a very particular humanitarian narrative. This narrative claimed that
rehabilitation was a necessary aim of immediate relief and made much
of UNRRA's effectiveness in providing it. The visual representation of
UNRRA's duties did not dwell on distressed victims and suffering bodies: images that might be expected to raise sympathy among the public.[2]
Rather, photographs focused on displaced men, women, and children
who – in the Administration's view – were being successfully rehabilitated both physically and spiritually. Should we regard portrayals of
children beaming with joy as they consumed their meals or of displaced
persons (DPs) being trained in the camps as examples of humanitarian
photography? I argue that UNRRA regarded them as such, since the
physical and spiritual rehabilitation of recipients was the heart of the
organization's humanitarian mission, and such pictures were intended

to show the job was being successfully accomplished. UNRRA's photographs call on us, as historians, to investigate the emergence of different humanitarian narratives and the role played by visual language in shaping them.

The United Nations Relief and Rehabilitation Administration was established in November 1943 by an agreement signed in Washington by forty-four countries, and it was presented to the world as the "humanitarian side" of the Great Alliance that was going to defeat the Axis Powers.[3] In the words of President Franklin Delano Roosevelt, UNRRA's job was to provide "relief and help in rehabilitation for the victims of German and Japanese barbarism."[4] In accomplishing this mission, the new organization aimed to bring about a sea change in the way aid had been traditionally conceived and administered. It sought to assume control of rescue operations, thanks to its privileged relationship with the Allied army in the liberated countries. Military authorities appointed UNRRA as the agency in charge of rescuing civilians, and it was engaged in food distribution, medical care, tracing missing people, and administering refugee camps.[5] Many voluntary agencies were also in the field, but it was UNRRA's job to coordinate and supervise them; the aim was to drive private philanthropy into the background, thus permitting the intergovernmental management of international aid to dominate.[6] UNRRA founders planned a complex machinery that was designed to modernize relief; institutionalization, secularization, and professionalization defined, to them, what modern humanitarianism was all about.

In the history of humanitarianism, there is a recurrent rhetoric of discontinuity and "new foundations." From Henri Dunant and the International Committee of the Red Cross onward, most newly founded institutions presented themselves as initiating a "new era."[7] Furthermore, the idea of professionalization was not new. In the aftermath of World War I, the values of professional qualifications and expertise had already emerged as main requirements for international relief workers.[8] However, after World War II, the United Nations agencies played up the idea of a "new beginning" in order to emphasize the break between the present and a past marked by "barbarism."[9] Of particular relevance for UNRRA founders was that information about the new agency be disseminated to the public and its activities be recorded. Here they had two aims in mind: to sell the public on the fact that UNRRA was doing its job effectively – thereby justifying the massive allocation of resources to international relief – and to create a public memory of the pathbreaking role played by UNRRA in pioneering a "new humanitarianism." In order to achieve these aims they established a Public Information Office, with a Visual Information section and created the Office of Historian tasked with documenting and writing the organization's history.[10] It was believed that the thousands of pictures taken in the different regions throughout the world would help persuade Western citizens of the major role played by UNRRA in bringing aid to peoples and countries devastated by the war.[11]

The shots of UNRRA official photographers filled the pages of the many booklets illustrating the organization's purposes and activities. The leaflet *Fifty Facts about UNRRA* is a good example of this type of publication. It was obviously meant for ordinary people who had little or no knowledge about international humanitarianism, and it addressed the supposedly "frequently asked questions" about the new organization, such as "How is UNRRA helping the Italian people?" or "With so many problems at home, why should we bother about UNRRA?" Answers were given in words and in pictures: photographs depicted UNRRA's activities in sixteen "receiving countries," most of them European.[12] *Fifty Facts about UNRRA* was reprinted several times and distributed in the main "contributing countries," as were other similar booklets. Thirty-eight governments participated in founding UNRRA operations, but contributions made by the United States, the United Kingdom, and Canada together accounted for 94 percent of the total budget.[13] There is little doubt that UNRRA "was one of the products of Anglo-American "post-conflict planning."[14]

Photographs were not only destined for UNRRA publications. UNRRA's Public Information Office handed over the pictures, along with news items, statistics, and reports to bureaus in the member states, which were committed to supporting the dissemination of information about the international agency.[15]

UNRRA headquarters considered images to be a great asset in familiarizing Western citizens with the new organizations, and a pool of professional photographers was recruited to make a record of relief operations. Of course, not all their pictures were published. Some of them were printed in UNRRA's brochures, but it is quite possible that others appeared in local newspapers or magazines, since the representatives of member states were charged with disseminating all the material dispatched by the UNRRA Information Office in their countries. This chapter analyzes photographs that illustrated UNRRA official publications, as well as other available shots, in order to outline the main narrative that, taken together, they suggest.

Photographers of Relief

UNRRA's visual policies should be seen in the light of both the historical development of narratives about humanitarianism and the increasing reliance of institutions on photography to document their activities throughout the twentieth century. In the United States, the Information Division of the government's Farm Security Administration (FSA) was a well-known milestone; New Deal social policies influenced the portrayal of people's poor living conditions in shots taken by a group of photographers under the direction of Roy Stryker. For example, the special attention devoted to migrant workers – photographed while eating, sleeping, or praying – was intimately connected to the plan to resettle them and to make land available to them.[16] A few years, later the Public Information Office of UNRRA – headed by Morse Salisbury, who was brought in from the identical position with the U.S. Department of Agriculture – assumed a similar mandate.[17] Such converging visual policies are one more reason to investigate the foundation of UNRRA as part of the U.S. program to internationalize the New Deal, a program that epitomized American multilateralism between the 1940s and the 1950s. From the FSA, UNRRA inherited the medium of photography to document and persuade, and it proceeded to employ photographers directly as staff, subjecting them to its requirements and directives. The U.S. Office of War Information (OWI) provided the link between the FSA and the UNRRA. As is well known, the OWI absorbed the FSA photographic section and made wide use of pictures in reporting from the frontline and in covering stories on the home front.[18]

Professional biographies of photographers reveal a lot about the entangled connections between various institutions. Arthur Rothstein – a leading figure among the professionals who took pictures for UNRRA – is one of the most interesting cases. Roy Stryker had hired him to help launch the FSA's photographic activities, and over the following five years Rothstein shot some of the most memorable pictures of rural America. In 1940, after a brief stint at *Look* magazine, Rothstein joined the OWI and then the U.S. Army as a photographer in the Signal Corps. The military assignment took him to China, where he remained between 1945 and 1947 as chief photographer of the local UNRRA mission.[19] His less famous colleague John Vachon followed a similar path. Vachon trained as photographer in his seven years with the FSA, traveling all around the States and photographing farmers' wives cooking meals for the family, kids playing in the fields, stockyard workers sitting on the fence during lunchtime, and the many other faces that "introduced America to

Americans." Between 1942 and 1943, he served in the Office of War Information, then moved with Roy Stryker to the Standard Oil Company for a couple of years. In November 1945 he joined UNRRA and was later dispatched to Poland.[20]

Many of the photographers who wore the UNRRA flash on their sleeve had previously worked for the military. Georges Dimitri Boria and Norman Weaver, for example, had served as photographers for the Allies, Boria in the U.S. Army Signal Corps and Weaver for the Supreme Headquarters of the Allied Expeditionary Force, Civil Affairs Division.[21] In 1945, both men began portraying humanitarian actions: Weaver among the displaced persons in Germany and Boria among DPs and local civilians in Austria, in Italy, and his native Balkans.[22] In Germany, Norman Weaver was on the same team as Maxine Rude, who had also served the U.S. Army during the war and in 1946 had traveled to several countries taking hundreds of exposures for UNRRA.[23]

Soldiers-turned-photographers were not isolated cases in UNRRA. The agency massively recruited former servicemen who, incidentally, also contributed to shaping the very practices and methods of relief work in the field.[24] According to one of the U.S. ex-soldiers hired to assist DPs, the new humanitarian agency needed "a cadre of people" who "talk[ed] militarized," since in the occupied countries of Europe UNRRA was supposed to deal with military authorities to implement aid programs.[25] UNRRA had to "talk militarized" in order to accomplish its tasks, and it relied on former army personnel, who consequently contributed to forging the language of relief.

Did the same also happen for the visual narrative about rescuing postwar Europe? The fact that UNRRA photographers had previously served in the army suggests that it might be productive to trace how war photography evolved into a new visual language intended to document humanitarianism. Photographers in the American army were commanded to report the fighting realistically. At the same time they were supposed to censor the horror of war and avoid frightening the public. Their shots were meant to convey the power and strength of the Allies' military operations. Once the war was over, pictures were supposed to perform the same functions: to engage people at home without frightening them. Only now the work of visual documentation focused on the new "humanitarian army," whose mission was not to defeat the enemy but to relieve his victims.[26]

UNRRA deployed a team of photographers in the field who had trodden similar paths but had different skill levels. In some cases, UNRRA was an important stepping stone to a longer professional career. Arthur Rothstein rejoined *Look* in 1947 and remained the director of photography until 1971, when the popular American magazine shut down. During the same period, John Vachon also worked for *Look*, where Rothstein was his boss; in 1956 he returned to Poland for a "ten years later" follow-up story for the magazine, though the memory of UNRRA and DP relief was quickly fading in the postwar economic boom. For other photographers, the skills acquired in visualizing the humanitarian narrative for UNRRA could lead to a new profession. Maxine Rude, for example, went on to work as photographer for the World Health Organization in Latin America in the 1950s. George Dimitri Boria's career shows how pathways between the military and humanitarian photography could lead in both directions. After his contract with UNRRA was over, Boria went back to the U.S. Army as supervisor of the color photographic laboratory of the Far East Command during the Occupation of Japan (1947–52).[27]

UNRRA dispatched most of its photographers to Europe, which was the core of the organization's rehabilitation mission. As General Dwight D. Eisenhower wrote in 1945 to Herbert H. Lehman, director general of UNRRA, the continent had gone through "one of the grimmest ordeals of history,"[28] and its reconstruction was crucial for the postwar world order. In the European theater of humanitarian operations, camera lenses were trained on Germany, and in particular on the millions of displaced persons the organization cared for.[29] In the immediate aftermath of the war, DPs were deemed to be the quintessential victims of "German barbarism." According to the UNRRA's official historian, George Woodbridge, "no operations of the Administration were to get so much publicity – good and bad" as the relief of Europe's displaced.[30] Here Woodbridge was referring to the tense public debate over the massive employment of supplies and personnel for the assistance of the camp population in Europe. His remarks provide a good indication of the context of the time – and pictures taken in the assembly centers must be analyzed in the light of divided opinions about the effectiveness of the agency's DP operations and the symbolic meaning of European refugees in UNRRA's attempt to launch a "new humanitarianism" in the postwar period.

"Public Relation Stories"

In her personal account *The Wild Place*, UNRRA Welfare Officer Kathryn Hulme described her arrival at the displaced person camp of Wildflecken, in the American zone of Germany. Hulme emphasized the chaotic flows of people, the appalling lack of facilities, and the nightmare of overcrowded dwellings. She did not depict in any detail what she saw around her, but insisted on how what she had seen had affected her. "The sight of human beings crowded into cattle cars makes a singular first impression," she stated, referring to the massive arrivals and departure of DPs to and from the camp. She had seen similar sights in newspaper photographs published during World War I, "but like everything else where humans are concerned, it is one thing to read about it and quite another to witness it."[31] Kathryn Hulme wrote about her visual experience of displacement and how this affected her performance of relief. Three hundred kilometers to the south, not far from Munich, the former social worker Susan Pettiss described the beginning of her service for UNRRA as "unbelievable." In her journal she complained about the people "piled up" in the Assembly Centers, described rooms with "no beds, no covers," and noted that "everything else seemed to be chaos," although "things somehow got done."[32] Hulme, Pettis, and the authors of many reports drafted from the field described the reality surrounding them in order to get across how challenging their mission was. They also just wanted to record what they had seen in postwar Germany and DP camps, which were a far cry from anything they or their fellow citizens had imagined back home.

The visual narrative promulgated by UNRRA was of a very different type. Chaos, camp overpopulation, and poor living conditions of refugees were not salient features of the photographs released by the Administration, not even in the shots taken immediately after the end of the war.[33] Photos taken by Maxine Rude in 1945 are a good example. The row of trucks and the piles of sacks convey a sense of order and efficiency, while the open spaces and the few people around seem to contradict the very idea of overpopulation in the camps. We find the same features in the portrait of DPs getting ready for repatriation: they all stand at attention in ordered military formation (Figure 8.1).[34]

This is an interesting picture for several reasons. It comes from the UNRRA collection housed in the UN Archives, but the "Signal Corps – U.S. Army" logo is visible in the bottom right-hand corner. We can account for this in two ways. Photographic materials were always in short supply in occupied Germany, but the problem was particularly serious in the early days after the war, and UNRRA photographers frequently used the army's equipment; therefore the logo may have been added automatically when the film was printed. Another possible explanation is that in its initial phase, the UNRRA Public Information Office circulated the photographs taken by the army.[35] Whatever the case, the uncertain attribution

FIGURE 8.1. Men in the camp for Russian displaced persons, established in a former German barracks at Heidelberg, assembled on the drill grounds. Some of these were German prisoners of war, and others were used by the Germans as forced laborers. They receive basic drill under direction of their own camp committees, prior to repatriation to Russia. United Nations Archives (UNA), S-1058-0001-01-4.

of such early photos documenting relief reminds us of the collaboration between the UN agency and the military authorities in arranging the public information campaigns.

Assisting the military authorities in repatriating the DPs was one of UNRRA's main tasks in postwar Germany, and these efforts were widely documented. According to the final report on the Public Information Office in the U.S. zone, the intensive circulation of accounts and pictures on repatriation had a twofold purpose. On the one hand, it was aimed at "carrying on a campaign of constructive publicity" about the activity to which the UNRRA Council had given the highest priority; on the other, UNRRA sought to disseminate "information designed to acquaint displaced persons with the desirability of a return to their homelands."[36] Pictures were meant for two viewing publics: ordinary people in Western countries, who needed to be convinced that UNRRA was successfully returning the refugees home, and the refugees themselves, who had to be persuaded to accept repatriation. Norman Weaver's sequence on the repatriation of 1,400 Polish DPs is a good example of how this kind of information was visually choreographed. Weaver portrayed women and men sailing for Danzig: a tidy line of people embarking on the ship (Figure 8.2).[37]

Cases, sacks, and mattresses take center stage in the picture. This is not surprising: undoubtedly luggage is one of the "visual signs of refugeeness" which, according to the anthropologist Lisa Malkki, has played an important part in shaping the collective imagination about refugees.[38] However, here sacks, cases, and mattresses were meant to be positive rather than negative symbols, since they spoke of people's return rather than of their displacement. In the following picture we see a group of smiling men waving their hands from the ship's deck; their cheerful goodbyes conveyed the feeling that they were happy to be going home, as they had allegedly wished to do for a long time. At the same time, people's smiles and goodbyes showed that they were satisfied and, therefore, appreciative of the organization that had so efficiently arranged the massive departure. The following pictures were taken first in the Transit Center, which temporarily hosted the repatriating Polish DPs, and then at the train station. The story of refugee repatriation was reported by looking at its different stages. A sequence of shots made it easier for the public to grasp what was going on and to visualize relief, turning it from an abstract goal into concrete action.[39]

Of course, these pictures tell a largely incomplete and partial story. As is well known, many displaced persons from Eastern Europe actually

FIGURE 8.2. The repatriation of 1,400 Polish displaced persons by the United Nations Relief and Rehabilitation Administration, Germany, March 1946. Imperial War Museum (IWM), Photographs Collection, HU 92285. Many thanks to Sarah Starsmore for permission to reproduce this picture.

refused repatriation. Under the terms of the Yalta Agreement, British and American military authorities turned over most Soviet citizens to Moscow's representatives even if they were unwilling to go.[40] Kathryn Hulme was shocked when she learned from a colleague that Russians refugees "had slashed their wrists, stripped naked and hanged themselves rather than get into the repatriation train."[41] Balts claimed that they had no country to return to, since the Soviet Union had annexed Estonia, Latvia, and Lithuania; therefore, they violently rejected any negotiation with the Soviet representatives. Only half of the Poles voluntarily opted for return, and the Allies asked UNRRA to pressure the resisters to follow the example of their fellow-nationals.[42] What the UN agency's pictures showed – those taken by Weaver are just an example – was the very opposite of what repatriation really meant in many of the camps: disorder, confrontation, passive and active resistance. Moreover, the long journeys toward Eastern Europe were anything but smooth and well organized; UNRRA reports complained of the travelers' unruly behavior, of the lack of food and supplies, of continuously occurring accidents. Quite understandably, UNRRA photographers were not expected to document these sides of the story, which were evidence of the Administration's failings and which cast doubts on the very nature and sincerity of its humanitarian mandate. The humanitarian narratives implicit in these photographs warrant further analysis and can reveal a lot about both how UNRRA aimed to shape public opinion and the kinds of views they sought to advocate.

Toward the end of his life, Norman Weaver remembered that UNRRA had hired him because they "needed a photo-reporter in the field, covering repatriation from concentration camps, welfare, tracing bureaus, etc." His job was to produce "public relations stories for official publications [*sic*] such as *Life*, *Time*, *Ebony* and others."[43] As we have seen, pictures taken "in the field" were mainly meant for UNRRA publications and appropriate agencies in the member states, whose job was to distribute them to their own populations. Popular illustrated magazines were not a priority target, especially not *Life*, whose publisher – Henry R. Luce – was a Republican and very critical of Roosevelt's policy in Europe and UNRRA's mission.[44] Weaver merely wished to emphasize the prominence of UNRRA photographers' work, associating it with the most prestigious publications of the era. More important, by calling his assignments "public relations stories," he identified the core role of photography in forging a humanitarian narrative aimed at establishing a positive relationship between the institution, its stakeholders, and public opinion.

A considerable body of scholarly literature considers humanitarian representations to be characterized by a focus on an identifiably suffering victim. Scholars have convincingly analyzed the role of visual images in establishing narrative conventions that were historically central to the emergence of the humanitarian project, broadly construed as the mobilization of empathy for human beings in severe distress.[45] The well-known story of the "starving baby" leaflet, which in 1919 contributed to giving unexpected celebrity to Eglantyne Jebb's humanitarian project, is an excellent example of photography aimed at raising empathy. Jebb and a group of women activists stood on Trafalgar Square distributing a flyer bearing the image of an undernourished Austrian baby. Their intention was to publicly condemn the British embargo against the countries defeated in the First World War. Eglantyne Jebb was arrested, but the leaflet was reproduced in the most popular newspapers and the case provided an initial impetus to the founding of the Save the Children Fund (SCF). The image of the emaciated toddler became a powerful icon for the origins of the SCF and more generally, for aid in the aftermath of World War I.[46] It further reinforced the idea that humanitarian photography was about portraying suffering bodies, about creating images that had the power stir up emotions and play on the public's sympathy.

UNRRA "public relation stories" were aimed at shaping an altogether different type of narrative. They did not seek to stir up stark emotions. Instead, their purpose was to explain their mission and persuade, reassure, and familiarize the postwar public with a new vision of humanitarianism as modern, professional, and thoroughly international. Scholars have convincingly argued that photography played a prominent role in U.S. cultural diplomacy as the Cold War was getting under way by supporting American foreign policy in its efforts to "win hearts and minds."[47] The same philosophy inspired thousands of UNRRA official shots. Visual language – supposedly universal – was meant to persuade citizens in the member states to endorse the UN agency's operations and the new idea of humanitarianism that informed them. More broadly, photographic publications were intended to promote the idea that relief and rehabilitation were new duties for the democratic countries that first defeated Nazism with their armies and now were responsible for leading the reconstruction on a new basis. In UNRRA's view, international aid was the driving force for postwar renewal, and photography was meant to portray and to facilitate the process.

Rehabilitating Children

The chronicle of Peter's day is an excellent example of a "public relations story," along with the sequence of pictures on repatriation that we have already examined. This visual chronicle was based on shots taken at the unaccompanied children's center of Kloster Indersdorf, in South Germany. The author was Wlad Groman, one of UNRRA's official photographers. Peter was a fantasy name, and the first picture was meant to portray the beginning and the end of his story. The connection between the end of a gloomy past and the beginning of a new life was symbolized by Peter's goodbye to the "the woman who cared for him since 1944," while the UNRRA officer was leading him to the car[48] (Figure 8.3).

The long period that Peter had spent as a German child in a German family after he was abducted by the Schutzstaffel (SS) from a Russian orphanage was finally over. Peter was now beginning a new life with his real identity which he had regained thanks to UNRRA. The sequence of pictures referred to the program devoted to Eastern European children

FIGURE 8.3. Kloster Indersdorf, Germany. Peter, whose exact name is unknown (called Alecander Pecha or Siegfried Bruhns), was born 20 June 1939. According to German records, Peter was an orphan in Shitomir, Russia, and was found by an SS doctor, Dr. Bruhns, who thought that Peter might be of German birth. Peter waves goodbye to the woman who cared for him since 1944 as he is taken to the car by Andre Marx of Luxembourg. UNA, S-1058-0001-01-161.

who had been forcibly taken to Germany and handed over to foster families during the Nazi occupation. Locating these children and removing them from the German homes where they had spent several years was one of the most prominent among UNRRA duties. The number of cases the organization dealt with was not particularly large, but the issue of "lost children" held a special grip on the postwar imagination and it stood at the center of tense confrontations between the varied actors involved. Foster families did not want to let the children go, UNRRA officers were in charge of taking them to collective centers, military authorities had to face the complaints of both the German population and the representatives of the children's supposed countries of origin that wanted them back.[49] This picture presents as an amiable goodbye what in many cases was the transfer of children unwilling to leave their homes for specialized collective centers, while UNRRA officers had to deal with the resistance of German families. It is interesting to probe the visual chronicle of Peter's "rebirth" for its meanings and intentions rather than merely focus on the gap between representation and reality.

Peter's one-day transition to a new life was related visually in steps and explained in captions: the bath "before the medical exam," the rich meal to "get all of his calories," the dental checkup, the sculpture class as "an important part of UNRRA's work in rehabilitation," and at the end the peaceful rest in the "new home."[50] This is a typical "picture story" – a sequence of shots dramatized by captions. The "picture story" was a more sophisticated version of the simple sequence of photographs already seen in Norman Weaver's report about the repatriation of Polish DPs. The combination of the pictures with the details in the captions provided an explicit narrative, making it easier for the viewer to comprehend the events and to participate in the child's rehabilitation process.[51] This format seems to have been particularly successful. A picture story similar to Peter's was published under the title "Heaven for an Orphan" in the American magazine *Look* in September 1946. This time the fantasy name of the unaccompanied child was Anna and she was presented as Polish. However, the plot remained the same and the focus was again on the "rebirth" of the little girl thanks to UNRRA's effective intervention.[52]

In both Peter's and Anna's chronicles, the fact that the main character was a child made the story more poignant. Children figured recurrently in UNRRA's visual documentation of DPs, and few would dispute that this subject was overrepresented. Immediately after the war, adults, not children, made up most of the displaced population. This situation changed only when the baby boom arrived in the camps. One reason that boys and girls appeared so frequently in UNRRA portraits was because the agency had special programs in place for children. But UNRRA's portraits of children were also meant to give out a powerful message about the organization's overall mission. Recent studies have shown that today's humanitarian communication strategies generally portray children as the quintessential embodiment of human suffering.[53] But pain and grief were almost completely censored out of UNRRA's pictures. Indeed, they often portrayed children in the act of eating: joyfully rather than greedily, as in the pictures taken in Kloster Indersdorf by Maxine Rude[54] (Figure 8.4).

Here the children's hunger was downplayed in favor of portraying the effectiveness of an organization capable of feeding them. Contemporary humanitarian campaigns frequently associate children with food; hunger is represented as the quintessential human need.[55] In the case of

FIGURE 8.4. Supper for the two-year-olds at Kloster Indersdorf, an UNRRA Children's Center for Orphaned Displaced Persons, located in the Bavarian mountains. The UNRRA welfare worker is Greta Fisherova, a Czechoslovakian. The center is housed in an old monastery. UNA, S-1058-0001-01-94.

UNRRA's pictures, the emphasis was reversed: food was shown as the quintessential aid.

Furthermore, photographers recurrently portrayed children at play. The images of smiling little girls and boys having fun aimed to convey the idea of innocence, another component of humanitarian discourse's special preference for childhood. In fact, the pictures of little boys and girls contributed to reinforcing the view that displaced persons were the recipients most deserving of the United Nations' aid. This message was needed, especially toward the end of UNRRA's mandate, when the persistent refusal of the camp population to repatriate raised suspicions in Western countries, which were now inclined to view the DP camps as havens for parasites abetted by international aid.[56] However, images of refugees' innocence – epitomized by children – not only aimed to counter increasing criticism against UNRRA: they were meant to legitimize humanitarian operations by showing they were being conducted fairly. Current humanitarian appeals to the public often refer to suffering innocence since this immediately evokes the moral duty to relieve such suffering. The official shots of UNRRA remind us that the "need to think of [recipients] as *innocent* victims" which is an essential feature of contemporary humanitarian narrative, is a historical construction,[57] and the visual representation of humanitarian aid contributed to promoting it.

UNRRA's Angle

UNRRA's emphasis on childhood and innocence had several aspects and extended to adult recipients. Adult refugees were portrayed as innocent as children, but also as unwitting and immature. They were the deserving recipients of postwar relief, but it was the job of the humanitarians to decide what was good for DPs and to educate them.[58] In his final assessment of the history of DP Operations in Germany, George Woodbridge pointed out that UNRRA required huge funds and an enormous workforce because its aim went beyond merely rescuing refugees and providing them with basic assistance; it "also wanted to rehabilitate the individuals in the camps." To clarify his point he used a metaphor:

Any mother who has tried knows that, when she first teaches her children how to perform simple household tasks (bed-making, dishwashing, cleaning) it requires far more time to teach the children to do such work and to supervise their doing it than to do the work herself. That was precisely the situation that confronted the Administration.

Hundreds of pictures portrayed "mother UNRRA" teaching her "children" how to "perform simple household tasks." Photographers extensively recorded the training classes organized in the camps, showing women gardening, spinning, or sewing, and men learning carpentry or using bricks and mortar (Figure 8.5). In many other pictures DPs were on duty in the kitchen, in the garden, in the school or in the hospital, contributing to the assembly center's life and "learning by doing."[59] Photographs contributed to presenting employment programs and vocational training as the best remedies against apathy and idleness, which were deemed typical illnesses of uprooted people.[60] Portraits of women and men at work visualized how people who had been "diagnosed" as passive and careless were being reshaped into self-sustaining individuals. Rehabilitation through work was rooted in the distant past of humanitarianism,[61] but it acquired a specific meaning in UNRRA-administered DP camps, since it was regarded as crucial in transforming putatively apathetic and indolent refugees into people who "could again face the world as free human

FIGURE 8.5. Wool from the sheep at the Hohenfels farm is spun by Anna Czura and Marismroz and then made into socks and mittens by Polish girls at the center. UNA, S-1058-0001-01-184.

beings."[62] This process turned out to be particularly important when the massive repatriation of *displaced persons* ceased to be an option and Westward resettlement became the only solution.

UNRRA regarded work as the core of the rehabilitation process, and photography was intended to document this by showing how committed the refugees and how effective the agency's educational programs were. These pictures were meant as an integral part of UNRRA's humanitarian narrative, because work was the essence of rehabilitation, and rehabilitation was the essence of humanitarianism. As the organization's famous motto asserted: "help the people to help themselves."

Although the photos appeared to be telling the story of the women and men in the camps, the real protagonist was UNRRA itself. Sometimes it was present through the insignia or uniforms worn by personnel; more often it was invisible but still dominating through the idea of effectiveness and professionalism conveyed by the photos. Relief workers always appeared self-confident and relaxed, all the camp surgeries shown were well equipped, the canteens were working properly, and the warehouses were well stocked. This was exactly what photographer John Vachon referred to as the "UNRRA angle." In the letters to his wife he repeatedly complained about the agency's guidelines; he felt he was "inadequate at gathering facts, sensing stories, etc.," and regretted not being free to "wander in Poland a la Montana." The Public Information Office of UNRRA deployed the professional skills of the Farm Security Administration's photographers, but it wanted a different sort of picture from them, one that focused on the organization's sterling performance. Shots were supposed to "say UNRRA in block letters," as Vachon ironically observed. In April 1946 he was extremely disappointed by the feedback he had just received from the European Regional Office in London about some of his recent photographs. As he reported to his wife, he had been told that the pictures were good, "but hardly of use to UNRRA – only two of the 64 had any UNRRA angle – an UNRRA official with a flash on his shoulder in the picture." "The idea of good historical pictures for UNRRA in the Stryker manner is totally incomprehensible," concluded Vachon. "So from now on, for UNRRA I make only what I think they will use. The others I keep for myself."[63] The most important fact to emerge from Vachon's letters from Poland is not his nostalgia for photography "a la Montana," nor is it his criticism of the "good fake stories" that London and Washington were asking photographers to provide. It is that he clearly acknowledges the existence of a distinct UNRRA visual narrative, centered on the institution's successful outcomes and its relieved recipients.

Victims or Recipients?

The whole point of UNRRA photographs was to showcase pleased recipients, instead of suffering victims. In the pictures taken for UNRRA it is difficult to find the "compassionate gaze at Europeans" that was so common in most other postwar American and British documentary photography.[64] UNRRA shots aimed mainly to persuade public opinion of the soundness of its programs. Women and men of the world had just left behind the tragedy of the war and were grappling with the problems of reconstruction; they needed hopeful glimpses of the future, such as the idea of a new international body salving the wounds of the war and paving the way for a new kind of international cooperation. The visual representation of UNRRA operations was meant to expand consensus and support for a modern, professional, and rational humanitarianism – in other words, a humanitarianism founded on qualification and planning rather than on "good heart" and sensitivity. Qualification and planning did not focus on the distress of victims to be rescued: John Vachon was happy when he finally could get his "first good pictures of *really* hungry looking people" and his boss in London liked them.[65] Nonetheless, while staff rejected photographs they felt were unsuitable, they probably never drafted an explicit code or guidelines to define the standards of "humanitarian photography." However, the portraits of refugees sailing for home, of smiling children in collective centers, and of DPs trained in various jobs showed the success of the Administration in helping people – which meant not just relieving them but rehabilitating them. These pictures were a fitting vehicle for circulating the contents and objectives of the humanitarian mission UNRRA sought to promote. They also remind us that humanitarianism speaks in different languages. For example, it can play on the distress of the victims or on the efficacy of aid, it can evoke sympathy for suffering humanity or praise for the rescuers, and it can focus on relief of the body's pain or on the "healing of souls," as in the case of DPs' rehabilitation through work and professional training.

Visual narratives have historically played a crucial role in the development of different humanitarian languages, and they have circulated dissimilar, but not necessarily divergent, views on international aid. The disempowerment of the men, women, and children portrayed is one general result. In UNRRA's photos, modern humanitarianism appeared sterilized and aseptic, almost dehumanized. Even though the captions offered details about their supposedly personal stories, the portrayed recipients were in fact standardized and depersonalized by the overwhelming image of the "aid machinery" set up for their assistance. This machinery itself was what mattered and its depiction overshadowed any kind of agency the recipients themselves may have had. From this perspective, the visual narrative of humanitarianism promoted by UNRRA in postwar time is an important reminder of humanitarian discourses that center on suffering victims. In fact, in the current language of aid the emphasis on people's misery and their need to be taken care of ends up sounding like an insistence that they are helpless. As scholars have stated with regard to the representation of forced migrants, "[a] vision of helplessness is vitally linked to the constitution of speechlessness among refugees: helpless victims need protection, need someone to speak for them."[66] UNRRA's photographs downplayed this aspect of "people's misery" to focus on the pleased recipients of efficient rescuers. Yet the pictures provide a meaningful glimpse into the historical shaping of transnational imagination of recipients as human beings without agency.

Notes

1 Reinisch, ed., *Relief in the Aftermath of War*; Mazower, *No Enchanted Palace*.
2 On the historical construction of humanitarian narratives centered on suffering victims and sympathetic rescuers, see Laqueur, "Bodies" and "Mourning"; Halttunen, "Humanitarianism and the Pornography of Pain"; and Hunt, *Inventing Human Rights*.
3 Borgwardt, *A New Deal for the World*, 118–21.
4 "Address of the President of the United States," *United Nations Relief and Rehabilitation Organization Journal* 1 (10 November – 2 December 1943): 1.
5 Ben Shephard, *The Long Road Home. The Aftermath of the Second World War* (New York: Knopf, 2010), 43–61.
6 Cohen, "Between Relief and Politics; Salvatici, "Professionals of Humanitarianism."
7 Lachenal and Thaite, "Une généalogie missionaire," 45.
8 Watenpaugh, "League of Nations' Rescue of Armenian Genocide Survivors."
9 Mazower, *No Enchanted Palace*, 5–10.
10 The Historian's Office originated in September 1943 with the appointment of Grace Fox as historian of the Office of Foreign Relief and Rehabilitation Operations (OFRRO), Washington, DC. Fox moved to UNRRA in January 1944, and the Historian's Office was made a part of the Secretariat. In September 1946, George Woodbridge was appointed chief archivist and historian, with Dr. Fox remaining Woodbridge's deputy as headquarters historian. The chief function of the Historian's Office was to prepare the official history of UNRRA, which was later published. See George Woodbridge, *UNRRA. The History of the United Nations Relief and Rehabilitation Administration* (New York: Columbia University Press, 1950), 3 vols. On the development of the Office of Historian, see United Nations Archives (UNA, New York), S-0556-0005-09, Historical section – Progress reports 1944–1947.
11 UNRRA photographic collection held at the UNA consists of 3,530 shots (prints and films). Norman Weaver Private Collection consists of around 1,000 pictures; copies of some of them are in the Imperial War Museum (IWM), Photograph Collections. The United States Holocaust Memorial Museum (USHMM), Photo Archive, has some of Maxine Rude's pictures.
12 Receiving countries in Europe were Greece, Yugoslavia, Albania, Poland, Czechoslovakia, two Soviet Socialist Republics (Ukraine and Byelorussia), Italy, Austria, Finland, Hungary, and the Displaced Persons operation in Germany. Receiving countries outside Europe were Korea, the Philippines, and China.
13 Woodbridge, *UNRRA*, vol. 1, 107–8.
14 Jessica Reinisch, "Auntie UNRRA at the Crossroad," *Past and Present*, Supplement 8 (2013): 70.
15 Woodbridge, *UNRRA*, vol. 1, 282.
16 Many studies on the FSA have appeared since the early 1970s; for the "revisionist" school, which emphasizes the role played by New Deal ideology in

shaping documentary photographs, see Curtis, *Mind's Eye, Mind's Truth*. Production, reproduction, and circulation of the pictures are the main focus in the volume by Finnegan, *Picturing Poverty*.

17 Borgwardt, *A New Deal for the World*.

18 Moeller, *Shooting War*, 155–250.

19 Oral history interview with Arthur Rothstein, 25 May 1964, Archives of American Art, Smithsonian Institution, http://www.aaa.si.edu/collections/interviews/oral-history-interview-arthur-rothstein-13317.

20 J. Vachon, *John Vachon's America. Photographs and Letters from the Depression to World War II*, ed. M. Orvell (Berkeley: University of California Press, 2003; A. Vachon, ed., *Poland, 1946. The Photographs and Letters of John Vachon* (Washington, DC: Smithsonian Institution Press, 1995).

21 Before the outbreak of the war, Norman Weaver taught at the Central School of Arts and Crafts in London, http://www.normanweaver.com/index.htm, while Georges Dimitri Boria worked as a photographer first in Hollywood and then on cruise ships, http://users.rcn.com/laura2/about.html.

22 Boria was born in Albania and had migrated to the United States when he was seventeen.

23 For a biographical sketch of Maxine Rude, see *Maxine Rude. Displaced Europe 1945–1946 Photographs and Remembrances*, organized by the Center for Holocaust and Genocide Studies, University of Minnesota, http://www.chgs.umn.edu/museum/exhibitions/displaced/.

24 Silvia Salvatici, "An Army without Weapons. UNRRA Relief Officer in Europe," paper presented at conference *Humanitarianism in Times of War (1914–2012)*, Giessen, 11–13 October 2012.

25 USHMM, Oral History Interview with Theodore Feder, RG-50.030*0335, 4.

26 Roeder, *The Censored War*; Maslowski, *Armed with Cameras*.

27 Boria donated his collection of photographs from the Far East to the McArthur Memorial, http://www.macarthurmemorial.org/la_pc_georges.asp.

28 Herbert H. Lehman Collections, Columbia University, Letter from Eisenhower to Lehman, 7 November 1945.

29 About displaced persons in postwar Europe see, among many, Cohen, *In War's Wake*, and Anna Holian, *Between National Socialism and Soviet Communism: Displaced Persons in Postwar Germany* (Ann Arbor: University of Michigan Press, 2011); also the review essay Pamela Ballinger, "Impossible Returns, Enduring Legacies: Recent Historiography of Displacement and the Reconstruction of Europe after World War II," *Contemporary European History* 22, no. 1 (2013): 127–38.

30 G. Woodbridge, *UNRRA*, vol. 2, 470.

31 Kathryn Hulme, *The Wild Place* (London: Frederick Muller, 1954), 24.

32 Susan Pettiss with Lynne Taylor, *After the Shooting Stopped: The Story of an UNRRA Welfare Worker in Germany 1945–1947*, 54–57.

33 Unfortunately, most of UNRRA's photographs are undated; in some cases original captions can help to reconstruct the shots' chronology.

34 UNA, S-1058-0001-01-4.

35 Woodbridge, *UNRRA*, vol. 1, 281–2.

36 Ibid., 1.

37 "The repatriation of 1400 Polish Displaced Persons by the United Nations Relief and Rehabilitation Administration, Germany, March 1946," WM, Photographs Collection, HU 92285.

38 Malkki, "Speechless Emissaries," 386.

39 IWM, Photograph Collection, Norman Weaver, The Repatriation of 1400 Polish Displaced Persons by the United Nations Relief and Rehabilitation Administration, Germany, March 1946, UH 92281/2/3/4/5.

40 Mark R. Elliott, *Pawns of Yalta. Soviet Refugees and America's Role in Their Repatriation* (Urbana: University of Illinois Press, 1982); Wolfgang Jacobmeyer, *Vom Zwangsarbeiter zum Heimatlosen Ausländer. Die Displaced Persons in Westdeutschland, 1945–1951* (Göttingen: Vandenhoeck und Reprecht, 1985).

41 Hulme, *The Wild Place*, 44.

42 About UNRRA and the repatriation of Polish DPs, see Jessica Reinisch, "'We Shall Rebuild Anew a Powerful Nation': UNRRA, Internationalism and National Reconstruction in Poland," *Journal of Contemporary History* 43, no. 3 (2008).

43 Norman Weaver Personal Collection, Isle of Wight. Of course, *Life, Look,* and *Ebony* were not "official publications"; Weaver probably used this term to emphasize the relevance of the work they were doing.

44 See the editorial "The Trouble with UNRRA ... Is so Basic that We Had Best Wind It Up and Start Over," *Life,* 5 November 1945, 48.

45 Sontag, *Regarding*; Malkki, "Speechless Emissaries"; Boltanski, *Distant Suffering*; Stanley Cohen, *States of Denial. Knowing about Atrocities and Suffering* (Cambridge: Polity, 2001).

46 Mulley, *The Woman Who Saved the Children*; Mahood, *Feminism and Voluntary Action*, 142–3; Barnett, *Empires of Humanity*, 82–7.

47 On U.S. cultural diplomacy during the Cold War, see K. A. Osgood, "Hearts and Minds: The Unconventional Cold War," *Journal of Cold War Studies* 2 (2002): 85–107; Bezner, *Photography and Politics in America*; and Sandeen, *Picturing an Exhibition*.

48 UNA, S-1058-0001-01-161.

49 Tara Zahra, *The Lost Children. Reconstructing Europe's Families after World War II* (Cambridge, MA: Harvard University Press, 2011).

50 UNA, S-1058-0001-01-161/2/3/4/5/6/7/8.

51 Picture stories became very popular in the second half of the 1930s, thanks to the new weekly magazines such as *Life, Vu,* and *Picture Post.*

52 *Look,* September 1946, 38–9.

53 Suski, "Children, Suffering and the Humanitarianism Appeal"; Malkki, "Children, Humanity and the Infantilization of Peace."

54 UNA, S-1058-0001-01-94.

55 Malkki, "Children, Humanity and the Infantilization of Peace," 64.

56 Salvatici, "From Displaced Persons to Labourers," 219–29.

57 David Rieff, *A Bed for the Night. Humanitarianism in Crisis* (New York: Simon & Schuster, 2002), 24–5; Martínez and Libal, "The Gender of Humanitarian Narrative," 161–70.

58 Salvatici, "'Help the People to Help Themselves.'"
59 UNA, S-1058-0001-01-184.
60 Eduard Bakis, "D. P. Apathy," in *Flight and Resettlement*, by H. B. M. Murphy (Lucerne: UNESCO 1955), 80–91. On the construction of "DP-apathy" as "une pathologie de personne déplacée," see also Daniel Cohen, "Naissance d'une nation: les personnes déplacées de l'après-guerre 1945–1951," *Genèses* 38 (2000): 56–78.
61 An example is Barnardo's Home, founded by Thomas J. Barnardo in Victorian London, in which street children were trained in different skills in order to rehabilitate them. Barnardo was a pioneer in using photography and circulated among donors portraits of children who had been "transformed" from "vagrants" into "little workmen." Koven, "Dr. Barnardo's 'Artistic Fictions.'" The debate on rehabilitation was crucial also in the foundation and development of the Charity Organization Society (COS) in late nineteenth-century Britain; see Woodroofe, *From Charity to Social Work*.
62 *History of Employment and Vocational Training Division of UNRRA*, U.S. Zone, p. 1, UNA, S-1021-0080-10, UNRRA, Office of the Historian. Monographs, Documents and Publications 1942–1948, History of Employment Division (part I).
63 Vachon, ed., *Poland, 1946*, 53.
64 Hoffmann, "Gazing at Ruins."
65 Vachon, ed., *Poland, 1946*, 62.
66 Malkki, "Speechless Emissaries," 388. Peter Gatrell, *Free World?*, has recently argued that the disempowerment of refugees is not the outcome of the international organizations' policies during the 1970s; rather, it has complex origins rooted further in the past.

9

All the World Loves a Picture

The World Health Organization's Visual Politics, 1948–1973

Davide Rodogno and Thomas David

Introduction

The World Health Organization (WHO) is one of the original United Nations agencies and a direct successor of both the League of Nations Health Organization and of the United Nations Relief and Rehabilitation Administration (UNRRA). It became operational in 1948.[1] The WHO did not possess the means to implement its grandiose plan of assisting in the task of extending health services all over the world.[2] The WHO's mandate was to set standards, collect data, engage in epidemiological surveillance, training and research, emergency relief, and cooperative activities. Thanks to its growing membership and an open decision-making structure through the annual World Health Assembly, the WHO enjoyed more legitimacy and permanence than its predecessors.[3] The two Cold War superpowers agreed on WHO's authority, on its international reach (through central headquarters with six regional offices and regiments of in-country field staff) and its role in creating a new cadre of international health professionals.[4] To legitimize its existence and expand its reach, the organization strove to inform the broadest possible audience about its activities using various media outlets. As one regional director noted, the WHO was "entirely dependent upon the goodwill of the member countries and their understanding and knowledge of the work that is performed."[5]

We wish to thank Sunil Amrith, Anne-Emmanuel Birn, Nitsan Chorev, Heide Fehrenbach, Yitang Lin, Amalia Ribi, Clifford Rosenberg, Jessica Reinisch, Pierre-Yves Saunier and Ludovic Tournès for their comments. All responsibility for any mistakes is ours.

During the 1950s and 1960s the WHO heavily depended on the financial support of the United States.[6] The organization embraced the tenets of capitalist economic development; it was mainly an organization of the West. The WHO was most active in Asia, Africa, and Latin America and learned to navigate the troubled waters of decolonization. Initially at least, the WHO struggled to establish its legitimacy and faced stiff competition for prestige and resources, human and financial, from other international organizations and philanthropic foundations such as the United Nations International Children's Emergency Fund (UNICEF), the Rockefeller Foundation, or the Food and Agriculture Organization (FAO). The visual politics of the organization were, to some extent, determined by this struggle and by the part the organization would play in what Sunil Amrith calls the "*promise of development.*" This chapter does not assess whether or not the organization kept its promise; rather, it examines how the WHO visually and discursively represented such promise.

During the 1950s and 1960s, the editors of the WHO Newsletter emphasized the importance of technology as a way to improve public health worldwide; however, they quickly realized that technology alone would not sufficiently promote and "sell" the organization.[7] Moreover, since the early 1950s, WHO leadership understood that addressing the root causes of ill health or implementing institution-building programs were utterly utopian objectives given their limited human and financial resources. The WHO could offer only targeted, small-scale, interventions. Therefore, technical assistance appeared to be the perfect palliative to achieve the promise of development, which was also the case for other international organizations, such as the International Labour Organization and the Food and Agricultural Organization.[8] The Newsletter editors shrewdly adapted the iconologic contents of the magazine to this set of circumstances, introducing and blending technical assistance with humanitarian narratives.

WHO practices, especially in the ex-colonial and newly independent states, were difficult to render visually. Therefore, the photographers hired by the magazine's editors resorted to humanitarian narratives comprised of three tropes: the hapless victim in distress, the villain – which, in this case, is not human, but could be a mosquito, the environment, or even traditions – and the savior, the international organization and its agents in the form of doctors, nurses, or technical experts. A crucial ingredient was the representation of pain and suffering, which links victim and savior.[9] This narrative framework was not new or original; it was long established in adventure novels and fairy tales of the British, North American, and other European literature traditions. The combination of images and text was not new either; its origins are to be found in missionary societies' publications, in the Red Cross and League of Nations publications of the interwar period, and in the visual politics of UNRRA.[10] Like its predecessors, the WHO made abundant use of tropes involving the fight against disease or epidemics or, more broadly speaking, the fight for health. As concerns public health narratives, similarities between the WHO and public health and humanitarian organizations and philanthropic charities – whether secular or religious – is clear. The rhetoric employed by the WHO – of before and after, of conversion, of *the* mission, of progress and improvement, of health and wealth – was certainly not new.

What was new was the combination of humanitarian narratives and specific tropes developed for the purposes of a newly created, ambitious organization. The WHO also benefited from the rise of photojournalism, particularly visual practices of glossy prestige magazines like *Life* and *Look*, and from the visual and communication experiences of the Second World War. Humanitarian narratives, both visual and discursive, were a way to give a human dimension and a human face to the dullness, coldness, and dryness of technical assistance. They put the human being at the center of their visual stories. Especially during the 1950s, the photographers hired by the WHO brought along a specific aesthetic sensibility, professional backgrounds, and wartime experiences that heavily influenced their reportages. The same applies to WHO editors and authors who, in the frames and captions as well as in the articles of the magazine, systematically refer to the fights and war against epidemics, to warriors, knights, and shields, and to victims of diseases.

Like other UN agencies, the WHO relied on information policies and practices implemented by international organizations since the end of the First World War. The League of Nations, the American Red Cross, and other private organizations had set up publicity departments in charge of propaganda that made abundant use of photographic material.[11] Other UN organizations, such as the United Nations Educational, Scientific, and Cultural Organization (UNESCO), published a magazine, the *Courier*, that was as sophisticated as *World Health*. The High Commissariat of Refugees hired – often the same – photographers for its publications, as did the Food and Agricultural Organization and the United Nations International Children's Emergency Fund. To this day, no studies have examined the visual politics of the UN, an organization that has had an information department since its inception, nor have scholars attempted comparative analysis of the visual politics of international organizations.

This chapter focuses on the visual politics of the WHO during its first twenty-five years of existence, from 1948 to 1973. We argue that while the visual politics of the organization were sophisticated, they were not entirely original. In the 1950s and 1960s, the WHO focused on biomedical determinants and technological solutions. By the early 1970s, it had adopted a new agenda, based on an unprecedented commitment to address political, social, and economic causes of poor health and to attend to the rights of developing countries. As a WHO pamphlet from 1976 put it:

This means the end of well-intentioned international technical paternalism in health and its replacement by an era of international collaboration and cooperation.[12]

This chapter examines the period of "well-intentioned international technical paternalism" and offers an account of when, how, and why technical assistance mobilized humanitarian photography.

The Newsletter and World Health: Two Visual Outlets of the WHO

The WHO *Newsletter* was first published in 1949. During the 1950s and 1960s the magazine took various formats, and in 1958 the *Newsletter* was rechristened *World Health*, adopting a format and glossy style that deliberately recalled *Life* magazine. The WHO *Newsletter* and *World Health* were the primary outlets through which the organization implemented its visual politics.[13]

Since the early 1950s the WHO has realized the importance of photography. In 1952, the organization signed its first contract with professional photographers. The way photography was used in the Newsletter and later in *World Health* varied conspicuously. Photographs were used for illustrative and informational purposes; they were often used to corroborate statements and facts narrated in the articles.

The WHO had a broad mandate and the *Newsletter* and *World Health* covered virtually all aspects related to public health: from cancer to blood transfusion, from transmissible diseases to drug addiction and alcoholism, from venereal disease control projects in Europe to mental health in Africa, from leprosy to health safeguards for the Mecca pilgrims. Many of these topics had little to do with technical assistance and were not cast in humanitarian narratives.

Since the late 1940s, the WHO has put forward the idea that technical assistance would construct the conditions necessary to trigger the virtuous circle leading to prosperity. As Judith Tendler explains: "Development assistance was established on the premise that the developed world possessed both the talent and the capital for helping backward countries to develop. Development know-how was spoken about as if it were like capital – a stock of goods capable of being transferred from its owners to the less privileged."[14] Once the process was properly set in motion, technical assistance would be withdrawn and the now "enlightened" local populations would thrive.[15] Technical assistance relied on the older humanitarian credo: "helping peoples to help themselves," on which the American Relief Administration, the Quakers, and the UNRRA had built their "missions."[16] Veiled as self-help, the WHO could pretend to respect local and national cultures and thereby sell its action as neutral and not political (anti-political). Articles in the early 1950s highlighted the premise that local people are the agents in their development of their health and wealth, provided they followed the modernization precepts of the WHO.

To promote technical assistance, the editors of the *Newsletter* portrayed some of the myriad pilot projects (over 600 in 1959) as success stories. The reader of the WHO magazine was led to believe that the world was on the verge of a revolutionary improvement in health standards – was about to eradicate malaria, to win the fight against transmissible diseases and water pollution, and so on. Each alleged success story was dramatically narrated and visually staged.[17] The magazine continually moved on to further successes in order to raise awareness of further international health problems. Technical assistance propaganda came with the pretense – or for some, perhaps, the genuine belief – of the universal validity of *the* model.[18] The pages of the *Newsletter* and of *World Health* abound in examples of model cities, model vaccination campaigns, and the like, systematically presented as success stories that could – and should – be repeated.[19]

In 1953, the Public Information Department hired Robert Kee as photo editor. Kee, a British historian and prisoner of war during the Second World War, began his career in journalism working for the *Picture Post* and became a special correspondent for the *Sunday Times* and the *Observer*. One of his first actions was to contact John G. Morris, photo editor and agency administrator of Magnum, the international photographic cooperative founded by Robert Capa, David "Chim" Seymour, Henri Cartier-Bresson and others, to introduce himself, present the magazine, and discuss the crucial role of picture stories.[20] Kee wanted to foster a relationship between Magnum and the WHO. At that point, the two organizations had collaborated only once: Magnum co-founder and photographer David Seymour had done a reportage for the WHO on a premature baby in France that had been a great success. As Kee noted at the time:

> Very little has been done on the picture story side here up to now as there has been no-one specifically assigned to that job, but there seems to me to be considerable possibilities.... Our stories fall into two categories: 1) Those projects big enough to interest a group such as Magnum to do for us and sell for themselves – the Premature Baby was an example of such a story; – and 2) those stories on which we send our own photographers and for which we must have some means of distribution.[21]

Although the WHO worked with other photographers, its collaboration with Magnum was special. Throughout the 1950s and 1960s several Magnum photographers such as Ernest Scheidegger, Kris Taconis, David Seymour, and Marc Riboud collaborated with the WHO: "The Magnum boys are expensive but in the end they are worth it. And also they have the best release possible for real story material."[22] The fame and reputation of Magnum photographers was important for the WHO; their reportage ensured the organization a high visibility. They were used to traveling and working in difficult conditions. Most of them, as well as other photographers working for WHO (for instance Eric Schwab, Ralph Morse, and Dominique Darbois) had been or still were war photographers. More important, Magnum – and more generally photojournalists in the aftermath of World War II – shared the ethics, liberal internationalism, and cosmopolitanism of the international organization.[23] Finally, personal ties enhanced the collaboration between Magnum and WHO.[24] They had similar education trajectories and the same – often traumatic – experiences of war, totalitarianism, personal loss, misery, epidemics. This might explain their agreement on editorial content and aesthetic codes.[25]

David Seymour (Chim)'s assignment on the Premature Baby Series in the early 1950s – a photographic reportage on the work of the French Ministry of Health, Division of Social Hygiene, in the care of premature infants – illustrates the collaboration between WHO and Magnum.[26] It was the first reportage of Magnum for the WHO and was later published by *Life* and *Illustrated* and used for a big WHO traveling exhibit[27] (Figure 9.1).

In 1950, Mary Losey and George Ninaud, office manager of Magnum, set the stage for this reportage. As indicated by Losey the photographs were to cover these points:

1. Routine of day's care of a typical premature infant. This should emphasize the work of the nurse rather than the equipment since it

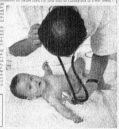

FIGURE 9.1. David Seymour, "The Baby Born Too Soon" in *WHO Newsletter*, February 1953. Several photos of different sizes and shape from the Premature Baby Series. © WHO/David Seymour.

is on the nurse that the minute to minute health and safety of the baby depend.

2. Training of doctors and nurses for the special problems of caring for prematures.

3. Service of Special Assistance which protects mother and baby both before delivery (a premature delivery is frequently anticipated and all arrangements made before it happens) and after the baby has been placed in a premature centre.[28]

The contract was very detailed and shows that the photographer was to emphasize the nurse and her work rather than the modern equipment. The human being was to take precedence over the technology.[29] The contract also mentioned the way Seymour should shoot his photos:

I talked to Pat Palmer [the WHO Public Information Officer for the Middle East and a friend of David Seymour] this morning and she told me all about your troubles and the ten pounds premature caesarean! Better luck next time and meanwhile don't despair. I know your agonies about getting pictures of the brats in incubators but assure you that whether you are satisfied with them or not, we will be satisfied if we can see the baby, see the nurse's hands, see what she is doing. Sometimes, believe it or not, those things even have a facial expression. I do not blame you if you would like to squash them all right now but don't let it have a permanent effect on your paternal instincts.[30]

Losey went as far as asking Magnum to retouch some photos and to remove one in order to conform to the expectations of the audience: "It is the opinion of WHO that it does no good to show pictures of infants, to the lay public, which refer to abnormalities [i.e. an infant with a deformity known as tunnel chest]. The second picture of this infant … also shows the deformity, but not so clearly. And in both reference is made to it in the text; it is thought that it will go unnoticed. However, if it is possible to retouch the negative enough to lessen the shadow in the depression in the chest we would recommend doing so."[31]

Little information exists concerning the distribution policy of the *Newsletter* and the *World Health* as well as the readership and reception of the magazine. The sketchy information we have indicates that the readers were public health professionals and semi-professionals, and middle-class literate audiences, male and female.[32] Since the time of the *Newsletter,* the publication was bilingual, French and English (it was called *O.M.S. Nouvelles*, and later *Santé du Monde*). Throughout the 1960s, it would be published in further languages, including Spanish, Arabic, Chinese, and Russian. WHO sold its magazine through its different regional offices, the offices of the UN, and its various agencies. The magazine was also sold and distributed through other intermediaries. For example, in 1962 WHO signed a contract with M. Jacques Rousseau who acted as agent in charge of the distribution of *World Health* (and of other publications) in France. His remuneration depended on the number of issues sold.[33] In Switzerland, however, the WHO sold 36,000 copies (20,000 in German and 16,000 in French) to the Swiss Society of Pharmacy, which would distribute the magazine for free through its network of drugstores. The Society was permitted to insert two pages of ads, which should be approved by WHO and should deal with the thematic topic of the issue.[34]

1949–1959: The Tale of Victory

The Second World War was an event that transformed a sense of the possible due to the revolutionary new technologies of disease control that it produced.[35] It was during the war that an almost blind faith in DDT and in vaccination began. War photographers hired by the WHO substantiated the idea that, just like Nazism and Fascism, diseases and epidemics could be wiped out. Moreover, the unresolved legacies of the Second World War and decolonization, as well as the intensifying Cold War, narrowed the definition of the relationship of health, medicine, hygiene, and economic development.[36] From 1946 to the mid-1950s, the new international agencies as well as national governments chose to concentrate on the piecemeal extension of their short-term emergency measures. This context favored the intertwining of technical assistance with humanitarian narratives, based on the idea of urgency and relief.

Photographic reportage on yaws, leprosy, trachoma, or malnutrition, where a – generally African – child was photographed before and after treatment are perfect examples of the idea the organization wished to convey: Western technology and science will triumph over disease. These photographs were intended to arouse the sympathy of readers in wealthy donor countries, especially in the United States, but they gave visual form to the worldview of which the agency's operation was an incarnation. Seymour's "Baby Born too Soon" suggests a common transnational humanity. However, contrary to previous pictures by Seymour (such as his well-known photo entitled "A Group of Children Await Food Rations, Greece (1948)"), here Chim pays attention – or is forced to pay attention – to the technical environment (i.e., the incubator) and to the technical assistance of the nurse, whose "dismembered" hands are clearly visible.

These before and after pictures are the quintessential embodiment of success stories: a child affected by yaws before and after treatment (Figure 9.2); a malnourished baby, before and after treatment; or the hygienic conditions of a farm before and after WHO had assisted local populations. This kind of photography was not new and had a long tradition related to missionary activities, colonial medicine, and humanitarian associations' missions.[37] Furthermore, these photographs show incontrovertible proof of the good work of the organization. They are not there to offer a perspective, but *the* perspective and *the* narrative. That is the story. There is no room for criticism, with rare exceptions of self-criticism.

Here the almost violent close-up images of the child with yaws (trachoma or leprosy) are tempered by the presentation and its contextualization. The bottle of penicillin shifts the focus from the child and its condition to the "magic" to cure it. Photographic traditions of sensationalist representation are diluted in a "progressive" medical text that celebrates what we can now do. In the case of Ede Nwaegbo, who made the cover page of the May–June 1957 issue of *World Health*, the primary photo is the happy "after" one. The smaller ones show the child with disease, followed by a celebratory one of the child participating in traditional practice of body painting by a happy mother, signaling the re-integration of the sick child back into family and community (Figure 9.3). A community forever changed, bettered, and improved by "modern" medicine: this is the intrinsic subliminal message.

Over the course of the 1950s, there were developments in the imagery used by the WHO At the same time, continuities prevail. The use of images was as sophisticated in 1953 as it was in 1959; however, the relation of the image to the text improved. The sensationalism of the early photo essays faded away, although later articles too sought to arouse readers' emotions. Attention to the environment, to technology, and to the agents of technical assistance remained. Throughout the 1950s, the editors of the *Newsletter* gave some agency to local intermediaries and go-betweens, though the focus remained on Western international health workers, especially nurses, doctors, and, to some extent, engineers and other experts.

Technical assistance was part of what anthropologist James Ferguson calls a "masculine version of modernity based on a hard, metallic, masculine industrialism" – this modernity was based, too, on hard, metallic cans of DDT, and physically fit men to carry them.[38] The visual representations of the WHO mostly confirm this. In the photographs, and in almost all of the field reports, the local characters are often male. However, the

WHO Newsletter

The Magic that is Wrought by One Shot of Penicillin

In this bottle (actual size, cost 25 US cents) is enough to clear away the disfiguring yaws lesions of five children

This amount of penicillin, 10 c.c., is enough to prevent ten children getting yaws, suffering like the boy on the right

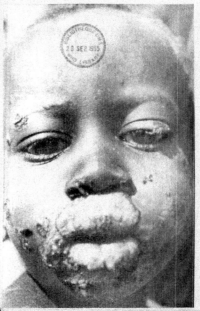

YAWS: TEN MILLION SUFFER NO MORE

By Dr. T. GUTHE
Chief, Venereal Diseases and Treponematoses Section, WHO

This issue of the Newsletter deals with the progress made in the world-wide battle against yaws, a disease often widespread in tropical rural areas.

Yaws begins in childhood. It destroys the skin and bones and frequently affects the face, body, legs and arms.

Lesions on the palms of the hands and soles of the feet are particularly important from an economic point of view because they reduce and often destroy the ability to do agricultural work. Yaws does not kill, but may condemn the victim to a lifetime of dependence on others.

Before the discovery of penicillin, it is estimated that there were 50 million yaws victims in the tropical regions of the world.

With the introduction of long-acting repository penicillin preparations, making it possible to cure yaws with a single injection, effective mass campaigns against this crippling disease could at last be organized. But it became equally important to find *all* the clinical cases in the community and to treat them, as well as the latent cases and contacts showing no overt signs of the disease, so that new epidemics would be prevented.

Yaws control has therefore in modern times become a matter in which the public health organization plays a considerable part.

Since 1948 campaigns against yaws and the other treponematoses (syphilis and pinta) have been carried out by a number of governments with the technical assistance of WHO and supplies from UNICEF.

Under this programme WHO has been engaged in 31 projects in 28 countries and involving a population, at risk, of more than a hundred and fifty million.

The programme has progressed so far that up to the middle of this year about 40 million people had been examined and about ten million had been treated with penicillin. Some governments have organized the campaigns so effectively that each field team of from 6 to 10 workers can examine as many as 25,000 people a month.

Modern public health methods have thus made it possible to eliminate yaws as a public health problem within a short time.

This has already been done in Haiti, where, in a rural population of some 3 million people—more than half of them victims of the disease—yaws was eradicated in the public health sense within three years.

The largest reservoir of yaws is tropical Africa, with an estimated 25 million cases, and WHO's work there is now being extended. Yaws control workers from more than 20 countries will be meeting next month in Nigeria in order to discuss modern yaws control methods.

It is a fact that there are few important diseases which can be cured more easily, more quickly or at less cost than yaws. Based on the experience of governments and WHO, the cost per person examined in mass yaws campaigns varies from about 10-20 US cents, and the cost per person treated from 30-80 US cents (in British currency 8½ d-1 s 5 d and 2 s 1½ d-5 s 8 d).

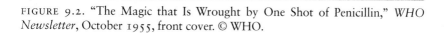

FIGURE 9.2. "The Magic that Is Wrought by One Shot of Penicillin," *WHO Newsletter*, October 1955, front cover. © WHO.

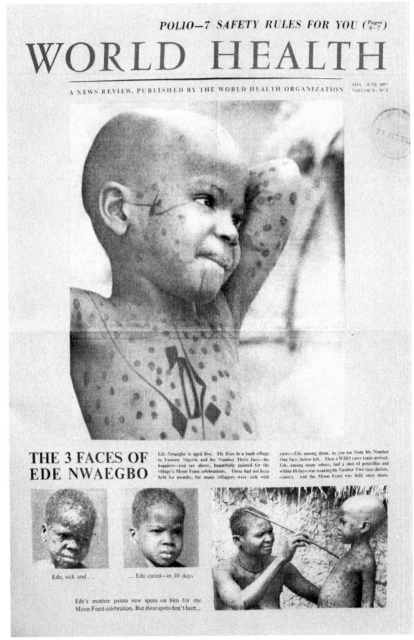

FIGURE 9.3. "Three Faces of Ede Nwaegbo." *World Health*, May–June, 1957.
© WHO.

Newsletter and *World Health* from the early 1950s also depict women, particularly nurses, European or North American, as well as local nurses as playing a central role. The maternal, quintessentially humanitarian presence of nurses counterbalanced the muscular and masculine technical assistance universe, (allegedly) showing that within it this gendered technical expertise was possible.[39]

Finally, the organization consistently concealed the high degree of improvisation that characterized virtually all internationally administered programs and the extent to which they relied – or had to rely – on local agents. Even during emergency operations, international health workers and planners were depicted as running smooth and cleverly devised operations. There is no trace of practical obstacles, broken-down trucks, interrupted supplies, or the eruption of politics into the domain of technical endeavors.[40] When harsh natural environments such as jungles, deserts, mountains, and further "extreme" landscapes were mentioned, their presence corroborated the heroism of doctors and nurses accomplishing their "missions" – yet another typically humanitarian term largely (ab) used in the magazine.

The year 1959 represented a rupture in many respects. The *Newsletter* became *World Health* and Joan Bush was appointed as photo editor. Bush, an English woman, had previously worked for Magnum and had joined the UN as visual media officer at the International Labour Organisation (ILO) in 1956; in 1957 she joined the WHO. Her job was to build up a photo library of the world health situation, to assign photo coverage in various parts of the world, and to enhance the magazine's visual appeal. Her early training at art school and experience with *Life* and Magnum bore fruit. The first issue was so well received that money was found to make it a permanent enterprise. Bush would continue doing the layouts for the magazine until 1963.[41]

1959–1973: A Script for Development

World Health turned a deaf ear to numerous criticisms coming from various quarters, including other UN agencies on disease control and eradication campaigns.[42] The editors and authors of the magazines preferred to leapfrog from one success story to another. What did change, by the turn of the 1960s with respect to the previous decade, was the increased visual space afforded local agents, local doctors, and local institutions often photographed working under the supervision of WHO team leaders. This was an attempt to emphasize the role of the organization in a post-colonial world and to show that in the aftermath of decolonization, the march toward progress, modernization, and development was unstoppable.

This new perspective is visible in the reportages of the November–December 1959 special issue of *World Health* on Africa. The magazine opened with a long article and photo reportage on "the era of the doctor and the engineer." The cover photo showed the construction of the port of Tema in Ghana. In the depths of the bush, in the village streets, in the offices of the administration, wrote Dr. F. J. C. Cambournac, the WHO regional director for Africa, a battle for health was waged. Without it, other undertakings would inevitably suffer. The photographs of Paul Almasy showed the new faces of Africa: local engineers and public health now at work. They perfectly embodied the triumph of self-help. The first article, by Swiss journalist C. H. Favrod, decreed that Africa had eventually moved "from the pastoral era to the age of engineers."[43]

In April 1964, another special issue of *World Health* focused on "New Africa." These articles show continuity with the previous special issue and let the voices of "new" Africa speak. In the opening article, "We Need Engineers and Economists More than Philosophers and Poets," philosophy and poetry were compared to magic and "magic cannot replace work" as the president of the Republic of Senegal, Léopold Sédar Senghor, said. The voices of "New Africa" are constrained and channeled by the narrator and author of the articles. The logics and dynamics of exclusion are inherent to these narratives. These are narratives of modernity, which "New Africans" are supposed to embody and give agency to. They are locals who understand tradition, preserve what is good about them (i.e., good for the WHO) and condemn everything magical, dirty, and unhealthy (i.e., everything the WHO condemns).[44] They have been educated in the "civilized" world, but now they educate, administer, and cure their own people. This explains the choice of a close-up photograph of their faces. By 1964, there is no trace of the previous decade's humanitarian narratives: children have apparently all been saved and now they are about to be educated; the educators themselves have been saved. The logic of emergency has disappeared; emergencies are now occluded, concealed, or overlooked. The new heroes of the magazine are locals, with the WHO appearing at a distance, though still paternalistically overseeing the enactment of the "promise of development." The photos of Africa are now those of smiling young people, pupils and professionals who embody the future of a "developing" continent; no pain or suffering are to be seen. A further special issue of *World Health* on Africa, published in

January 1967 would expand on the same themes, tapping into the abused rhetoric that the winds of change, having reached Africa, were now "shaking the structure of tradition." The rhetoric of a collaborative effort to lift the twin yokes of misery and disease persists.[45]

During the 1960s, the organization seized every opportunity to emphasize the progress made in the professionalization of international health workers, on the increased place and empowerment of women, especially from non-Christian and non-Western countries. The accounts became more professional and less emotional. Humanitarian narratives faded away, even when they could have been used, for instance, during the early stages of the anti-colonial struggle in Congo (1960–1966). During the 1960s, the organization studiously avoided mentioning conflicts, focusing instead on themes such as the history of medicine; the use of the atom for medical and health-related purposes a broad range of health issues related to industrialization, urbanization, leisure, and mental health, especially in Europe and North America. Every now and then, the magazine celebrated some pilot projects: water supplies in Kenya, a campaign against tuberculosis in India, another against typhus in Egypt or against yaws in some Pacific islands, as well as better hospital administration in Europe.

From 1969 to 1973 *World Health* published more articles on Europe – systematically portrayed as the locus where technology thrived and research was done – and on labor, environmental health, and scientific progress, including space medicine. One finds fewer articles on the "underdeveloped" world as such; an increase of special issues on progress in "underdeveloped" countries; and articles whose contents would have been unthinkable in 1949 or even in 1959, such as "Tropical Heart Research" (November 1969). Within the WHO "there have always been tensions between social and economic approaches to population health and technology – or disease-focused approaches.... The emphasis on one or the other waxes and wanes over time, depending on the larger balance of power, the changing interests of international players, the intellectual and ideological commitments of key individuals, and the way that all of these factors interact with the health policymaking process."[46] These tensions were equally perceptible in the visual politics of the organization.

The disappearance of humanitarian narratives in *World Health* was accompanied by a reduction in heroic images and narratives. Rather than a photo reportage on a specific project, the magazine's editors preferred to cluster them into a single article. As in the previous decade, however, the readers of the magazine were left wondering whether all these projects had been successful. On the issue of success, *World Health* did not elaborate too much, except on projects led jointly with other UN agencies.[47] One exception was the narrative structured around malaria. In this case, the ongoing struggle to eradicate it, and the joint efforts of the international organizations and various donors, allowed the editors and authors of *World Health* to set up a narrative of waves of progress and failures. This was an admittedly unfinished war; losing a battle was an inherent part of the portrayed heroism of the organization's broader campaign against the disease.

Technical Assistance and Humanitarian Narratives, a Strange Union

In the final section of this chapter, we wish to expand on a union that, in our view, was far from ineluctable. First, we would like to underscore that one of the constituent tenets of the WHO went unrepresented in the pages of the magazine: health as a fundamental human right. The organization had no means to relate its policies and practices to such an aspiration.[48] It was far beyond its reach, and linking technical assistance to human rights was a seriously risky operation that could expose the organization to all sorts of criticism. Nonetheless, at each major anniversary of the Universal Declaration on Human Rights, the fifth, the tenth, or the twentieth, the WHO dusted off its discourse on the organization's original ambition to address the root causes of ill health and to guarantee the enforcement of health as a fundamental human right. Systematically, these words were not accompanied by deeds. Moreover, attempts to provide an articulated and visual definition of health were never seriously pursued by the organization.

Second, by 1954, the organization had fully embraced the ideology and rhetoric of the vicious circle of "poverty-breeds-sickness-and-increases poverty" and of its alter ego, health is wealth, which overshadowed the idea of health as a fundamental right. Technical assistance was shaped by many of the same assumptions underlying modernization theories that international health experts shared with economists, demographers, and sociologists. These experts linked poverty and underdevelopment with pre-rational, superstitious modes of thought and believed the transition to rationality would accompany the process of urbanization, industrialization, and the diffusion of education[49] (Figure 9.4).

Technology dispensed by technical experts was the tool the organization chose to make health (ergo, wealth) available in many parts of the

When the poor man is sick his sickness increases his poverty. The aim of WHO is to make and keep the sick healthy, thus enabling them to fight and conquer their poverty.

But the vicious circle of "poverty-breeds sickness-increases poverty" can be broken at other points through the work of other international agencies. The Food and Agriculture Organization can help the farmer increase the productivity of his land by teaching him modern methods and providing him with mechanised tools. UNESCO can help him and his children learn to read and to open up to them vast new fields of knowledge. The International Labour Organization may, for example, teach him how to found and operate village co-operatives for the marketing of his produce. And the International Bank for Reconstruction and Development lends money for development projects... no less than 302 million dollars in the form of 24 loans to thirteen countries within a period of nine months.

It is the policy of "WHO Newsletter" to give, from time to time, articles on the work of other international organizations—for WHO's work could never be completely successful if conducted in isolation—and on Page Three we print extracts from an address by Eugene R. Black, President of the International Bank, in which he points out that at the end of last year, more than 3,000 technical experts were at work, under international auspices, in all parts of the world

"participating in what is undoubtedly the greatest technological education campaign ever undertaken".

The picture above, from Pakistan, is a symbol of an economy in transition and represents the kind of much-needed development in many parts of the world which could not be undertaken without the help of such an organization as the International Bank. Through the pipeline will flow water to make fertile what is now arid ground and to make possible the development of new industries.

More food means better health, new industries mean less poverty. And so the aims of the World Health Organization are furthered by the work of its sister agencies.

FIGURE 9.4. "Pipeline to Prosperity," *WHO Newsletter*, May 1954, front cover. © WHO.

world. The premises on which the WHO should have enforced technical assistance would have led the organization to minimize contact with individual bodies by working, wherever possible, on the environment. This was a deliberate policy adopted by the organization to depoliticize and de-culturalize its work: to appear neutral and professional, and to appeal to a growing number of post-colonial governments. Yet, even a very superficial glance at the *WHO Newsletter* reveals how often doctors, nurses, and health workers touched the bodies of the recipients of international health care. The bodies of recipients were visually indistinguishable from those of the victims (of war or natural disasters) to be saved. It was in this unplanned and rather spontaneous way that humanitarian narratives prominently appeared and eventually "contaminated" the magazine, particularly during the period from 1949 to 1959. The victims to be saved were often non-white peoples; and the heroes and saviors were white doctors and nurses (Figure 9.5). Our point is that these narratives coexisted, in tension and contrast, with the official discourse of technical assistance.

Humanitarian narratives appearing in the *Newsletter* and in *World Health* did not differ markedly from the tropes and arguments put forward for over fifty years, during the age of imperial humanitarianism and the Second World War. These narratives were not always clearly distinguishable from civilizing mission narratives. In the *Newsletter* and in *World Health*, WHO attempted to distinguish itself from colonial powers and colonial medicine. As Sunil Amrith argues: "access to the latest international expertise and the latest international technologies, denied to them under colonial rule, was a democratic right claimed by Asian (and African) nations. But the architects of technical assistance, too, envisaged their task in opposition to the epidemiological and epistemological legacies of colonial medicine."[50] Nonetheless, when the editors and authors of the *Newsletter* or *World Health* sought to illustrate these assumptions, the visual (and discursive) outcome resembled stereotypical paternalistic, colonial, and humanitarian representations. Despite the rhetoric of respecting local cultures and traditions and the alleged efforts to combine tradition with technology, the results were not always persuasive. More important, they coexisted, somewhat ambiguously, with virulent attacks against non-Western conceptions of health and medicine.[51]

The task of the *Newsletter* and, later, of *World Health* was to promote the projects of the organization and make the work of technical experts administering assistance visible. Visibility was supposed to enhance the legitimacy and authority of the organization with Western

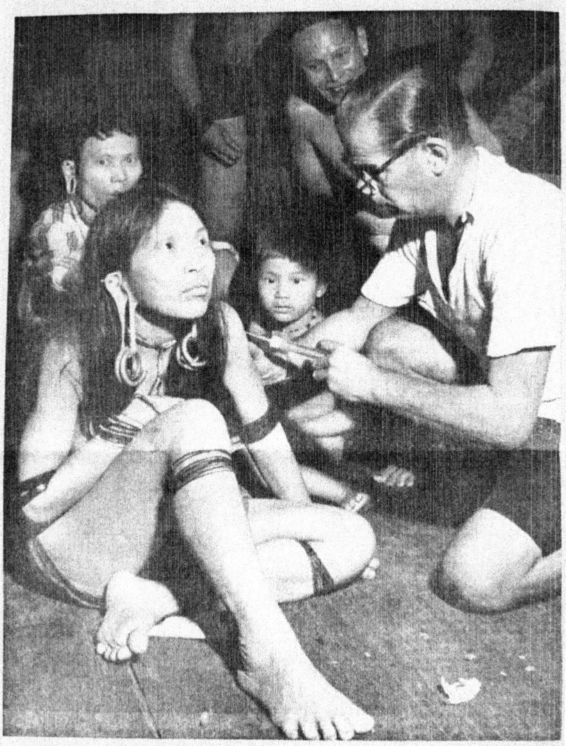

FIGURE 9.5. "The Girl from the Forest," WHO *Newsletter*, February–March 1955, p. 4. © WHO. At the center of the page is the doctor who came by dugout canoe to Sarawak where the organization assisted in a malaria pilot project. The

donors. Especially during the 1950s, the magazine resorted to the logic of emergency – typical of humanitarian operations and largely used by humanitarian organizations[52] – to demonstrate that it was possible to obtain immediate results. The latter were very prominently staged as successes in the pages of the magazine, in a sensational and dramatic way.

The WHO needed to legitimize its action in donor countries as well as in countries where assistance was delivered. To persuade "less-than-fully-rational" peoples to accept vaccination or house spraying, technical assistance revolved around rapid, tangible, and visible results. Technical experts conceived of the problem in terms of a gap between faith and reason; their challenge was to make their work as visible and thus as able to stimulate belief as possible.[53] The iconologic discourse of the WHO magazine referred to faith and belief. This was not really the consequence of an attempt by the organization to dialogue with "less-than-fully-rational" communities, societies, or public authorities, for as we know, the audience of the magazine was located in the West. It seems that the editors and authors of the magazine considered religious rhetoric a persuasive and efficient way to show the miracles of technology. The editors and authors of the *Newsletter* recycled or adapted a strategy frequently and successfully used by humanitarian organizations, faith-based as well as secular, to support and "sell" the actions of the organization.

Had the logic of technical assistance been applied without compromises and in a fully successful way, the WHO would have not needed to show bodies in pain and suffering. After all, the "closed" language of technical assistance was unable to accommodate pain or suffering, and it was particularly unsuited to recognizing that the technical assistance itself could be a source of pain and suffering (as in the case of adverse reactions from vaccinations or side effects from drug treatments, which the organization hardly recorded, let alone acknowledged).[54] In the end, however,

FIGURE 9.5. (*cont.*)

heroic aspect of the journey is suggested in the textual description of the "force of the wide, strong river." The team, entirely composed of men, encountered "the girl from the forest": "deep into the dense forest bordering the Baram River in Sarawal filtered the news that doctors were visiting a longhouse of the riverside dwellers. This girl, receiving penicillin for a skin disease from a WHO malaria team member, Dr. R.J.G. Hogg, had never before found herself under a roof." In the excerpts of the field report local population are described with all the virtues of the *bons sauvages* including "instinctive" hospitality and being "naturally friendly." The field report emphasized the doctors' humanity for working long hours without taking a lunch break.

such a project failed; therefore the *Newsletter* and *World Health* became the locus where technical assistance encountered the human being. As a consequence, in the pages of the magazine, pain and suffering found an important place, which allowed the editors to strengthen and elaborate on the salvific action of the WHO.

Conclusion: All the World Loves a Picture

The WHO photographed technical assistance, its pilot projects, and demonstration sites. It visually represented health, and set up a distinct narrative, visual and discursive, that linked technical assistance to modernity, ergo prosperity. Through a magazine that represented its public face, the WHO introduced, mixed and blended, used and instrumentalized humanitarian narratives to enhance its authority and legitimacy both with donor states and with colonial and post-colonial states, where it deployed the majority of actions and implemented its practices and projects. Humanitarian narratives promoted technical assistance; they gave it a human face: that of the expert, of the nurse, and of the international health worker, of the doctor and of the recipient of aid.

The opening page of the February 1953 *Newsletter* reads: "All the World Loves a Picture" (Figure 9.6). With this caption and the photograph of a veiled Indian woman, the WHO announced its visual strategy. It was a powerful message signaling that the veil of tradition and religion was not the veil of ignorance.[55] In an accompanying editorial, the organization made it clear that photographs and films would become "the most useful tool of education" and would prove "of enormous value to the United Nations and its Special Agencies in making their work understood by the man in the streets." The editors announced that the following issue of the *Newsletter* would contain a special picture supplement. The topic would be the latest advances made in the care of premature babies. This supplement would be the first of a series intended for wall display in schools and institutions and as an aid to lecturers and discussion groups.

If humanitarian narratives faded away over time, photographs remained the preferred means of expression of the official magazine of the WHO. Photographs allegedly told the truth; they gave incontrovertible evidence of the progress made. They stood as perfect companions to articles and captions, although sometimes they altered the meanings of the narrative, adding ambiguity or blurring the lines of the organization's policies. In the end, if "all the world loves a picture" and if a picture – as

FIGURE 9.6. "All the World Loves a Picture," *WHO Newsletter*, February 1953, front cover. © WHO.

the WHO leaders and editors believed – was worth a thousand words, it was equally worth relying on good photographers, such as the Magnum boys. Through their pictures they could keep the promise of development alive; a single shot could capture the dream of humanity achieving the utopian objective of better health for everybody, everywhere.

Notes

1   Iris Borowy, *Coming to Terms with World Health. The League of Nations Health Organisation 1921–1946*,(Frankfurt am Main, Peter Lang, 2009); Paul Weindling, ed., *International Health Organisations and Movements, 1918–1939* (Cambridge: Cambridge University Press, 1995); Clifford Rosenberg, "The International Politics of Vaccine Testing in Interwar Algiers," *American Historical Review* 117, no. 3 (2012): 671–97; Sivlia Salvatici in this volume; Jessica Reinisch, "'We Shall Rebuild Anew a Powerful Nation': UNRRA, Internationalism and National Reconstruction in Poland," *Journal of Contemporary History* 43, no.3 (July 2008): 451–76; "Internationalism in Relief: The Birth (and Death) of UNRRA," in Mark Mazower, Jessica

Reinisch and David Feldman, eds., *Past and Present*, Supplement No. 6 (Oxford: Oxford University Press, 2011), 258–89; "Auntie UNRRA at the Crossroads," in Rana Mitter and Matthew Hilton, eds., *Past and Present*, Supplement No. 8 (Oxford: Oxford University Press, 2013), 70–97, 73.

2 Sunil Amrith, *Decolonizing International Health. India and Southeast Asia, 1930–65* (Basingstoke: Palgrave Macmillan, 2006); Nitsan Chorev, *The World Health Organization between North and South* (Ithaca, NY: Cornell University Press, 2012).

3 Anne-Emmanuel Birn, "The Stages of International (Global) Health: Histories of Success or Successes of History?" *Global Public Health: An International Journal of Research, Policy and Practice* 4, no. 1 (2009): 50–68, 56.

4 Birn, "The Stages of International (Global) Health," 56. (WHO regional offices for Africa, the Americas, Southeast Asia, Europe, Eastern Mediterranean, and Western Pacific).

5 Archives WHO, Geneva, Switzerland, Workfiles-Events-General, Fol. 2, Magnum Photos INC, 1950–1968, letter from HB (most likely Harold Ballou, regional office for the Americas of the WHO), to Dr. Sacha Leviathan, UNICEF/WHO Yaws eradication program, Haiti, Division of Public Health, 19 March 1951.

6 Socrates Litsios, "Malaria Control, the Cold War, and the Postwar Reorganization of International Assistance," *Medical Anthropology* 17, no. 3 (1997): 255–78; Randall Packard and P. J. Brown, "No Other Logical Choice: Global Malaria Eradication and the Politics of International Health in the Postwar Era," *Parassitologia* 40, no. 1–2 (1998): 217–230; Erez Manela, "A Pox on Your Narrative: Writing Disease Control into Cold War History," *Diplomatic History* 34, no. 2 (2010): 299–323.

7 Amrith, *Decolonizing International Health*, 3. Also S. Amrith and Patricia Clavin, "Feeding the World: Connecting Europe and Asia, 1930–1945," in Rana Mitter and Matthew Hilton, eds., *Past and Present* 218, Supplement 8 (Oxford: Oxford University Press, 2013), 29–50; Arturo Escobar, *Encountering Development. The Making and Unmaking of the Third World* (Princeton, NJ: Princeton University Press, 1995); Frederick Cooper and Randall Packard, eds., *International Development and the Social Sciences. Essays on the History and Politics of Knowledge* (Berkeley: University of California Press, 1997).

8 Amy Staples, *The Birth of Development: How the World Bank, Food and Agriculture Organization, and World Health Organization Changed the World, 1956–1965* (Kent, OH: Kent State University Press, 2006).

9 Laqueur, "Bodies, Details and the Humanitarian Narrative" and "Mourning, Pity, and the Work of Narrative in the Making of Humanity."

10 See the chapters by Heather Curtis, Kevin Grant, and Silvia Salvatici in this volume.

11 See chapter by Francesca Piana in this volume.

12 From *Introducing WHO*, presumably written by Director-General Halfdan Mahler. See Chorev, *The World Health Organization* 6–7, and 42–85; and Birn, "The Stages of International (Global) Health," 58–9, for Mahler's quote. In the 1970s the organization embraced a new approach to public health

known as Primary Health Care. This approach rejected the costly high-technology, urban-based, and curative care that led to skewed resource allocation in the national health systems in many developing countries and prioritized equity and universal access to essential health services provided at the community level, by nonprofessional workers trained for that activity.

13 The WHO also made extensive use of posters during public events organized all over the world to illustrate its policies and practices. Since the late 1940s, the organization has made abundant use of film documentaries, shown in the cinema and public spaces. Radio programs were also broadcast and special collections of stamps were among tools of WHO propaganda. It is worth mentioning that the *Chronicle*, a more scientific outlet at the disposal of the WHO, did not aim to compete against specialized medical journals, though it integrated technical information and was intended for public health experts and specialists. Marcos Cuéto, "Imágenes de la salud, la enfermedad y el desarrollo: fotografías de la Fundacion Rockefeller en Latinoamérica," *Historia, Ciências, Saude-Manguinhos* 5, no. 3 (1999).

14 Judith Tendler, *Inside Foreign Aid* (Baltimore, MD: Johns Hopkins University Press, 1975), 10; George M. Foster, "Bureaucratic Aspects of International Health Programs," in Robert A. Hahn, ed., *Anthropology in Public Health. Bridging Differences in Culture and Society* (Oxford: Oxford University Press, 1999), 345–64, 349.

15 Michele Alacevich, "The World Bank and the Politics of Productivity: The Debate on Economic Growth, Poverty and Living Standards in the 1950s," *Journal of Global History* 6 (2011): 53–74.

16 See Reinisch, "Auntie UNRRA at the Crossroads," 2013,77–9.

17 We could refer to the numerous articles and special issues on malaria – for example the February 1954 issue of the WHO *Newsletter*, 2–4.

18 On a closely related topic, see Nicole Sackley, "The Village as Cold War Site: Experts, Development and the History of Rural Reconstruction," *Journal of Global History* 6 (2001): 481–504.

19 David Webster, "Development Advisors in a Time of Cold War and Decolonization: The United Nations Technical Assistance Administration, 1950–59," *Journal of Global History* 6, no, 2 (2011), 249–72.

20 WHO also tried to use Magnum as an agency to sell its reports or photos on the U.S. market. Archives WHO, Workfiles-Events-General, Fol. 2, Magnum Photos INC, 1950–1968, letter from Mary Losey to Harold Ballou, 17 February 1955.

21 Archives WHO, Workfiles-Events-General, Fol. 2, Magnum Photos INC, 1950–1968, letter from Robert Kee to John Morris, 27 January 1953.

22 Archives WHO, Workfiles-Events-General, Fol. 2, Magnum Photos INC, 1950–1968, Mary Losey to Mr. Field Horine [PIO, Regional Office of WHO for South East Asia], 3 November 1953.

23 Bear, "Magnum Orbis: Photographs from the End(s) of the Earth"; also Mitchell, "World Pictures. Globalization and Visual Culture," 49–59; Michael Ignatieff, *Magnum Degrees* (London: Pahidon, 2000); Bondi, *Chim*.

24 Tess Taconis, the photo editor between 1954 and 1957, was married to Kryn Taconis, a photographer who worked for Magnum. Gertraud Lessing who

worked for the Public Information Department during the 1950s was married to Erich Lessing, a photographer who joined Magnum in 1951. Mary Losey, film officer at the PI Department during the 1950s, was close to Robert Capa. Joan Bush, who had worked for the PI since 1957, had worked for Magnum. OMS Archives, Joan BUSH Taylor (WHO 1957–1982), see http://www.who.int/formerstaff/history/bush_taylor_joan2306.pdf (accessed on 27 June 2013).

25 Further research on ties, connections, education, and professional and military experiences is necessary to determine whether our working hypotheses are correct.

26 This collaboration also caused some tension; see Archives WHO, Workfiles-Events-General, Fol. 2, Magnum Photos INC, 1950–1968, Joseph Handler, Director, Division of Public Information to Mrs. Gloria Hoffmann, Magnum Phot, New York, 4 February 1953.

27 Placing the report into *Life* was a great success for WHO, Archives WHO, Workfiles-Events-General, Fol. 2, Magnum Photos INC, 1950–1968, Mary Losey to David Seymour (Chim), 14 February 1951.

28 Archives WHO, Workfiles-Events-General, Fol. 2, Magnum Photos INC, 1950–1968, Mary Losey to George Ninaud, 5 October 1950.

29 Archives WHO, Workfiles-Events-General, Fol. 2, Magnum Photos INC, 1950–1968, Mary Losey to George Ninaud, 19 December 1950.

30 Archives WHO, Workfiles-Events-General, Fol. 2, Magnum Photos INC, 1950–1968, Mary Losey to David Seymour (alias Chim), 18 October 1950.

31 Archives WHO, Workfiles-Events-General, Fol. 2, Magnum Photos INC, 1950–1968, Mary Losey to George Ninaud, 20 December 1950. These amendments also concerned the photos and the captions. Indeed, WHO hired, on short-term contracts, numerous specialists and/or journalists to write articles and captions for the *Newsletter* (see Archives WHO, P/10/37/1 for copies of these agreements).

32 Archives WHO, Workfiles-Events-General, Fol. 2, Magnum Photos INC, 1950–1968, letter from Tess Taconis to John Morris, 29 September 1953.

33 Archives WHO, P 10/438/2, Policy on Distribution and Sale of "World Health," Contrat entre l'OMS et M. Jacques Rousseau.

34 Archives WHO, P 10/438/2, Policy on Distribution and Sale of "World Health," Contrat entre l'OMS et la Société Suisse de Pharmacie, 19 avril 1968. The figures of the print run concern 1972.

35 Amrith, *Decolonizing Health*, 2.

36 Amrith, *Decolonizing Health*, 72.

37 See chapter by Kevin Grant in this volume.

38 Amrith, *Decolonizing Health*, 113.

39 In 1953, for instance, Mary Losey explained to John G. Morris the importance of nurses for the international organization at a time when the shortage of medical personnel was acute all over the world. Losey pointed out the adventurous life since of most of the nurses would be "sent to places where medical science has hardly begun to penetrate." She also explained that nurses paved the way for doctors and other technicians who have less contact with the people and less understanding of their day-to-day problems (Archives

WHO, Workfiles-Events-General, Fol. 2, Magnum Photos INC, 1950–1968, Mary Losey to John Morris, 18 August 1953).

40 Amrith, *Decolonizing Health*, 121. There is also no trace of the criticisims of international health planning, which rose from various quarters after the mid-1960s. See Nevin S. Scrimshaw, "Myths and Realities in International Health Planning," *American Journal of Public Health* 64, no. 8 (1974):792–8.

41 OMS Archives, Joan BUSH Taylor (WHO 1957–1982), see http://www.who.int/formerstaff/history/bush_taylor_joan2306.pdf (accessed on 27 June 2013).

42 For some exceptions, see Tibor Mende, "Conversation with Food and Health Hunger," *World Health*, September–October 1962, Special Issue (the author had previously published "Conversation with Nehru").

43 *World Health*, November–December 1959, Special Issue: *Africa – The Era of the Doctor and the Engineer.*

44 This condemnation of superstition and witchcraft is a frequent topic in the magazine. See, for instance, Traudl Lessing, Division of Public Information, to Trudy Feliu, Magnum. Archives WHO, Workfiles-Events-General, Fol. 2, Magnum Photos INC, 1950–1968, 5 September 1955.

45 "Africa: Its Health and Development," *World Health*, January 1967; text by C. H. Favrod and pictures taken by Didier Henrioud during his four years service in Africa with the WHO.

46 Theodore M. Brown, Marcos Cuéto, and Elizabeth Fee, "The World Health Organization and the Transition from 'International Health' to 'Global' Public Health," *American Journal of Public Health*, special issue *Public Health Then and Now*, 96, no. 1 (2006): 62–72, 66.

47 Take, for instance, "Anatomy of a Project: Ethiopia 9," *World Health* (July–August 1962): 20–7, or the special issue of November 1963 entitled *With the Refugees of Palestine*, which elaborated on a joint project of the Health Organization with UNRRA, UNICEF, and other organizations.

48 A visual attempt to render health as a human right was done in November 1958, for the tenth anniversary of the Declaration of Human Rights. The photographic interpration was an *una tantum*. The effort of the magazine was not particularly creative as it recycled photographs that had been taken for other purposes.

49 Amrith, *Decolonizing Health*, 135.

50 Amrith, *Decolonizing Health*, 106.

51 See, for instance, WHO *Newsletter*, "Africa Sets a Problem and This Is How WHO Plans to Help in Solving It" May 1953, 2.

52 See Irwin, *Making the World Safe.*

53 Amrith, *Decolonizing Health*,135.

54 Amrith, *Decolonizing Health*,136–7.

55 This was the caption for that photograph in the French edition of the *Newsletter*.

10

"A" as in Auschwitz, "B" as in Biafra

The Nigerian Civil War, Visual Narratives of Genocide, and the Fragmented Universalization of the Holocaust[*]

Lasse Heerten

In early July 1968, Holy Ghost Fathers Anthony Byrne, Raymond Kennedy, and Fintan Kilbride left their West African parishes to cross the Atlantic. The Irish missionaries had embarked for the United States to campaign for the interconfessional aid operation established to help the population of Biafra, the former Eastern Region of Nigeria, which had declared its independence in May 1967. Now, the secessionist state was threatened by famine. In spring 1968, Federal Nigerian troops had completed their blockade of the breakaway region. With the supply situation in the enclave becoming increasingly serious, the International Committee of the Red Cross (ICRC) and Christian relief organizations mounted airlifts to provide the Biafran population with food and medicine.[1]

On arrival in New York, the Catholic priests met with the leadership of the American Jewish Committee (AJC). The Irishmen reported on the humanitarian crisis, urging the AJC to lobby for the cause in the American Jewish community and to employ their resources for the aid operation. At the meeting, the missionaries spread photographs of emaciated "Biafran Babies" on the table: "starving children with bloated bellies and matchstick legs." Afterward, the AJC's director of Interreligious Affairs, Rabbi Marc H. Tanenbaum, noted that the photographs were "to Jewish eyes, 1968 versions of photographs of Jewish children taken in the 1940's in such other notorious sites [as] Bergen-Belsen, Thereisenstadt [*sic*],

---

[*] This chapter is a revised English version of "A wie Auschwitz, B wie Biafra: Der Bürgerkrieg in Nigeria (1967–1970) und die Universalisierung des Holocaust," *Zeithistorische Forschungen* 8, no. 3 (2011), http://www.zeithistorische-forschungen. de/site/40209178/default.aspx.

Auschwitz." According to Tanenbaum, the Irish fathers had made this
connection in an effort to underline the urgency of the crisis. The rabbi
noted that Father Kilbride repeatedly resorted to analogies with the
events of the 1930s and 1940s.

"To our eternal shame," he said in his soft, compelling Irish accent, "we sat by
while millions of Jewish people and others were put to death before our very eyes.
We did practically nothing then." Then his Irish fire broke out, "Have we learned
nothing from those days?"

For the AJC, this felt like déjà vu:

To the AJC staff gathered around the conference table, Father Kilbride's voice was
like a replay of the voices of the few Jews who managed to flee from Germany,
Hungary, and Poland to Paris, London, and New York in the early 1940's to stir
the world's conscience to come to the aid of their doomed brothers. Back then,
the cries for succor fell on unbelieving ears. Just 25 years later, this could not be
allowed to happen again.

The photographs and reports of the Catholic priests fulfilled their function: the crisis in Biafra became the first non-Jewish event for which the
AJC engaged. Within a few weeks, twenty-one American Jewish organizations combined their forces and created the American Jewish Emergency
Effort for Biafran Relief.[2]

The Irish-Jewish joint venture was only one link in a large network
of humanitarian activists that emerged around Biafra in mid-1968.
Throughout the summer, newspaper and magazine readers and TV viewers across the West were shocked by relentless images of starving Biafran
children[3] (Figure 10.1). Biafra committees mushroomed across Western
Europe and North America. The publics in France, Germany, the United
Kingdom, and the United States – the countries on which this chapter
focuses – were among the most active. Campaigners united in transnational protest networks, harshly criticized governments for their inaction, and raised funds for relief operations. The civil war between Nigeria
and Biafra, which had eluded journalistic attention for a year, became an
international media and protest event.[4]

In recent historical scholarship the "power of images" is a commonly
evoked topos.[5] Art historian Horst Bredekamp coined the term "image
acts" to emphasize the performative function of images: that they can
make us think, feel, or even act.[6] According to various observers, television and print images transmitted from Biafra horrified contemporaries and stirred them to action.[7] In view of the tangible effects that the
images' global dissemination exerted on the war's course of events, this

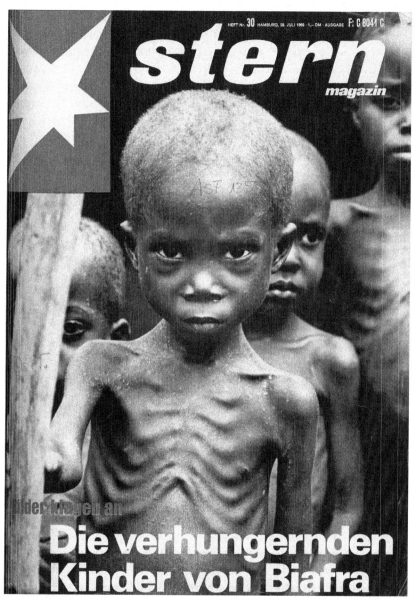

FIGURE 10.1. "The Starving Children of Biafra," *Stern*, 28 July 1968 cover. Photographer: Hubert Lecampion.

chapter interprets these photographs as such an "image act. "However, what exactly was it about these pictures that produced such an impact?

As the opening episode of this chapter suggests, the particular power of these images stemmed from their association with the Holocaust.[8] The images from Biafra reminded countless contemporaries in Western Europe and the United States of the photographs taken during the liberation of the Nazi concentration camps; fears of an "African Auschwitz" abounded. These associations were also cultivated by Biafran propaganda, which relied heavily on allegations of genocide and a language of comparisons connecting the Biafran crisis with the fate of Europe's Jews during World War II.[9]

Photographs do not stand by themselves. They become intelligible only through textual contextualization and references to other pictures; the potentially boundless space of meanings can thus be limited. This holds true especially for images that horrify. Their shock effect is often due to associations with images we already know – and fear.[10] The reading of the remembered images does not remain untouched either: through these associations they are called to mind again, and comparisons with other pictures may cast them in a new light.

Recent work by literary theorist Michael Rothberg offers a model by which to study such entanglements. In his writings about "multidirectional memories," he connects the history of Holocaust memory to other events. Most studies of Holocaust memory sketch rather linear routes of memorialization; according to this narrative, the major moments in the "discovery" of the Holocaust after the fact were the Eichmann trials in Jerusalem in the early 1960s, the Auschwitz trials in Frankfurt between 1963 and 1965, and the 1978 TV show *Holocaust*. However, Rothberg has shown how memories of the Second World War, the *résistance,* and the Holocaust have been central to French discussions regarding the colonial war in Algeria. Such a model, which understands collective memories as open, fluid entities, allows us to acknowledge how the perception of contemporary events and different forms of memory intertwine and inform each other.[11] In the late 1960s, "the Holocaust" had not yet emerged as the symbolic core of a memory culture focused on genocidal violence. At the time, the evocation of the Nazi genocide did not have the cultural power these analogies hold today. Rather, the language of genocide comparisons during the Biafran conflict helped constitute the meanings and public understanding of both events. Such comparisons gave clearer shape and cultural resonance to two events that so far had been only vaguely contoured – the Nigerian civil war as well as the Nazi mass murder of Europe's Jews.[12]

In the following, I analyze the entanglements between the Nigerian civil war and the cultural memory of the Holocaust. I argue that the shared space of associations made both Biafra and the Holocaust visible in a distinct manner. In the process, however, parts of both phenomena also became invisible. In Western societies, the Nigerian civil war was perceived as a humanitarian crisis threatening to culminate in genocide; that this was a complex political conflict escaped most contemporaries. The Holocaust also emerged in a particular manner. Through comparisons with Biafra, the mass murder of the European Jews was singled out as a unique event from a larger complex of National Socialist crimes. Moreover, the visual interconnection between Biafra and the Holocaust was a decisive step for the establishment of a rhetoric of Holocaust comparisons that has become essential for the perception of genocides until today.[13]

The aim of this chapter is to elucidate the entangled shifts in transnational discourses about Biafra and the Holocaust that emerged once contemporaries started to think of Nazi genocide when they were confronted with the war in Nigeria. To grasp these interconnections, I trace these analogies in the wealth of mass media reports on Biafra and in activist publications. Many of these reports were heavily illustrated and relied on the interplay of texts and images in their representations of the conflict. The differences of contexts in the four countries I focus on are substantial with regard to both the Biafran crisis and to Holocaust memory. However, since my goal is to identify broad patterns in the interwoven representations of Biafra and the Holocaust in Western Europe and the United States, I do not explore such differences here.[14] Rather, I examine how the Nigerian civil war was turned into the international media event "Biafra" and analyze the iconographic patterns into which the pictorial reports about the conflict have been inscribed. Then I explore the rhetoric of Holocaust comparisons in the political communication about the war. In the conclusion, I situate the Biafran episode in what I call the fragmented universalization of the Holocaust.

The International Media Event "Biafra"

The Nigerian civil war was primarily the result of ethnicized political conflict, aggravated by economic factors. As a unified territory, Nigeria was created through the amalgamation of Britain's colonial possessions in the region in 1914. British colonialism had left two calamitous legacies: the colonial system had divided the population along lines of ethnic demarcation but had united them in a centrally governed federal state. The Nigerian federation was divided into three larger regions, each of them dominated by one ethnic group: the Islamic Hausa-Fulani in the north, the Yorubas in the southwest, and the Igbos in the southeast.[15] The latter two were predominantly Christian. The territorial and ethnic borders that divided Nigerian society were still in place in 1960 when the country achieved independence. The growing participatory options for the population after independence further weakened the post-colonial state. The groups that assumed power defended their positions vehemently. On the regional level, a system of patronage was thus created; on the national level the three "mega-tribes" were pitted against each other in their competition for state resources.[16]

Nigeria was soon struck by a severe political crisis. In late summer 1966, after a series of coups, countercoups, and the onset of military rule, up to 30,000 Igbos living in the north were killed. The northern-dominated military government, which had come to power in July, had failed to prevent the massacres. The violence drove a stream of approximately one million Igbo refugees to the Eastern Region, the "homeland" of their diasporic community. In reaction to the "pogroms," as their propagandists instantaneously called them, the Eastern Region called for more autonomy. After failed negotiations, the region declared its independence as the Republic of Biafra on 30 May 1967. A few weeks later, hostilities erupted. On 6 July 1967, the Nigerian civil war began.[17]

The Biafran leadership was confronted with the problem of uniting the heterogeneous population of the secessionist state: the nation of "Biafra" still had to be turned into an imaginable community. Only roughly half of the fourteen million inhabitants were Igbo; the rest belonged to different ethnic minorities. An analogy that originated in ethnological genealogies cast the Igbos as the "Jews of Africa," one of Israel's lost tribes. The Biafran leadership drew on this representation, which many eastern Nigerians had adopted as their self-perception. This analogy, combined with the charge of genocide, was used by the leadership to secure the support of the population; their strategy was to build loyalty to Biafra by emphasizing the threat from a common enemy. The secessionists drew on Holocaust memory as a script to project Biafran group identity through narratives of victimization. At the core of this rhetoric was the concept of genocide as the negative founding myth of a new nation: an "African Israel."[18]

This rhetoric of genocide was addressed to the international community as well as to would-be Biafrans. The secessionists tried to gain diplomatic advantage through intensive propaganda. As the "diplomatic revolution" of Algeria's anti-colonial fight demonstrated, militarily futile Third World conflicts could be won through their successful internationalization.[19] Biafra engaged public relations agencies in Europe and the United States to coordinate their propaganda efforts internationally.[20] Biafran expatriates abroad also campaigned for the secessionist cause.[21] However, competing for media coverage with the Prague Spring, the Vietnam War, and student protest, the conflict did not attract a lot of international interest during its first year.[22]

This changed dramatically in the summer months of 1968 when journalists began to report on famine in the secessionist republic. Missionaries in Biafra, fearful that the conflict would result in genocide against their fellow believers in the mostly Christian breakaway state, were the first to alert the press to the crisis.[23] Biafran public relations agents organized the flight of foreign media representatives into the enclave. Soon journalists and photographers flocked into the crisis area. The first front page report of a major newspaper was published on 12 June 1968 in the British *Sun* – still a reputable newspaper back then – which described the secessionist republic as a "Land of no hope, where children wait to die."[24] In the following weeks, countless reports followed in the Western press, on TV and radio. Between June and October 1968, Biafra hit the headlines of international news reporting.[25]

Thus Biafra heralded the "age of televised disaster."[26] More to the point, it was the interplay of television images and photojournalistic reports that created the event – and Biafra's iconography. In the late 1960s, TV and photojournalism entered a "relationship of mutual influence"; together, they defined the visual landscape of faraway crises.[27] Photojournalists increasingly focused on capturing decisive moments or symbolically laden compositions. Photojournalism thus created the iconic images of Third World wars, images that defined both their contemporary perception and their afterlife in cultural memory.[28]

Media reports left a lasting imprint on the minds of many contemporaries, who described them as nightmarish, inconceivably horrific – and yet so real. Responding to these first visual reports, Lady Violet Bonham Carter noted in her diary that "Biafra is the ghost – no alas reality – which haunts me at present."[29] By August she was convinced of the veracity of these apparitions. In a House of Lords emergency debate, the grand dame of British liberalism underlined: "Thanks to the miracle of television we

see history happening before our eyes. We see no Ibo propaganda; we see
the facts."[30] Other commentators argued similarly. Novelist Günter Grass
explained that the "Völkermord" in Biafra was happening publicly as an
everyday spectacle: "after dinner we watch how people starve and die in
Biafra."[31] Witnessing these scenes in full color, motion, and sound – the
TV reports usually featured the children crying – amplified the excruciat-
ing impression they left.[32] The representational force of TV and photographs lent a ghastly "reality effect" to the reports.[33]

At the core of this event was the icon of the starving "Biafran Babies,"
skeletal infants deformed by malnourishment and illness. The children's
bodies were in the focus of this "humanitarian lens"; their deformations
were described in lurid detail in the texts.[34] This humanitarian narrative
relied on bodily details to render the pain of others tangible – and on an
iconography that aimed at the audience's emotions.[35] The wide opened
eyes are one of the recurrent motifs of the photographic staging of the
"Biafran Babies," which seem to beg for the beholder's help. Moreover,
the observer of these images was himself observed, questioned about his
inaction as a mere consumer of the imagery.[36] In one book account, the
authors have a group of children in a photograph ask: "Why, yes, why do
you let us die of hunger?"[37] Here the journalists speak *for* the children –
but the objects of pity themselves remain silent. They are never given a
voice of their own in these texts. The agency to speak – and to act – lies
entirely with the Western observers.

The journalists frequently addressed their readers – and themselves – as
"us." Thus they created a shared collective identity, an "emotional community" of Western observers – of journalists in the field and audiences
at home.[38] According to captions and headlines, this collective of Western
witnesses is confronted with "looks of children which condemn us"; the
pictures "accuse" them (Figure 10.1).[39] In a gesture of self-accusation,
journalists questioned the passivity of Western observers, and readers
found themselves standing in the dock of a media campaign which heavily employed a language of rights and religiously charged terms to arouse
guilt.[40]

For the "emotional community" thus evoked, the detailed descriptions
of eyewitnesses' emotional reactions to the suffering of the children provide what may be called "templates of emotion."[41] These protocols of sentiment are characteristic for many of these texts.[42] "Eyewitness reports"
regularly featured accounts of Western humanitarian workers or journalists who were unable to gulp back their tears in view of the famine-
stricken dying children.[43] Emotional reactions of the victims, however,

were seldom emphasized. Rather, the apathy with which they awaited their impending fate was commonly mentioned. Images and texts focused on the torpid state of fatality preceding the children's death.[44] These children "demand nothing, want nothing, feel nothing. They have become living dead."[45]

Many photographs featured children or other Biafrans in tightly packed groups. Individual victims dissolve into what Lisa Malkki calls a "sea of humanity," a common trope in visual representations of humanitarian crisis[46] (Figure 10.2). When individual children are depicted or described in texts, the readers are not told their names. One caption to the image of a Biafran boy reads: "He is Ibo. He is eight years old." The boy's age and ethnic belonging suffice to evoke his tragic fate. The children in these texts exist almost solely as part of a collective subject, that of the Biafran "people."[47]

Biafra and the Rhetoric of Holocaust Comparisons

At an interconfessional protest rally at Saint Patrick's Cathedral in Manhattan on 26 October 1968, Rabbi A. James Rudin blended images of Biafra and the Nazi genocide of the Jews: "In my mind's eye the smokestacks of Auschwitz blur into the cities and the bush country of Biafra. In my wakeful and terrible visions I see the mass Jewish graves of Europe rapidly filling with starving and dying Biafrans." By linking the events, the Jewish cleric summoned an imperative to act. The particular fate of the European Jewry and a moral universalism dovetail seamlessly: "When the fires of the Nazi crematoria were finally extinguished twenty-three years ago, a stunned and traumatized Jewish people cried from the very depths of its being: human destruction must never happen again to any people at any time in any place."[48] Rabbi Tanenbaum considered remaining silent incompatible with Jewish ethics in a world after Auschwitz: "Silence, indifference, spectatorship to human suffering are the cardinal sins in the Jewish value system today. 'Thou shall not stand idly by the blood of thy brother' has become virtually the eleventh commandment in contemporary Judaism."[49]

Representations of the Biafran crisis shared a set of similarities with representations of the Holocaust. In their apathy, the Biafran children resemble the figure of the "Mussulman" in German concentration camps: "people of a determined fatalism," as Eugen Kogon wrote.[50] Similarly, Holocaust victims were also represented as archetypical figures rather than individuals in contemporary accounts – as nameless "inmates"

FIGURE 10.2. "Biafra: Death Sentence for a People," *Spiegel*, 19 August 1968 cover. Photographer: Romano Cagnoni.

doomed to die in the "univers concentrationnaire." Again, victims were not portrayed as individuals, but as groups.[51] These tropes – of apathetic victims represented as part of a collective rather than as individuals – are common features in humanitarian narratives. However, for most contemporaries the photographs from Biafra evoked images taken during the liberation of the camps in 1945 – and seldom those of other humanitarian crises or genocides.[52] The nascent public memory and historical centrality of the Holocaust was not yet fully formed in the late 1960s. Yet it provided contemporaries with means to render the Biafran conflict legible and comprehensible. This emerging visual narrative of genocide simultaneously brought a faraway crisis and the Holocaust into the focus of international media attention.

For Biafra, there were no photographs of heaps of corpses similar to those found in Bergen-Belsen. This time, mass death still seemed to be preventable. The estimates of victim counts were regularly used to emphasize the need for immediate action. An ad that the American Committee to Keep Biafra Alive ran in the New York–based *Jewish Press*, for example, predicted that the death toll in Biafra would match that of the Holocaust, exclaiming: "Dear God, not again"[53] (Figure 10.3).

The photographs of individual infants' bodies also boded ill for the conflict by invoking visual parallels with Nazi mass murder. In a volume edited by German Biafra activists, an image of a dead child was reprinted that resembled the photographs of heaps of bodies in Bergen-Belsen so closely that it could have been taken in a Nazi concentration camp (Figure 10.4). According to the caption, this was one of the 8,000 victims of the "KZ Ikot Ekpene" (Concentration Camp Ikot Ekpene). This referred to the prison in the city of the same name where, after it was captured by Federal Nigerian troops, thousands were reportedly slaughtered. But mostly, the dying had not yet happened. These photographs brought home the news about pending mass death that looked like a genocide of the past.[54] But in the present, the worst could still be averted. The photographs were employed to try instigate a humanitarian campaign.

In other texts, the Biafran refugee camps were described as "Dachaus or Mauthausens of famine" or as a "Buchenwald for children."[55] A member of the Comité d'action pour le Biafra, former Gaullist minister Jacques Marette, explained to the French national assembly: "Biafra – that is the camp of Belsen at its liberation."[56] Auberon Waugh, member of the "Britain-Biafra Association," also deemed that comparison appropriate, since "the method of destruction is much the same," even if "the numbers involving Biafra are much greater."[57] Auschwitz, the most well-known site of mass annihilation, was repeatedly referred to; yet comparisons were also made with the concentration camps Dachau, Buchenwald, and Bergen-Belsen. These camps had been liberated by U.S. and British Allied troops, and photos of them had circulated in Western media since 1945. Auschwitz and the other extermination centers in the east were

6 million

Dear God, not again.

Does this scene look familiar? It should. It was only twenty-five years ago that similar scenes scarred the face of Europe, while nations turned their heads and said they did not know. You don't have that excuse.

Today Nigeria is engaged in the genocide of eight million Biafrans, calling it an "internal problem" and a "political solution." The Nigerian army which rapes, pillages and burns everything in its path is supported by Russian Mig's flown by Egyptian pilots who are training for the next war with Israel.

The world stood silent while 6,000,000 Jews died. Are you going to stand by now?

The scene above exists today. Help today before it is too late. Write your senators and congressmen and insist on an immediate cease-fire and send contributions now to the American Committee To Keep Biafra Alive, Inc.

1234 Broadway - Hotel Hadson
New York, New York 10001
(212) 736-2040

FIGURE 10.3. "Six Million." Swarthmore College Peace Collection, Swarthmore, PA, Clearing House for Nigeria–Biafra Information Records, Clearing House, DG 168, Box 10.

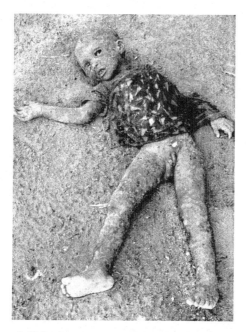

Im KZ Ikot Ekpene starben 8000 Ibibios Der Fernsehberichterstatter Klaus
Stephan hat in seinen Berichten im ARD auch diesen Massenmord, wie zahlreiche
andere von der nigerianischen Armee, an den kleineren Völkern Biafras begangene
Greuel unterschlagen.   Photo: Alex Klemkens

FIGURE 10.4. "In the concentration camp Ikot Ekpene, 8000 Ibibios have starved." Tilman Zülch and Klaus Guercke, eds., *Soll Biafra überleben? Dokumente – Berichte – Analysen – Kommentare* (Berlin: Lettner, 1969), between pp. 128 and 129. Photographer: Alex Klemkens.

liberated by Soviet forces, and photographs taken there did not reach Western media outlets in greater numbers. The iconography of the Nazi camps, at least in the West, was thus defined by the concentration camps and not the extermination centers.[58] Oddly, the visual narratives of genocide that emerged during the Biafran crisis evoked the memory of the Holocaust through images that depict Nazi crimes, but not necessarily Nazi genocide.

The connections between Biafra and the Holocaust were also a product of representation strategies. Not only Biafran propagandists but also the secessionists' sympathizers around the globe tried to secure the "right" interpretation of the "facts." Andreas Olie Chegwe, a Biafran student at Mainz University, self-published a collection of documents on the conflict. In his commentaries, Chegwe repeatedly draws on the cultural memory of the Holocaust. He explains that the images from Biafra "speak for themselves": "They tell us so clearly and precisely about the more than three years of bitter misery and cruelty that adding one further word to it is hardly necessary." Still, to make sure that the observers interpreted the images along the lines intended, he adds more than one word: "Dear reader, you see an 'Anne Frank' show in Biafra," and continued: "a people dies while the world looks on.... That is our tragic destiny – IGBOS, the Jews of Africa."[59]

However, the Biafrans were not the only ones who felt obligated to speak out against the suffering of the "Jews of Africa." Networks of Jewish activists and organizations elsewhere were also vital for the establishment and coordination of transnational Biafran protest.[60] Jewish heritage was part of the motivation to commit to the Biafran cause for numerous activists. Prominent examples include the pilot Abie Nathan, who assumed a highly active role in the delivery of food and medicine to Biafra,[61] and Bernard Kouchner. Part of a team of young Parisian doctors, Kouchner went to Biafra in 1968 with the French Red Cross. Critical of the regulations of the ICRC which was dependent on the acquiescence of the Nigerian government, the young French medics founded the Comité de Lutte contre le Génocide au Biafra, which in 1971 developed into "Médecins sans Frontières." Kouchner, whose grandfather was killed in Auschwitz, was the figurehead of *sans-frontiérisme*, the human rights movement which, as its myth of origin has it, emerged in the hospitals of Biafra.[62]

Numerous non-Jewish contemporaries reacted similarly. Günter Grass felt it was a particular responsibility of his fellow countrymen to react:

As Germans, we should know what we say when we use the word "genocide." This biggest of all crimes weighs heavily on the past of our people. Not moralizing condescension, but the knowledge of Auschwitz, Treblinka and Belsen obligates us to speak out publicly against the culprits and accessories of the genocide in Biafra.... [S]ilence – we had to learn that as well – turns into complicity.[63]

Many West German commentators agreed that "after Auschwitz, to which Biafra had been rightfully likened," the Federal Republic of Germany bore "a special responsibility."[64]

This responsibility was not West Germany's alone, however. Bishop Heinrich Tenhumberg, head of the Catholic Church's liaison office with the Bonn government, explained that the "principle of non-intervention is outdated in our time when the protection of fundamental human rights is at stake." "Civilized states" cannot remain passive in a world after Auschwitz given that modern communication technology automatically transformed internal conflicts into international crises.[65] The international community of states would need to react, the *Spiegel* argued as well. The UN has "defined what is happening in Biafra as criminally liable. The Nazi genocide of the Jews prompted the world organisation in 1946 [*sic*] to declare genocide an international crime." Yet the organization would lack the instruments to enforce this norm in practice. Without an international court that could open a trial, the Anti-Genocide Convention remains a fiasco – "the genocide allegations against Nigeria would have to be judged by a Nigerian court."[66] In view of Biafra, the lessons to be drawn from the Holocaust were to create international norms to prevent similar crimes in the present and the future.

The associations with the Holocaust became especially virulent in the United Kingdom. Because of the entanglements with the former colony, discussions in Britain had been intensive from the beginning of the conflict. Harold Wilson's Labour government came under heavy rhetorical fire.[67] Wilson's critics in the Biafra lobby, in the press, and in the two houses of the English parliament accused Whitehall of complicity in genocide. Auberon Waugh argued that the "mass starvation to death of innocent civilians" was "the most hideous crime against humanity in which England has ever been involved."[68] The staunchly pro-Biafran journalist Frederick Forsyth censured Wilson equally harshly. In his 1969 Penguin *Biafra Story*, the first edition of which sold out in weeks, the later author of bestselling crime novels explained that Britain was culpable of supporting Nigeria's genocidal persecution of the Biafrans which resembled the treatment of the Jews in World War II. Forsyth likened the Biafran territory in Eastern Nigeria to the "eastern resettlement area" European Jews had been relocated to by force.[69]

Although the Biafran lobby exerted strong pressure on London, the prime minister upheld support of the military regime in Lagos. British and Nigerian diplomats and state officials initiated a public relations counterattack.[70] References to National Socialism also played a role in this pro-Federal offensive. When debates of the arms trade with Nigeria were set for both houses of the British parliament in June 1968, the Nigerian head of propaganda Anthony Enahoro circulated a letter to the delegates warning that "indiscriminate and ill-founded use of the highly emotional word 'genocide' would remind the British of the fate of the Jews in Nazi Germany." However, there could be no question of genocide against the Igbo of Biafra. The Biafran claims should be understood as mere propaganda, since the "rebel command" represents a regime comparable to "the Hitler-Goebbels phenomenon."[71] The pro-Biafran rhetoric of Holocaust comparisons was turned on its head: the "Jews of Africa" were changed into "African Nazis." Analogies drawn between Biafran propaganda and that of the Nazis became a cornerstone of pro-Nigerian rhetoric.[72]

Pro-Federal efforts to de-legitimize Biafra as a political actor revolved around the rebuttal of the genocide allegations. An effective stroke was London's move to convince Lagos to invite a team of international observers to examine the conduct of the Nigerian troops. The team consisted of military personnel from the United Kingdom, Poland, Sweden, and Canada, all of which looked favorably on Nigeria. In their reports, which they started issuing in October 1968, the observer team concluded that no genocide had been perpetrated.[73] Lagos and London thus secured a major diplomatic success. The reports received a good amount of international attention, and in the eyes of many contemporaries, invalidated the genocide claims. These allegations were now increasingly understood as an invention of Biafran propagandists.[74]

Despite its biased approach, the observer team's assessment was perhaps not entirely incorrect. Numerous Igbos lived widely unmolested in Federally held territory. The end of the war did not lead to the "kill off" of the Igbo that many of their sympathizers had expected.[75] In spite of the 1966 massacres, the ruthless conduct of war, and the famine that cost countless lives, "genocide," as it is widely understood, as the intentional mass killing of a people, may not be the right term to describe what happened to the Igbos. The annihilation of the Igbos/Biafrans does not seem to have been a foremost goal of their adversaries.[76] The Nigerian civil war was, in the first place, indeed a civil war: a complex political conflict. Moreover, the Biafran leadership discredited itself, as it seemed to accept the suffering of its population. Even in discussions about a land corridor for the transport of relief supplies, the secessionists were reluctant to make concessions at the negotiation table. The airlift, which provided a lifeline to the global media, humanitarian aid, and the international arms trade were too valuable to give up. Put cynically, it was the famine that had secured international media attention.[77] International attention to the conflict abated after the publication of the observers' reports. Although the war continued until early 1970, the international media event "Biafra" ended with the rebuttal of the genocide allegations.

Conclusion: Biafra and the Fragmented Universalization of the Holocaust

The media and protest event "Biafra" happened during a time when the perception of National Socialism was changing slowly, but decisively. In the first ten years after the end of the war, the Holocaust played only a marginal role in dominant understandings of Nazism. While it is misleading to talk of a deliberate silencing of references to Nazi criminality in the immediate postwar years, the mass murder of the European Jews remained peripheral in representations of National Socialism and the war. The voices of camp survivors did not receive ample public hearing.[78] In the 1960s, Nazi mass crimes were increasingly discussed in Western publics. Intellectuals and protesters associated with the New Left likened French politics in Algeria and American involvement in Vietnam to Nazi terror.[79] However, these analogies were part of distinct intellectual traditions of anti-fascism: this rhetoric did not universalize the Holocaust; it compared imperialist powers.[80] More decisively, media coverage devoted to the Eichmann trial and the Six-Day War, for instance, helped to make the annihilation of the European Jews legible as genocide. A new rhetoric of genocide comparisons evolved during the war between Israel and Egypt: with the Egyptian President Gamal Abdel Nasser deemed a "new Hitler," some feared a "second Holocaust."[81]

This space of resonance had already been opened up when, in the summer months of 1968, newspaper readers and TV viewers in the West were confronted with images of starving children in a West African civil war. They were reminded of the genocide of the Jews in World War II or, more likely, of the *photographs* that were taken during the Allied liberation of the camps that appeared in newspapers and magazines in the immediate postwar period and have returned into public view since the late 1950s. Thus contemporaries had a reservoir of imagery of Nazi victims at their disposal to make sense of the pictures from Biafra. Although most of the photographs from 1945 were taken in concentration camps – and not in the death factories – they were nevertheless increasingly understood to "show" the genocide of the Jews.[82]

In representations of Biafra, both complexes – the Nigerian civil war and the crimes of Nazi Germany – were interpreted as genocide and thus given rhetorical equivalence. The "Jews of Africa" were no Jews, but (mostly) Christians – the connecting line was drawn on a purely metaphorical basis. Biafra was interpreted using models that derived from the evolving cultural memory of National Socialism. Conversely, Biafra also influenced historical and public perceptions of Nazi rule. The African civil war contributed to the consolidation of a pattern of memorialization and helped to establish a new understanding of National Socialism. The murder of European Jews ceased to be merely one entry on a long list of Nazi crimes and became "the Holocaust": the historical and symbolical *core* of a new understanding of National Socialist rule and the Second World War. Biafra thus represented an important step in this process of cultural and historical reinterpretation.

Photographs often visually define our memory of past events. We remember the photo and not the event: the event, in a sense, is eclipsed by its photographic representation.[83] Similarly, contemporaries in the late 1960s "remembered" the Holocaust in terms of images that showed the result of Nazi mass crimes, but not necessarily the genocide itself. Through the Auschwitz-Biafra analogy, parts of the object behind these visual representations (such as Nazi rule as a political system) were eclipsed: what remained for the eye to see was "genocide" in Nazi Europe and in postcolonial West Africa.

The bilateral effects of the images from Biafra can be illustrated with a drawing first printed on a flyer of the Comité de lutte contre le genocide au Biafra. On one half is the drawing of an inmate, reduced to a skeleton, sitting on a plank bed. The sketch strongly echoes the iconography of concentration camps, in particular photographs taken by Margaret Bourke-White at the liberation of Buchenwald.[84] Yet the drawing is captioned "Auschwitz" – the site of the genocidal annihilation of the Jews. The void that the absence of photographic representations of Auschwitz has left is filled with ink – the drawing, as a visual representation, is not as dependent on the object represented as a photograph is. Roland Barthes calls the person or thing photographed "the *Spectrum* of the Photograph." "This word retains," he explained, "a relation to 'spectacle' and adds to it that rather terrible thing which is there in every photograph: the return of the dead."[85] The dead of Auschwitz returned in representations of the bodies of starving Biafrans, or so many contemporaries felt. The photographs of the original dead, of the victims of the Nazi genocide, were missing. However, the representations of other dying people filled this void: the Biafrans, a people doomed to die in present but who evoked a different genocidal past.

The other half of the drawing shows one such dead of the present: a standing figure which is equally emaciated and whose age and sex can scarcely be identified – it could be a child as much as a dotard. Precision is added only through the caption "Biafra." Like the "Auschwitz," written with a capital "A," this is a Biafra with a capital "B."[86] This "alphabet of horror," as the caption to the French flyer dubbed it, resonated with Biafra activists in Germany who adopted the image nearly unchanged. The Gesellschaft für bedrohte Völker, which had evolved out of the Hamburg-based Aktion Biafra-Hilfe, used a similar drawing

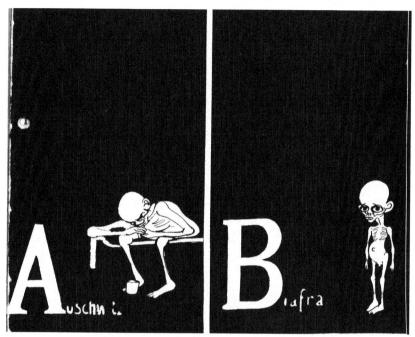

FIGURE 10.5. "Auschwitz – Biafra" in *Pogrom* 1, no. 4/5, August/September 1970, cover page.

on the cover of the first issue of their aptly named periodical *Pogrom*[87] (Figure 10.5).

A German proverb can help to open up the particular meanings of this source. It translates as: "Who says A, also has to say B." Apparently for the pro-Biafran Germans the drawing suggested that who says "Auschwitz" also has to say "Biafra." It also echoes Max Horkheimer's dictum, "whoever does not want to talk about capitalism should also remain silent about fascism."[88] Yet in the Biafran version, fascism and capitalism were dropped from the equation. What remained was genocide.

The Nigerian civil war was inscribed into an iconography and rhetoric of genocide comparisons, with the Holocaust as its Ur-Gestalt. This analogy did not leave a lot of space for the analysis of complex political systems. But in the course of the war, it became apparent that the Nigerian civil war could not be contained by simple narratives: the Biafrans were not mere "innocent victims" but a party in a complicated conflict. Confronted with the political complexities of a barely known world region, Western interest in the war quickly diminished. The case is characteristic for the ambivalent effects of Holocaust comparisons: for some time, this rhetoric may help to focus the attention of the media and the public on a certain topic. Sometimes it may also help to create political pressure to act. Yet the Holocaust is such an extreme crime that the demands it poses to any event compared to it are almost never met. And the international community is free to turn away from bloody conflicts fought somewhere in the more distant parts of our world if they are not "like Auschwitz." Setting aside the intricate question of whether intervention is reasonable or not in a given case,[89] the question remains whether Holocaust memory culture is as effective at raising awareness as many commentators claim.[90] It certainly does not contribute to a nuanced perception of conflicts and mass crimes.

Part of the problem may be the fixation on visual icons. Indeed, there are "image acts" that make history, but not because of a force inherent in them. In a certain sense, an "image act" has to be written. The meanings ascribed to images depend on, for instance, those ascribed to other images and events associated with them. The photographs from Biafra were understood as images of a "new Auschwitz." Within the shared visual and semantic space of associations and entanglements that developed, both complexes became visible in a similar manner: as genocides. When it turned out that this frame of reference did not match the Nigerian civil war, the image act "Biafra" lost its power.

Notes

1 On the relief operation see Desgrandchamps, "Entre coopération et concurrence," and Laurie S. Wiseberg, "Humanitarian Intervention: Lessons from the Nigerian Civil War," *Revue des Droits de l'Homme / Human Rights Journal* 7, no. 1 (1974): 61–98. The Irish missionaries played a key role in the internationalization of the conflict. See Kevin O'Sullivan, *Ireland, Africa and the End of Empire* (Manchester: Manchester University Press, 2013), chapters 4–5.

2 Marc H. Tanenbaum, "Biafran Tragedy Accelerates: Christian Jewish Cooperation," *Religious News Service*, 14 August 1968, American Jewish Committee Archives, New York, Blaustein Library, Interreligious Affairs 1968, Biafra, Box 71, quotes on p. 4.

3 The conflict was also featured on the cover pages of *Life*, 12 July 1968; *Paris Match*, 20 July 1968; *Spiegel*, 19 August 1968; and *Time*, 23 August 1968.

4 For accounts of the international history of the war see John J. Stremlau, *The International Politics of the Nigerian Civil War 1967–1970* (Princeton, NJ: Princeton University Press, 1977); Laurie Sheila Wiseberg, "The International Politics of Relief: A Case Study of the Relief Operations Mounted during the Nigerian Civil War (1967–1970)," PhD dissertation, University of California at Los Angeles 1973, and Lasse Heerten, "Spectacles of Suffering."

5   See Brink, "Bildeffekte, 104–29.

6   Bredekamp, *Theorie des Bildakts.*

7   "Nur beten," *Spiegel*, 19 August 1968, 71.

8   I use the term "Holocaust" even though it was not in wide usage at the time; it has since become the standard designation for the Nazi mass murder of the European Jews.

9   Stremlau, *International Politics*, 109–17.

10 Valentin Groebner, "Zeige deine Wunde! Gewaltbilder und ihre Betrachter – in historischer Perspektive," *Neue Zürcher Zeitung*, 13 February 2010.

11 Rothberg, *Multidirectional Memory.*

12 Since comparisons with the Holocaust as genocide were a new phenomenon, these analogies were free of the frictions that emerged when its universalization aroused fears of a denigration of the Holocaust as the *ur*-genocide. See Jeffrey C. Alexander et al., *Remembering the Holocaust: A Debate* (Oxford: Oxford University Press, 2009); Peter Novick, *The Holocaust in American Life* (Boston: Mariner Books, 1999); Jan Eckel and Claudia Moisel, eds., *Universalisierung des Holocaust? Erinnerungskultur und Geschichtspolitik in internationaler Perspektive* (Göttingen: Wallstein, 2008); Annette Wieviorka, *The Era of the Witness* (Ithaca, NY: Cornell University Press 2006, first ed. French: *L'ère du témoin*, Paris 1998).

13 On the afterlife of images of the Holocaust in media reports on late twentieth-century genocides, see Zelizer, *Remembering to Forget.*

14 See Heerten, "Spectacles of Suffering."

15 Nigeria was separated into four states in 1963 when the multi-ethnic Midwestern State was carved out of parts of the Western Region.

16 J. D. Y. Peel, "The Cultural Work of Yoruba Ethnogenesis," in Elizabeth Tonkin et al., eds., *History and Ethnicity* (London: Routledge 1989), 198–215, quote on 200; Michael Crowder, *The Story of Nigeria* (London: Faber and Faber, 1978), chapters 12–14, and Toyin Falola and Matthew M. Heaton, *A History of Nigeria* (Cambridge: Cambridge University Press, 2008), chapter 7.

17 The best accounts are still Anthony H. M. Kirk-Greene, "January 1966: The Political Prologue," in Kirk-Greene, ed., *Crisis and Conflict in Nigeria*, Vol. I: *January 1966 – July 1967* (Aldershot: Gregg Revivals, 1993 [1971]), 1–24; Anthony H. M. Kirk-Greene, "War and Peace: July 1967–January 1970," in Kirk-Greene, ed., *Crisis and Conflict in Nigeria*, Vol. II: *July 1967–January 1970* (Aldershot: Gregg Revivals, 1993 [1971]), 1–144; and Albert Wirz, *Krieg in Afrika: Die nachkolonialen Konflikte in Nigeria, Sudan, Tschad und Kongo* (Wiesbaden: Steiner, 1982), 134–50.

18 Heerten, "Spectacles of Suffering," chapter 3; Tudor Parfitt, *Black Jews in Africa and the Americas* (Cambridge, MA: Harvard University Press, 2013), 102–16.

19 Matthew Connelly, *A Diplomatic Revolution: Algeria's Fight for Independence and the Origins of the Post–Cold War Era* (Oxford: Oxford University Press, 2002).

20 Morris Davis, *Interpreters for Nigeria: The Third World and International Public Relations*, (Urbana: University of Illinois Press, 1977).

21 The most active group was the Biafra Union of Great Britain and Ireland; see their "Statement on British Arms Supplies" in Kirk-Greene, *Crisis and Conflict,* Vol. 2, 151.

22 In July 1968, French readers were still told that this would be a forgotten war, "too remote and confusing" to draw the interest of the European public. Jean Finois, "Horreurs et tractations," *Le Nouvel Observateur,* 15 July 1968, 19.

23 O'Sullivan, *Ireland,* chapters 4–5; Nicholas Ibeawuchi Omenka, "Blaming the Gods: Christian Religious Propaganda in the Nigeria-Biafra War," *Journal of African History* 51 (2010): 367–89.

24 *Sun,* 12 June 1968, 1–3.

25 Heerten, "Spectacles of Suffering," chapter 4.

26 Michael Ignatieff, *The Warrior's Honor: Ethnic War and the Modern Conscience* (New York: Henry Holt, 1997), 124.

27 Kennedy, "'A Compassionate Vision,'" 180.

28 Hariman and Lucaites, *No Caption Needed,* chapter 6.

29 Mark Pottle, ed., *Daring to Hope: The Diaries and Letters of Violet Bonham Carter 1946–1969* (London: Weidenfeld & Nicolson, 2000), 348.

30 *Hansard Lords,* 27 August 1968, column 700–701, http://hansard.millbank-systems.com/lords/1968/aug/27/nigeria (last accessed 14 May 2013).

31 Günter Grass, "Völkermord vor aller Augen: Ein Appell an die Bundesregierung," *Die Zeit,* 11 October 1968, 5. See, for instance, Hans Gresmann, "Mord ohne Gericht," *Die Zeit,* 9 August 1968, 1.

32 See Jacques Siclier, "A la télévision: Un peuple en train de mourir de faim," *Le Monde,* 15 August 1968, 4.

33 Roland Barthes, "The Reality Effect," in Barthes, *The Rustle of Language,* 141–8. Also Marshall McLuhan, *The Gutenberg Galaxy: The Making of Typographic Man* (London: Routledge and Kegan Paul, 1962), 31.

34 Knoch, "Mediale Trauer." As source examples, see "Nur beten," *Spiegel,* 19 August 1968, 71–6, and Pascal Grellety-Bosviel, "Bloc-notes d'un médecin au Biafra," *La Croix,* 14 March 1969, 10.

35 Laqueur, "Bodies," 179. This is not necessarily a successful strategy. The bodily disfigurations of the Biafran children could also be perceived as a dehumanization and thus an obstacle to compassion. Similarly, the inhumane appearance of the victims of the Holocaust impeded empathic reactions among Allied soldiers during the liberation of the camps. Jeffrey C. Alexander, "The Social Construction of Moral Universals," in Alexander et al., *Remembering,* 3–102, 6.

36 See Figure 10.1, this chapter, and for instance *L'express,* 7 October 1968, cover page.

37 *La Mort du Biafra: Photographies de Gilles Caron, Présentation de F. de Bonneville* (Paris: Solar, 1968), 14.

38 Rosenwein, "Worrying about Emotions in History."

39 Jean Buhler, *Tuez-Les Tous! Guerre de Sécession au Biafra* (Paris: Flammarion, 1968), between 46 and 47.

40 On the languages of human rights employed during Biafra, see Heerten, "Dystopia."

41 This term is a variation on a formulation by Frank Bösch and Manuel Borutta, "Medien und Emotionen in der Moderne," 13.

42 See, for instance, "Augenzeugenbericht einer jungen katholischen Schwester aus Europa zu den Massakern der Bundestruppen im Mittelwesten (Mid-West-Nigeria)," in Tilman Zülch and Klaus Guercke, eds., *Soll Biafra überleben? Dokumente – Berichte – Analysen – Kommentare* (Berlin: Lettner, 1969), 106; James R. Shepley, "A Letter from the Publisher," *Time*, 23 August 1968, 9.

43 For a particularly evocative passage, see Buhler, *Tuez-Les*, 80–81.

44 See "Die verhungernden Kinder von Biafra," *Stern*, 28 July 1968, 14.

45 Buhler, *Tuez-Les*, 85–6. More detailed were only medical treatises. See Bruno Gans, "A Biafran Relief Mission," *Lancet*, 29 March 1969, 660–5.

46 Malkki, "Speechless Emissaries," 387, 388.

47 Hans Gresmann, "Mord ohne Gericht," *Die Zeit*, 9 August 1968, 1.

48 A. James Rudin, "Talk Given at Biafra Interfaith Rally, St. Patrick's Cathedral, New York, 26 October 1968," American Jewish Committee Archives, New York, Blaustein Library, Interreligious Affairs 1968, Biafra, Box 72, Biafra Responses Folder, 1.

49 Tanenbaum, "Biafran Tragedy," 4.

50 Eugen Kogon, *Der SS-Staat: Das System der deutschen Konzentrationslager* (Frankfurt a.M.: Europäische Verlagsanstalt, 1964 [1946]), 380.

51 David Rousset, *L'univers concentrationnaire*, Paris: Éditions de Minuit, 1965 [1946]; also Brink, *Ikonen der Vernichtung*, 161–4, 170–3.

52 Understandings of the Holocaust have also been formed with recourse to the Armenian genocide. The inventor of the term "genocide," Raphael Lemkin, is a case in point. On the Armenian case, see Balakian, in this volume. Representations of Biafra also share a lot with older humanitarian narratives, but these traditions were rarely evoked. For one notable exception see International Witnesses against Genocide, "Genocide in Biafra: Fifty Years Ago – the Armenians, Twenty-five Years Ago – the Jews, Now – the Ibo," August 1968 (World Council of Churches Archives Geneva, 42.3.007, WCC General Secretariat, Nigeria / Biafra, 3).

53 American Committee, "6 Million," Swarthmore College Peace Collection (SCPC), Swarthmore, PA, Clearing House for Nigeria / Biafra Information Records, 1968–1970, DG 168, Box 10. See for instance also Marion Gräfin Dönhoff et al., "An die Adresse der Regierungen," *Die Zeit*, 23 August 1968, 3, or John D. Campbell, Letter to N. Gaydon, 29 January 1969, UK NA FCO 26/300, 1.

54 From a range of possible examples, see Heinrich Tenhumberg to the members of the budget committee of the German Bundestag, 20 June 1968. Political Archives of the German Foreign Office Berlin: B 34/747.

55 Buhler, *Tuez-Les*, 114; Raymond Offroy, "Editorial," *Biafra: Bulletin du comité d'action pour le Biafra*, April 1969, No. 1, 1.

56 "Le témoignage de Monsieur Jacques Marette devant l'assemblée nationale française," *Biafra: Bulletin du comité d'action pour le Biafra*, Supplement to No. 5, I-VI.

57 Auberon Waugh, *Britain and Biafra: The Case for Genocide* (London: Britain-Biafra Association, 1969), 20. Numerous similar examples could be added. See Jean Cau, "Un camp de concentration où des kapos noirs assassinent des juifs noirs," in Alexandre Sosnowsky, ed., *Biafra: Proximité de la mort continuité de la vie* (Paris: Fayard, 1969), unpaged, and Paul Connett, "Statement for Immediate Release," 14 November 1968. SCPC Clearing House for Nigeria / Biafra Information Records, 1968–1970, DG 168, Box 10.

58 The most influential publication in West Germany was Gerhard Schoenberner, *Der gelbe Stern: Die Judenverfolgung in Europa 1933–1945* (Hamburg: Rütten & Loening, 1960). On the blurring of the differences between the camps, see Brink, *Ikonen*, 161–4, 170–3, and for a diverging opinion, Knoch, *Die Tat als Bild*, 699–721. On Soviet Holocaust photography, see Shneer, *Through Soviet Jewish Eyes*.

59 Andreas Olie Chegwe, ed., *Biafra: Tragödie eines Volkes, Ein Volk stirbt und die Welt sieht zu* (Wiesbaden: self-published, no date [ca. 1969]), commentaries on the pictures between 48 and 49.

60 Large parts of the Israeli population also sympathized with the Biafrans. Michal Givoni, "Des victimes pas comme les autres: Réactions israéliennes face a la catastrophe du Biafra," in William Ossipow, ed., *Israël et l'autre* (Geneva: Labor et Fides, 2005), 195–242.

61 Ibid.; "Twin Circle Headline: Aid to Biafra," SCPC, Swarthmore, PA, Clearing House for Nigeria – Biafra Information Records, 1968–1970, DG 168, Box 5.

62 Marie-Luce Desgrandchamps, "Revenir sur le mythe fondateur de Médecins Sans Frontières: les relations entre les médecins français et le CICR pendant la guerre du Biafra (1967–1970)," in *Relations internationals* 146, no. 2 (2011): 95–108.

63 Grass, "Völkermord," 5.

64 J. Rudolph/H. Menzel, "Information für die Teilnehmer der Podiumsdiskussion 'Biafra – Testfall für eine neue Politik,' Heidelberg, 27 January 1969," Evangelisches Zentralarchiv in Berlin, 87/1119.

65 Heinrich Tenhumberg, "Massenmord trotz Völkerrecht? Zur Problematik Nigeria / Biafra," in Zülch and Guercke, eds., *Soll Biafra überleben?*, 229.

66 "Nur beten," 72. The UN Genocide Convention was adopted in 1948.

67 John W. Young, *The Labour Governments 1964–1970*, Vol. 2: *International Policy* (Manchester: Manchester University Press, 2003), 193–217.

68 Waugh, *Britain and Biafra*, 5, 7.

69 Forsyth, *The Making of an African Legend: The Biafra Story* (Harmondsworth: Penguin, 1977 [1969]), 267–8.

70 Lagos enlisted the services of the PR agency Galitzine. Davis, *Interpreters*.

71 Nigeria High Commission, *Chief Enahoro Writes to British M.P.s on Nigerian Civil War*, London, 12 June 1968, Churchill College Archives, Cambridge, NBKR 4/41, 4, 6.

72 See, for instance, "Editorial: The Bigger the Lie," *United Nigeria*, 11 October 1968, No. 4, 2.

73 Karen E. Smith, "The UK and 'Genocide' in Biafra," *Journal of Genocide Research* 16, Nos. 2–3 (2014), 247–62.

74 On the changing perception of the Biafran regime, see "Ein Kavalierskrieg," *Spiegel*, 19 January 1970, 82–7.

75 Stremlau, *International Politics*, 366–7.

76 For a more thorough discussion of these questions, see Lasse Heerten and A. Dirk Moses, "The Nigeria-Biafra War: Postcolonial Conflict and the Question of Genocide, 1967–1970," *Journal of Genocide Research* 16, nos. 2–3 (2014), 169–203.

77 Heerten, "Dystopia."

78 See Richard Bessel and Dirk Schumann, eds., *Life after Death: Approaches to a Cultural and Social History of Europe during the 1940s and 1950s* (Cambridge: Cambridge University Press, 2003); Tony Judt, *Postwar: A History of Europe Since 1945* (London: Pimlico, 2007 [2005]), 803–31; Pieter Lagrou, *The Legacy of Nazi Occupation: Patriotic Memory and National Recovery in Western Europe, 1945–1965* (Cambridge: Cambridge University Press, 2000).

79 Christoph Kalter, *Die Entdeckung der Dritten Welt: Dekolonisierung und neue radikale Linke in Frankreich* (Frankfurt a.M.: Campus, 2011), chapter 4; Wilfried Mausbach, "Auschwitz and Vietnam. West German Protest against America's War during the 1960s," in Andreas W. Daum et al., eds., *America, the Vietnam War, and the World. Comparative and International Perspectives* (Cambridge: Cambridge University Press, 2003), 279–8.

80 Anson Rabinbach, *Begriffe aus dem Kalten Krieg: Totalitarismus, Antifaschismus, Genozid* (Göttingen, Wallstein, 2009); Kirsten Fermaglich, *American Dreams and Nazi Nightmares: Early Holocaust Consciousness and Liberal America, 1957–1965* (Waltham, MA: Brandeis University Press, 2006).

81 Idith Zertal, *Israel's Holocaust and the Politics of Nationhood* (Cambridge: Cambridge University Press, 2005), 115–27.

82 See Knoch, *Die Tat*; Brink, *Ikonen* and Zelizer, *Remembering*. On the changing perceptions of the camps since 1945, see Samuel Moyn, "In the Aftermath of Camps," in Frank Biess and Robert G. Moeller, eds., *Histories of the Aftermath* (New York: Berghahn, 2009), 49–64.

83 Barthes, *Camera Lucida*.

84 Dagmar Barnouw, *Germany 1945: Views of War and Violence* (Bloomington: Indiana University Press 1996).

85 Barthes, *Camera Lucida*, 9.

86 "L'alphabet (á suivre) de l'horreur," April 1969. SCPC, Swarthmore, PA, Clearing House for Nigeria–Biafra Information Records, 1968–1970, DG 168, Box 12.

87 *Gesellschaft* dubbed their journal, in which the fate of "threatened peoples" around the world was discussed, "Pogrom." See, for instance, Tilman Zülch, "Auschwitz – Biafra – Bengalen," in *Pogrom* 2, no. 11 (1971): 2–3.

88 Max Horkheimer, "Die Juden und Europa," *Zeitschrift für Sozialforschung* 8 (1939): 115–37, 115.

89 On the problems connected with a pro-interventionist stance, see Stephen Wertheim, "A Solution from Hell: The United States and the Rise of Humanitarian Interventionism, 1991–2003," *Journal of Genocide Research* 12, Nos. 3–4 (2010): 149–72.

90 That is the thesis in Daniel Levy and Natan Sznaider, *The Holocaust and Memory in the Global Age* (Philadelphia: Temple University Press, 2006, first ed. German: Erinnerung im globalen Zeitalter. Der Holocaust, Frankfurt a. M., 2001), and, in a more reflected manner, Alexander, "Social Construction."

II

Finding the Right Image

*British Development NGOs and the Regulation of Imagery**

Henrietta Lidchi

It may be difficult now to recall with what passion and persistence the question of imagery was discussed among development practitioners in the late 1980s and 1990s. The history of development is a comparatively short one; the largest and most prominent development organizations in the United Kingdom – Oxfam, Christian Aid, Save the Children Fund – have institutional histories confined to the last century. Conceived as small social justice organizations that emerged as a response to the need for peace and reconstruction in Europe, rather than elsewhere, they saw their role in development secured in the 1960s. Yet the proper use of images was a preoccupation that emerged only in the 1980s.

This chapter examines the image of development – in visual and verbal terms – and considers why it became an issue of concern in the 1980s for British development NGOs. Focusing on an advertising campaign produced by the British-based Christian Aid, I explore how images of development mobilized and represented complex ideas about development process and practice in seemingly ingenuous ways.

The first to address the question of representation and imagery was Jørgen Lissner in a thesis entitled *The Politics of Altruism* (1977). Radical for its time, this book effectively delineated the parameters of a debate that would subsequently emerge in the aftermath of the Ethiopian famine in the mid-1980s. Lissner's argument was based on the following

* This chapter was originally published in *Culture and Global Change*, edited by Tracey Skelton and Tim Allen (London: Routledge, 1999), 87–101. The editors thank Henrietta Lidchi and Taylor & Francis for permission to reprint an edited and condensed version of the original essay.

premises: (1) that development nongovernmental organizations in the North (NNGOs) were harboring a destructive internal conflict between fundraising and education, (2) that this was symbolized in the images and messages these discrete groups of professionals produced, and (3) that the image of development fundamentally impacted on development practice: *negative* images of development encouraged *negative* development practice and vice versa. Lissner characterized the activities of fundraising and education as conflictual and competing. Fundraising, in his view, was a primarily economic activity dedicated to raising money, with no further goal, and ensured the long-term institutional survival of the organization. Development education, on the other hand, was a morally oriented pursuit, committed to increasing global awareness of development and conscience-raising among Northern audiences. Fundraisers had short-term goals: the ends (money) justified the means (advertising); the best methods were quite simply those with the largest profit margins. Development educationalists were more visionary and means-oriented, their work was a practical application of ideals of solidarity with the poor, and they were, furthermore, particular about the types of messages and images they produced.[1]

These differing priorities were rendered most visibly manifest, for Lissner, in the distinct images of development these groups produced. Fundraisers were crude behaviorists content to flatter or shame the donor, either by showing how cost-effective their donations could be or by dwelling on the despair and devastation in the global South. Because there was nothing sexy about development in advertising terms, fundraisers sought to elicit donations by making full and constant use of a narrow range of images – utilizing, in the main, distressing portraits of malnourished young children: starving baby images.[2] For Lissner, whose sympathies lay squarely with education and social justice, it was simply a question of opting to show the truth. Starving baby images, he held, were neither true nor accurate pictures of reality overseas, but a reflection of the laziness of fundraisers who chose to feed Northern prejudices for profit. Lissner defined these images as *negative* – demeaning, lacking dignity, and untruthful. In this manner Lissner gave voice to an argument stating that *negative* images were the product of a power imbalance between those *representing* – the NNGOs, the North – and those being *represented* – the poor, the South.

The public display of an African child with a bloated kwashiorkor-ridden stomach in advertisements is pornographic because it exposes something in human life that is as delicate and deeply personal as sexuality, that is, suffering. It puts people's bodies, their misery, their grief and their fears on display with all the details and all the indiscretion that a telescopic lens will allow.[3]

Lissner's drawing of an analogy between negative imagery and pornography at this early point was particularly prescient because he linked knowledge to power through the visual image.[4] Such an argument was not mainstream to development thinking, but drew much from work on photography in other disciplines.

Lissner advocated that imagery, most particularly photographs, should be regulated. His analysis tacitly acknowledged what Elizabeth Edwards later stated: that all photography works on the basis of spatial and temporal dislocation.[5] A photograph is of the past, it freezes a moment that has ceased to be; yet it functions in the present, transforming the "there-then" into the "here-now." Moreover, its immediacy and realism can be replayed an infinite number of times: "the photography repeat[s] mechanically what could never be repeated existentially."[6] It is this combination of factors that allows photographs to stand for, and symbolize, historical events, while failing to disclose within the frame the conditions under which these events came to exist. The existence of a photograph does not allow the viewer to distinguish whether what he or she is looking at is the result of a candid or posed shot of the subject.[7] Temporal dislocation is coupled with spatial dislocation. Photography frames and shapes the moment, exposing it to historical scrutiny. Furthermore it travels. Photography can make familiar what is spatially distant, and what may never be personally encountered – famine, for instance. Consequently, the most basic characteristic of the documentary snapshot is that it simultaneously appropriates an image and decontextualizes it. The camera, then, rather than being seen as a *medium* that represents the "real" can be best characterized as an *instrumentality*.[8] It is instrumental in the sense that not only does it construct meaning but that, as a tool of representation, it is intrusive: it has the power to observe at close proximity and to remove the image absolutely from its original context (Figure 11.1).

For these reasons, it has been argued that photography as a medium combines voyeurism and control, because visual images are taken *by* the powerful *of* the powerless; the *subjects* of the photograph are transformed into *objects* by virtue of being "shot."[9] So photography can produce the colonized and the powerless as fixed realities: entirely knowable and visible, but equally "other," irreconcilably different – the *objects* of desire and derision. Photography constitutes subjects not only as objects of knowledge, but also as fetishistic objects, docile and visible bodies.[10]

FIGURE 11.1. "Keep the health service going" advertisement. Courtesy of Christian Aid.

All these reservations underlay Lissner's critique of *negative* images. For him, images of starving children demeaned the *subjects* of development because they represented them as being devoid of dignity: they were transformed into *objects* of representation, and by implication *objects* of development. For Lissner, representation – the image of development – was decisively linked to intervention – the methodology of development. The wrong type of image could elicit the wrong type of development. Consequently Northern NGOS (NNGOs) were in a crucial position. Northern audiences were particularly susceptible to negative and exotic images of the South because they had no chance to double check their veracity, nor did they have a ballast of the normal with which to compare them.[11] When NNGOs reproduced charity images that dwelt on disaster and despair, or promoted a dependent view of the South, they conspired with the media to undermine their own capabilities to increase either global awareness or democracy.[12] So Lissner advocated consistency between images and practice. By reflecting a dated charitable approach based on a modernization view of development, fundraisers constituted poverty as an inescapable fact of the global order. But development organizations, he believed, ostensibly favored a more recent structural view of poverty causation and advocated social change and global social justice. This agenda was reflected and disseminated only in poorly resourced, infrequently produced educational material. Fundraising targeted the sin of omission – the failure of the rich to give to the poor – promoting an idea of charity. Education, on the other hand, sought to address the sin of commission – the manner in which the rich North constantly appropriated wealth from the poorer South – advancing the more desirable view of potential social justice. Development education had an agenda driven by moral values, not profit margins.[13]

Lissner's account described Northern NGOs as sites of internal conflict: in his fatalistic narrative, fundraisers were a parasitic and increasingly dominant force.[14] NNGOs were in turn characterized as lacking the institutional will to navigate the tension between pursuing institutional growth and a vocal commitment to global development and social justice. Lissner's portentous warning – of at best an impasse, at worst an erosion of principle – did not forecast the possibility of a major alteration in the state of affairs. Yet the extraordinary events that surrounded the Ethiopian famine in the mid-1980s ushered in a cultural revolution that proved the tensions delineated in Lissner's account to be far more blurred.

The Story Breaks: Imagining the Ethiopian Famine in
1984–1985 and Its Consequences

The Ethiopian famine of 1984–5 was a revolutionary moment for development NGOs in two significant respects. First, in the realm of development practice: for development NGOs the events of 1984–5 marked a coming of age evidenced by their unprecedented leap in income and prestige.[15] The crisis in Ethiopia seemed to be *the* example of "development in reverse" that NNGOs had long been warning governments about. Its effect was to secure a loss of faith in the ability of official aid institutions and their programs to relieve or alleviate poverty in the long term.

> Mass death by starvation in Africa was the most emphatic proof possible that the development era had been a washout, that most official aid served to impoverish communities rather than to enrich them and that such reassuring notions as the "trickle-down" theory of development were a cruel deception.... Only the private agencies emerged with any credit from the catastrophe.[16]

Throughout the famine, it appeared, NGOs had remained true to their principles and steadfast in their priorities. The events in Africa in the mid-1980s convinced many that an NGO contribution was more effective, professional, and caring than anything governments in the larger aid organizations could hope to provide. NGOs emerged as the new hopeful instruments of development, representing a new model of what development could mean and how it should be conducted.[17] In a situation of dire need, NGOs had promised and delivered salvation; they represented and carried through a more human/e alternative.

The events surrounding the Ethiopian famine of 1984–5 also had profound cultural effects. They forced NNGOs to consider their own image – how they looked and were identified as NGOs as well as how they represented their partners in development. Questions of representation moved to the fore; it was no longer a question of gilding the lily, it was now a principal concern.

One consequence of the Ethiopian famine was to increase confidence in NGOs and ensure their survival, through exponentially increasing their income and popularity. This was achieved through a barrage of powerful if disturbing imagery: that of starving masses and doomed individuals. The fate and fortune of the development NGOs could not be divorced from the power of the media. This recognition caused development organizations to reassess their responsibility in representational terms. They came to the unsettling realization that popularizing the right images might ensure their institutional survival, increase their political leverage, and promote their kind of development by mobilizing popular support.

The Ethiopian famine gained global recognition in October 1983 when a report filmed by the late Mohammed Amin, then Visnews' Africa Bureau Chief, and filed by Michael Buerk of the BBC, was screened on the Nine O'Clock News. Up to that point, despite repeated warnings, detailed official accounts, a Disasters Emergency Committee appeal,[18] and news reports, the famine did not occupy center stage. It was judged to be marginal and largely un-newsworthy. That Amin and Buerk worked together was largely a product of good fortune and sound journalistic instinct. Buerk had, in fact, been to Ethiopia in July of 1983 to report back on the success of the Disasters Emergency Committee appeal but had only filmed in the southern part of Ethiopia, which was comparatively lush and suffering the effects of famine to a lesser degree. In October 1983, Amin and Buerk focused on the northern towns of Korem and Makelle, the epicenters of the famine. They were unprepared for the scale of the human distress they encountered and emerged in a profound state of shock.[19] This was a notable feature of the visual and verbal images that were subsequently broadcast on the BBC's evening news of 23 October 1984.

Dawn, as the sun breaks through the piercing chill of night on the plain outside Korem, it lights up a biblical famine, now, in the 20th century. This place, say workers here, is the closest thing to hell on earth. Thousands of wasted people are coming here for help. Many find only death.... Death is all around.... Korem, an insignificant town, has become a place of grief.[20]

The footage is said to have hushed newsrooms, producing tears and unprompted donations from a habitually hardened news staff. Carried by 425 of the world's major broadcasting agencies, in Britain, it jammed the Oxfam's switchboard for three days. Even British tabloids such as the *Sun* joined the fray with a two-inch headline "Race to Save the Babies" (28 October 1983). An enormous aid operation ensued, fueled by popular support. Aid workers were now swamped with clumsy news teams eager for a story. It was the biggest news item to come "out of Africa" in the 1980s.[21]

Extraordinary though these events were, they did not secure the cultural revolution in NGOs. This was left up to the pop star – Bob Geldof – who saw the Amin-Buerk footage. He responded by recording the single *Do They Know It's Christmas?*, a record that sought to "save the world at Christmas time," under the name "Band Aid."[22] Geldof's energy fueled a media circus around the famine; he emerged as the self-appointed voice of the people. As a concerned, independent, and active citizen, he considered himself to be empowered and entitled to confront politicians and governments on the level of their commitment to the South. Geldof's abrasive approach opened a surprising number of doors, to the consternation of more established and experienced development professionals.[23]

The Band Aid saga culminated in the legendary Live Aid Concert of July 1985. Staged simultaneously at Wembley Arena and the JFK Stadium in Philadelphia, it was sixteen hours long, beamed via thirteen satellites to 120 nations and an estimated 1.6 billion people, a third of the world's population. It was the "biggest [philanthropic] music concert in history."[24] Frenzied performances were punctuated with appeals from an exhausted Geldof bullying people to part with their money now and the by-now iconic footage of starving people, including, most particularly, the Amin/Buerk report.[25] Substantial quantities of money poured in during and after the event to the tune of U.S. $60,000 a month in 1985.[26] The Band Aid Trust eventually raised £144 million worldwide.[27] Live Aid secured populism a place in charity fundraising and spawned a succession of similar events, but for development NGOs it created a precedent both alarming and seductive. It showed how people could be mobilized behind development. The crucial question was, at what price?

For many who worked in the development field, particularly those who had striven against public indifference, the success of Band Aid warranted investigation, in part because it seemed that the media and the NNGOs had dehistoricized, depoliticized, and trivialized the complex and life-threatening issue of famine by reducing it to an issue of money and food. By opting for money over truth, they had privileged a *negative* image of Africa. Once more constituted as "other" – the "Dark Continent" – it was lastingly inscribed in the minds of millions as a timeless space where a biblical famine, an event alien to the modern industrial West, could unfold without resistance.[28] Ethiopia, which became synonymous with Africa, was depicted as a country, poor to begin with, brought to its knees by famine, and needing outside assistance to feed itself on a scale without historical precedent.[29]

Northern audiences, whose popular belief was that Africa was poor and underdeveloped, now had proof. African nations were visually depicted as passive nations constantly threatened by the possibility of a "natural disaster" and dependent on Western goodwill and assistance.[30] Both the media and the NGOs made full and frequent use of images of starving Africans, most particularly women and children.[31] They used and popularized a predominantly negative image of Africa and Africans.

Africans were mostly photographed when they were powerless to refuse. Repeatedly, individual African subjects went unidentified in photos and were used to incarnate the timeless mass of starving Africans.[32] For a respected Southern partner who prepared a Zimbabwe report on news coverage of the Ethiopian famine, these images were disturbing:

Images represent people.... Images should not be applied en masse, but to individuals; to people with dignity, with an identity. When images lose their identity, they become a way of looking down on people.... It seems to be that if you respect somebody you want to learn their name ... you want to know them as individuals. But the way that ... African people [were portrayed] is as if they were not people at all.[33]

African *subjects* were represented as the passive recipients of aid – *objects* of development – who had no voice, no identity, and no contribution to make during the crisis. The West, in contrast, appeared full of active subjects: development workers, fundraisers, journalists, or world citizens.[34] Such critics argued, echoing Lissner, that these negative images were both counterproductive and untrue. Untrue, because the peoples of Africa were active and resourceful, engaged in diverse and effective strategies to circumvent the possibility of starvation. Counterproductive, because negative images were self-fulfilling prophecies. They attracted the wrong type of development and development agencies: those that encouraged dependence rather than "empowerment," "dialogue," or "self-reliance."[35]

In response to such criticism, thirteen countries participated in the *Images of Africa* survey, which attempted to understand why these images were produced.[36] They concluded that none of the image-purveyors – NGOs, the media, or Band Aid – had made a concerted effort to address and broadcast positive indigenous efforts to allay the crisis. NNGOs had produced educational materials, but only after the event. Less resourced, less attractive, with more restricted circulation than their fundraising counterparts, these more enlightened images and messages had not reached a comparable audience.[37] These *positive* images of development – in which subjects participated, were self-reliant, and were self-determined – had simply not been available to Northern publics.[38] The *Images of Africa* report concluded that although NNGOs had had the opportunity to portray the crisis in a different light, they had not done so.

This moment marked a decisive shift. Response to the coverage of the Ethiopian famine moved the question of image to center stage. It caused NNGOs to reconcile the agendas of education and fundraising by making the images that both these sections produced consistent with institutional image and development practice. Beginning in the late 1980s, the more visionary NGOs came to be guided by the belief that "the problem of images and perception cannot be separated from the methodology of intervention."[39]

Media and NGO response to the Ethiopian famine also showed that money had saved lives, and that a broad level of popular concern regarding the developing world could be – and was – stimulated.[40] The events of 1984–5 convinced NGOs that image and practice were causally linked. This engendered several transformations: (1) in development organizations, which now viewed broadcasting the right image as a priority; (2) in the images themselves, with noticeable increase in the production of *positive* images or balanced messages; (3) in representational practice, and in particular the creation of formal or informal guidelines that sought to impose constraints on the content and regulate the production of images. Finally, there was a reconsideration of the value of a more populist approach; indeed, NNGOs were loath to lose the constituency and support they had gained from Band Aid and Live Aid.

Positively the Truth: New Turns in the Imaging of Development

Having briefly considered the historical context in which the question of imagery achieved saliency, we can now consider the impact of such criticism on imagery itself. This section offers a reading of the *positive* image emergent in the early 1990s. The reasons are threefold: First, to show how the codes and conventions of images of development are designed to "make sense." Second, to suggest why positive images and negative images are, in effect, two sides of the same coin, buttressed by a realist understanding of representation. Finally, to propose that this adherence to the criterion of realism prevents new modes of representation from emerging.

The poster image and press advertisement discussed here (Figures 11.2 and 11.3) were produced by the British NGO Christian Aid for "Christian Aid Week" in 1990. As the priming April communication materials for its major annual fundraising drive, they occupied a prominent place in Christian Aid's fundraising calendar that year. These advertisements were deliberately designed to be positive; they represented the first step toward new strategies of representation for Christian Aid at the time.[41]

Christian Aid became well known for its distinct methods of communication and its adherence to new development ideals, which emphasized

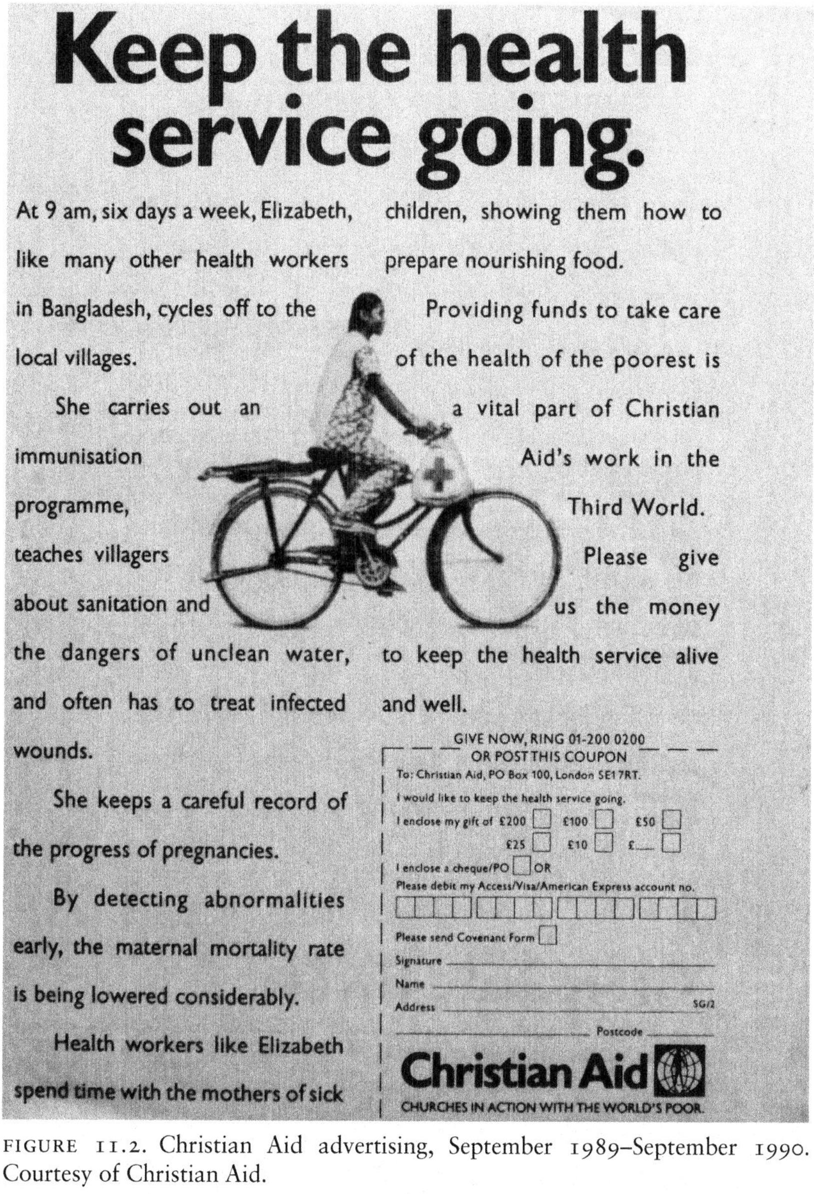

Keep the health service going.

At 9 am, six days a week, Elizabeth, like many other health workers in Bangladesh, cycles off to the local villages.

She carries out an immunisation programme, teaches villagers about sanitation and the dangers of unclean water, and often has to treat infected wounds.

She keeps a careful record of the progress of pregnancies.

By detecting abnormalities early, the maternal mortality rate is being lowered considerably.

Health workers like Elizabeth spend time with the mothers of sick children, showing them how to prepare nourishing food.

Providing funds to take care of the health of the poorest is a vital part of Christian Aid's work in the Third World.

Please give us the money to keep the health service alive and well.

GIVE NOW, RING 01-200 0200
OR POST THIS COUPON
To: Christian Aid, PO Box 100, London SE1 7RT.
I would like to keep the health service going.
I enclose my gift of £200 [ ] £100 [ ] £50 [ ]
£25 [ ] £10 [ ] £___ [ ]
I enclose a cheque/PO [ ] OR
Please debit my Access/Visa/American Express account no.
[ ][ ][ ][ ][ ][ ][ ][ ][ ][ ][ ][ ][ ][ ][ ][ ]
Please send Covenant Form [ ]
Signature _____
Name _____
Address _____ SG/2
_____ Postcode

Christian Aid
CHURCHES IN ACTION WITH THE WORLD'S POOR.

FIGURE 11.2. Christian Aid advertising, September 1989–September 1990. Courtesy of Christian Aid.

partnership, empowerment, and participation as principal development goals. These materials, although not typical of Christian Aid's fundraising strategies in the long term, were definitively of the moment. They received widespread approval from other members of the British NGO

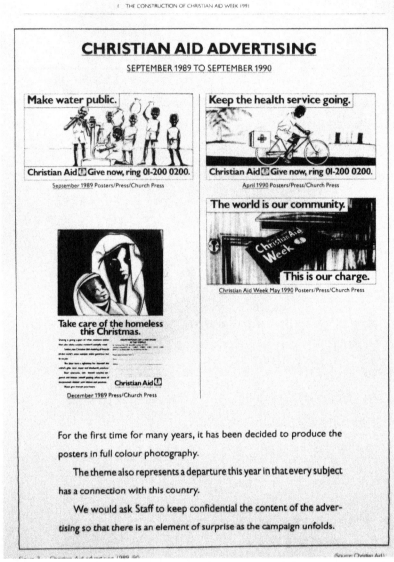

FIGURE 11.3. "Keep the health service going. Supporting health care in the Third World." Courtesy of Christian Aid.

community, who embraced these images as positive and as making the right kind of statement. This was partly attributable to their perceived political nature. The 1989–90 series of Christian Aid appeals, of which the poster and press advertisement formed a significant component, had a theme of bringing Third World problems closer to home (Figure 11.3). While the 1989 September poster and press advertisement urged "Make Water Public" (in reference to the privatization of water in the United Kingdom), the Christian Aid Week statement was "The World Is Our Community, This Is Our Charge."

The most striking aspect of the poster image (Figure 11.1) is its documentary appearance. It is as if the photographer just happened to be there as the woman was riding by, early in the morning, on her way to work. She seems to have taken him by surprise, and he "froze her in time."[42] The photograph has a literal content; it appears to reproduce mechanically, repeatedly, and literally the moment that was fortuitously caught. This is amplified by the quizzical look on the faces of the men, seemingly interrupted, the temporarily immobilized cow, and the fact that the bike and its rider are slightly out of focus.

This realistic style and the image's usage encourage the impression that it is simply *denotation*, that it depicts reality, and this validates it as evidence: as an objective document. To have taken the photograph, the photographer must "have been there." It appears to be an authentic record of what happened: an unprompted, representative visual image of the everyday in the global South and Christian Aid's work there. The *connotation* is that this photograph was the result of a lucky find – for the photographer – a fortunate *trouvaille*.[43]

The viewer is then struck by the linguistic message, the poster's obvious caption and explanation "Keep the Health Service Going." This linguistic message locates the visual image and navigates the reader through it. It ostensibly exists purely at the level of *denotation* because, although it does not describe the photograph, it seems to amplify it, the only noticeable construction being the pun (something more evident in the press advertisement).

Conversely, the linguistic message of "Keep the Health Service Going" is illustrated by the visual image; the woman ("Elizabeth") represents and embodies the health service which is denoted by her bag with a green cross on it (clearly connoting the Red Cross and its medical services). The bicycle suggests mobility and dynamism. For the British viewer in 1990 there was the added *connotation* that drew on parallels between the underfunded British Health Service and the similar plight of public health services overseas (affected by structural adjustment programs). This is, therefore, a humanitarian and a universalist message: a testament of similarity, of common struggle, over and above difference. All world citizens, we are given to understand, should have access to adequate health care, and all those who have it within their power to do so should ensure that public provision of health services is sustained, as Christian Aid does.

In the poster, the short verbal message leaves room for a richer, polysemic visual image. First, one is struck by the fanfare and intensity of color. Strongly contrasted with the sepia tones, or black and white coding of negative images, and their habitually desiccated and desert environments, this is an upbeat rural tableau where the scenery is green and lush. The hut, the cow (complete with pats), the young woman in a white, black, and red *shalwaar kameez* (in the three colors of Christian Aid's logo), the white flowing scarf, the yellow flip-flops, the "sit up and beg" bike, the old umbrella (black with a red handle) and the rudimentary medical equipment (one bag with a green cross suffices to contain all that she needs) all serve to *connote* spatial location. It achieves this in particular by evoking local color – what Barthes might call "Indian-ness"[44] – and perhaps a feeling of community (is she smiling at those inside or outside the frame, or both?), but most especially by invoking "authenticity" (the photographer and the subjects were there and, what is more, Elizabeth has mud on the tires of her Phoenix bike).

Second, it equally denotes a different reality, a distinct type of health care, where the health worker's medical technology is contained in the one bag and her transport is a bicycle. This could have the positive connotations of primary health care – grassroots, appropriate, and participatory – or the negative ones of rudimentary health provision – technologically backward and ineffective. The reading depends on the viewer. The latter reading, however, would be somewhat contradictory since the image's tone is clearly joyous and the connotations of success and dynamism are conveyed by both visual images and verbal messages.

What makes the poster compelling, what might be called the *punctum*[45] – that something that draws the viewer in and commands attention, and which presumably distinguished this image from others during the selection process – is the central *subject*: "Elizabeth" (identified and depicted alone in the press advertisement) despite the fact that she is not centrally placed. This glowing image depicts her in a neat and clean *shalwaar kameez*, with a whiter than white scarf casually draped over her shoulders, and wearing a beaming smile. She connotes health, a certain set of standards, purposefulness. She knows where she is going. There may also be an element of feminine liberation, the *connotations* of mobility, professional status, and public participation defined in opposition to consensual notions (in the North) of Muslim/Asian women as restricted to the domestic sphere.

The selection of this image was not accidental. It was likely selected because it was oppositional and nonstereotypical. The visual image and the verbal message combine to constitute her not as the *object* of development – helpless and despairing – but as its empowered *subject*. The visual connotations can be read against the text of the press advertisement, which focuses quite explicitly on her diligence. In a number of respects she symbolizes many of the key aspects of NGOs' new development thinking: the active citizen/participant who through her own self-realization empowers others.

In addition, "Elizabeth" is notable in being a *named* subject: she incarnates partnership while satisfying the need for a human touch in advertising. She rises above sheer statistics; she appears to be a genuine person, embodying the triumphs and tragedies of the developing world. Elizabeth is what Barthes calls the "mythical signifier": part analogy, part motivation.[46] She purposefully hails the viewer in the name of "Third World health/development/empowerment" and insists on recognition as a self-determining subject. This naming device therefore encourages a convenient slippage between representation and intervention. By being the identified/identifiable subject of representation, Elizabeth is concomitantly the identified/iable "partner" in development. She is not the recipient of charity or pity; and although these visual images are intended to elicit donations, the British donor is not misled into thinking that Elizabeth is exclusively dependent upon his or her magnanimity.

Nonetheless, Elizabeth's status is a somewhat uncertain. It is clear that she is not one of the poorest of the poor (compare her with the old man). Yet she could be a "do-gooding" charity worker instead of a more politically motivated, empowered, and self-realizing subject. Ambiguity permeates at another level, evident in the text of the press advertisement (Figure 11.2). Care work is habitually feminized, so the particular roles being accorded to Elizabeth in maternity, pregnancy, nutrition, immunization, and sanitation work are hardly controversial. Although this image was hailed as "positive" and "political," it focuses on traditional arenas of charity concern. This image is advantageously ambivalent: its message could as easily be read as a humanitarian message with charitable referents or as an exhortation for solidarity with the global poor. There are also some intriguing, unanswered questions: Elizabeth's identity, for instance. This is a Christian name in a predominantly Muslim country. What does this imply about Christian Aid's selection of beneficiaries or representatives?

This short analysis suggests how an ostensibly clear image ("Elizabeth") can be read on a number of levels. To evaluate the value, content, and signification of individual representational documents, there is need to explore their hidden histories, which might address the context of image production, the motivations of those who produce them, the reasons they attain the status of truth.[47] Unsurprisingly, despite appearances, this photograph's existence was not entirely fortuitous:

> This picture ... was part of a series of pictures. I mean, there was the health issue and ... we'd agreed that we would ... take local community health workers ... and X [the person from the advertising agency] had been looking at old ... stuff and he'd pick up ... the bike, you know, cycling around.... He thought that would be a good idea, to have one of them cycling around.... So I shot loads of pictures of ... these health workers riding around all over the place.... We ... thought we'd got it and then we were walking back from one village and we passed this little scene and I thought, that looks ... almost archetypal ... the ... old man and the cow and the little grass hut and ... the banana tree.... And so he said, "Okay, well look, get on your bike, cycle past this one ... say three or four ... [times]." (Author's interview)

Though the setting of the image was partly attributable to luck, the image was largely constructed – scripted and framed – before it was finally executed and selected. If this was a representation of reality, it operated purely in a generic manner, in the sense that while it is true that health workers *did* ride on bikes through the Bangladeshi countryside, in this instance this "truth" was deliberately caught by the camera. It might be referred to as a *technical truth*,[48] something which in all probability could happen, rather than something that actually did happen unprompted.

What is more, this image must be considered in relation to previous communication images and messages created by Christian Aid: it was evaluated in relation to these, and proved to be a stepping stone to a new type of fundraising that ultimately led to a subsequent revision in Christian Aid's communications strategy. Christian Aid, as its name implies, is an ecumenical organization with strong links overseas that it fosters through a network of "partners" who are mostly church-based. In 1990, the guiding document was the social justice–oriented pamphlet *To Strengthen the Poor*.[49] Throughout the 1980s, Christian Aid acquired a well-deserved reputation for its bold and innovative style of advertising and communication, which favored depictions of single, and mostly inanimate, objects in its press and poster work. Strong messages drew on a sophisticated discourse of development and justice in the form of religious metaphor or allusions and wordplay. This enabled Christian Aid to develop "political" but nonconfrontational messages in conjunction with iconographic and symbolic, black-and-white representations of woks, bread, plows, rocks, arms, and feet but also the ubiquitous Christian Aid Week envelope, red with the logo "slim jim" in a diagrammatic world.[50]

The 1989–90 series was only the second to feature identifiable people, the first and only in the series to use full-color posters. These images of Elizabeth were therefore different and *positive* because they distinguished themselves from previous Christian Aid communication strategies; at the same time they contrasted with *negative* images used by other NGOs.[51] They did not in any way reify the desperate condition of the poor with the connotations of "all past and no future."[52] The image was positive due to its active nature and upbeat tone. By choosing a woman as the main subject, Christian Aid exhibited openness to reversing certain other stereotypes about participation and development. "Elizabeth" was the image of an empowered, independent, competent, "industrious and self-determined" subject.[53] The image was clearly a response to the prevalent argument that the practice of development – intervention – was reflected in and influenced by the images produced of it.

Attention to an image's production brings into focus the intentionality of its construction. Positive images are not, in any sense, closer to the "truth." They were, and are, deliberate, highly motivated answers to the truth claims and immediacy of negative images. Departing from the proposition that representation and intervention were linked, they took as their specific task to counteract certain assumptions about development, developing countries, and development agencies. It is this connection, made between image and practice, that creates a realistic impasse in images of development. Development NGOs rely heavily on documentary photography. In large part this is due to the assumption that such photographs can provide transparency, an unmediated window on the world that fixes "reality" or "truth." There is also the assumption that *positive* images are somehow closer and more representative of the truth than *negative* ones. After the mid-1980s a great deal of effort was expended on ensuring that the photographer, the lens, and the processing did not allow power to corrupt the integrity of the initial image and therefore its essential truth[54] – the basic supposition being that a photograph is somehow indexically linked to truth, and can, therefore, provide evidence of it. Such assumptions have been questioned by film and photography scholars such as Bill Nichols and Alan Sekula. They argue that the deceptiveness of documentary or realistic photography lies in its deliberate ingenuousness: "The [only] ... 'objective' truth that photographs offer is the assertion that somebody or something – in this case an automated camera – was somewhere and took a picture. Everything else, everything beyond the imprinting of a trace, is up for grabs."[55]

Photography's persuasiveness derives from its rhetorical strategies and stylistic form. Nichols contended that visual representations combine argument and evidence, merging representations *of* the world with those *about* the world. As such, photography in the realistic or documentary mode functions both as a *reflection* of reality and as a *discourse* on it. Though the viewer may engage in the structure and meaning of the image, what she or he recognizes, and inevitably responds to, is its realism.[56]

Nichols's critique consequently undermines the polarities created between negative and positive images. They cannot be oppositional entities that, respectively, mobilize falsehoods or truths since, according to Nichols, *all* representations are quotations from, rather than samples of, reality. Every image has the ambivalent status of both evidence and argument. By favoring positive images over negative ones, NGOs denied positive and negative images the same level of motivation. To NGOs, positive images were not, ostensibly, concerned with money but primarily with ethics. As a result, they were thought to be better and truer. However, this discourse of accuracy and truth tells us more about how these representations are used to validate intervention – development practice – than about their ability to depict accurately or truthfully.[57] In considering NGO representational practices, the most pertinent question becomes, Why is a realist, or documentary mode, of representation judged the most appropriate for development NGOs?

A possible answer might lie in the fact that documentary photography invests the discursive assertions of NGOs with immediacy, poignancy, and most important, authority. The audience is encouraged to witness (distant) subjectivity and believe the analog of overseas reality with which they are presented. An objective depiction functions as evidence of NGO experience: it demonstrates that these development organizations "were/are-really-there" and acts as conclusive proof that they "were/are-really-doing-something." Documentary/realist representations work simultaneously as the basis for knowledge, the validation for the correctness of NGO discursive assertions, but they work equally as inspirational images: images that require some form of active response. They anchor and limit the conditions of truth and, therefore, meaning.

There is a final aspect worth considering. By privileging the documentary photograph, NGOs present photography primarily as a medium, not an instrumentality, thereby covertly dissociating representation from power. The recognition of power is made in institutional terms, in the form of guidelines. The guidelines drafted after 1984–5 by Oxfam (1987), Save the Children Fund (1988, 1991), and the NGO-EC Liaison Committee (1989) emphasized the need for greater accuracy and truth in tandem with substantial verbal contextualization, dialogical production, and appropriately controlled methods of reproduction. Development organizations know that representations fuse power with knowledge, but this is not something that is conveyed to their audiences, who are presented with apparently unmediated realities.

Cultural Consequences

The outcome of the events of 1984–5 initiated a fundamental reconsideration of the content and process of production of visual images by British development charities. The most immediate result was a move toward positive imaging, producing images that possessed the strength, dignity, and self-determination of the human subject in the face of adversity that development work sought to create rather than images that objectified and dehumanized the subject of development.[58] Debates about imagery called into question the quality and the quantity of NGO images as well as their techniques of production and reproduction. Such debates decisively linked the *practice of representation* – the image of development – with the *practice of development* or intervention. But this operated according to a realist premise, positing that "out there" there was one real truth or reality ready to be captured and conveyed in visual images. Yet, as we have seen, all visual images – *positive* or *negative* – articulate something very different from dry truth or reality.[59]

Development NGOs are reproductive cultural institutions that generate visual and material products. They perceive development as a practice that defines problems and prescribes methods for achieving certain delineated goals. As organizations they have a certain way of seeing the world, generating discourses on how the world is and how they wish it to be. These understandings change over time and differ across the gamut of organizations. Nevertheless, as organizations involved in a common project, development, they articulate sophisticated understandings of it as a practice, which allows them to be perceived and understood as a moral and intellectual community of practitioners. They do not confine a discussion of these understandings and beliefs to themselves. Indeed it is in their interest not to. They are actively engaged in creating meaningful images and messages on the subject of the developing world for the purposes of dissemination, conversation and conversion. Only by reaching a wide variety of people and ensuring that they take on board the challenge and the need for development can development NGOs ensure their ultimate survival. As prolific cultural producers, they search constantly to circumscribe and fix meaning, most tellingly perhaps through the use of reportage and the regulation of documentary photography.

Notes

1 Lissner, *Politics of Altruism*, 145–7; J. Lissner, "Merchants of Misery."

2 Lissner, *Politics*, 189; Lissner, "Merchants." This image was developed quite early by Northern NGOs to denote the raw urgency of "need" in the developing world; see M. Black, *A Cause for Our Times: Oxfam the First 50 Years* (Oxford: Oxfam, 1992), 195; "Changing Charity: 50 Years of Oxfam," *New Internationalist* (1992), 228 (Plate 1); also the chapter by Lasse Heerten in this volume.

3 Lissner, "Merchants," 23.

4 For a similar account, see P. Adamson, "Charity Begins with the Truth," *The Independent*, May 18, 1993.

5 Elizabeth Edwards, "Introduction," in Edwards, *Anthropology and Photography 1860–1920*, 7.

6 Barthes, *Camera Lucida*, 4.

7 Nichols, *Representing Reality*, 150–1; R. Barthes, *Image-Music-Text*, trans. S. Heath (New York: Hill and Wang, 1977).

8 V. Burgin, "Something about Photographic Theory," in A. L. Rees and F. Borzello, eds., *The New Art History* (London: Camden Press, 1986), 43.

9 For Susan Sontag the camera is a sublimation of the gun, something that is "loaded," "pointed," and "shot" at subjects, capturing their image for the purposes of consumption. Sontag, *On Photography*, cited in Pinney, 1992.

10 R. Young, *White Mythologies: Writing History and the West* (London: Routledge, 1990), 143.

11 Lissner, "Merchants," 24; P. Adamson, Speech to UNICEF National Committee, Geneva, 1991.

12 Lissner, "Merchants."

13 Lissner, *Politics*, 159–60, 167–71, 173; B. Whitaker, *A Bridge of People* (London: Heinemann, 1983), 160; S. Arnold, "Constrained Crusaders: British Charities and Development Education," *British Charities and Education*, Education Network Project Occasional Paper, 1, University of Sussex (1988), 14.

14 Lissner, *Politics*; Lissner, "Merchants"; Whitaker, *Bridge*, 177–8.

15 "Changing Charity"; R. Poulton, "On Theories and Strategies" in R. Poulton and M. Harris, eds., *Putting People First: Voluntary Organisations and Third World Development* (Basingstoke, UK: Macmillan, 1988); P. Gill, "Conclusion: Helping Is Not Enough," in *Putting People First*; A. G. Drabek, "Editor's Preface," *World Development* 15 (Autumn 1987, Supplement); A. G. Drabek, "Development Alternatives: The Challenge for NGOs – An Overview of the Issues," *World Development* 15 (Autumn 1987, Supplement). In its

1987 report, the Charities Aid Foundation, which gathers statistics on giving in Britain, concluded that between 1977 and 1986 the underlying trend of giving to international aid was steadily rising, from just over 11 percent of the total voluntary income in 1984 to 22 percent in 1985. Oxfam's income from 1981–2 to 1990–1 leaped from £16.26 million to £69.223 million. By 1988, of the total $51 billion in aid received by developing countries, $3.6 billion was provided by voluntary agencies, of which Britain contributed $239 million. See L. Rajan, "Charity Statistics 1977–1986: An Analysis of Trends," in *Charity Trends 1986/7* (Tonbridge: Charities Aid Foundation, 1987), 88; Burnell, *Charity, Politics and the Third World*, 292, 24; and *Oxfam Review 1990–1991* (Oxford: Oxfam).

16 P. Gill, "Conclusion," 169.

17 R. Chambers, "Normal Professionalism, New Paradigms and Development," *IDS Discussion Paper*, University of Sussex (1986): 227; J. W. Sewell, "Foreward," in J. P. Lewis, ed., *Strengthening the Poor: What Have We Learned?* (New Brunswick: Transaction, 1988), ix; Drabek, "Development Alternatives," vii; Poulton and Harris, *Putting People First*, 4. This new development thinking advocated a more equitable and active role for Southern partners in development, with methodologies that spoke of the rights and entitlements of the poor. J. Boyden and B. Pratt, eds., *Field Directors' Handbook: An Oxfam Manual for Development Workers* (Oxford: Oxford University Press, 1985), 13.

18 The Disaster Emergency Committee (DEC) appeals are group-held. At this time, the main actors were Christian Aid, Save the Children Fund, Oxfam, the British Red Cross, and the World Wildlife Fund for Nature.

19 M. Amin, "A Vision of the Truth," *Refugees* (October 1989): 22–5.

20 Michael Buerk's commentary quoted in Harrison and Palmer, *News Out of Africa*, 122.

21 Harrison and Palmer, *News*, 110.

22 D. Hebdige, "Post-Script 1: Vital Strategies," in Hebdige, *Hiding in the Light* (London: Comedia/Routledge, 1988), 216.

23 In January 1985, Geldof visited six capital cities in the Sahel, accompanied by the world's press. He met Mother Theresa in an airport lounge and had flights arranged, compliments of the Ethiopian government, to areas previously closed off for "security" reasons; see Burnell, *Charity*, 122–3; Harrison and Palmer, *News*, 131; Philo and Lamb, *Television and the Ethiopian Famine*, 26.

24 Philo and Lamb, *Television*, 26.

25 Harrison and Palmer, *News*, 131–3; A. Hart, "Consuming Compassion: The Live Aid Phenomenon," *Links* 28 (1987): 15–17.

26 R. Allen, "Behind the News 2: Bob's Not Your Uncle," *Capital & Class* 30 (Winter 1986): 32.

27 These statistics come from Burnell, *Charity*, 203–4. The Band Aid Trust was wound up in 1991; see Benthall, *Disasters, Relief and the Media*, 84–6, 235.

28 Van Der Gaag and Nash, *Images of Africa*, 30.

29 Horgan, *Images of Africa*, 18.

30 Van Der Gaag and Nash, *Images*, 1; S. Nyoni, "Images of Poverty," 9; Hart, "Consuming Compassion"; A. Hart, "Images of the Third World," *Links* 34 (1989):12–18.

31 Kaida-Hozumi, "The Role of NGOs," 26; *Dialogue* (September–October 1988), also Plate 1.

32 P. Stalker "Infotainment," *New Internationalist* 222 (1991): 8–9.

33 Nyoni, "Images," 7.

34 Hart, "Images of the Third World"; D. A. Bailey, "The Black Subject at the Centre: Repositioning Black Photography," *Links* 34 (1989): 31–8.

35 Nyoni, "Images," 7–8.

36 "The Image of Africa," *Dialogue* (September–October, 1988): 1–2.

37 Van Der Gaag and Nash, *Images*.

38 A. Simpson, "Charity Begins at Home" in *Ten8* 19 (1985): 21–26, here 21; "The Image of Africa"; Nyoni, "Images."

39 Van Der Gaag and Nash, *Images*, 77.

40 Black, *Cause*, 265; Burnell, *Charity*, 12.

41 Lidchi, "All in the Choosing Eye."

42 Hall, "The Determinations of News Photographs," 79. The photographer was a male and a regular Christian Aid photographer.

43 Barthes, *Camera Lucida*, 33.

44 Barthes, "Rhetoric of the Image."

45 Barthes, *Camera Lucida*, 27–60; Graham-Brown, *Images of Women*, 3.

46 Barthes, *Mythologies*, 134–5.

47 Edwards, "Introduction," 12.

48 P. Adamson, Speech to UNICEF National Committee, Geneva, 1991.

49 M. Taylor, *The Strengthen the Poor: A Statement of Commitment Adopted by the Board of Christian Aid July 1987 as a Basis for Action and Reflection* (London: Christian Aid, 1987).

50 Christian Aid's logo has since been changed.

51 Christian Aid produced an educational leaflet outlining its view on images in 1988; see Christian Aid, *Images of Development*.

52 Taylor, "General Theory of Icebergs," 50.

53 Hart, "Images of the Third World," 14.

54 For formal guidelines that sought to regulate all the stages in photographic production and reproduction, see Oxfam, "What Makes an Appropriate Picture"; Save the Children Fund, *Impact of Image Guidelines*, and Save the Children Fund, *Focus on Images*; and *Code of Conduct* (1989).

55 Sekula, *Photography against the Grain*, 57; also Nichols, *Representing Reality*.

56 Nichols, *Representing Reality*, ix–x, 177.

57 I. Hacking, *Representing and Intervening* (Cambridge: Cambridge University Press, 1983), 146.

58 A. Montague, "The Changing Face of Charity," *New Society* 13 (May 1988): 22–4; Hart, "Images of the Third World."

59 D. Chaney, "Photographic Truths," *Discourse Social (Social Discourses)* 1, no. 4 (1988).

Dilemmas of Ethical Practice in the Production of Contemporary Humanitarian Photography

Sanna Nissinen

Setting the Scene: En Route to Shoot

In a Lexus on the road in Bangladesh between Dhaka and Brahmanparia with the Country Director and the commissioned photographer, 31 March 2010.[1]

Following my line of questioning he leans over to Saikat who is in the front seat and says: "I want an iconic photo." Saikat nods his head and does not respond and I cannot tell if this is uncomfortable silence or annoyance at an unreasonable request.

When we get out of the car for a pit stop I ask Zaki privately, what he meant by that [iconic photo]. He replies that photo shoots produce the same type of photos and he wants something different. I probe further and ask what could be different and how. He thinks for a brief moment: "I don't know, I don't know exactly what it is. But when I see it I will know" and lights his cigarette.

The pursuit and ethics of these elusive photographs have attracted discussion and controversy for decades, most prominently since the Ethiopian famine of 1984–5.[2] Critics charge that such charity images raise funds by providing a voyeuristic spectacle of suffering and passivity for Western audiences. Such practices continue to attract ethical questions and political debate concerning the rights of photographic subjects, the duties of producers, and the extent and degree of harm or benefit these images generate.

Although these ethical concerns allude to photographic practice, photographic ethics has not been investigated as a *practical* problem.[3] This chapter is based on research I undertook in 2010 in Bangladesh.[4] It draws on interviews with communications managers working inside major aid agencies and photographers commissioned to procure images for humanitarian campaign projects. My focus is the examination of the tensions that arise at the level of practice when NGO staff and photographers attempt to operationalize ethics in the context of humanitarian photography. My analysis is based upon ethnographic notes taken in the field during the filming of assignments and highlights the complexity of issues involved in producing ethical photographs and regulating ethical photographic practice.

The Birth of Regulation

Photography has been used, and manipulated, for purposes of public persuasion in the humanitarian sector from its beginnings.[5] It was the pivotal event of the Ethiopian Famine of 1984–5 that alerted a wider public to issues of ethics in representations of humanitarian events and prompted unified action on the part of the NGO community to formulate regulatory image codes. As the first global mediatized event, the Ethiopian Famine raised ethical and political questions regarding image content and image sourcing. This reflected poorly on the media organizations that distributed graphic images of suffering, on the photographers who were seen to be abusing their power over vulnerable famine victims, and on the values of the humanitarian organizations that relied on such images for fundraising.[6]

NGOs were accused of capitalizing on suffering, which prompted questioning among their management regarding whether their use of imagery challenged or confirmed racist stereotypes of Africa and Africans.[7] A central question was how to represent subjects with dignity and how to change the focus from negative images that "conveyed the helplessness and the passivity of Ethiopians" to images that conveyed their partnership in development.[8] Another area of criticism was aimed at individual photographers and accused them of abusing their power by disrespecting both the rights of their subjects in distress and the mandate of their agency in the filming process.[9] The influential *Images of Africa Report* written in the wake of coverage of the Ethiopian famine asked, "Had the subjects been aware they were being photographed? Had they had the choice, or the capacity, to protest or exercise informed consent given their emotional and physical state?"[10]

Post-Ethiopia discussions prompted a distinct shift in humanitarian imagery from negative depictions of passive, suffering, innocent victims to narratives of the resilient victims told through "positive" imagery.

This was widely considered an "ethical" solution to the problem of humanitarian imaging.[11] In 1989, a broader collective movement emerged to standardize representational practices across the NGO industry. The General Assembly of European NGOs adopted a *Code of Conduct on Images Related to the Third World* to provide standard guidelines for fundraising NGOs and to encourage discussion among stakeholders on the appropriateness of materials produced. The Code affirmed the values of representing subjects to emphasize their equality and dignity and recommended including the opinions of Southern partners in the representational process. This marked a major shift in representational strategy and a new emphasis on the agency of the people portrayed. In 2006, a revised *Code of Conduct on Images and Messages* provided a framework of guiding principles that was designed to be more workable in practice in comparison to the previous prescriptive code, which emphasized what *not* to do.[12] In addition, it specifically addressed the rights of children in NGO photography.

Contemporary Communications and the Image Industry

The role of NGOs in global politics and the visual economy of humanitarianism are increasingly significant.[13] The mandates of humanitarian NGO are expanding and now include projects once considered to be functions of states or major international nongovernmental organizations, such as education, the protection of human rights, economic development, democracy promotion, and peace building.[14] This has encouraged the adoption of new forms of communications designed for multiple purposes, whether raising awareness, raising funds, and/or increasing support for particular programs. With growing competition among nonprofit organizations for funding, practices are becoming more commercialized and NGOs have increasingly undertaken organizational branding strategies.[15] Such strategies establish key frameworks for transmitting the desired values that organizations wish communicated to targeted audiences.[16] They do not strictly determine or define how such values are interpreted in practice; they indicate the desired aims of how organizations wish to operate and to be seen as operating.[17]

NGOs have developed communications formats with new methods of distribution that are now called by the industry term, "visibility projects." Increasingly this "visibility work" exploits social media, blogs, and even downloadable applications on mobile devices. For example, in 2011, UNICEF launched an iPhone App to showcase the extensive photography archives documenting their work. Photo competitions have become more frequent and have attracted submissions by photographers while providing free content for the sponsoring organizations.[18] Another notable trend is the merging of NGO visibility projects with cultural sectors: NGOs cooperate with artists, art organizations, and galleries to stimulate "positive" media coverage instead of the "negative" crisis coverage.[19] Humanitarian and Aid NGOs raise their public profiles by commissioning the work of leading photographers who are able to provide positive exposure with high-profile campaigns linked to them.[20]

In the recent volatile economic climate,[21] photographers and filmmakers have turned to charities, foundations, and companies with corporate social responsibility (CSR) agendas for sponsorship of their issue-driven work. Photographic reportages, exhibitions, and printed work that previously would have been self-financed by the artist are now being produced with grant aid and sponsored by NGOs. With organizational agendas driving these projects, the editorial independence of the photographer is called into question. The degree of a photographer's freedom of observation available on such photographic assignments, given the sponsors' agendas, is arguably lessened and can generate tensions between the photographer and sponsor.[22] Photographers struggle with how to position their work and maintain their reputations within the framework of NGOs' ethical and institutional guidelines. Photographer Bitan explains this challenge:

This is the NGO sector showing happy faces to say that we have achieved development. We [photographers] have the power to portray that but that is the Bangladesh that I don't want forced on my pictures. Then on the other side, you have many photographers, showing black and white images of poverty and saying that this is indigenous photography – this to me is not right and this is a dangerous line we walk.

Photographers I encountered in the Bangladeshi photographic community work under the risk of being accused of promoting the familiar negative depictions of the country, even though they consciously organize to battle Western media hegemony and its tendency to depict the global South either through the lens of exoticism or victimhood.[23] Even the most politically active photographers whose social documentary projects and working ethos aim to rebuke and challenge stereotypes are not immune to this social critique.[24] The professional success of some photographers attracts criticism; they are accused of having appropriated neo-Orientalist perspectives, continually recycling representations of poverty and despair under the label of "indigenous photography." As a result, questions have been raised about photography's ability to produce positive social change.

Professional photographers who wish to secure a living must adapt and expand their repertoires by actively promoting their work through multiple means, particularly in the competitive environment of today's digital world. In order to build a reputation and a firm standing in the industry, photographers need to pursue assignments with elite publications, representation with elite agencies, and photographic prizes and scholarships, many of which are sponsored by humanitarian organizations. Positioning their work as socially and politically relevant is an important part of securing assignments with NGOs.

As a result, the professional identities of photographers are flexible and are responsive to the market demands and the varying interests of stakeholders. Photojournalist and documentarian roles overlap and most photographers engage in both.[25] Despite a focus on humanitarian subject matter in their work, few photographers embrace the label of "humanitarian photographer." Rather, this designation is only begrudgingly employed and then mostly as a marketing strategy to compete for the limited and lucrative assignments of humanitarian organizations. In fact, the label "humanitarian photographer" is considered by photographers to have derogatory associations. It is understood as attached to those assignments that follow strict client protocol and organizational guidelines, thereby constraining the independence, artistic vision, and professional skills that photographers consider essential to their work. Most photographers I met in my fieldwork described themselves as social documentarians or activist photographers.

Regulating an Exploitative Medium

Photography has been theorized in two contradictory ways: as a tool of exploitation and as a realistic recording device.[26] Power and politics have been viewed as inseparable from photography and its functions.[27] The theoretical focus on the relations of power in photography makes assumptions about the ways social actors are positioned in the production of images and how power operates at the level of practice.

Critics have used concept of the gaze to theorize photographic interactions, arguing that photographic subjects lack power, which is invested in those holding the camera, framing and fixing the images.[28] The theory of the gaze inadvertently places photographers in assumed positions of domination in the field: as the all-seeing and all-powerful actors in the interaction.[29] Writ globally, this emphasis on photographic exploitation and objectification has been understood in political terms as the colonizing and dominating gaze of the West toward the global South. It suggests that being poor and disadvantaged automatically makes one unaware of the camera and the potential impact of images: a very much outdated notion, particularly given the ubiquity of mobile technologies.[30] It also suggests a lack of awareness of non-Western photographic histories.[31]

Photographers justify their roles as "bearing witness."[32] Unlike theorists, working photographers believe in referential accuracy and neutrality; these have become convictions of principle in the work of professional photographers and are associated with the genres of documentary and photojournalism by audiences.[33]

An ambiguity surrounds the photographic image: on the one hand, there is a belief in its potential to foster social change; on the other, there is a belief in its capacity for exploitation. In the humanitarian context, this has resulted in a polarized and narrow framing of photography according to the binaries of the true/false, positive/negative, ethical/unethical divide without consideration of the more complex issues involved in photographic practice.[34]

To avoid, or counteract, accusations that NGOs and their photographers were engaging in exploitative practices, NGOs began adopting institutional guidelines to regulate ethical image making and ensure the protection of subjects. Regulatory codes are generally based on the values of dignity, authenticity, and solidarity, which are intended to guide practice and production, including the content and sourcing of images.

Concerning image content, NGO codes emphasize the need to adopt more positive and dignified representations of subjects in their communications work; however this has not eliminated the demands to communicate "need" in order to provoke audience response. This remains a persistent tension: how to depict need without infringing on ethical principles. As the Regional Communications Director of World Vision explained:

Showing people as helpless would not be appropriate simply because you are trying to convey the power they do have. However in certain cases, depending on the advocacy message, maybe on the issue of the children on the street or begging ... the ability to show the problem images can potentially be quite powerful. I think people need to see the problem. And it's probably always the case that "the problem shot" is the most difficult shot, because when you show the problem you also show people at their most vulnerable.

NGO imagery can generally be characterized as simple, direct, and emotive. It combines two consistent components: people and activity, with subjects in the frame addressing viewers directly. This is exemplified in a comment by the Country Director of World Vision: "a photograph without a person is useless to me," and his further demand for the photographer to include some form of activity, especially if the purpose of communication is to show the effectiveness of the organizational program. Content guidelines are sensitive to levels of audience tolerance and ban the use of dead bodies or subjects in sexually suggestive poses. Such content directives are relatively straightforward. However, other ethical issues that relate to the sourcing of images– such as accompanying text, informed consent, image manipulation, and identity protection – are more complex to assess.

The role of text and tag lines attached to images is one of the most significant and strategic omissions in organizational branding and image regulation. The use of captioning and surrounding text anchors the meanings of the image while offering flexibility to alter meanings for multiple contexts or campaigns. Although strict protocols acknowledging copyright of photographs exist, the content of the captions is less clearly outlined and enforced despite its power to alter meaning. The impact this has in communication, and the potential to mislead through text, was expressed by the Head of External Relations of the World Food Programme.

Simple photographs, sometimes, have impact. But with a concise caption, it makes the photograph even more interesting. For example, when you have a woman working in a field, and you just put the caption "a widow" even if we don't know if that woman is a widow, her status, or if she has had three meals. Or if you put: "widow had one meal today trying to get something from the ground" – now you know and you can relate. We are now asking photographers to add captions to their work and this has started giving us results.

The textual component attached to images to guide audience interpretation is often omitted from regulation; written texts can create the shock/ horror-work that graphic imagery was able to do before ethical governance. The multimodal technique of combining images and text, or "mixed messaging,"[35] facilitates the use of positive imagery and negative taglines and vice versa. This makes distinctions between positive and negative largely unproductive categories for analysis.

Informed consent is an ethical and practical concern when sourcing images, and different organizations adopt varying degrees of formality in the process. These positions vary from legislated demands to use formalized written consent forms to the less formal verbal notification of the purposes of filming. The use of written consent forms (or subject release forms) is thought to protect photographic subjects from false or nonconsensual commercial use of their image. However, misleading captions over which the subject has no control can easily undermine these protocols, and the final placement of photographs is generally not known at the time of filming. The forms are documents that protect the organizations from potential legal repercussions and ensure that subjects do not legally challenge their veracity; they do little to protect the subject. The premise of the consent forms may be misleading, particularly in cases where photographic subjects are illiterate or living in areas with histories of land disputes and cases of child trafficking. The mandated signing of forms may in fact be unethical.[36]

Permission and tolerance for the digital manipulation of images also varies across organizational literature and raises issues about the protection of reputations of organizations and of photographic subjects. Misleading and inaccurate messages, which digital manipulation can produce, are to be avoided, but some allowances for minor manipulation are made.[37] The levels of manipulation condoned are based on balancing the loss of credibility to the organization against the gain in the impact of images on audiences.

The alteration of images is connected to issues of identity protection, an important ethical consideration for organizations working with vulnerable populations. Some forms of photo-manipulation for the purpose of protecting identities, such as the blurring out of faces and placing a black bar across the eyes, have been rejected as criminalizing the subject. These have been replaced with alternatives, such as the use of silhouette shots, or a focus on body parts, such as a close-up image of holding hands or a long shot with an adult's arm over the child's shoulder in a protective stance.

Photographers on these types of assignments have criticized how some of these organizational mandates work in practice. Photographer Chandran gives the example concerning identity protection that caused a conflict between him, a commissioner, and the subjects he was photographing. In this case, the commissioner claimed that using pseudonyms in the captions was sufficient to protect the photographic subjects. Chandran thought this was illogical if protecting identities is a priority:

You are showing the images so what is the point of omitting her name. I think it is much better to put her name, just as she requested.... The commissioner said to use the photos of sex workers but to change their names. In my opinion, in that case you should not disclose their faces either.

Identity protection protocols can undermine the dignity and agency of the subjects as this example shows. Such judgments implicitly deem the subjects incapable of making informed decisions about how they are represented, something that many organizational branding policies purport to be promoting.

Operationalizing Ethics

The majority of NGO assignments are not primarily concerned with aesthetics but stand as evidence-oriented documentary. Content and composition are largely determined before the photographer enters the field. Whether the organization needs single images based on pre-scripted narratives, or more in-depth case study formats, the NGO commissioner attempts to dictate the terms and the frames required. The format focus is either an individual beneficiary of the NGO or a particular activity. As the Regional Information Officer of the Humanitarian Aid and Civil Protection Department of the European Commission (ECHO) explains:

Every frame is written out.... [E]ither I need an image of a woman, with a child, in that hut, at that time because of the sun [light]. We want to tell this story. She [the woman] has been briefed and we follow her around. Or then there is a distribution on a particular day – and these are the five shots: a shot of the bag, with logo, opening the bag, distribution of rice, and the people at distribution will do [the scene] ten times in front of you so you get that shot.

For these types of highly structured assignments, photographers are allowed only limited freedom to express creativity or to pursue in-depth reports of the situation. Even on lengthy assignments, a default narrative guiding communications is implicitly understood as one that "advertises the story of hope, the story of struggle, the story of resistance and resilience," explains photographer Greer. Photographers generally understand their responsibility to operate within these restricted parameters and capture the grand "silent" narrative for their NGO client. As photographer Ahmed summarized:

The job of communications teams is to sell projects by presenting proof that past ones worked; they [communications messages] need to have a human touch to them, they [communications staff] also need to keep it fresh by finding new problems and new solutions.

The increased influence of development organizations on representational practices and the promotion of their own ethical guidelines need not necessarily contradict photographers' desires to represent subjects with dignity. However, there are subtle and silent restraints, which are implicitly understood by the photographers and prove difficult to negotiate in practice. The double-bind of working for an international agency and accepting commissioner directives may at times conflict with personal preferences and understandings of the situation. Some question the moral boundaries of their photographic practice in these situations. Photographer Bitan describes how he struggled with one assignment:

I have been to the Sidr area after the cyclone and I couldn't take photos because people were holding my arms and crying because they had lost their children. In one village everyone had lost their children – how can I take a picture of these people in this state? Am I a vulture?

However, at other times, negotiation between the demands of the client and one's ethical and professional preferences is not a problem, as Photographer Chandran noted:

It depends on the assignment you send me to. If I work for the donor agency then I want to portray poverty to make the donor happy. Immediately my vision will be theirs. Honestly speaking, we are all human, so if I am paid by the donor agency, I want to give them what they want.

One strategy for portraying negative situations in a dignified, positive way is to emphasize activity and the resilience of the photographic subjects, despite the negative and vulnerable circumstances they live in. It is felt this not only makes for more interesting images – and ones to which multiple narratives can be attached – but it also suggests that the positive, human-rights based work of the organizations is empowering their beneficiaries. An example of the choices available in the field is provided senior photographer Akil during the floods in the north of Bangladesh in 2004. He expressed how he was able to satisfy the demands of the commissioners and align them with his personal ethics to show the resiliency of the subjects. He explained his decision on assignment as follows:

I found refugees and saw a family who came with their house. Their roof was in a boat along with their essentials, and believe me, within two hours they had rebuilt their house. I was amazed how the family of five or six members, without any knowledge of engineering, built a house. So that is a positive story instead of people dying of diarrhoea or no food for several days. There is always the potential for stories which show power and struggle such as this family building the house. The focus of the pictures was on the muscles to communicate how powerful they are.

Commissioned photographers are aware of the ethical protocols and regulation of the NGOs they work with and the types of images that would satisfy the aims of their communications projects. Ahmed reveals the commonly understood silent guidelines that coexist with, and sometimes contradict, regulations:

[most NGOs he has worked with] always say they want positive images of people and children being active, but if they were to only portray that, they wouldn't have funding for the next project. It is always positive (read, our programmes work), ending on a negative (read, there is so much more to do), so we need funding.

The most obvious conflicts arise when demands are placed on photographers to capture conditions and situations that do not exist, which creates pressure to stage or reconstruct events to meet the demands of the assignment. This undermines the core concept of authenticity and the journalistic principles of accuracy in reporting, placing the photographer in an ethical dilemma. As photographer Faisal explains:

The main objective was to take footage and make it emotional. They [NGOs] need to collect money abroad and what they wanted to show was what was happening with the money. That was the objective for this assignment and I find the same objectives every time ... to make the images emotional even if it is not real. The actual situation is often different from the official situation.

He explained how he comes to terms with his decisions in these situations and admits that staging events is sometimes necessary to satisfy the client's demands.

Sometimes I find it very complicated to make photographs, when what they want is not there. In one case they did not even start the project but they wanted the photographs. They got the funds a week previously but immediately had to show the project had started, so we had to construct the scene. In situations such as this I am confused ... but if I am told it will be happening say, in one month, then I can accept the project request.

Staging and reconstructing events do not belong to the ethos of the documentary tradition nor are they encouraged in NGO regulations. However, on assignment the distinction between staging and guiding subjects can become blurred. The photographer is faced with the dilemma of interpreting the ethical boundary of how much to intervene in the situation to get more powerful or provocative images. This was explained on a photography assignment I participated in with senior photographer Ahmed. The situation involved an elderly man who had undergone surgeries leading to severe mental distress. His wife explained he had a tendency to wander and cause great worry for his family. He sat on a bench with his foot chained to a tree, wearing a lungi – a sarong-like garment wrapped around the waist that extends to the ankle. His wife made it clear that she wanted pictures taken and their story told. My field notes recorded what happened:

> Ahmed pulls me aside to explain the choices available to the photographer in this situation: this would be a great shot. We take his picture with him in chains. But some photographers who want a better one would pull up his lungi over his knees so we can see his thin legs. If you feel that is unethical, then all you have to do is wait. Wait for him to do it himself and be ready for the shot. It's a waiting game.

This raises the ethical questions: how actively do you target unfolding scenarios in the field to get a more dramatic image? How far do you push boundaries before it becomes a misrepresentation?

The photographer's need to achieve proximity and build an emotional connection with the subject provokes another personal tension. Most assignment photography commissions are on a tight filming schedule that necessitate the fast building of often superficial yet meaningful relationships. Diego explained:

> If your purpose is to achieve your end regardless of means, then get the person to believe you have good intentions when you don't (or maybe you do). For me getting to know a person takes time and you just cannot go and forcibly make a connection.

The following section explores the interactions that happen in the field in the process of filming. I accompanied Ahmed on assignment for a charity to document the organization's activities and to record the benefits they provide to their beneficiaries. The scenes, recorded in my field notes, illustrate the numerous considerations photographers face, such as making connections with subjects, gaining their consent to be photographed, and leading or guiding subjects, and how these interactions evolve and are negotiated on location.

> Minara fetches her baby with a worried look on her face. The baby is hungry. She takes the lead for the approximate three kilometre walk across the dry fields to their home which she shares with her brother-in-law's family. It is a family homestead and Akimunesa's house is located next door. She shields the baby from the sun with her dupatta – a scarf worn draped over the chest resting over the shoulders. Akimunesa cannot walk as quickly so she strays behind but in the

steady flow of labourers all leaving at the same time there is a sharp wind blowing the women's saris – which gives movement to the images and Ahmed takes a few shots.

At the house we follow Minara to the cooking area where she prepares porridge for the baby while her older daughter of twelve takes the baby (Figure 12.1). She sits next to her mother comforting the baby and is keenly aware of the camera: she is clearly posing for us but the sullen expression is quite opposite to the rambunctious entrance she made. She doesn't speak and only rocks the baby.

When complete, Minara swiftly takes the baby and moves into the house, upon which Ahmed follows and asks her to sit in the doorway so he can take advantage of the light to shoot some pictures. The doorway is narrow and I stay back but Ahmed calls for me to join – "the light is fantastic, come and take some shots." It is a good light and Minara's six-year-old daughter joins us with a pet chicken to add to the scene (Figure 12.2). Minara then tells us her story of her four children: her eldest daughter being deaf and her six-year-old having developmental problems. Her eldest son has had to take the role of the man in the family as her husband has gone to work in Dhaka and they haven't seen him for years. She has benefited from the charity programmes and the livestock programme in particular. She said that one of the proudest moments in her life was going alone to the cattle fair to pick up a cow, which was given to her as part of this programme.

Ahmed asks when are the cows given water and Minara replies: "Now – the kids can take you" and we go. Nine children join and they pose with the water bucket. The older boys are told to kneel in front and the others in the back. They pose stiffly and are told "Don't look at me – look at what you are doing" and the process is over in five minutes (Figure 12.3).

Consent to work with and film the activities of Minara and her family was not formalized; it did not follow a structured protocol or involve consent forms. Rather, there was continuous negotiation of consent which the photographer was aware could change at any time. The initial consent was made through the meeting of Akimunesa, the mother of Minara, arising from a casual encounter made earlier in the day. As described in my field notes:

Sitting next to Ahmed in the day shelter built by the charity is an older woman, with her eyes downcast and not looking at the commotion next to her. Her heavy composure is in stark contrast with the violet coloured sari she is wearing. Ahmed turns to her with his camera pointing but doesn't shoot, and instead takes his eyes from the viewfinder and waits for the woman to look up. She eventually does and raises her head as consent – and he then takes a few close-up portraits (Figure 12.4), after which he puts down the camera and starts talking with her. Akimunesa points out her grandchildren from the crowd and her daughter Minara, who is comforting a baby, about five months old. Next to her is her eldest grandchild, a pre-teen boy who has been watching the interaction and is fascinated by Ahmed and his equipment. He has big observant eyes and a cheerful exterior. Ahmed half-jokes, half-rebukes: why aren't you in

FIGURE 12.1. Minara prepares porridge ©Nissinen.

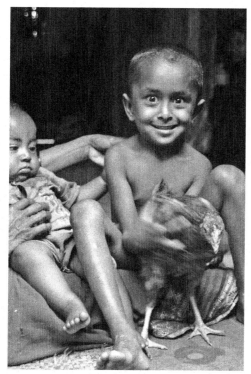

FIGURE 12.2. Sitting in the doorway ©Nissinen.

school! Akimunesa lets out a subdued smile as she glances at her grandson and confirms they live together just across the field. "We'll follow them home later" states Ahmed.

Making these connections is the marker that permission has been gained. There are situations in which photographers ask directly and others where they only show their camera, implying their intentions. In other cases, they use the technique of taking the first shot as the permission shot. If the subject does not show disapproval, this implies permission is granted to continue. The formalized consent forms are considered by photographers to alter and hinder the natural progression of making connections with subjects. Obtaining consent ethically becomes more complex when dealing with children, people with disabilities, and those under extreme distress. In these situations, more subtle assessments are needed about whether potential subjects are willing to participate, or if they feel coerced, uncomfortable, or decide to change their minds during the process. Photographer Shehab spoke of his concern and the precarious

FIGURE 12.3. Feeding the cow ©Nissinen.

FIGURE 12.4. Approaching Akimunesa ©Nissinen.

situation he faced when attempting to gain permission from a group of street dwellers:

These people did not even look towards the next moment; their existence is a struggle for each moment. And when I spoke to them, they could not understand why someone like me wanted to photograph them. First, they rejected my requests and the next moment they came to ask if I could. It is tough to predict their actions and preferences.

On assignment, moreover, tensions can exist between the conceptual criteria of dignity and authenticity that become irreconcilable at the level of practice. The potential for conflict arises if either the photographer assesses the situation as too negative to photograph or if the situation on the ground does not support the assignment demands. A field case study example that took place at the home of a beneficiary family illustrates this dilemma:

Back at the house, we receive an invitation from the doorway to enter the home of Akimunesa. We enter and sit on one of the beds in the room to see the sight of a thin man in a foetal position on the floor on a blue plastic sheet. He is unable to lift his head for long but glances in our direction for a moment and lets his head fall back on the floor. Akimunesa lets out a command for the children to keep the noise down. The man on the floor is her husband of 43 years who has been paralysed for the last two. She looks at him with sadness and kneels down and smoothes his hair. She tells of her struggle and how the doctors cannot do anything. He is incontinent and she struggles to find enough energy to care for him. The man then lifts his head and she says "your food is coming" to him while she looks at us with a smile, "he is hungry." Minara brings rice and spinach she has prepared and Akimunesa feeds him, wiping the sides of his mouth with her dupatta and we sit motionless in silence. Ahmed then turns to me cautiously, looks me in the eye this time, shaking his head and says "how is it possible for this to be allowed?" He then asks Akimunesa if he can take a few pictures, because people should see this. She complies and looks confused at the question as if to imply that is why she asked us there in the first place. I sit and watch – Ahmed moves slowly, takes a position in the back of the house, and takes three shots in slow succession telling them to keep on eating. Within eye shot of Akimunesa he places some money under some clothes on the bed and taps it. This was the only time Ahmed gave money during our assignment. She mouths thank you and we quietly leave.

In the yard Ahmed says, "you didn't take pictures?" I answer no, for the needs of my project I didn't think this necessary. He replies "I had to. This is real. I need to capture what I see. They need to know."

Ahmed's assignment brief emphasized the need for positive and encouraging photographs evidencing program success. The images of Akimunesa's husband are in stark contrast to the dignified and positive criteria the NGO commission requested. In this case, the photographer felt that the need for an authentic depiction of the situation overrode the case for dignity and that to take the picture is in fact the most ethical decision in the circumstances. His actions are a reflection of his self-imposed sense of responsibility toward Akimunesa and her family, a result of the relationship that has developed over the day of filming and his duty to document accurately. This case exemplifies the way in which conceptual regulatory criteria can clash with situational ethics. The decision to take or *not* take a photograph can be experienced by the photographer as a confrontation with personal and professional principles of ethical conduct.

Dominant theories of photographic practice assume the importance of the all-powerful photographer and a subject without agency or power to negotiate terms of participation. In practice, however, challenges to this assumed power dynamic arise frequently, highlighting more micro-level ethical considerations. Faisal explains:

Typically the annual reports for NGOs are made after the project has been completed and in the field no one will help you, because there is no money. The photographer has no control. As an example from my assignment for an NGO, after a five-year project had finished, the community was not motivated to participate because the project had ended. In this situation you have to make good relations with the people and give them hope like, "I am doing this documentation because the next project is coming," even though you don't know this. They are daily labourers, so if they gave you their time, one day would mean 200 Taka. During the project it is easy because they are getting paid [and] when they think you are the evaluator and you have the power to make the project continue.

The power to mislead exists. However, this case also illustrates how positions can be reversed: the photographer often needs the community to be able to deliver his assignments, as much as or more than the community needs the photographer. Photographic subjects' awareness of this potential power – and of the misrepresentations that assignment images can make – should not be underestimated and is a definite concern of photographers. On assignment I was witness to an altercation that highlights this:

The market place is male dominated, with men hanging outside the various stalls that sell rice, vegetables and other foodstuffs. Each of the case study women frequent different stalls, remaining loyal to whichever shopkeeper gives them credit. Khalida walks up to her shop and Ahmed takes shots of the transactions, the measuring of rice, the mustard oil and other goods she buys. The crowd congregates and pushes in – with Minara's eldest son acting as guard and pushing people back. They crowd around and Ahmed politely asks them to get back and give him space. The crowds follow and comment on events – Khalida is unbothered, as are the children.

The next stall is where pictures are taken of Minara and her mother, Akimunesa, shopping. At this end of the market the crowds have multiplied and they get slightly more intrusive. Men, some intentionally and some unintentionally, come into the frame, pushing their friends in as a joke and putting their faces in. Comments fly around such as: "look he's selling our poverty again" and "he's going to make a lot of money with those pictures." At this stage Ahmed loses his temper and yells for the crowd to shut up and mind their business, following which a momentary silence descends and Minara looks embarrassed. The crowd murmur picks up again and we leave quickly to the tea shop for some sweets.

The photographer can be placed in precarious positions if the community feels threatened or exploited. Approaching situations and people with respect becomes not only an ethical and regulatory imperative but also a practical one for ensuring one's safety and access. The picture-making process is one of fast-paced, spontaneous events unfolding in the field. The interactions that ensue are a matter of serendipity and unpredictability; they are haphazard affairs that cannot be explained only by reference to power and politics in representational practices. Although current regulatory guidelines for the content and sourcing of photographs conform to rights-based principles, the production of humanitarian imagery is highly complex. Photographic practice reveals contestation from the very people the critics claim are being objectified and silenced.

Ethical Tensions

As these examples from the field illustrate, evaluation of ethics is a complex and situation-specific process covering numerous considerations that develop on site. The photographer negotiates for participation in the configuration of events, and negotiation becomes a balance between the varying needs of the professional, the NGO client, the community, and the individual in front of the camera. The considerations and perspectives of the image-producers are framed within wider social – and more immediate professional – pressures that are characterized by unpredictability and the disorganized evolution of events in the field.

Photographic ethics in humanitarian imaging is at once organization-specific and, in practice, highly situational and open to interpretation. The production of humanitarian imagery is strewn with ethical considerations that make the notion of an ethical photograph unhelpful as a singular prescriptive concept. The issues involved in the production of humanitarian imagery are much broader and more numerous than accounted for in regulations. Such image-making involves a human element and a complex of social dynamics that are insufficiently recognized in the codes and among theorists alike. Codes and theorists fail to account for what ethics means in practice.

Organizational codes for photography are written in ways that suggest that the codes are applicable to all filming contexts; they are based on the idea that the photographer is in charge of the environment in which he or she operates. They do not take into account how the relationship between the photographer and his subjects develops in situ and how this might potentially alter ethical considerations and decision making. Even if practice is guided by regulation of photographic ethics, it is the human capacity that constructs the interactions of filming.

Neither ethical guidelines nor good intentions can support claims of ethical imagery since they do not account for the complexity and variety of decisions that occur in the process. The process of production involves constraints and decisions, such as how identities are maintained and promoted, how personal responsibilities for representations circulated, and the need to build trust and credibility with both subjects and consumers while abiding as closely as possible to the regulatory requirements. In light of the multiple and sometimes contradictory interests of those involved in production practices, the main incentive for ethical regulation and image guidelines is to provide a mechanism to protect photographic subjects from harm by shielding their identities, obtaining their consent in the process, and in general producing and distributing a more "balanced" imagery of the global South in the international image economy. This ethical enthusiasm has led to the promotion of certain representational tropes. It has simplified visual messages and in doing so continues to work within notions of a positive/negative divide of imagery. It can also be argued that the more formal and sanitized the images, the less information they relay: they become symbolic markers of the conventional narratives that NGOs feel safe in promoting. While they may aid organizational branding, they do not fulfill any descriptive or political function. The result is a flat and narrow horizon of representation that perpetuates predictable images of victims or grateful recipients of aid.

The fact that the photographic subjects are often in dire circumstances and are therefore considered poor and marginalized has fostered a tendency to view all photographic subjects as lacking agency and needing protection. Yet it is patronizing to discount the willingness of subjects to participate or their ability to confront and to alter self-representations. In many of these case studies, subjects participated in filming in the hope that some form of assistance or benefit would result and their participation was based on evaluations of possible risks and gains. The denial of the agency, in photographic theory and regulation, disempowers the subjects that organizations and photographers strive to document and contradicts the desired visual messages of subjects' resiliency and empowerment.

To argue for the incorporation of human agency into analyses of photographs and their uses is not to suggest that the resulting images would communicate something more balanced or offer a singular resolution of the issue. Rather it is to suggest that understanding the social lives and relationships of the actors outside of the frame may affect how audiences consume these images.

There are always risks of exploitation and deception in human interaction when power relations are disproportionate. However, increased reliance on regulatory ethical codes poses potential danger for the ways image-making in the humanitarian sphere operates. Making the ethics frameworks prescriptive homogenizes the image economy. It also undermines individual agency and the personal code of accountability by image producers, creating a system of inflexible conformity to protocol rather than relying on, or promoting, individual accountability. Ethical considerations at the macro and micro levels are central to practice, yet this responsibility should not be relegated to organizational codes guided by NGO branding strategies. Regardless of how comprehensive guidelines may be, the ethical decisions of its producers are highly subjective and guidelines can be interpreted to suit various interests. As such, definitions of what is "ethical" and "unethical" must be understood as contextual and institution-specific.

The ongoing emphasis on the politics of photography, which focuses on representations and the truth/proof value of images, has lost traction and may distract from what is really at stake. Altering representations is less complex than combating issues of social inequality, structural violence, and inequality in the distribution of wealth. A disproportionate emphasis on the truth value of images can have the consequence of securing representation as the main areas of concern rather than the actual inequalities and injustices that images are depicting. Polarizing humanitarian photographic practice into positive/negative and ethical/unethical limits the potential and opportunities of the medium. Such potential may best be realized by reinserting a consideration of the social lives that occur outside the frame into our view of the photograph.

Notes

1   This opening vignette is from field notes of a conversation between the charity commissioner, the professional photographer, and the author en route to a filming location in Bangladesh on 31 March 2010.
2   See Van der Gaag and Nash, _Images of Africa_; Benthall, _Disasters, Relief, and the Media_; Voluntary Services Overseas, _The Live Aid Legacy_; and the chapter by Henrietta Lidchi in this volume.
3   Pinney, "Introduction" in Pinney and Peterson, eds. _Photography's Other Histories_, 14.
4   To explore practical tensions in the production of imagery, I used ethnographic methods that combined analysis of branding strategies and photographic guidelines of nine international NGOs, in-depth semi-structured interviews with eleven professional photographers and fifteen senior communications professionals from the NGO sector in Bangladesh. I went on three photographic assignments as an observer and was commissioned as the photographer for one NGO assignment. The comments from photographers and case study descriptions in this chapter are all drawn from my field notes made during these assignments. Nissinen, "In Search of Visibility."
5   See Tagg, _Burden_, 85; also chapters by Twomey, Grant, and Curtis in this volume.
6   See Lidchi chapter in this volume.
7   Van der Gaag and Nash, _Images of Africa_.
8   Lidchi, "All in the Choosing Eye," 110.
9   Several years later, in 1993, a controversy over Kevin Carter's Pulitzer Prize–winning photo taken in southern Sudan of a starving child stalked by a vulture raised the same issues, including photographers' responsibilities to the people they photograph and their accountability in the situations they witness.

10 Van der Gaag and Nash, *Images of Africa*; Lidchi, "All in the Choosing Eye," 111. Such criticism was disputed by many photographers. In an interview, the photographer Wossan, who had been on assignment during the disaster, remarked "The people of Korem were desperate and my impression was there was no objection to being filmed. Presuming they did not have the capacity to make a judgement in itself is demeaning." Clark, *Representing*, 272.

11 Van der Gaag and Nash, *Images of Africa*; Lidchi, "All in the Choosing Eye"; Benthall, *Disasters*; Dogra, "Reading NGOs Visually."

12 Manzo, "Imagining Humanitarianism," 637.

13 In 2012 the political effect of imagery was exemplified in the diplomatic incident between Britain and India. In a leaked memo, published in the *Telegraph* on 4 February 2012, the Indian foreign minister, Nirumpama Rao, proposed rejecting "further DFID [British] assistance" because of "negative publicity of Indian poverty promoted by DFID." The controversy did not center solely on such representations but suggested deeper anxieties about aid, national interests, and commercial gain in which imaging of poverty played an important role.

14 Smith and Yanacopulos, *Public Faces*; M. Abélè, "Rethinking NGOs: The Economy of Survival and Global Governance," *Indiana Journal of Global Legal Studies*, 15, no. 1 (2008): 241–58; Barnett and Weiss, *Humanitarianism in Question*.

15 Vestergaard, "Humanitarian Branding." Guidelines include imagery and formal fixed elements such as logotype, colors, strap-line positioning, and typefaces designed to reflect the values the organization wishes to promote.

16 The UNICEF brand tool kit defines the style based on characteristics that are simple, optimistic, bold, and contemporary. United Nations Children's Fund, *Brand Tool Kit*, 2008. http://pdfcast.org/pdf/unicef-branding-toolkit. Accessed 29 November 2009.

World Vision branding is aimed to symbolize hope. World Vision, *One Voice for the Whole World: Corporate Identity Standards*, 2007. http://wvuscontracts.org/WVUS_Branding_Guidelines.html. Accessed 30 August 2011.

ActionAid brand guidelines present the key values as mutual respect, equity, transparency, solidarity, independence, courage of conviction, and humility – values that reflect the desired organizational identity of "togetherness.: ActionAid Brand Guidelines, 2007. http://www.austcare.org.au/media/67200/actionaid%20brand%20guidelines%20part%201.pdf Accessed 31 August 2011.

17 Manzo, "Imaging Humanitarianism."

18 For example, the prestigious annual *UNICEF Photo of the Year Award* by UNICEF Germany and GEO magazine since the year 2000; also *Click about It Photography Competition* sponsored by European Journalism Centre (EJC), Oxfam International, and the European Commission.

19 Nissinen, "Children in Conflict."

20 Examples are Oxfam's campaign commissions to Martin Parr (2009), Rankin (2011), Alejandro Chaskielberg (2012) in order to leave "clichéd, sensationalist images of the past behind." Christian Aid joined with Magnum

photographers in 2011 to "record powerful testimonies of discrimination" for an AIDS stigma prevention campaign.

21 Pressures of the industry were reported by Reporters sans Frontières (RSF), an international NGO based in France that advocates freedom of the press and freedom of information. RSF launched an exhibition in Paris, announcing that the photojournalistic profession was under threat due to a media industry crisis. J.-F. Julliard, "Freedom to Observe and Public Support" in *Pierre and Alexandra Boulat: 100 Photos pour la Liberté de la Presse (Paris: Reporters sans frontiers,* 2010), 9. The experiences of leading photographers during the 2010 Haiti crisis were cited. Their work could not be sold due to a decline in media budgets of newspapers and news magazines and the emergence of the "citizen journalist." As technology spreads, more people are claiming to be photographers and provide cheaper or free content, thereby competing with the professionals.

22 R. Harrington et al., "Documentary Foundations: The New Quangocracy? The Battle for Editorial Independence," in *Proceedings of the Battle of Ideas* (6 November 2010) http://www.battleofideas.org.uk/2010/session_detail/4711> Accessed 1 September 2014; Julliard, "Freedom to Observe and Public Support."

23 One example is the DRIK organization founded in 1989; see S. Alam, "The Majority World Looks Back," *New Internationalist,* Issue 403 (2007): 4–17. Their efforts include the expansion of the media infrastructure and revision of visual content, a photography school, and a festival of photography called the Chobi Mela. Such efforts are controversial and critics argue they have not changed traditional documentary and photojournalistic conventions where hegemonic assumptions remain intact. L. Hoek, "The DRIK Picture Library: Images for Change," *Visual Communication,* 4 (2005): 333–6, here 336.

24 For example, the contemporary arts review magazine *Depart* criticized "empathy images" by Wasif, a photographer who gained international reputation photographing Bangladeshi topics, questioning whether his work is a response to "the First World's demand for the Third World crisis image, or … a genuine investment in understanding human condition." M. Zaman, "New Flashpoints in the Continuous Drama of Brief Encounters with the Homo Incognitus," *Depart,* 1, no. 3 (2010): 20–7.

25 See Rosler, "Post Documentary?" for an attempt to define the characteristics of each, suggesting that documentary photographers have more freedom to select their subjects and influence how the story is presented and distributed; in photojournalistic assignments, content and subjects are largely predetermined and priority lies with the assignment rather than building a relationship with the subjects. Both are guided by principles of accuracy.

26 Walter Benjamin noted the propensity of photography to trivialize human suffering as early as 1936; Susan Sontag criticized photography's "predatory" qualities. Walter Benjamin, "The Work of Art in the Age of Mechanical Reproduction," in Benjamin, *Illuminations,* edited by H. Arendt (New York: Schocken Books, 1969), 217–52, orig. 1936. Sontag, *On Photography,* 14; also Barthes, *Camera Lucida,* 91. For a recent ethnographic study that perpetuates the idea of photography as a form of domination, see L. Henderson,

"Access and Consent in Public Photography," in Wells, ed., *The Photography Reader*, 285.

27 Tagg, *The Burden of Representation*; Rose, *Visual Methodologies*.

28 Such a view limits the possibility of a multiplicity of gazes. Lutz and Collins complicate the framework of the duality of gazes, arguing instead for the polysemic nature of images in which a multiplicity of gazes, including that of the subject, contribute to the ambiguous status of photography. C. Lutz and J. Collins, "The Photograph as an Intersection of Gazes," in Wells, ed., *The Photography Reader*, 371.

29 Van de Ven, "The Eyes of the Street Look Back."

30 Even before mobile technology and social media, Edward Said admonished: "I would like to think that we [Palestinian people] are not just the people seen or looked at in these photographs: We are also looking at our observers.... [W]e too are looking, we too are scrutinizing, assessing, judging. We are more than someone's object." Said and J. Mohr, *After the Last Sky: Palestinian Lives* (New York: Columbia University Press, 1998), 156.

31 For example, Munem Wasif and Tansim Wahab, eds., *Kamra* (Dhaka: Oitijya Press, 2012), which documents the evolution of Bangladeshi photography.

32 Tait, "Bearing Witness," 1221.

33 Szarkowski, *The Photographer's Eye*; Rosler, "Post Documentary?"; Wells, ed., *Photography Reader*.

34 Dogra, *Representations*.

35 Dogra, "Reading NGOs Visually."

36 Nissinen, "In Search of Visibility."

37 Action Aid Brand Guidelines; World Vision, *One Voice*; UNICEF, *UNICEF Photography*, personal communication 25 November 2009.

Select Bibliography

Abruzzo, Margaret. *Polemical Pain: Slavery, Cruelty, and the Rise of Humanitarianism*. Baltimore, MD: Johns Hopkins University Press, 2011.

Akcam, Taner. *The Young Turks' Crime against Humanity: The Armenian Genocide and Ethnic Cleansing in the Ottoman Empire*. Princeton, NJ: Princeton University Press, 2012.

Amrith, Sunil. *Decolonizing International Health. India and Southeast Asia, 1930–65*. Basingstoke, UK: Palgrave Macmillan, 2006.

Apel, Dora and Shawn Michelle Smith. *Lynching Photographs*. Berkeley: University of California Press, 2008.

Arnold, S. "Constrained Crusaders: British Charities and Development Education." *British Charities and Education*, Education Network Project Occasional Paper, 1, University of Sussex (1988), 5–33.

Baer, Ulrich. *Spectral Evidence: The Photography of Trauma*. Cambridge, MA: MIT Press, 2002.

Balakian, Peter. *The Burning Tigris: The Armenian Genocide and America's Response*. New York: HarperCollins, 2003.

Bank, Andrew. "Anthropology and Portrait Photography: Gustav Fritsch's 'Natives of South Africa,' 1863–1872," *Kronos* 27 (November 2001): 43–76.

Banks, Marcus and Jay Ruby, eds. *Made to Be Seen: Perspectives on the History of Visual Anthropology*. Chicago: University of Chicago Press, 2011.

Barnett, Michael. *Empire of Humanity: A History of Humanitarianism*. Ithaca, NY: Cornell University Press, 2011.

Barnett, Michael N. and Thomas George Weiss, eds. *Humanitarianism in Question: Politics, Power, Ethics*. Ithaca, NY: Cornell University Press, 2008.

Barthes, Roland. *Camera Lucida: Reflections on Photography*. Translated by Richard Howard. New York: Hill and Wang, 1982.

Mythologies. Translated by A. Lavers. London: Paladin, 1989.

"The Rhetoric of the Image." *Working Papers in Cultural Studies* 1 (1971): 37–51.

The Rustle of Language. Translated by Richard Howard. Berkeley: University of California Press, 1989.

Barton, James L. *Story of Near East Relief*. New York: Macmillan, 1930.

Batchen, Geoffrey, Mick Gidley, Nancy K. Miller, and Jay Poster, eds. *Picturing Atrocity: Photography in Crisis*. London: Reaktion Books, 2012.

Baughan, Emily. "'Every Citizen of Empire Is Emplored to Save the Children!' Empire, Internationalism and the Save the Children Fund in Inter-war Britain." *Historical Research* 86, no. 231 (February 2012): 116–37.

Bear, Jordan. "Magnum Orbis: Photographs from the End(s) of the Earth." *Visual Studies* 25, no. 2 (2010): 111–23.

Benthall, Jonathan. *Disasters, Relief and the Media*. London: I. B. Tauris, 1993.

Berkhoff, Karel C. "'Total Annihilation of the Jewish Population': The Holocaust in the Soviet Media, 1941–45." *Kritika* 10, no. 1 (Winter 2009): 61–105.

Bezner, L. C. *Photography and Politics in America: From the New Deal to the Cold War*. Baltimore, MD: Johns Hopkins University Press, 1999.

Bösch, Frank and Manuel Borutta, "Medien und Emotionen in der Moderne: Historische Perspektiven." In Frank Bösch and Manuel Borutta, eds., *Die Massen bewegen: Medien und Emotionen in der Moderne*, 193–213. Frankfurt am Main: Campus, 2006.

Boltanski, Luc. *Distant Suffering: Morality, Media and Politics*. Cambridge: Cambridge University Press, 1999.

Bolton, Richard, ed. *The Conflict of Meaning: Critical Histories of Photography*. Cambridge, MA: MIT Press, 1989.

Bondi, Inge. *Chim. The Photographs of David Seymour*. Boston: Bulfinch Press, 1996.

Borer, Tristan Anne. *Media, Mobilization and Human Rights: Mediated Suffering*. New York: Zed Books, 2012.

Borgwardt, Elizabeth. *A New Deal for the World. America's Vision for Human Rights*. Cambridge, MA: Belknap Press of Harvard University Press, 2005.

Bornstein, Erica and Peter Redfield, eds. *Forces of Compassion: Humanitarianism between Ethics and Politics*. Santa Fe, NM: School for Advanced Research Press, 2011.

Bourdieu, Pierre, ed. *Photography: A Middle-Brow Art*. Oxford: Polity Press, 1990.

Bredekamp, Horst. *Theorie des Bildakts*. Frankfurt am Main: Suhrkamp, 2010.

Brennan, Bonnie and Hanno Hardt, eds. *Picturing the Past: Media, History, and Photography*. Urbana: University of Illinois Press, 1999.

Briggs, Laura. "Mother, Child, Race, Nation: The Visual Iconography of Rescue and the Politics of Transnational and Transracial Adoption." *Gender & History* 15, no. 2 (August 2003): 179–200.

Brink, Cornelia. "Bildeffekte: Überlegungen zum Zusammenhang von Fotografie und Emotionen." *Geschichte und Gesellschaft* 37 (2011): 104–29.

Ikonen der Vernichtung: Öffentlicher Gebrauch von Fotografien aus nationalsozialistischen Konzentrationslagern nach 1945. Berlin: Akademie Verlag, 1998.

"Secular Icons: Looking at Photographs from Nazi Concentration Camps." *History and Memory* 12, no. 1 (Spring/Summer 2000): 135–50.

Brothers, Caroline. *War and Photography*. New York: Routledge, 1997.

Burman, Erica. "Innocents Abroad: Western Fantasies of Childhood and the Iconography of Emergencies." *Disasters* 19, no. 3 (1994): 238–53.

Burnell, P. *Charity, Politics and the Third World*. Hemel Hempstead: Harvester Wheatsheaf, 1992.

Burroughs, Robert M. *Travel Writing and Atrocities: Eyewitness Accounts of Colonialism in the Congo, Angola and the Putuyamo*. London: Routledge, 2010.

Cabanes, Bruno. *The Great War and the Origins of Humanitarianism*. New York: Cambridge University Press, 2014.

Calain, Philippe. "Ethics and Images of Suffering Bodies in Humanitarian Medicine." *Social Sciences and Medicine* xxx (2012): 1–8.

Calhoun, Craig. "The Imperative to Reduce Suffering: Charity, Progress, and Emergencies in the Field of Humanitarian Action." In Michael Barnett and Thomas G. Weiss, eds., *Humanitarianism in Question: Politics, Power, Ethics*, 73–97. Ithaca, NY: Cornell University Press, 2008.

Campbell, D., D. J. Clark, and Kate Manzo. *Imaging Famine*. London: Guardian, 2005. Accessed July 7, 2012. http://www.imaging-famine.org/images/pdfs/famine_catalog.pdf.

Chaney, D. "Photographic Truths." *Discourse Social (Social Discourses)* 1, no. 4 (1988): 397–422.

"Changing Charity: 50 Years of Oxfam." Special issue, *New Internationalist* 228 (1992).

Chaudhary, Zahid R. *Afterimage of Empire: Photography in Nineteenth-Century India*. Minneapolis: University of Minnesota Press, 2013.

Checkland, Olive. *Humanitarianism and the Emperor's Japan*. New York: Palgrave Macmillan, 1994.

Chouliaraki, Lilie. *The Ironic Spectator. Solidarity in the Age of Post-Humanitarianism*. Malden, MA: Polity Press, 2013.

"The Symbolic Power of Transnational Media: Managing the Visibility of Suffering." *Global Media and Communication* 4 (2008): 329–51.

Christian Aid. *Images of Development, Links between Racism, Poverty and Injustice*. (Insight Series) London: Christian Aid, 1988.

Clark, D. J. "Representing the Majority World: Famine, Photojournalism and the Changing Visual Economy." PhD diss., University of Durham, 2009.

Clark, Elizabeth B. "'The Sacred Rights of the Weak': Pain, Sympathy, and the Culture of Individual Rights in Antebellum America." *Journal of American History* 82, no. 2 (September 1995): 463–93.

Cmiel, Kenneth. "The Recent History of Human Rights." *American Historical Review* 109, no. 1 (2004): 117–35.

Code of Conduct: Images and Messages Relating to the Third World. Produced by the General Assembly of the Liaison Committee of Development NGOs to the European Communities, 1989. Accessed December 28, 2013. http://www.imaging-famine.org/papers/CODE_OF_CONDUCT_on%20Images_and_Messages_1989.pdf.

Code of Conduct on Images and Messages. Produced by Dochas (the Irish Association of Non-Governmental Development), 2006. Accessed December 28, 2013. http://www.dochas.ie/Shared/Files/5/Images_and_Messages.pdf.

Cody, Jeffrey W. and Frances Terpak, eds. *Brush and Shutter: Early Photography in China*. Los Angeles: Getty Institute, 2011.

Cohen, Daniel G. "Between Relief and Politics: Refugee Humanitarianism in Occupied Germany 1945–1946." *Journal of Contemporary History* 43, no. 3 (2008): 437–49.

In War's Wake: European Refugees in the Postwar Order. Oxford: Oxford University Press, 2011.

Coleman, A. D. *Depth of Field: Essays on Photography, Mass Media, and Lens Culture*. Albuquerque: University of New Mexico Press, 1998.

Collins, Kathleen, ed. *Shadow and Substance: Essays in the History of Photography*. Bloomfield Hills, MI: Amorphous Institute Press, 1990.

Conklin, Alice. *A Mission to Civilize: The Republican Idea of Empire in France and West Africa, 1895–1930*. Palo Alto, CA: Stanford University Press, 1997.

Curti, Merle. *American Philanthropy Abroad: A History*. New Brunswick, NJ: Rutgers University Press, 1963.

Curtis, James. *Mind's Eye, Mind's Truth: FSA Photography Reconsidered*. Philadelphia: Temple University Press, 1989.

Curtis, Neal. *The Pictorial Turn*. New York: Routledge, 2010.

Daniel, Pete et al. *Official Images: New Deal Photography*. Washington, DC: Smithsonian Institution Press, 1987.

Daughton, J. P. *An Empire Divided: Religion, Republicanism, and the Making of French Colonialism*. (New York: Oxford University Press, 2006).

Dauphinée, Elizabeth. "The Politics of the Body in Pain: Reading the Ethics of Imagery." *Security Dialogue* 38 (2007): 139–55.

Davis, Morris. *Interpreters for Nigeria: The Third World and International Public Relations*. Urbana: University of Illinois Press, 1977.

Dean, Carolyn. *The Fragility of Empathy after the Holocaust*. Ithaca, NY: Cornell University Press, 2004.

Desgrandchamps, Marie-Luce. "Entre coopération et concurrence: CICR, Unicef et organisations religieuses au Biafra." *Relations internationales* 152, no. 4 (2012): 51–62.

"Revenir sur le mythe fondateur de Médecins Sans Frontières: les relations entre les médecins français et le CICR pendant la guerre du Biafra (1967–1970)." *Relations internationals* 146, no. 2 (2011): 95–108.

Dewitz, Bodo von and Roland Scotti, eds. *Alles Wahrheit! Alles Lüge! Photographie und Wirklichkeit im 19. Jahrhundert: Die Sammlung Robert Lebeck*. Cologne: Museum Ludwig, 1997.

Dikovitskaya, Margarita. *Visual Culture: The Study of Visual Culture after the Culture Turn*. Cambridge, MA: MIT Press, 2005.

Dogra, Nandita. "'Reading NGOs Visually' – Implications of Visual Images for NGO Management." *Journal of International Development* 19 (2007): 161–71.

Representations of Global Poverty: Aid, Development and International NGOs. London: I. B. Taurus, 2012.

Doherty, Robert J. *Social-Documentary Photograph in the USA*. New York: Amphoto, 1976.

Douzinas, Costas. "The Many Faces of Humanitarianism." *Parrhesia* 2 (2007): 1–28.

Edgerton-Tarpley, Kathryn. *Tears from Iron: Cultural Responses to Famine.* Berkeley: University of California Press, 2008.

Edwards, Elizabeth, ed. *Anthropology and Photography 1860–1920.* London: Yale University Press/Royal Anthropological Institute, 1992.

Edwards, Elizabeth and Janice Hart, eds. *Photographs, Objects, Histories: On the Materiality of Images.* New York: Routledge, 2004.

Evans, Jessica and Stuart Hall. *Visual Culture: The Reader.* New York: Sage, 1999.

Falconer, John. "'A Pure Labour of Love': A Publishing History of *The People of India*." In by Eleanor M. Hight and Gary D. Sampson, eds., *Colonialist Photography: Imag(in)ing Race and Place,* 51–83. New York: Routledge, 2002.

Farré, Sébastien and Yan Schubert. "L'illusion de l'objectif. Le délégué du CICR Maurice Rossel et les photographies de Theresienstadt." *Le Mouvement Social* 227 (avril–juin 2009): 65–83.

Fassin, Didier. *Humanitarian Reason: A Moral History of the Present.* Berkeley: University of California Press, 2011.

Fehrenbach, Heide. "From Aid to Intimacy: The Humanitarian Origins of International Adoption." In Johannes Paulmann, ed., *The Dilemmas of Humanitarian Aid in the Twentieth Century.* London: Oxford University Press, 2015.

"War Orphans and Postfascist Families: Kinship and Belonging after 1945." In Frank Biess and Robert G. Moeller, eds., *Histories of the Aftermath: The Legacies of the Second World War in Europe,* 175–95. New York: Berghahn Books, 2010.

Festa, Lynn. "Humanity without Feathers." *Humanity* 1, no. 1 (Fall 2010): 3–19.

Finnegan, Cara A. *Picturing Poverty: Print Culture and FSA Photographs.* Washington, DC: Smithsonian Institution, 2003.

Forsythe, David P. *The Humanitarians, the International Committee of the Red Cross.* Cambridge: Cambridge University Press, 2005.

Forsythe, David P. and Barbara Ann J. Rieffer-Flanagan. *The International Committee of the Red Cross: A Neutral Humanitarian Actor.* London: Routledge, 2007.

Fuller, Pierre. "North China Famine Revisited: Unsung Native Relief in the Warlord Era, 1920–1921." *Modern Asian Studies* 47, Part 3 (May 2013): 820–50.

Gatrell, Peter. *Free World? The Campaign to Save the World's Refugees, 1956–1963.* Cambridge: Cambridge University Press, 2011.

Gidal, Tim N. *Modern Photojournalism: Origins and Evolution, 1910–1933.* New York: Macmillan, 1973.

Gill, Rebecca. "'The Rational Administration of Compassion': The Origins of British Relief in War." *Le Mouvement Social* (April–June 2009): 9–26.

Godby, Michael. "Confronting Horror: Emily Hobhouse and the Concentration Camp Photographs of the South African War." *Kronos* 32 (2006): 34–48.

Goldberg, Vicki, ed. *Photography in Print: Writings from 1816 to the Present.* Albuquerque: University of New Mexico Press, 1981.

Goldberg, Vicki. *The Power of Photography: How Photographs Changed Our Lives.* New York: Abbeville Press, 1991, 1993.

Goldsworthy, Simon. "English Noncomformity and the Pioneering of the Modern Newspaper Campaign including the Strange Case of W. T. Stead and the Bulgarian Horrors." *Journalism Studies* 7, no. 3 (2006): 387–402.

Grant, Kevin. "The British Empire, International Government, and Human Rights." *History Compass* 11, no. 8 (2013): 573–83.

"Christian Critics of Empire: Missionaries, Lantern Lectures, and the Congo Reform Campaign in Britain." In Martin Shipway, ed., *The Rise and Fall of Modern Empires,* Vol. IV: *Reactions to Colonialism,* 91–122 (London: Ashgate, 2013).

A Civilized Savagery: Britain and the New Slaveries in Africa, 1884–1926. New York: Routledge, 2005.

Grimshaw, Anna. *The Ethnographer's Eye. Ways of Seeing in Anthropology.* New York: Cambridge University Press, 2001.

Hall, Stuart. "The Determinations of News Photographs." *Working Papers in Cultural Studies.* Birmingham Centre for Cultural Studies 3 (Autumn 1972): 53–87.

Halttunen, Karen. "Humanitarianism and the Pornography of Pain in Anglo-American Culture." *American Historical Review* 100, no. 2 (1995): 303–34.

Hannigan, William and Ken Johnston. *Picture Machine: The Rise of American News Pictures.* New York: Abrams, 2004.

Hariman, Robert and John Louis Lucaites. *No Caption Needed: Iconic Photographs, Public Culture, and Liberal Democracy.* Chicago: University of Chicago Press, 2007.

Harris, Michael D. *Colored Pictures: Race and Visual Representation.* Chapel Hill: University of North Carolina Press, 2003.

Harrison, Paul and Robin Palmer. *News Out of Africa: Biafra to Band Aid.* London: Hilary Shipman, 1986.

Haskell, Thomas L. "Capitalism and the Origins of Humanitarian Sensibility, Parts 1–2." *American Historical Review* 90 (April 1985): 339–61; (June 1985): 547–66.

Haver, Gianni. *Photos de Presse: Usage et Pratique.* Lausanne: Antipodes, 2009.

Heerten, Lasse. "The Dystopia of Postcolonial Catastrophe: Self-Determination, the Biafran War of Secession and the 1970s Human Rights Moment." In Jan Eckel and Samuel Moyn, eds., *The Breakthrough: Human Rights in the 1970s.* Philadelphia: University of Pennsylvania Press, 2013.

"Spectacles of Suffering: The Biafran War of Secession and International Human Rights in a Postcolonial World, 1967–1970." PhD diss., Freie Universität Berlin, 2013.

Hicks, Wilson. *Words and Pictures: An Introduction to Photojournalism.* New York: Harper and Brothers, 1952.

Hight, Eleanor M. and Gary D. Sampson, eds. *Colonialist Photography: Imag(in)ing Race and Place.* New York: Routledge, 2002.

Hochschild, Adam. *King Leopold's Ghost.* Boston: Houghton Mifflin, 1998.

Hodgson, Pat. *Early War Photographs*. Boston: New York Graphic Society, 1974.

Hoffmann, Stefan Ludwig. "Gazing at Ruins: German Defeat as Visual Experience." *Journal of Modern European History* 9 (2011): 328–50.

Hoffmann, Stefan Ludwig, ed. *Human Rights in the Twentieth Century: A Critical History*. New York: Cambridge University Press, 2011.

Hoffmann, Tessa and Gerayer Koutcharian. "'Images that Horrify and Indict': Pictorial Documents of the Persecution and Extermination of the Armenians from 1877 to 1922." *Armenian Review* 45, no. 1–2 (Spring/Summer 1992): 53–184.

Horgan, J. *Images of Africa: Interim Research Report*. Dublin: School of Communication, National Institute for Higher Education, Ireland, 1986.

Humanitarian Action and Cinema. ICRC Films in the 1920s. Memoriav, J.-B. Jonod, 2005.

Hunt, Lynn. *Inventing Human Rights: A History*. New York: W. W. Norton, 2007.

Hunt, Nancy Rose. "An Acoustic Register, Tenacious Images, and Congolese Scenes of Rape and Repetition." *Cultural Anthropology* 23, no. 2 (May 2008): 220–53.

Hutchinson, John. *Champions of Charity: War and the Rise of the Red Cross*. Boulder, CO: Westview, 1996.

"Disasters and the International Order: Earthquakes, Humanitarians, and the Ciraolo Project." *International History Review* 22 (2000): 1–36.

Irwin, Julia. *Making the World Safe: The American Red Cross and a Nation's Humanitarian Awakening*. Oxford: Oxford University Press, 2013.

Jay, Martin and Sumathi Ramaswamy, eds. *Empires of Vision: A Reader*. Durham: Duke University Press, 2014.

Johnston, Patricia, ed. *Seeing High & Low: Representing Social Conflict in American Visual Culture*. Berkeley: University of California Press, 2006.

Kaida-Hozumi, M. K. "The Role of NGOs and the Media in Development Education." M.Phil. diss., IDS, Sussex University, 1989.

Kaplan, Daile, ed. *Photostory: Selected Letters and Photographs of Lewis W. Hine*. Washington, DC: Smithsonian Institution Press, 1992.

Keller, Ulrich. *The Ultimate Spectacle: A Visual History of the Crimean War*. New York: Routledge, 2001.

Kennedy, Denis. "Selling the Distant Other: Humanitarianism and Imagery – Ethical Dilemmas of Humanitarian Action." *Journal of Humanitarian Assistance* (February 2009). Accessed 23 May 2014. http://sites.tufts.edu/jha/archives/411.

Kennedy, Liam. "'A Compassionate Vision': Larry Burrows's Vietnam War Photography." *Photography & Culture* 4, no. 2 (July 2011): 179–94.

Kévonian, Dzovinar. "Photographie, génocide et transmission: l'exemple arménien." *Les Cahiers de la Shoah* 1, no. 8 (2004): 119–49.

Kleinman, Arthur and Joan Kleinman. "The Appeal of Experience, the Dismay of Images: Cultural Appropriations of Suffering in Our Times." *Daedalus* 125, no. 1 (1996): 1–24.

Kloian, Richard D., ed. *The Armenian Genocide: News Accounts from the American Press 1915–22*. Berkeley: Anto, 1987.

Knightley, Phillip, ed. *The Eye of War: Words and Photographs from the Front Line.* Introduction by John Keegan. Washington, DC: Smithsonian Books, 2003.

Knightley, Phillip. *The First Casualty: The War Correspondent as Hero and Myth-Maker from the Crimea to Kosovo.* Baltimore, MD: Johns Hopkins University Press, 2002.

Knoch, Habbo. "Mediale Trauer: Bildmedien und Sinnstiftung im 'Die Zeitalter der Extreme.'" In Frank Bösch and Manuel Borutta, eds., *Die Massen bewegen: Medien und Emotionen in der Moderne*, 193–213. Frankfurt am Main: Campus, 2006.

Die Tat als Bild: Fotografien des Holocaust in der deutschen Erinnerungskultur. Hamburg: Hamburger Edition, 2001.

Koven, Seth. "Dr. Barnardo's 'Artistic Fictions': Photography, Sexuality, and the Ragged Child in Victorian London." *Radical History Review* 69 (Fall 1997): 7–45.

Slumming: Sexual and Social Politics in Victorian London. Princeton, NJ: Princeton University Press, 2004.

Krikorian, Abraham D. and Eugene L. Taylor. "Achieving Ever-Greater Precision in Attestation and Attribution of Genocide Photographs." In Tessa Hofmann, Matthias Bjørnlund, and Vasileios Meichanetsidis, eds., *The Genocide of the Ottoman Greeks: Studies on the State-Sponsored Campaigns of the Christians of Asia Minor, 1912–1922 and Its Aftermath: History, Law, Memory*, 394–96. Scarsdale, NY: Aristide D. Caratzsas, 2011.

La Capra, Dominick. *Writing History, Writing Trauma.* Baltimore, MD: Johns Hopkins University Press, 2001.

Lachenal, Guillame and Bertrand Thaite. "Une généalogie missionaire et coloniale de l'humanitaire: le cas Aujoulat au Cameroun, 1935–1973." *Le Mouvement Social* 227, no. 2 (2009): 45–63.

Lagrou, Pieter. *The Legacy of Nazi Occupation: Patriotic Memory and National Recovery in Western Europe, 1945–1965.* Cambridge: Cambridge University Press, 2000.

Laqua, Daniel, ed. *Internationalism Reconfigured: Transnational Ideas and Movements between the World Wars.* New York: Tauris Academic Studies, 2011.

Laqueur, Thomas. "Bodies, Details, and the Humanitarian Narrative." In Lynn Hunt, ed., *The New Cultural History*, 176–204. Berkeley: University of California Press, 1989.

"Mourning, Pity, and the Work of Narrative in the Making of Humanity." In Richard Ashby Wilson and Richard D. Brown, eds., *Humanitarianism and Suffering: The Mobilization of Empathy*, 31–57. Cambridge: Cambridge University Press, 2009.

Lau, Grace. *Picturing the Chinese: Early Western Photographs and Postcards of China.* Hong Kong: Joint Publishing, 2008.

Lebeck, Robert and Bodo von Dewitz. *Kiosk: A History of Photojournalism.* Göttingen: Steidl, 2001.

Lewinski, Jorge. *The Camera at War: A History of War Photography from 1848 to the Present Day.* New York: Simon & Schuster, 1980.

Lidchi, Henrietta. J. "All in the Choosing Eye: Charity, Representation and the Developing World." PhD diss., Open University, 1993.

Linfield, Susie. *The Cruel Radiance: Photography and Political Violence*. Chicago: University of Chicago Press, 2010.

Lissner, Jørgen. "Merchants of Misery." *New Internationalist* 100 (1981): 23–25. *The Politics of Altruism*. Geneva: Lutheran World Federation, 1977.

Lutz, Catherine and Jane Collins. "The Photograph as an Intersection of Gazes: The Example of National Geographic." In Liz Wells, ed., *The Photography Reader*, 354–74. Oxford: Routledge, 2003.

Lydon, Jane. "'Behold the Tears': Photography as Colonial Witness." *History of Photography* 34, no. 3 (August 2010): 234–50. *The Flash of Recognition: Photography and the Emergence of Indigenous Rights*. Sydney: University of New South Wales Press, 2012.

MacDougall, David. *The Corporeal Image: Film, Ethnography and the Senses*. Princeton, NJ: Princeton University Press, 2006.

Mahood, L. *Feminism and Voluntary Action. Eglantyne Jebb and Save the Children, 1876–1928*. London: Palgrave Macmillan, 2009.

Mahood, Linda and Vic Satzewich. "The Save the Children Fund and the Russian Famine, 1921–23: Claims and Counter-Claims about Feeding "Bolshevik" Children." *Journal of Historical Sociology* 22, no 1 (March 2009): 55–83.

Malkki, Liisa. "Children, Humanity and the Infantilization of Peace." In I. Feldman and M. Ticktin, eds., *In the Name of Humanity. The Government of Threat and Care*, 58–85. Durham, NC: Duke University Press, 2010. "Speechless Emissaries: Refugees, Humanitarianism and Dehistoricization." *Cultural Anthropology* 11, no. 3 (1996): 377–404.

Manzo, Kate. "Imaging Humanitarianism: NGO Identity and the Iconography of Childhood." *Antipode* 40, no. 4 (2008): 632–57.

Marshall, Dominique. "Children's Rights and Children's Action in International Relief and Domestic Welfare: The Work of Herbert Hoover between 1914 and 1950." *Journal of the History of Childhood and Youth* 1, no. 3 (2008): 351–88. "The Construction of Children as an Object of International Relations: The Declaration of Children's Rights and the Child Welfare Committee of the League of Nations, 1900–1924." *International Journal of Children's Rights* 7 (1999): 103–47. "Humanitarian Sympathy for Children and the History of Children's Rights, 1919–1959." In James Marten, ed., *Children and War: A Historical Anthology*. New York: New York University Press, 2002.

Marien, Mary Warner. *Photography: A Cultural History*, 2nd ed. Upper Saddle River, NJ: Pearson Prentice Hall, 2006.

Martínez, Samuel and Kathryn Libal. "Introduction: The Gender of Humanitarian Narrative." *Humanity* 2, no. 2 (Fall 2011): 161–70.

Maslowski, Peter. *Armed with Cameras. The American Military Photographers of World War II*. New York: Maxell Macmillan International, 1993.

Maxwell, Anne. *Colonial Photography and Exhibitions: Representations of the Native and the Making of European Identities*. Leicester: Leicester University Press, 2000.

Mazlish, Bruce. *The Idea of Humanity in a Global Era*. New York: Palgrave Macmillan, 2008.

Mazower, Mark. *No Enchanted Palace. The End of Empire and the Ideological Origins of the United Nations*. Princeton, NJ: Princeton University Press, 2009.

McCabe, Linda Rose. *The Beginnings of the Halftone*. Chicago: Inland Printer, 1924.

Mirzoeff, Nicholas. *The Visual Culture Reader*. New York: Routledge, 1998.

Mitchell, Mary Niall. *Raising Freedom's Child: Black Children and Visions of the Future after Slavery*. New York: New York University Press, 2008.

Mitchell, W. J. T. *Iconology: Image, Text, Ideology*. Chicago: University of Chicago Press, 1986.

   What Do Pictures Want? Chicago: University of Chicago Press, 2005.

   "World Pictures. Globalization and Visual Culture." *Neohelicon* 34, no. 2 (2007): 49–59.

Moeller, Susan D. *Shooting War: Photography and the American Experience of Combat*. New York: Basic Books, 1989.

Mohammad, Fania Khan and Daniel Palmieri. "Des morts et des nus: le regard du CICR sur la malnutrition extrême en temps de guerre (1940–1950)." In Renée Dickason, ed., *Mémoires croisées autour des deux Guerres mondiales*, 85–104. Paris: Mare & Martin, 2012.

Moorehead, Caroline. *Dunant's Dream: War, Switzerland, and the History of the Red Cross*. New York: Carroll and Graf, 1998.

Moorehead, Caroline, ed. *Humanity in War: Frontline Photography since 1860*. Introduction by James Nachtwey. Geneva: ICRC, 2009.

Morgan, David. "The Look of Sympathy: Religion, Visual Culture, and the Social Life of Feeling." *Material Religion* 5, no. 2 (2009): 132–54.

   Protestants and Pictures. Religion, Visual Culture, and the Age of the American Mass Production New York: Oxford University Press, 1999.

Morris, Rosalind C., ed. *Photographies East: The Camera and Its Histories in East and Southeast Asia*. Durham: Duke University Press, 2009.

La Mort du Biafra: Photographies de Gilles Caron, Présentation de F. de Bonneville. Paris: R. Solar, 1968.

Moyn, Samuel. *The Last Utopia: Human Rights in History*. Cambridge, MA: Harvard University Press, 2010.

Mulley, Clare. *The Woman Who Saved the Children. A Biography of Eglantyne Jebb, Founder of Save the Children*. Oxford: Oneworld Book, 2009.

Natale, Enrico. "Quand l'humanitaire commençait à faire son cinema: les films du CICR des années 1920s." *Review of the International Committee of the Red Cross (RICRC)* (2004): 415–37.

Nichols, Bill. *Representing Reality*. Bloomington: Indiana University Press, 1991.

Nissinen, Sanna. "Children in Conflict: Visual Rhetoric in Advocacy." *Systemic Therapy* 1, no. 2 (2008).

   "In Search of Visibility: The Ethical Tensions in the Production of Humanitarian Photography." PhD diss., Open University, 2012.

Nyoni, S. "Images of Poverty: A View from Zimbabwe." *Poverty* 71 (Winter 1988–1989): 6–10.

Omenka, Nicholas Ibeawuchi. "Blaming the Gods: Christian Religious Propaganda in the Nigeria-Biafra War." *Journal of African History* 51 (2010): 367–89.

Oxfam. *What Makes an Appropriate Picture for Oxfam?* Oxford: Oxfam, 1987.

Paschalidis, Gregory. "Perseus' Shield: The Politics of the Body in Humanitarian Campaigns." Accessed August 20, 2014. http://www.enl.auth.gr/gramma/gramma03/Paschalidis.pdf.

Paulmann, Johannes. "Conjunctures in the History of International Humanitarian Aid during the Twentieth Century." *Humanity: An International Journal of Human Rights, Humanitarianism, and Development* 4, no. 2 (2013): 215–38.

Peffer, John. "Snap of the Whip/Crossroads of Shame: Flogging, Photography, and the Representation of Atrocity in the Congo Reform Campaign." *Visual Anthropology Review* 24, no. 1 (2008): 55–77.

Philo, G. and R. Lamb. *Television and the Ethiopian Famine – From Buerk to Band Aid*. London: Television Trust for the Environment, 1986.

Piana, Francesca. "Towards the International Refugee Regime. Humanitarianism in the Wake of the First World War." PhD diss., Graduate Institute of International and Development Studies, Geneva, Switzerland, 2012.

Pinney, Christopher. *Camera Indica: The Social Life of Indian Photographs*. Chicago: University of Chicago Press, 1997.

"The Parallel Histories of Anthropology and Photography." In Elizabeth Edwards, ed., *Anthropology and Photography 1860–1920*. London: Yale University Press/Royal Anthropological Institute, 1992.

Photography and Anthropology. London: Reaktion Books, 2011.

Pinney, Christopher and N. Peterson, eds. *Photography's Other Histories*. Durham, NC: Duke University Press, 2003.

Poole, Deborah. *Race & Modernity: A Visual Economy of the Andean Image World*. Princeton, NJ: Princeton University Press, 1997.

Poulton, R. and M. Harris, eds. *Putting People First: Voluntary Organisations and Third World Development*. Basingstoke, UK: Macmillan Press, 1988.

Przyblyski, Jeanene and Vanessa Schwartz, eds. *The 19th Century Visual Culture Reader*. New York: Routledge, 2004.

Raeburn, John. *A Staggering Revolution: A Cultural History of Thirties Photography*. Urbana: University of Illinois Press, 2006.

Reeves, Caroline. "The Changing Nature of Chinese Philanthropy in Late Qing China." *Papers on Chinese History*, Vol. 5. Cambridge: Harvard University, 1996.

"The Power of Mercy." PhD diss., Harvard University, 1998.

Reinhardt, Mark, Holly Edwards, and Erina Duganne. *Beautiful Suffering: Photography and the Traffic in Pain*. Chicago: University of Chicago Press, 2007.

Reinisch, Jessica, ed. "Relief in the Aftermath of War." Special issue, *Journal of Contemporary History* 43, no. 3 (2008).

Roberts, Claire. *Photography and China*. London: Reaktion Books, 2013.

Robinson, D., S. Herbert, and R. Crangle, eds. *Encyclopedia of the Magic Lantern*. London: Magic Lantern Society, 2001.

Rodogno, Davide. *Against Massacre: Humanitarian Interventions in the Ottoman Empire, 1815–1914*. Series in Human Rights and Crimes against Humanity. Princeton, NJ: Princeton University Press, 2011.

Roeder, G. H. Jr. *The Censored War. American Visual Experience during World War II*. New Haven, CT: Yale University Press, 1993.

Rose, G. *Visual Methodologies: An Introduction to the Interpretation of Visual Materials*. London: Sage, 2007.

Rosenblum, Naomi. *A World History of Photography*, 3rd ed. New York: Abbeville Press, 1997.

Rosenwein, Barbara H. "Worrying about Emotions in History." *American Historical Review* 107, no. 3 (2002): 821–45.

Rosler, M. "Post Documentary?" In R. Raatikainen, ed., *Photo.doc: Documents of Documentary Photography*. Helsinki: Musta Taide, 2000.

Rothberg, Michael. *Multidirectional Memory: Remembering the Holocaust in the Age of Decolonization*. Stanford, CA: Stanford University Press, 2009.

Rozario, Kevin. "'Delicious Horrors': Mass Culture, the Red Cross, and the Appeal of Modern American Humanitarianism." *American Quarterly* 55, no. 3 (September 2003): 417–55.

Ryan, James R. *Picturing Empire: Photography and Visualization of the British Empire*. Chicago: University of Chicago Press, 1997.

Salvatici, Silvia. "From Displaced Persons to Labourers. Allied Employment Policies towards DPs in Post-war West Germany." In Jessica Reinisch and Elizabeth White, eds., *The Disentanglement of Populations: Migration, Expulsion and Displacement in Post-War Europe, 1944–1949*, 219–29. London: Palgrave, 2011.

"'Help the People to Help Themselves.' UNRRA Relief Workers and European Displaced Persons." *Journal of Refugee Studies* 3, no. 25 (2012): 452–73.

"Professionals of Humanitarianism. UNRRA Relief Officers in Post-war Europe." In Johannes Paulmann, ed., *The Dilemmas of Humanitarian Aid in the Twentieth Century*. Oxford: Oxford University Press, forthcoming.

Sandeen, E. J. *Picturing an Exhibition. The Family of Man and 1950s America*. Albuquerque: University of New Mexico Press, 1995.

Save The Children Fund (SCF). *Focus on Images*. London: SCF, 1991.

Impact of Image Guidelines for Writers, Editors, Advertisers and Photographers. London: SCF, 1988.

Scarry, Elaine. *The Body in Pain: The Making and Unmaking of the World*. New York: Oxford University Press, 1987.

Schwartz, Vanessa and Jeannene Przyblyski. "Visual Culture's History." In Vanessa Schwartz and Jeannene Przyblyski, eds., *The 19th Century Visual Culture Reader*, 3–14. New York: Routledge, 2004.

Sekula, Alan. *Photography against the Grain*. Halifax, Canada: Press of the Nova Scotia College of Art and Design, 1984.

Shneer, David. *Through Soviet Jewish Eyes: Photography, War, and the Holocaust*. New Brunswick, NJ: Rutgers University Press, 2011.

Shore, Stephen. *The Nature of Photographs*. Baltimore: Johns Hopkins University Press, 1998.

Simpson, Donald. "Missions and the Magic Lantern." *International Bulletin of Missionary Research* 21, no. 1 (January 1997): 13–15.

Slide, Anthony, ed. *Ravished Armenia*. Lanham, MD: Scarecrow Press, 1997.

Sliwinski, Sharon. "The Childhood of Human Rights: The Kodak on the Congo." *Journal of Visual Culture* 5, no. 3 (2006): 333–63.

Human Rights in Camera. Chicago: University of Chicago Press, 2011.

Sluga, Glenda. *Internationalism in the Age of Nationalism*. Pennsylvania Studies in Human Rights. Philadelphia: University of Pennsylvania Press, 2013.

Smith, Joanna Handlin. *The Art of Doing Good: Charity in Late Ming China*. Berkeley: University of California Press, 2009.

Smith, M. and H. Yanacopulos. "The Public Faces of Development: An Introduction." *Journal of International Development* 16 (2004): 657–64.

Smith, Shawn Michelle. *American Archives: Gender, Race, and Class in Visual Culture*. Princeton, NJ: Princeton University Press, 1999.

Sontag, Susan. *On Photography*. New York: Farrar, Straus and Giroux, 1977.

Regarding the Pain of Others. New York: Picador, 2003.

Stange, Maren. *Symbols of Ideal Life: Social Documentary Photography in America, 1890–1950*. New York: Cambridge University Press, 1989.

Stott, William. *Documentary Expression and Thirties America*. New York: Oxford University Press, 1973.

Struk, Janina. *Photographing the Holocaust: Interpretations of the Evidence*. New York: I. B. Tauris, 2004.

Suski, Laura. "Children, Suffering and the Humanitarianism Appeal." In R. Ashby Wilson and R. D. Brown, eds., *Humanitarianism and Suffering: The Mobilization of Empathy*, 202–21. Cambridge: Cambridge University Press, 2010.

Szarkowski, John. *The Photographer's Eye*. New York: Museum of Modern Art, 2007, 1966.

Tagg, John. *The Burden of Representation: Essays on Photographies and Histories*. Minneapolis: University of Minnesota Press, 1993.

Tait, S. "Bearing Witness, Journalism and Moral Responsibility." *Media Culture Society* 33, no. 8 (2011): 1220–35.

Taylor, John. *Body Horror: Photojournalism, Catastrophe, and War*. New York: New York University Press, 1998.

"The General Theory of Icebergs or What You Can't See in Political Advertisements." *Ten8* 26 (1987): 44–53.

"The Problems of Photojournalism: Realism, the Nature of the News, and the Humanitarian Narrative." *Journalism Studies* 1, no. 1 (2000): 129–43.

Thiriez, Régine. *Barbarian Lens: Western Photographers of the Qianlong Emperor's European Palaces*. New York: Routledge, 1998.

"Photography and Portraiture in Nineteenth-Century China." *East Asian History*, nos. 17/18 (June/December 1999): 77–102.

Thomas, Julia Adeney. "The Evidence of Sight." *History and Theory* 48 (December 2009): 151–68.

"Power Made Visible: Photography and Postwar Japan's Elusive Reality." *Journal of Asian Studies* 67, no. 2 (May 2008): 365–94.

Thomas, Lew, ed. *The Restless Decade: John Gutmann's Photographs of the Thirties*. New York: Harry N. Abrams, 1984.

Thompson, T. Jack. *Light on Darkness? Missionary Photography of Africa in the Nineteenth and Early Twentieth Centuries*. Grand Rapids, MI: William B. Eerdmans, 2012.

Troyon, Brigitte and Daniel Palmieri. "The ICRC Delegate: An Exceptional Humanitarian Player?" *International Review of the Red Cross* 89, no. 865 (March 2007): 97–111.

Twain, Mark. *King Leopold's Soliloquy: A Defence of his Congo Rule*. Boston: F. R. Warren, 1905.

Twomey, Christina. "Severed Hands: Authenticating Atrocity in the Congo, 1904–13." In Geoffrey Batchen, Mick Gidley, Nancy K. Miller, and Jay Poster, eds., *Picturing Atrocity: Photography in Crisis*, 39–50. London: Reaktion Books, 2012.

Tucker, Anne Wilkes et al. *War/Photography: Images of Armed Conflict and Its Aftermath*. Houston, TX: Museum of Fine Arts, 2012.

Tucker, Jennifer. *Nature Exposed: Photography as Eyewitness in Victorian Science*. Baltimore, MD: Johns Hopkins UP, 2005.

Tyrrell, Ian. *Reforming the World: The Creation of America's Moral Empire*. Princeton, NJ: Princeton University Press, 2010.

Van der Gaag, N. and C. Nash. *Images of Africa – The UK Report*. Oxford: Oxfam, 1987.

Van de Ven, A. "The Eyes of the Street Look Back: In Kolkata with a Camera around My Neck." *Photographies* 4, no. 2 (2011): 139–55.

Vernon, James. *Hunger: A Modern History*. Cambridge, MA: Belknap Press of Harvard University Press, 2007. See esp. chap. 2, "Humanitarian Discovery of Hunger."

Vestergaard, A. "Humanitarian Branding and the Media: The Case of Amnesty International." *Journal of Language and Politics* 7, no. 3 (2008): 471–93.

Voluntary Service Overseas. *The Live Aid Legacy: The Developing World through British Eyes – A Research Report*. 2002. Accessed December 28, 2013. http://www.eldis.org/vfile/upload/1/document/0708/DOC1830.pdf.

Walker, Peter, and Daniel Maxwell, *Shaping the Humanitarian World*. New York: Routledge, 2009.

Watenpaugh, Keith David. "The League of Nations' Rescue of Armenian Genocide Survivors and the Making of Modern Humanitarianism, 1920–1927." *American Historical Review* 115, no. 5 (December 2010): 1315–39.

Weindling, Paul, ed. *International Health Organisations and Movements, 1918–1939*. Cambridge: Cambridge University Press, 1995.

Wells, Liz. *Photography: A Critical Introduction*. 4th ed. New York: Routledge, 2009.

Wells, Liz, ed. *The Photography Reader*. London: Routledge, 2003.

Wexler, Laura. *Tender Violence: Domestic Visions in an Age of U.S. Imperialism*. Chapel Hill: University of North Carolina Press, 2000.

Willis, Deborah and Barbara Krauthamer. *Envisioning Emancipation: Black Americans and the End of Slavery.* Philadelphia: Temple University Press, 2013.

Wilson, Ann Marie. "In the Name of God, Civilization, and Humanity: The United States and the Armenian Massacres of the 1890s." *Le Mouvement Social* 227 (avril–juin 2009): 27–44.

Wilson, Michael. "Visual Culture: A Useful Category of Historical Analysis." In Vanessa Schwartz and Jeannene Przyblyski, eds., *The 19th Century Visual Culture Reader*, 26–33. New York: Routledge, 2004.

Wilson, Richard Ashby and Richard D. Brown, eds. *Humanitarianism and Suffering: The Mobilization of Empathy.* New York: Cambridge University Press, 2009.

Wiseberg, Laurie S. "The International Politics of Relief: A Case Study of the Relief Operations Mounted during the Nigerian Civil War (1967–1970)." PhD diss., University of California at Los Angeles, 1973.

Yochelson, Bonnie and Daniel Czitrom. *Rediscovering Jacob Riis: Exposure Journalism and Photography in Turn of the Century New York.* New York: New Press, 2007.

Young, Cynthia, ed. *We Went Back: Photographs from Europe 1933–1955 by CHIM.* New York: International Center of Photography and Delmonico Books, 2013.

Young, R. *White Mythologies: Writing History and the West.* London: Routledge, 1990.

Zelizer, Barbie. *About to Die: How News Images Move the Public.* Oxford: Oxford University Press, 2010.

   Remembering to Forget: Holocaust Memory through the Camera's Eye. Chicago: University of Chicago Press, 1998.

Index

CPSIA information can be obtained
at www.ICGtesting.com
Printed in the USA
LVOW01s1555200916

505435LV00018B/1617/P